# War crimes and crimes against humanity in the Rome Statute of the International Criminal Court



MANCHESTER
1824
Manchester University Press

**Melland Schill Studies in International Law**
*Series editor* Professor Dominic McGoldrick

The Melland Schill name has a long-established reputation for high standards of scholarship. Each volume in the series addresses major public international law issues and current developments. Many of the Melland Schill volumes have become standard works of reference. Interdisciplinary and accessible, the contributions are vital reading for students, scholars and practitioners of public international law, international organisations, international relations, international politics, international economics and international development.

# War crimes and crimes against humanity in the Rome Statute of the International Criminal Court

Christine Byron

Manchester University Press
Manchester and New York
distributed in the United States exclusively by Palgrave Macmillan

*Published by* Manchester University Press
Oxford Road, Manchester M13 9NR, UK
*and* Room 400, 175 Fifth Avenue, New York,
NY 10010, USA
www.manchesteruniversitypress.co.uk

*Distributed in the United States exclusively by*
Palgrave Macmillan, 175 Fifth Avenue, New York,
NY 10010, USA

*Distributed in Canada exclusively by*
UBC Press, University of British Columbia, 2029 West Mall,
Vancouver, BC, Canada V6T 1Z2

*British Library Cataloguing-in-Publication Data*
A catalogue record for this book is available from the British Library

*Library of Congress Cataloging-in-Publication Data applied for*

ISBN 978 0 7190 7389 2 *hardback*

First published 2009

18 17 16 15 14 13 12 11 10 09 10 9 8 7 6 5 4 3 2 1

Typeset in 10/12pt Times
by Graphicraft Limited, Hong Kong
Printed in Great Britain
by CPI Antony Rowe, Chippenham, Wiltshire

In memory of my father
Dr John F. Byron

# Contents

# General introduction

The international Criminal Court was the first international institution established in the twenty-first century. It embodied the hope that the new century will not be marked by the culture of impunity that characterised the last one. In the nature of criminal courts their substantive jurisdiction has to be very precise. Publication of this book coincides with the appearance of the first defendants before the new court. It provides a critical analysis of the definitions of war crimes and crimes against humanity as construed in the Rome Statute and developed by the Elements of Crimes. It will be an invaluable aid to those involved in proceedings before the Court and before other national, international or internationalised courts that have to apply substantive international criminal law. It will also appeal to those with a more general interest in the limits of international law and the functioning of international institutions.

Dominic McGoldrick

# Acknowledgements

As this book is based on my PhD thesis obtained from the University of Liverpool in 2003, I would like to thank my supervisor, Professor Dominic McGoldrick, for his help, advice and friendship, during my time as a postgraduate student. Further, I am grateful for his continuing support, as series editor, to develop my thesis into a research monograph in the 'Melland Schill studies in international law' series. In this respect I would like to thank everyone at Manchester University Press, especially with respect to their flexibility over deadlines.

Whilst preparing this monograph I have been based at the University of Manchester and I am very grateful to my colleagues for their support and to the law library staff at the University for their assistance. I would also like to thank the law library staff at the University of Liverpool, the London School of Economics and the Institute of Advanced Legal Studies. I would especially like to express my appreciation to Professor Rob Cryer who was kind enough to read and comment upon the manuscript at an earlier stage and to Stephie Fehr, a postgraduate student at the University of Manchester, who has been of great help in the final stages of preparation of the manuscript.

Finally, I will always be grateful to my family for their love and support especially my mother and my husband, David Turns.

# List of abbreviations

**Periodicals**

| | |
|---|---|
| AFLR | Air Force Law Review |
| Am J Comp L | American Journal of Comparative Law |
| AJIL | American Journal of International Law |
| Am U Int LR | American University International Law Review |
| Am UJ Int'l L & Pol'y | American University Journal of International Law and Policy |
| Am ULR | American University Law Review |
| ARIEL | Austrian Review of International and European Law |
| Ariz J Int'l & Comp L | Arizona Journal of International and Comparative Law |
| Army Lawy | The Army Lawyer |
| ASIL Proceedings | American Society of International Law Proceedings |
| Austrian JPIL | Austrian Journal of Public International Law |
| BCL Rev | Boston College Law Review |
| BC Third World LJ | Boston College Third World Law Journal |
| Berkeley J Int'l L | Berkeley Journal of International Law |
| Buff Hum Rts LR | Buffalo Human Rights Law Review |
| BYIL | British Yearbook of International Law |
| BYU J Pub L | Brigham Young University Journal of Public Law |
| Calif West ILJ | California Western International Law Journal |
| Can YBIL | Canadian Yearbook of International Law |
| Cardozo JL & Gender | Cardozo Journal of Law and Gender |
| Cas W Res JIL | Case Western Reserve Journal of International Law |
| Catholic ULR | Catholic University Law Review |
| Chi J Int'l L | Chicago Journal of International Law |
| Chi-Kent LR | Chicago–Kent Law Review |
| Chinese J Int'l L | Chinese Journal of International Law |
| Colum Hum Rts L Rev | Columbia Human Rights Law Review |
| Colum J Transnat'l Law | Columbia Journal of Transnational Law |
| Conn JIL | Connecticut Journal of International Law |
| Cornell Int'l LJ | Cornell International Law Journal |
| Crim LF | Criminal Law Forum |
| Crim LR | Criminal Law Review |

| | |
|---|---|
| DePaul LR | DePaul Law Review |
| Dick J Int'l L | Dickinson Journal of International Law |
| Duke J Comp & Int'l L | Duke Journal of Comparative and International Law |
| EJIL | European Journal of International Law |
| Emory Int'l L Rev | Emory International Law Review |
| Fla J Int'l L | Florida Journal of International Law |
| Fletcher F World Aff | Fletcher Forum of World Affairs |
| Fordham Int'l LJ | Fordham International Law Journal |
| Geo LJ | Georgetown Law Journal |
| Georgia J Int Comp L | Georgia Journal of International and Comparative Law |
| Geo Wash JIL & Econ | George Washington Journal of International Law and Economics |
| Germ Yrbk Int'l L | German Yearbook of International Law |
| Hague Yrbk Int'l L | Hague Yearbook of International Law |
| Hamline LR | Hamline Law Review |
| Harv HRJ | Harvard Human Rights Journal |
| Harv ILJ | Harvard International Law Journal |
| Hastings Int & Comp LR | Hastings International and Comparative Law Review |
| Hof LPS | Hofstra Law and Policy Symposium |
| Hous LR | Houston Law Review |
| HR Brief | Human Rights Brief |
| HRLJ | Human Rights Law Journal |
| HRQ | Human Rights Quarterly |
| Hum Rts L Rev | Human Rights Law Review |
| ICLQ | International and Comparative Law Quarterly |
| ILF | International Law Forum |
| ILQ | International Law Quarterly |
| Int Com JR | International Commission of Jurists Review |
| Int Law | International Lawyer |
| Int'l Enforcement L Rep | International Enforcement Law Reporter |
| Int Rel | International Relations |
| IRRC | International Review of the Red Cross |
| Israel Yrbk Hum Rts | Israel Yearbook on Human Rights |
| JACL | Journal of Armed Conflict Law |
| JCL | Journal of Criminal Law |
| JCSL | Journal of Conflict and Security Law |
| J Int'l Crim Just | Journal of International Criminal Justice |
| Jur Rev | Juridical Review |
| LJIL | Leiden Journal of International Law |
| Loy LA Int & Comp LR | Loyola of Los Angeles International and Comparative Law Review |
| L & Pol Int Bus | Law and Policy in International Business |
| Melb J Int'l L | Melbourne Journal of International Law |
| Mich J Gender & L | Michigan Journal of Gender and Law |
| Mich J Int'l L | Michigan Journal of International Law |
| Mich SU-Detroit Col L | Michigan State University–Detroit College of Law |
| JIL | Journal of International Law |

| | |
|---|---|
| Milit LR | Military Law Review |
| MLR | Modern Law Review |
| Nav LR | Naval Law Review |
| NCJIL & Com Reg | North Carolina Journal of International Law and Commercial Regulation |
| NILR | Netherlands International Law Review |
| NLJ | New Law Journal |
| NYIL | Netherlands Yearbook of International Law |
| NYL Sch J Int'l & Comp L | New York Law School Journal of International and Comparative Law |
| NYUJ Int L & Pol | New York University Journal of International Law and Politics |
| NYUR | New York University Review |
| Pace ILR | Pace International Law Review |
| Pac Rim LPJ | Pacific Rim Law and Policy Journal |
| Penn St Int'l L Rev | Penn State International Law Review |
| RADIC | African Journal of International and Comparative Law |
| Rdi | Rivista di diritto internazionale |
| Rec des Cours | Recueil des Cours, Académie de Droit Internationale de la Haye (Netherlands) |
| RECIEL | Review of European Community and International Environmental Law |
| Rev dr milit | Revue de droit pénal militaire et de droit de la guerre |
| SAJHR | South African Journal on Human Rights |
| Scholar: St Mary's LR Min Issues | The Scholar: St Mary's Law Review on Minority Issues |
| San Diego Int'l LJ | San Diego International Law Journal |
| St John's JLC | Saint John's Journal of Legal Commentary |
| Suffolk Transnat'l LR | Suffolk Transnational Law Review |
| SYBIL | Singapore Yearbook of International Law |
| Sy J Int L | Syracuse Journal of International Law and Commerce |
| Texas Int'l LJ | Texas International Law Journal |
| Thomas Jefferson LR | Thomas Jefferson Law Review |
| Transnat'l L & Contemp Probs | Transnational Law and Contemporary Problems |
| UC Davis J Int'l L & Pol'y | University of California at Davis Journal of International Law and Policy |
| U Col LR | University of Colorado Law Review |
| U Miami Int'l & Comp L Rev | University of Miami International and Comparative Law Review |
| Va Envt'l LJ | Virginia Environmental Law Journal |
| Va JIL | Virginia Journal of International Law |
| Vand J Transnat'l L | Vanderbilt Journal of Transnational Law |
| Yale HR & Dev LJ | Yale Human Rights and Development Law Journal |
| Yale J Int'l L | Yale Journal of International Law |
| Yale LJ | Yale Law Journal |
| YIHL | Yearbook of International Humanitarian Law |

## *List of abbreviations*

### Law reports

| | |
|---|---|
| AC | Appeal Cases (UK) |
| AD | Annual Digest and Reports of Public International Law Cases |
| All ER | All England Law Reports |
| CMR | Court Martial Reports (US) |
| EHRR | European Human Rights Reports |
| ICJ Rep | International Court of Justice Reports |
| IHRR | International Human Rights Reports |
| ILM | International Legal Materials |
| ILR | International Law Reports |
| Iran–US CTR | Iran–US Claims Tribunal Reports |
| LRTWC | Law Reports Trials of War Criminals |
| RIAA | Reports of International Arbitral Awards |
| YB ECHR | Yearbook of the European Court of Human Rights |

# 1

# Introduction

As the first defendants appear before the International Criminal Court it is now more important than ever to gain a proper understanding of the crimes with which they have been charged. The purpose of this study is to provide a critical analysis of the definitions of war crimes and crimes against humanity as construed in the Rome Statute and developed by the Elements of Crimes.

## Background to the ICC

The origins of the ICC are mainly rooted in the events of the twentieth century. Whilst attempts to create an international tribunal prior to the Second World War failed dismally,[1] the horrific atrocities committed in that conflict led to the Nuremberg and Tokyo Tribunals to try German and Japanese war criminals.[2] Despite criticism of these tribunals for applying victors' justice and *ex post facto* law, it is undeniable that they greatly contributed to international criminal law and the prospects of a permanent international criminal court.[3] In particular, they revealed the potential of international criminal justice, when given political backing and sufficient resources.[4]

[1] See proposals for a 'High court of international justice', PCIJ Advisory Committee of Jurists, Procès-verbaux of the Proceedings of the Committee, 16 June to 24 July 1920, reprinted in B. Ferencz, *An International Criminal Court, a Step Toward World Peace: A Documentary History and Analysis*, Vol. I (New York: Oceana Publications, 1980), 193–224, and the adoption of a Convention on the Creation of an International Criminal Court to try those accused of terrorism (never ratified) at the International Conference on the Repression of Terrorism, 1–16 November 1937, Geneva, reprinted in B. Ferencz, *ibid.*, 355–98.

[2] London Agreement and Nuremberg Charter, 8 August 1945.

[3] H. von Hebel, 'An international criminal court: a historical perspective', pp. 13–38 in H. von Hebel, J. Lammers and J. Schukking (eds), *Reflections on the International Criminal Court* (The Hague: Asser, 1999), pp. 20–2.

[4] M. Bassiouni, 'Establishing an international criminal court: historical survey', Milit LR, 149 (1995), 49–63, p. 55.

However, the momentum towards the formation of a permanent ICC, created in the wake of the International Military Tribunals, was soon mired in Cold War politics. The International Law Commission's Draft Code of Offences was given priority over the creation of an international jurisdiction to deal with such crimes and the Draft Code could not be considered until aggression was defined, so the question of an international criminal court was postponed indefinitely.[5] The issue was lost in silence as the years went by and only the work of academics and some non-governmental organisations kept the topic from being forgotten completely.[6]

Nevertheless, towards the end of the twentieth century barriers impeding an ICC began to tumble one by one. First, the General Assembly managed to adopt a definition of aggression,[7] allowing the International Law Commission (ILC) to resume work on its Draft Code of Crimes.[8] Second, the end of the Cold War created a 'new political climate that favoured international cooperation'.[9] This, in particular, enabled the General Assembly to react favourably to the request of the Prime Minister of Trinidad and Tobago for consideration of an international court to deal with transnational drug offences, and so it mandated the ILC to consider this under the umbrella of its work on the Draft Code of Crimes.[10]

The third factor was the instability of areas such as the Balkans and massive violations of human rights.[11] These atrocities, combined with the media coverage, which bombarded the public with images of death and destruction in their living rooms, created a groundswell of public pressure that 'something must be done'.[12] The non-governmental organisations dedicated to fighting for an international criminal court were quick to capitalise on this.[13] The *ad hoc* international tribunals

[5] M. Bassiouni, 'From Versailles to Rwanda in seventy-five years: the need to establish a permanent international criminal court', Harv HRJ, 10 (1997), 11–62, p. 53, and C. Tomuschat, 'A system of international criminal prosecution is taking shape', Int Com JR, 50 (1993), 56–70, p. 57.

[6] B. Ferencz, *An International Criminal Court, A Step Toward World Peace: A Documentary History and Analysis*, Vol. II (New York: Oceana Publications, 1980), p. 56, comments on the calls of academics for an international criminal court in the 1960s. P. Marquardt, 'Law without borders: the constitutionality of an international criminal court', Columbia J Transnat'l Law, 33 (1995), 73–148, p. 87, comments on the work of academics in the 1970s. B. Graefrath, 'Universal criminal jurisdiction and an international criminal court', EJIL, 1 (1990), 67–88, p. 71, comments on the work of NGOs in the 1970s.

[7] General Assembly Resolution (GA Res.) 3314 (XXIX), 14 December 1974.

[8] See the 1996 ILC Draft Code.

[9] M. Leigh, 'Evaluating present options for an international criminal court', Milit LR, 149 (1995), 113–28, p. 113, and see A. Cassese, 'On the current trends towards criminal prosecution and punishment of breaches of international humanitarian law', EJIL, 9 (1998), 2–17, p. 7.

[10] GA Res. 44/39, 4 December 1989.

[11] A. Cassese, 'On the current trends towards criminal prosecution', n. 9 *supra*, p. 8.

[12] See J. Crawford, 'The ILC adopts a statute for an international criminal court', AJIL, 89 (1995), 404–16, p. 407.

[13] See L. Caflisch, 'Toward the establishment of a permanent international criminal jurisdiction', International Peacekeeping, 5:6 (1998), 110–11.

for Yugoslavia and Rwanda were born out of the post-Cold War co-operation of the Security Council and public pressure following media coverage of the conflicts.[14] Undoubtedly the existence and successful operation of the tribunals greatly increased support for the creation of an International Criminal Court.[15]

Influenced by these events, the ILC Draft Statute for an ICC envisaged jurisdiction over the crimes of genocide, aggression, serious violations of the laws and customs applicable in armed conflict and crimes against humanity, in addition to other exceptionally serious crimes of international concern contained in an Annex.[16] The crimes themselves were not further defined, as the Draft Statute addressed issues of procedure rather than substantive law issues.[17]

Acting on the advice of the Sixth Committee, the General Assembly established an *Ad Hoc* Committee to review 'the major substantive and administrative issues arising out of the draft statute' and to consider arrangements for an international convention.[18] However, the *Ad Hoc* Committee report in 1995 left many issues undecided, although it raised the issue of limiting the subject matter jurisdiction of the Court to crimes under general international law, as it was felt that limiting the Court to the most serious crimes would enhance its moral credibility and authority and promote a broader acceptance of the Statute.[19] Nevertheless, whilst the Committee had expressed concern at the lack of definition of the crimes in the Draft Statute, it had not attempted to address this issue.[20]

The difficult task of defining the subject matter jurisdiction and working towards an acceptable statute for the Court fell to the Preparatory Committee, a body created by the General Assembly to finalise issues and work towards a diplomatic conference.[21] The task before the Preparatory Committee was described as 'daunting' by Kirsch, '[g]iven the widely divergent views as to the appropriate scope and powers for the ICC, and the need to reconcile aspects of the world's legal systems'.[22] Indeed, the committee spent over two years debating and refining proposals for a workable ICC and moving towards an acceptable

[14] The ICTY and ICTR were created by Security Council Resolution 827, 25 May 1993, and 955, 8 November 1994, respectively.

[15] A. Bos, 'The International Criminal Court: recent developments', pp. 39–46 in H. von Hebel *et al.*, *Reflections on the ICC*, n. 3 *supra*, p. 45.

[16] Article 20, ILC Draft ICC Statute.

[17] See B. Broomhall, 'Looking forward to the establishment of an international criminal court: between State consent and the rule of law', Crim LF, 8 (1997), 317–34, p. 324.

[18] GA Res. 49/53, 9 December 1994.

[19] Report of the *Ad Hoc* Committee on the Establishment of an International Criminal Court, GA Official Records, Fiftieth Session, Supplement No. 22 (A/50/22), p. 3.

[20] *Ibid.*, pp. 11–12.

[21] GA Res. 50/46, 11 December 1995.

[22] P. Kirsch, 'Introduction', pp. 1–10 in H. von Hebel *et al.*, *Reflections on the ICC*, n. 3 *supra*, p. 1.

statute.[23] The UN Diplomatic Conference of Plenipotentiaries on the Establishment of an International Criminal Court finally took place at the headquarters of the Food and Agriculture Organisation in Rome, from 15 June to 17 July 1998.[24] Despite 'deep divides, a substantial volume of work and limited time',[25] the Rome Statute was eventually adopted on 17 July 1998.[26]

Articles 7 and 8 of the Rome Statute set out the eleven crimes against humanity and fifty war crimes. The Elements of Crimes, developed by the Preparatory Commission established under the Final Act of the Conference,[27] set out the elements of war crimes and crimes against humanity in detail over thirty-nine pages.[28] Nevertheless, there still remains a need for further analysis of these offences. First, the Rome Statute draws strongly upon international humanitarian law, but the interpretation of provisions drawn from this source can prove problematic, as they were primarily enacted with thoughts of the prevention of war crimes and gross abuses of human rights, rather than as a basis for their prosecution.[29] Second, there is a vagueness inherent in customary international law, which is also often present in treaties, owing to compromises during negotiations. The Rome Statute, itself a product of political compromises, is not immune from this.[30]

Therefore, an in-depth analysis of the crimes contained within Articles 7 and 8 is essential to understand how the ICC will interpret these offences as the trials commence. Such analysis is particularly crucial in light of the Rome Statute's *de facto* codification of part of humanitarian law and the importance of effective national implementation of this law by States Parties to the ICC.[31] The definitions of crimes in the Rome Statute and Elements of Crimes (EOC)

[23] See C. Hall, 'The first two sessions of the UN Preparatory Committee on the establishment of an International Criminal Court', AJIL, 91 (1997), 177–87; C. Hall, 'The third and fourth sessions of the UN Preparatory Committee . . .', AJIL, 92 (1998), 124–33; C. Hall, 'The fifth session of the UN Preparatory Committee . . .', AJIL, 92 (1998), 331–9; C. Hall, 'The sixth session of the UN Preparatory Committee . . .', AJIL, 92 (1998), 548–56, and see the Report of the Preparatory Committee on the Establishment of an International Criminal Court, Draft Statute and Draft Final Act, UN Doc. A/Conf.183/3/Add.1, 1998.

[24] GA Res. 52/160, 15 December 1997.

[25] P. Kirsch, 'Introduction', pp. 1–10, n. 22 *supra*, p. 2.

[26] A hundred and twenty voted in favour, twenty-one abstained and seven voted against this compromise package, see <http://www.un.org/icc/docs.htm>.

[27] Final Act, UN Doc. A/Conf.183/10, Annex 1, Resolution F.

[28] See C. Byron and D. Turns, 'The Preparatory Commission for the International Criminal Court', ICLQ, 50 (2001), 420–35.

[29] W. Fenrick, 'International humanitarian law and criminal trials', Transnat'l L & Contemp Probs, 7 (1997), 23–43, p. 26.

[30] See L. Sadat, 'Custom, codification and some thoughts about the relationship between the two: Article 10 of the ICC Statute', DePaul LR, 49 (2000), 909–23, p. 910, and K. Ambos, 'General principles of criminal law in the Rome Statute', Crim LF, 10 (1999), 1–32, p. 1.

[31] See D. Turns, 'Prosecuting violations of international humanitarian law: the legal position in the United Kingdom', JACL, 4 (1999), 1–39; C. Kreß and F. Lattanzi (eds), *The Rome Statute and Domestic Legal Orders*, Vol. I, *General Aspects and Constitutional Issues* (Fagnano Alto: Editrice il Sirente Piccola, 2000) and discussion *infra*, pp. 246–51.

will not only be pertinent to cases before the ICC but, owing to the principle of complementarity, are likely to influence national trials of those who commit war crimes and crimes against humanity across the globe.[32]

## Default mental element for offences in the Rome Statute

It is necessary at this point to explain that the delegates at Rome felt that whilst the definition of specific crimes set out the material elements or *actus reus* clearly, they did not always articulate the mental element or *mens rea* to be proved by the prosecutor. Whilst those offences which include a mental element usually adopt the language used in the treaty from which the offence has been drawn, other offences have not previously been set out in treaty form or do not include an express mental element.[33] Therefore, Article 30 was included in Part 3 of the Rome Statute on 'General Principles of Criminal Law'.

### Article 30 of the Rome Statute

Article 30 essentially acts as a default mental element setting out that 'unless otherwise provided' the accused will not be found criminally responsible unless he or she has committed the 'material elements', or *actus reus* of the crime, with both 'intent and knowledge'. Article 30 does not explain where else the *mens rea* may be 'provided', it is submitted that that an alternative mental element could be found in the language of the Statute, the EOC, applicable treaties or customary international law.[34]

#### 'Intent' in relation to conduct

Intent is defined in relation to conduct, where the *actus reus* of the offence forbids a certain behaviour,[35] when a person 'means to engage in the conduct'.

[32] W. Schabas, *An Introduction to the International Criminal Court* (Cambridge: Cambridge University Press, 2001), p. 19.

[33] R. Clark, 'The mental element in international criminal law: the Rome Statute of the International Criminal Court and the elements of offences', Crim LF, 12 (2001), 291–334, p. 314, and J. Van der Vyver, 'The International Criminal Court and the concept of *mens rea* in international criminal law', U Miami Int'l & Comp L Rev, 12 (2004), 57–149, pp. 110–13.

[34] See R. Clark, 'The mental element in international criminal law', p. 321; G. Werle and F. Jessberger, '"Unless otherwise provided": Article 30 of the ICC Statute and the mental element of crimes under international criminal law', J Int'l Crim Just, 35 (2005), 35–55, pp. 45–6, and K. Dörmann, 'Preparatory Commission for the International Criminal Court: the elements of war crimes', IRRC, 839 (2000), 771–95, p. 776. However, this proposed understanding is not uncontentious, R. Lee (ed.), *The International Criminal Court: Elements of Crimes and Rules of Procedure and Evidence* (New York: Transnational, 2001) (hereinafter: Lee (ed.), *ICC: Elements*), pp. 29–30.

[35] For example the offence of 'declaring that no quarter will be given', under Article 8(2)(b)(xii).

This suggests, according to Piragoff, that the conduct 'must be the result of a voluntary action on the part of an accused' and also connotes some element 'of desire or willingness to do the action'.[36] It is a basic principle of criminal law that the *actus reus* of an offence must be committed voluntarily,[37] and so this phrase must connote something more than mere voluntariness, such as deciding upon and initiating the conduct.[38]

It is uncertain whether the expression 'conduct' in Article 30 includes omissions in addition to actions. This uncertainty results from the fact that the article on criminal liability for omissions, included in earlier drafts, was omitted from the final Statute.[39] Ambos suggests that its removal confirms that the offences in the Rome Statute may not be committed by omission, except in the case of command responsibility, which is expressly allowed for in Article 28.[40] Piragoff, however, considers that there is still scope for the Court to decide whether a particular offence may be committed by omission and under what circumstances.[41] The latter opinion is persuasive, as the reasons for removal of the article in question are unclear.[42] Therefore, in deciding whether a particular offence may be committed by omission, the Court should consider the history and jurisprudence of the particular offence in international law and principles drawn from national legal systems.[43]

### 'Intent' in relation to a consequence

Intent is defined in relation to a consequence, where the *actus reus* of the offence forbids a particular result,[44] in two ways. First, when a person 'means to cause that consequence'. This would describe the situation where it was the accused's aim or objective to cause the result. Second, a person is taken to intend a consequence when he or she 'is aware that it will occur in the ordinary course of events'. This would describe the situation where the accused aimed to achieve

[36] D. Piragoff, 'Article 30, mental element', pp. 527–35 in O. Triffterer (ed.), *Commentary on the Rome Statute of the International Criminal Court, Observers' Notes, Article by Article* (Baden-Baden: Nomos, 1999), p. 533.

[37] See W. Wilson, *Criminal Law Doctrine and Theory* (London: Longman, 1998), p. 220.

[38] Taken from the dictionary definition of 'to will', in the *Concise Oxford Dictionary* (Oxford: Clarendon Press, 9th edn, 1995).

[39] D. Piragoff, 'Article 30, mental element', n. 36 *supra*, p. 532.

[40] K. Ambos, 'General principles of criminal law in the Rome Statute', n. 30 *supra*, p. 19.

[41] D. Piragoff, 'Article 30, mental element', n. 36 *supra*, p. 532.

[42] *Ibid.* See Draft Article 28, Report of the Preparatory Committee on the Establishment of an International Criminal Court, 14 April 1998, UN Doc. A/Conf.183/2/Add.1, pp. 54–5. The *travaux préparatoires* do not disclose the reasons for its exclusion from the final statute at the Rome Conference.

[43] For a discussion of criminal omissions in English and French law see P. Palmer, 'Attempt by act or omission: causation and the problem of the hypothetical nurse', JCL, 63 (1999), 158–65, and A. Ashworth, 'Criminal omissions and public duties: the French experience', Legal Studies, 10 (1990), 153–64.

[44] For example 'wilful killing', Article 8(2)(a)(i).

another result but knew that the criminal result was a prerequisite or necessary side effect of the desired objective.[45]

With regard to this second type of intent, it is necessary to understand the expression 'ordinary course of events'. In English criminal law intention may be inferred from an undesired but foreseen result only when the forbidden consequence is foreseen by the accused as virtually certain to occur as a result of his or her actions.[46] Piragoff comments that this virtual certainty test is common to 'most legal systems'[47] and suggests that foreseeing a consequence as a virtual certainty, or foreseeing a consequence as occurring in the ordinary course of events, amounts to the same thing.[48]

However, the wording of the phase 'will occur in the ordinary course of events' appears to allow of more uncertainty than the phrase 'will occur as a virtual certainty'. A hypothetical example of the possible difference can be shown in the offence of 'enlisting children' under the age of fifteen. An army recruitment officer who strongly desires to meet a high recruitment target for a popularly supported conflict may recruit hundreds of individuals who stated that they were fifteen, and appear to be *about* that age, without checking identity papers to confirm it. The recruitment officer could argue that it was not his objective to recruit under-fifteen-year-olds simply to reach the recruitment target, and that he did not foresee under-age recruitment as virtually certain to result from his actions. However, it would be much more difficult for him to claim that he was unaware that, in the ordinary course of events, some of the individuals recruited in such a fashion would be under-age.[49]

## Knowledge

Knowledge is defined by Article 30 as 'awareness that a circumstance exists or a consequence will occur in the ordinary course of events'. It is hard to see how the requirement of knowledge, when defined as being aware that 'a consequence will occur in the ordinary course of events', adds to the notion of intent when this is one of the definitions of *intent* in Article 30(2)(b). Ambos criticises

[45] For a discussion of intention in English law see: A. Simester and W. Chan, 'Intention thus far', Crim LR, 43 (1997), 704–19; A. Norrie, 'After *Woollin*', Crim LR, 45 (1999), 532–44, and W. Wilson, 'Doctrinal rationality after *Woollin*', MLR, 62 (1999), 448–63.

[46] See the Court of Appeal decision in *R. v. Nedrick* [1986] 3 All ER 1, pp. 3–4 and the House of Lords decision in *R. v. Woollin* [1998] 4 All ER 103, p. 113.

[47] But see discussion of *dol éventuel* and *dol spécial* in C. Elliott, 'The French law of intent and its influence on the development of international criminal law', Crim LF, 11 (2000), 35–46, p. 41.

[48] D. Piragoff, 'Article 30, mental element', n. 36 *supra*, pp. 533–4.

[49] Note that, whilst the statute does not provide for a mental element in respect of the age of the child, which would suggest that the default mental element of Article 30 applies, the EOC sets a 'knew or should have known' standard, Elements of Crime, Assembly of State Parties to the Rome Statute of the ICC, Official Records, First Session, ICC-ASP/1/3, 3–10 September 2002 (hereinafter: EOC), p. 144.

this wording, stating that 'article 30 ignores the difference between "intent" and "knowledge" and mixes up two different categories of conduct'.[50]

However, 'awareness that a circumstance exists' does add to the *mens rea* requirement if the offence requires awareness of a particular circumstance in addition to the intention to act. For example, in the case of wilful killing under Article 8(2)(a)(i) the accused must *intend* to kill a person and have *knowledge* of both the factual circumstances establishing the protected status of the person and those establishing the existence of an armed conflict.

### General *mens rea* issues

The introduction to the Elements of Crimes makes it clear that 'intent and knowledge' do not have to be express but may be 'inferred from relevant facts and circumstances'.[51] Additionally the introduction states that when the *mens rea* involves 'elements involving value judgements' such as 'inhumane' or 'severe' it is not necessary, unless indicated, 'that the perpetrator personally completed a particular value judgement'.[52]

## Applicable law

The law to be applied by the judges of the ICC when adjudicating cases and interpreting the definition of crimes is given in Article 21 of the Rome Statute.[53] Whilst the sources of general public international law according to Article 38 of the International Court of Justice Statute are well known, Article 21 'constitutes the first codification of the sources of international *criminal* law'.[54] According to Article 21 the primary source of law will be the Statute, the EOC and the Rules of Procedure and Evidence (RPE). However, it must be noted that according to Article 9 of the Rome Statute, the Elements are intended only to '*assist* the Court in the interpretation and application' of the definitions of crimes and so are to be used as an interpretative aid only, rather than being binding upon the Court.[55]

[50] K. Ambos, 'General principles of criminal law in the Rome Statute', n. 30 *supra*, p. 22.

[51] EOC, pp. 108–55, 'General introduction', p. 112, para. 3.

[52] *Ibid.*, para. 4.

[53] See M. McAuliffe deGuzman, 'Article 21, applicable law', pp. 435–46, in O. Triffterer (ed.), *Commentary on the Rome Statute*, n. 36 *supra*, and A. Pellet, 'Applicable law', pp. 1051–84 in A. Cassese, P. Gaeta and J. Jones (eds), *The Rome Statute of the International Criminal Court: A Commentary* (Oxford: Oxford University Press, 2002).

[54] Original emphasis, M. McAuliffe deGuzman, 'Article 21, applicable law', n. 53 *supra*, p. 438.

[55] K. Dörmann, *Elements of War Crimes under the Rome Statute of the International Criminal Court: Sources and Commentary* (Cambridge: Cambridge University Press and International Committee of the Red Cross, 2002), p. 8, emphasis added. Dörmann comments on the disagreement over the EOC at the Rome diplomatic conference and states that 'Article 9 appears to be the *lex specialis* with regard to Art. 21(1)', *ibid.* Note also that Article 51(5) states that, in the event of a conflict between the Rome Statute and the RPE, the Statute shall prevail.

Second, applicable treaties and the principles and rules of international law may be applied 'where appropriate'. This gives the Court a discretion, in certain cases, to look beyond the Rome Statute itself, perhaps when interpreting the crimes, to the treaties which formed the basis of Articles 6, 7 and 8.[56] The reference to 'principles and rules of international law' clearly allows the Court to refer to international customary law to assist its interpretations where necessary.[57]

Third, in the absence of the above sources, general principles of law derived 'from national laws of legal systems of the world' may be applied. Both Pellet and deGuzman comment that recourse to this provision would not require the judges to enter into an exhaustive comparison of all legal systems but rather a representative number.[58] The Court 'may' also apply principles and rules of law as interpreted in its previous decisions, but, as there is no system of precedent in international law, the Court is permitted, not required, to apply its previous decisions. Nevertheless, in the words of the *Aleksovski* Appeal Chamber in the International Criminal Tribunal for the former Yugoslavia (ICTY), it is 'in the interests of certainty and predictability' for the Judges to apply previous case law unless there are 'cogent reasons in the interests of justice' to depart from it.[59] Finally, the interpretation of law pursuant to this article must also be consistent with 'internationally recognized human rights'.[60]

## Analysis of crimes

The analysis in this study of war crimes and crimes against humanity will not follow the order of applicable law in Article 21 of the Statute sequentially. The participants at the ICC Diplomatic Conference in Rome, their forerunners in the Preparatory Committee and the delegates in the post-conference Preparatory Commission were not working in a vacuum. Rather, they were drawing from and, to a great extent, codifying existing conventional and customary law.[61]

This analysis will consist, first, of an examination of the original meaning of the text in the convention or customary source from which each offence in the

[56] M. McAuliffe deGuzman, 'Article 21, applicable law', n. 53 *supra*, p. 440, but see A. Pellet, 'Applicable law', n. 53 *supra*, pp. 1067–70.

[57] A. Pellet, 'Applicable law', n. 53 *supra*, p. 1071.

[58] M. McAuliffe deGuzman, 'Article 21, applicable law', n. 53 *supra*, pp. 443–4, and A. Pellet, 'Applicable law', n. 53 *supra*, pp. 1073–4.

[59] *Aleksovski*, Appeal Judgement, para. 107.

[60] For comments on this provision see A. Pellet, 'Applicable law', n. 53 *supra*, pp. 1079–82.

[61] See P. Kirsch, 'Introduction', n. 22 *supra*, p. 4; T. Meron, 'Crimes under the jurisdiction of the International Criminal Court', pp. 47–55, in H. von Hebel *et al.*, *Reflections on the ICC*, n. 3 *supra*, p. 48, and D. Robinson and H. von Hebel, 'War crimes in internal conflicts: Article 8 of the ICC Statute', YIHL, 2 (1999), 193–209, p. 194, but see L. Sadat, 'Custom, codification and some thoughts about the relationship between the two', n. 30 *supra*, pp. 915–16, and R. Clark, 'Methods of warfare that cause unnecessary suffering or are inherently indiscriminate: a memorial tribute to Howard Berman', Calif West ILJ, 28 (1998), 379–89, pp. 380–1.

Rome Statute was drawn. This will be undertaken by examining the wording and *travaux préparatoires* of conventional sources, and evidence of customary sources. All conventional sources will be analysed following Articles 31 and 32 of the Vienna Convention on the Law of Treaties of 1969. Whilst the Vienna Convention does not formally apply to treaties concluded prior to 1980,[62] nevertheless it codified the customary international law approach to treaty interpretation in use throughout the twentieth century. So this interpretation will also be applied, *inter alia*, to the 1949 Geneva Conventions and 1977 Additional Protocols.[63] Reference to interpretative declarations made to these conventions will also be considered inasmuch as they elucidate the customary international law interpretation of these crimes.[64]

Second, the development of these crimes through national and international prosecutions and work by UN bodies will be considered. The jurisprudence of the ICTY and International Criminal Tribunal on Rwanda (ICTR) and 'internationalised tribunals' such as the Special Court for Sierra Leone (SCSL) and their contribution to the development of these crimes will be examined in some detail. Whilst the ICC will not be bound by the decisions of previous international tribunals, such decisions and those of national courts can shed light upon the treaties and customary law from which the offences in the Rome Statute are drawn. However, although some national decisions will be examined, this is not a comparative law study.[65]

Decisions of human rights bodies will also be drawn upon in order to expand the meaning of terms used in both humanitarian and human rights treaties. Human rights law is relevant not only because the non-derogable portions of human rights law remain applicable even in times of armed conflict, as the ICJ affirmed in the *Nuclear Weapons* case,[66] but, in Meron's words, 'the recognition as customary of norms rooted in international human rights instruments has affected the interpretation, and eventually the status, of the parallel norms in instruments of

[62] Article 4, 1969 Vienna Convention on the Law of Treaties.

[63] See C. Greenwood, 'Customary law status of the 1977 Geneva Protocols', pp. 93–114 in A. Delissen and G. Tanja (eds), *Humanitarian Law of Armed Conflict: Challenges Ahead* (Dordrecht: Nijhoff, 1991), p. 99.

[64] See discussion *infra*, pp. 251–2.

[65] For comments on the limited usefulness of national law decisions see G. Mettraux, 'Crimes against humanity in the jurisprudence of the international criminal tribunals for the former Yugoslavia and for Rwanda', Harv ILJ, 43 (2002), 237–316, p. 277, and P. Hwang, 'Defining crimes against humanity in the Rome Statute of the International Criminal Court', Fordham Int'l LJ, 22 (1998), 457–504, p. 489.

[66] *Legality of the Threat or Use of Nuclear Weapons*, Advisory Opinion, ICJ Rep. (1996) 226, para. 25, and see the Inter-American Commission of Human Rights decisions in *Abella v. United States* (1997), IA Com HR Case 11.137, Report No. 55/97, para. 158, and *Coard et al. v. United States* (1999), IA Com HR Case 10.951, Report No. 109/99, para. 39. See also D. Stephens, 'Human rights and armed conflict: the advisory opinion of the International Court of Justice in the Nuclear Weapons case', Yale HR & Dev LJ, 4 (2001), 1–24.

international humanitarian law'.[67] Indeed, the relevance of human rights law to the definition of crimes before the ICC is confirmed by Article 21 on applicable law.

Finally, the wording of the relevant offences in the Rome Statute, and the EOC developed by the Preparatory Commission, will be examined. The analysis will take into account the fact that under Articles 9(1) and 51(5) the EOC and RPE are to assist the Court, but that the Statute should prevail in the case of a conflict.[68] Nevertheless, the EOC are an important interpretational aid, considered by some to represent customary international law.[69] They are especially useful, given the lack of detailed *travaux préparatoires* for the Rome Statute, as official records of debates were not taken in order to facilitate compromises during delicate negotiations.[70]

[67] T. Meron, 'The humanization of humanitarian law', AJIL, 94 (2000), 239–78, p. 244.

[68] Article 51(5), Rome Statute, states '[i]n the event of a conflict between the Statute and the Rules of Procedure and Evidence, the Statute shall prevail'. Article 9(1), Rome Statute, states that the EOC 'shall assist the Court' and see para. 1 of the 'General introduction', EOC, p. 112. See also K. Dörmann, 'Contributions by the *ad hoc* tribunals for the former Yugoslavia and Rwanda to the ongoing work on elements of crimes in the context of the ICC', ASIL Proceedings, 94 (2000), 284–6, p. 284; W. Rückert and G. Witschel, 'Genocide and crimes against humanity in the elements of crimes', pp. 59–93 in H. Fischer, C. Kreß and S. Lüder (eds), *International and National Prosecution of Crimes under International Law: Current Developments* (Berlin: Berlin Verlag, 2001), p. 61, and M. Politi, 'Elements of crimes', pp. 443–473, in A. Cassese *et al.*, *The Rome Statute of the International Criminal Court*, n. 53 *supra*, p. 447.

[69] C. Hall, 'The first five sessions of the UN Preparatory Commission for the International Criminal Court', AJIL, 94 (2000), 773–89, p. 788, notes that the US delegate considered that the EOC document 'correctly reflects international law'.

[70] See R. Lee, 'Creating an international criminal court: of procedures and compromises', pp. 141–52 in H. von Hebel *et al.*, *Reflections on the ICC*, n. 3 *supra*, pp. 145–6.

# 2

# War crimes (I): grave breaches

## Background to war crimes[1]

While the origins of the laws of war stretch back centuries,[2] the nineteenth and twentieth centuries were the first to see multilateral conventions on the law of armed conflict,[3] and the twentieth century was the first to see significant prosecutions for breaches of this law.[4] Following the prosecution of a small number of Germans after the First World War by the Supreme Court of the Reich in Leipzig,[5] the aftermath of the Second World War saw the prosecution by the Allies of Axis citizens in the International Tribunals of Nuremberg and Tokyo, and the prosecution of countless more accused in national military tribunals throughout Europe.[6] Towards the end of the century the *ad hoc* tribunals for Yugoslavia and Rwanda were established by the Security Council resolutions under Chapter VII and commenced prosecuting persons accused of war

[1] See generally L. Green, 'The law of war in historical perspective', pp. 38–78, in M. Schmitt (ed.), *The Law of Military Operations: Liber Amicorum Professor Jack Grunawalt*, 72 *US Naval War College International Law Studies* (Newport RI: Naval War College, 1998).

[2] L. Green, *The Contemporary Law of Armed Conflict* (Manchester: Manchester University Press, 2nd edn, 2000), pp. 20–33.

[3] Roberts and Guelff, *Documents*, pp. 4–6, and C. Greenwood, 'Historical development and legal basis', pp. 1–38, in D. Fleck (ed.), *Handbook of Humanitarian Law in Armed Conflict* (Oxford: Oxford University Press, 1999), para. 106.

[4] Notable exceptions include the 1474 trial of Peter von Hagenbach by the Hanseatic cities of Breisach, see G. Schwarzenberger, *International Law as applied by International Courts and Tribunals*, Vol. II, *The Law of Armed Conflict* (London: Stevens, 1968), pp. 462–6, and the trial of Captain Wirz of the Confederate army for crimes committed in a Union prisoner of war camp, described by L. Laska and J. Smith, ' "Hell and the devil": Andersonville and the trial of Captain Henry Wirz, C.S.A., 1865', Milit LR., 68 (1975), 77–132 – although the crimes in both cases could be characterised as crimes against humanity, rather than war crimes *per se*.

[5] See H. von Hebel, 'An international criminal court: a historical perspective', pp. 13–38, in H. von Hebel *et al.*, *Reflections on the International Criminal Court* (The Hague: Asser, 1999), pp. 15–16.

[6] *Ibid.*, pp. 19–22, and see the LRTWC series (London: HMSO, 1947–49).

crimes.[7] The beginning of this century has also seen the prosecution of war crimes in 'internationalised' courts and tribunals such as the Special Panel for Serious Criminal Offences in East Timor and the Special Court for Sierra Leone.[8]

Despite the significance of these prosecutions, and the proliferation of treaties on the law of armed conflict, it is nevertheless true that enforcement of the laws of armed conflict has 'limped along behind the developmental pace of rules on warfare'.[9] The International Criminal Court (ICC) is a vital step forward in addressing this imbalance, as remedying the culture of impunity for war crimes cannot be achieved through the selective justice of *ad hoc* or 'internationalised' tribunals alone.[10] It is therefore important that the Rome Statute's provisions on war crimes under Article 8 are clearly interpreted in order to promote deterrence of the crimes within, and to assist the prosecution and defence of those accused of breaches of the law.

[7] The ICTY and ICTR were created by SC Res. 827, 25 May 1993 and 955, 8 November 1994, respectively. See R. Clark and M. Sann (eds), *The Prosecution of International Crimes: A Critical Study of the International Tribunal for the Former Yugoslavia* (New Brunswick NJ: Transaction, 1996); J. Jones, *The Practice of the International Criminal Tribunals for the Former Yugoslavia and Rwanda* (New York: Transnational, 1998); V. Morris and M. Scharf, *An Insider's Guide to the International Criminal Tribunal for the former Yugoslavia: A Documentary History and Analysis* (New York: Transnational, 1995), and V. Morris and M. Scharf, *The International Criminal Tribunal for Rwanda* (New York: Transnational, 1997).

[8] On 6 March 2000 the UN Transitional Administration in East Timor (UNTAET) promulgated UNTAET/REG/2000/11, a regulation providing for the Dili District Court (a domestic East Timorese tribunal) to have exclusive jurisdiction over 'serious criminal offences', namely genocide, war crimes, crimes against humanity, murder, sexual offences and torture (later amended by UNTAET/REG/2001/21 of 14 September 2001). Following this, the Transitional Administrator, on 6 June 2000, promulgated UNTAET/REG/2000/15, a regulation on the establishment of panels with exclusive jurisdiction over serious offences. These panels were not separate courts but panels of judges within the institutional framework of the District Court, comprised of two international judges and one East Timorese judge; the appeals were heard by a mixed international/national bench of the Court of Appeal in Dili. The relevant documents are available at: <http://www.jsmp.minihub.org/Language_English/legislation_english.htm>. The Special Court for Sierra Leone was established on 16 January 2002 following an agreement between the government of Sierra Leone and the United Nations. The relevant documents are available at: <http://www.sc-sl.org/documents.html>. For academic comment on 'internationalised' tribunals see D. Turns, '"Internationalized" or *ad hoc* justice for international criminal law in a time of transition: the cases of East Timor, Kosovo, Sierra Leone and Cambodia', ARIEL, 6 (2001), 123–80, and S. Linton, 'Cambodia, East Timor and Sierra Leone: experiments in international justice', Crim LF, 12 (2001), 185–246.

[9] R. Wolfrum, 'Enforcement of international humanitarian law', pp. 517–50, in D. Fleck (ed.), *Handbook of Humanitarian Law*, n. 3 *supra*, p. 518.

[10] See G. Skillen, 'Enforcement of international humanitarian law', pp. 205–16 in H. Durham and T. McCormack (eds), *The Changing Face of Conflict and the Efficacy of International Humanitarian Law* (The Hague: Kluwer, 1999), pp. 210–11, and G. Triggs, 'National prosecutions of war crimes and the rule of law', pp. 175–91 in H. Durham and T. McCormack, *The Changing Face of Conflict*, p. 190.

## Nexus with an armed conflict

For each of the crimes under Article 8 there must be a nexus between the crime itself and the armed conflict. The Elements of Crimes lay down that the conduct for each offence within Article 8 must take place 'in the context of' and be 'associated with an [international or non-international] armed conflict'.[11] The necessity of this link was also recognised by the International Criminal Tribunal for the former Yugoslavia (ICTY) in the Appeal Chamber's Interlocutory Decision on Jurisdiction in the *Tadić* case, where the Court explained 'in the context of an armed conflict' as meaning 'that the alleged crimes were *closely related* to the hostilities'.[12]

The Trial Chamber in *Tadić* suggested that this close relationship between the hostilities and the crime could be demonstrated by proving that 'the crime was committed in the course of or as part of the hostilities in, or occupation of, an area controlled by one of the parties'.[13] The Judgement further held that it was not necessary to show that 'armed conflict was occurring at the exact time and place of the proscribed acts',[14] nor that it was 'part of a policy or of a practice officially endorsed or tolerated by one of the parties to the conflict', nor even 'in the actual interest of a party to the conflict'.[15]

The Women's Caucus for Gender Justice have strongly argued, particularly in respect of crimes of sexual violence, that the phrase 'associated with an . . . armed conflict' in the Elements of Crimes (EOC) should be read widely enough to include crimes committed in the aftermath of war or taking advantage of the situation of war.[16] This approach was taken in the *Kunarać* case, where the Trial Chamber stated that 'Muslim civilians were killed, raped or otherwise abused as a direct result of the armed conflict and because the armed conflict apparently offered blanket impunity to the perpetrators'.[17] It further held that '[t]he

[11] EOC, Assembly of States Parties to the Rome Statute of the ICC, Official Records, First Session, ICC-ASP/1/3, 3–10 September 2002 (hereinafter: EOC), pp. 125–44. For a discussion of the temporal and geographical extent of armed conflicts see *infra*, p. 173.

[12] *Tadić*, Interlocutory Appeal Decision, para. 70, emphasis added.

[13] *Tadić*, Trial Judgement, para. 573. See also the *Stakić* Appeal Judgement statement that 'a geographical and temporal linkage between the crimes ascribed to the accused and the armed conflict' must be established, para. 342.

[14] *Tadić*, Trial Judgement, para. 573; see also *Kordić and Čerkez*, Trial Judgement, para. 27, and C. Rottensteiner, 'The denial of humanitarian assistance as a crime under international law', IRRC, 835 (1999), 555–82, p. 561.

[15] *Tadić*, Trial Judgement, para. 573. This approach was endorsed by the Trial Chambers in *Čelebici* and *Blaškić*; *Čelebici*, Trial Judgement, paras 193–5, and *Blaškić*, Trial Judgement, paras 69–70. See *Furundžija*, Trial Judgement, para. 65, for an example of where this nexus was found and *Kayishema and Ruzindana*, Trial Judgement, para. 621, for an example of where it was not.

[16] Women's Caucus for Gender Justice, 'Recommendations and commentary for the Elements annex', submitted to the 26 July–13 August 1999 Preparatory Commission for the International Criminal Court. Available at: <http://www.iccwomen.addr.com/icc/pc199907/elements.htm>.

[17] *Kunarać*, Trial Judgement, para. 568.

requirement that the act be closely related to the armed conflict is satisfied if, as in the present case, the crimes are committed in the aftermath of the fighting, and until the cessation of combat activities in a certain region, and are committed in furtherance or take advantage of the situation created by the fighting'.[18]

This approach was elaborated by the *Kunarać* Appeal Chamber, which held that '[t]he armed conflict need not have been causal to the commission of the crime, but the existence of an armed conflict must, at a minimum, have played a substantial part in the perpetrator's ability to commit it, his decision to commit it, the manner in which it was committed or the purpose for which it was committed'.[19] The Appeal Chamber also suggested factors which could be taken into account in order to decide whether a nexus between the acts in question and the armed conflict existed, including 'the fact that the perpetrator is a combatant; the fact that the victim is a noncombatant; the fact that the victim is a member of the opposing party; the fact that the act may be said to serve the ultimate goal of a military campaign; and the fact that the crime is committed as part of or in the context of the perpetrator's official duties'.[20] This list was approved by the *Rutaganda* Appeal Chamber, which commented that 'the determination of a close relationship between particular offences and an armed conflict will usually require a consideration of several factors, not just one' and warned that particular care is needed in determining a nexus with the conflict when the accused is a noncombatant.[21]

The nexus between the acts of the perpetrator and the armed conflict should not be too readily acknowledged, as it is this relationship which raises the status of an act from an ordinary domestic crime to a war crime and so a breach of international law. However, it is submitted that the ICC should bear in mind the comments of the *Kunarać* Trial Chamber above and make certain that their interpretation of the conflict nexus is broad enough to ensure that when dealing with offences of sexual violence they do not create a loophole to be exploited by defendants by defining such offences as 'private' even when committed in the course of an armed conflict.[22]

The EOC for all offences in Article 8 require, in addition to a nexus between the armed conflict and the crime, that the perpetrator 'was aware of factual circumstances that established the existence of an armed conflict'.[23] In respect of this, the introduction to the elements for Article 8 states that there is no requirement for a legal evaluation by the perpetrator as to either the existence of an

[18] *Ibid.*

[19] *Kunarać*, Appeal Judgement, para. 58.

[20] *Ibid.*, para. 59. Followed by the Special Court for Sierra Leone in *Fofana and Kondewa*, Trial Judgement, para. 130.

[21] *Rutaganda*, Appeal Judgement, para. 570.

[22] In the case of institutionalised sexual violence a nexus to the conflict would, of course, be undeniable, see C. Chinkin, 'Women's international tribunal on Japanese military sexual slavery', AJIL, 95 (2001), 335–41, p. 340.

[23] EOC, pp. 125–44.

armed conflict or whether it is international or non-international.[24] Therefore, it seems that the perpetrator must merely be sufficiently aware of the circumstances which objectively establish an armed conflict to comprehend the context in which he commits his offence.[25] This interpretation is supported by the approach taken by the *Naletilić and Martinović* Appeal Chamber, which held that '[i]t is a general principle of criminal law that the correct legal classification of a conduct by the perpetrator is not required' but asserted that the principle of individual guilt 'demands sufficient awareness of factual circumstances establishing the armed conflict and its (international or internal) character'.[26]

## Article 8(1)

### Jurisdiction in respect of war crimes

The Court is to deal with war crimes, particularly when they are committed 'as part of a plan or policy', or as part of a 'large-scale commission of such crimes'. This *chapeau* was introduced at the third Preparatory Committee meeting,[27] in a proposal by the United States,[28] taking into account delegates' concern that war crimes should be 'limited to exceptionally serious violations of international concern'.[29] The threshold clause was intended to prevent the Court from 'becoming overburdened by minor or isolated cases'.[30]

Askin comments that the language of the *chapeau* 'effectively prevents random acts, isolated crimes, or less serious offenses from coming within the jurisdiction of the Court'.[31] However, the use of the word 'particularly' demonstrates that the Court may nevertheless deal with isolated incidents if they are sufficiently grave, and indeed Fenrick comments that 'plan, policy and scale are

[24] *Ibid.*, p. 125.

[25] K. Dörmann suggests that the awareness of the perpetrator with respect to the existence of an armed conflict is below the level required by Article 30 of the ICC, K. Dörmann, *Elements of War Crimes under the Rome Statute of the International Criminal Court: Sources and Commentary* (Cambridge: Cambridge University Press and ICRC, 2002), pp. 21–2, and K. Dörmann, 'Contributions by the *ad hoc* tribunals for the former Yugoslavia and Rwanda to the ongoing work on elements of crimes in the context of the ICC', ASIL Proceedings, 94 (2000), 284–6, p. 285.

[26] *Naletilić and Martinović*, Appeal Judgement, para. 119.

[27] Decisions taken by the Preparatory Committee at its session held from 11 to 21 February 1997, UN Doc. A/AC.249/1997/L.5, 1997, p. 6.

[28] H. von Hebel and D. Robinson, 'Crimes within the jurisdiction of the court', pp. 79–126, in R. Lee (ed.), *The International Criminal Court: The Making of the Rome Statute: Issues, Negotiations, Results* (The Hague: Kluwer, 2001), p. 107.

[29] See the concerns expressed at the first Preparatory Committee meeting, Summary of the Proceedings of the Preparatory Committee during the Period 25 March to 12 April 1996, UN Doc. A/AC.249/1, 1996, p. 14.

[30] H. von Hebel and D. Robinson, 'Crimes within the jurisdiction of the court', n. 28 *supra*, p. 107.

[31] K. Askin, 'Crimes within the jurisdiction of the International Criminal Court', Crim LF, 10 (1999), 33–59, p. 50.

not elements or jurisdictional prerequisites, they are factors which should be taken into account by the Prosecutor'.[32]

### Differentiation between international and non-international armed conflicts under the Rome Statute

Although the ICC will have jurisdiction over offences committed in both international conflicts, under Article 8(2)(a) and (b), and non-international armed conflicts, under Article 8(2)(c) and (e), the *travaux préparatoires* to the Rome Statute do not explain how the ICC should differentiate between the two situations.[33] Common Article 2 of the 1949 Geneva Conventions gives an insight into the definition of an international armed conflict by stating that the Conventions should apply 'to all cases of declared war or of any other armed conflict which may arise between two or more of the High Contracting Parties, even if the state of war is not recognized by one of them' and to 'all cases of partial or total occupation', even if such occupation does not meet with armed resistance.

The ICTY has expanded upon this definition in the *Tadić* Appeal Judgement, which set out three situations which would constitute an international armed conflict.[34] First, a conflict is indisputably international if it takes place between two or more States.[35] Second, a conflict taking place on the territory of one State may be internationalised by the intervention of the military forces of a second State. Third, a conflict taking place on the territory of one State between nationals of that State may be internationalised if 'some of the participants in the internal armed conflict act on behalf of that other [second] State'.[36]

The test to distinguish this third type of international armed conflict from a purely internal conflict has been analysed in depth in the jurisprudence of the ICTY.[37] The present approach taken by the ICTY is set out in the *Tadić* Appeal Judgement,[38] which held that the correct test for the internationalisation of a conflict owing to the influence of a foreign State over a military group in another State is the same as the test of State responsibility of that State for violations of

[32] M. Cottier, W. Fenrick, P. Viseur Sellers and A. Zimmermann, 'Article 8, war crimes', pp. 173–262 in O. Triffterer (ed.), *Commentary on the Rome Statute of the International Criminal Court: Observers' Notes, Article by Article* (Baden-Baden: Nomos, 1999, hereinafter Cottier *et al.*, 'Article 8'), p. 181, and R. Lee (ed.), *The International Criminal Court: Elements of Crimes and Rules of Procedure and Evidence* (New York: Transnational, 2001, hereinafter Lee (ed.), *ICC: Elements*), p. 110.

[33] *Thomas Lubanga Dyilo*, Pre-trial Chamber Decision on the Confirmation of Charges, para. 205.

[34] *Tadić*, Appeal Judgement, para. 84.

[35] This may be a very low-level affair, see Cottier *et al.*, 'Article 8', p. 182.

[36] *Tadić*, Appeal Judgement, para. 84. *Thomas Lubanga Dyilo*, Pre-trial Chamber Decision on the Confirmation of Charges, para. 209, follows *Tadić* here.

[37] C. Byron, 'Armed conflicts: international or non-international?', JCSL, 6 (2001), 63–90, pp. 66–79.

[38] This has been followed by the *Aleksovski* and *Čelebici* Appeal Judgements, paras 134 and 26 respectively, and the *Blaškić* and *Kordić and Čerkez* Trial Judgements, paras 75 and 111 respectively.

international law by the military group.[39] This had been the approach of the *Tadić* and *Aleksovski* Trial Chambers, which had based their reasoning on the Judgement of the International Court of Justice (ICJ) in *Nicaragua*.[40] However, the *Tadić* Appeal Judgement did not find the reasoning of the ICJ on State responsibility in the *Nicaragua* case persuasive.[41]

The majority in the *Tadić* appeal propounded a test of control over rebels which differentiated between private individuals and individuals making up an organised and hierarchically structured group such as a military unit.[42] They found that only in the case of private individuals would it be necessary to show that the State had 'issued specific instructions concerning the commission of the breach',[43] whereas in order to attribute State responsibility for the actions of a military unit it would be sufficient to show that the group as a whole was under the 'overall control' of the State.[44] Therefore, a conflict within one State between the government of that State and rebels is internationalised if a foreign State has 'overall control' of those rebels, which means that the foreign State must have '*a role in organising, coordinating or planning the military actions* of the military group, in addition to financing, training and equipping or providing operational support to that group'.[45]

Although this approach has now gained ascendancy in the ICTY, it does not bind the ICC to adopt the same reasoning in the future, there being no principle of *stare decisis* in international law.[46] A possible alternative was

[39] *Tadić*, Appeal Judgement, para. 104.

[40] See *Tadić*, Trial Judgement, paras 585–8, and *Aleksovski*, Trial Judgement, Joint Opinion of the Majority, para. 11.

[41] *Tadić*, Appeal Judgement, para. 115. For a criticism of this approach see M. Sassòli and L. Olson, 'International decisions: Prosecutor *v.* Tadić (Judgement)', AJIL, 94 (2000), 571–8, p. 575.

[42] *Tadić*, Appeal Judgement, paras 118–21.

[43] *Ibid.*, para. 118. To support this argument the cases of *United States Diplomatic and Consular Staff in Tehran*, ICJ Rep (1980), 3, and *Alfred W. Short v. Islamic Republic of Iran*, Iran–US Claims Tribunal, 16 Iran–US CTR, 1987, 76, were cited in paras 132–5.

[44] *Tadić*, Appeal Judgement, para. 120. To support this argument the cases of *United States v. Mexico (Stephens case)*, Mexico–US General Claims Commission, RIAA, Vol. IV, 266; *Kenneth P. Yeager v. Islamic Republic of Iran*, Iran–US Claims Tribunal, 17 Iran–US CTR, 1987, Vol. IV, 92; *Loizidou v. Turkey (Merits)*, ECHR, Judgement, 18 December 1996 (Merits), 26 Reports of Judgements and Decisions, 1996-VI, 2217, and the *Jogic* case, Oberlandesgericht, Düsseldorf, 26 September 1997, 2 StE 8/96 (unpublished typescript, on file with the ICTY library, see *Tadić*, Appeal Judgement, para. 129, and fns 154–6) were cited in paras 125–9.

[45] *Tadić*, Appeal Judgement, para. 137, original emphasis.

[46] Under Article 21 of the Rome Statute the Court will apply first the Statute, EOC and Rules of Procedure and Evidence (RPE), Assembly of States Parties to the Rome Statute of the ICC, Official Records, First Session, ICC-ASP/1/3, 3–10 September 2002, pp. 10–107, secondly applicable treaties and principles and rules of international law (including the established principles of the international law of armed conflict) and thirdly general principles of law derived from national laws of legal systems of the world. Nowhere are the decisions of other international tribunals mentioned except, perhaps, where they authoritatively expound the principles and rules of international law. See also M. Greenspan, *The Modern Law of Land Warfare* (Berkeley CA: University of California Press, 1959), p. 7.

suggested by Judge Shahabuddeen in his Separate Opinion in the *Tadić* Appeal Judgement, where he expressed the view that the *Nicaragua* Judgement was correctly decided.[47] He argued persuasively that in order to discover whether there is an international armed conflict, the question to be asked is not whether the foreign State has State responsibility for the actions of rebels in another State, but whether the foreign State has *used force* against the other State through the rebels.[48] Judge Shahabuddeen suggested a flexible test of 'effective control' to determine whether the foreign State had sufficient control over the rebel military to constitute a use of force against the other State and in the case of *Tadić* found that Yugoslavia was using force against Bosnia-Herzegovina through the Bosnian Serb army, 'even if such control did not rise to the level required to fix the FRY with state responsibility for any breaches of international humanitarian law committed by the VRS'.[49]

However, Judge Shahabuddeen's interpretation of the test for the internationalisation of a conflict in this situation was not followed by the ICC Pre-trial Chamber in the *Thomas Lubanga Dyilo* case.[50] Here the Court found that the conflict in Ituri in the Democratic Republic of the Congo was in fact international as a result of the intervention of Uganda, which was an Occupying Power in the region because of the actions of its armed forces, which had established and exercised authority there.[51] Nevertheless the Court also commented that a conflict could be internationalised in circumstances when armed forces act on behalf of a foreign State and followed the approach of the *Tadić* Appeal Judgement, stating that 'where a State does not intervene directly on the territory of another State through its own troops, the overall control test will be used to determine whether armed forces are acting on behalf of the first State'.[52]

[47] *Tadić*, Appeal Judgement, Separate Opinion of Judge Shahabuddeen, para. 5.

[48] *Ibid.*, para. 17, and *Blaškić*, Trial Judgement, Declaration of Judge Shahabuddeen. See also T. Meron, 'Classification of armed conflict in the former Yugoslavia: *Nicaragua's* fallout', AJIL, 92 (1998), 236–42, pp. 236–7.

[49] *Tadić*, Appeal Judgement, Separate Opinion of Judge Shahabuddeen, para. 19. Judge Shahabuddeen comments that in *Nicaragua* the Court found that 'the arming and training of the *Contras* in the circumstances of the case amounted to a use of force' by the United States against Nicaragua, but that the United States were not liable for the breaches of humanitarian law committed by the Contras, *ibid.*, paras 8–11 (see *Case concerning Military and Paramilitary Activities in and against Nicaragua (Merits)*, Judgement, *Nicaragua v. United States*, ICJ Rep (1986) 14, especially paras 288 and 292). Nevertheless, Judge Shahabuddeen noted in his Declaration appended to the *Blaškić* Trial Chamber Judgement that a conflict thus internationalised may also retain some internal aspects, and therefore may be mixed in status. On this see C. Greenwood, 'International humanitarian law and the Tadić case', EJIL, 7 (1996), 265–83, pp. 271–3.

[50] *Thomas Lubanga Dyilo*, Pre-trial Chamber Decision on the Confirmation of Charges, paras 205–20.

[51] *Ibid.*, paras 213–17.

[52] *Ibid.*, paras 210–11.

Perhaps this failure to rethink the ICTY jurisprudence on the test for internationalisation of an armed conflict in such situations is not surprising, given the influence of former judges from the *ad hoc* tribunals in the ICC.[53] Indeed, in the *Dyilo* case the Presiding Judge of the Pre-trial Chamber, Judge Jorda, was formerly Presiding Judge of the *Blaškić* Trial Chamber at the ICTY, where the judgement followed *Tadić* on this issue. There is, however, no reason why a differently constituted trial or appeal Chamber at the ICC should not look at this issue in another context and take a different view.[54]

A fourth type of internationalised conflict not contemplated by the *Tadić* Appeal Judgement, but relevant for the States Parties to Additional Protocol I (AP I), is the situation described in Article 1(4) of the Protocol 'where peoples are fighting against colonial domination and alien occupation and against racist regimes in the exercise of their right of self-determination'.[55] The exercise of self-determination in such circumstances would turn what would otherwise be viewed as an internal conflict into an international one for the States Parties to AP I, provided that the rebel group had undertaken to apply the Geneva Conventions and Protocol.[56]

The type of armed conflict internationalised by AP I may pose problems for the ICC. The Rome Statute does not specifically incorporate AP I and so the ICC, when dealing with an individual alleged to have committed crimes in this situation, would be faced with two alternatives. The Court could make a finding of the nature of the conflict dependent upon whether or not the State involved had ratified AP I,[57] or it could consistently apply the same law to all States Parties to the Rome Statute irrespective of their participation in other international humanitarian law instruments. It is submitted that the latter approach would be

[53] Currently, out of the eighteen judges at the ICC, four have previously served as judges at either the ICTY or the ICTR.

[54] See the discussion of this test by the ICJ in *Application of the Convention on the Prevention and Punishment of the Crime of Genocide*, Judgement of 26 February 2007 (Bosnia and Herzegovina *v.* Serbia and Montenegro), available at <http://www.icj-cij.org/>, paras 398–407.

[55] H. Gasser, 'An appeal for ratification by the United States', AJIL, 81 (1987), 912–25, pp. 916–17; H. McCoubrey and N. White, *International Law and Armed Conflict* (Aldershot: Dartmouth, 1992), pp. 197–9, and H. Wilson, *International Law and the Use of Force by National Liberation Movements* (Oxford: Clarendon Press, 1988), pp. 162–80, suggest that Article 1(4) is very limited in scope. E. Kwakwa, *The International Law of Armed Conflict: Personal and Material Fields of Application* (Dordrecht: Kluwer, 1992), pp. 49–66, and G. Abi-Saab, 'Wars of national liberation in the Geneva Conventions and Protocols', 165 Rec des Cours (1979) IV, 353–445, argue for a more liberal interpretation.

[56] Article 96(3), AP I. See G. Aldrich, 'Progressive development of the laws of war: a reply to criticisms of the 1977 Geneva Protocol I', Va JIL, 26 (1986), 693–720, pp. 701–2, and Y. Dinstein, 'Interstate armed conflict and wars of national liberation: commentator', Am ULR, 31 (1982), 849–53, pp. 849–51.

[57] See M. Bothe, 'War crimes', pp. 379–426, in A. Cassese *et al.*, *The Rome Statute of the International Criminal Court: A Commentary*, Vol. I (Oxford: Oxford University Press, 2002), p. 391.

preferable, but it would entail a decision upon whether the internationalisation of conflicts in such a situation constitutes customary international law.[58]

A final type of armed conflict which may be internationalised derives from the situation of a State which is fighting an internal conflict against a rebel movement and invites a neighbouring State to send armed forces to assist in defeating the rebels.[59] This type of conflict does not immediately appear to come within the description given in Common Article 2 of the Geneva Conventions, not being 'between' two contracting parties, and may not give rise to an occupation of territory by the neighbouring State's forces.

It is, however, arguable that such a conflict would be internationalised. First, the 'request' may not be genuine at all, and may be a mere device used by the neighbouring State to mask an invasion, or it may be made by an individual not constitutionally capable of speaking for the State.[60] Second, it is strongly argued by some publicists that, once a civil war is under way, there can be no valid request for external assistance in any case, as 'there is no authority competent under international law to invite assistance from other states'.[61] Finally, a purposive interpretation of the Geneva Conventions could lead to the conclusion that the substantial intervention of foreign troops in an armed conflict would convert the conflict into an international one.

## Article 8(2)(a)

### Persons or property protected under the 'grave breach' provisions of the Geneva Conventions

The 'grave breach' provisions of the Geneva Conventions, as reproduced in Article 8(2)(a) of the Rome Statute, apply only in international armed conflicts.[62] This,

[58] C. Greenwood, 'Customary law status of the 1977 Geneva Protocols', pp. 93–114 in A. Delissen and D. Tanja, *Humanitarian Law of Armed Conflict: Challenges Ahead* (Dordrecht: Nijhoff, 1991), at pp. 111–12, and the same author, 'Scope of application of humanitarian law', pp. 39–63 in D. Fleck (ed.), *Handbook of Humanitarian Law*, n. 3 *supra*, para. 202(4), suggests that Article 1(4) does not represent customary international law. This is supported by C. Murray, 'The 1977 Geneva Protocols and conflict in Southern Africa', ICLQ, 33 (1984), 462–70, p. 465. However, of the 159 States Parties to AP I (September 2002), none has made a reservation or declaration with regard to Article 1(4). (See ICRC website at <http://www.icrc.org/>.)

[59] See H. Gasser, 'International non-international armed conflicts: case studies of Afghanistan, Kampuchea, and Lebanon', Am ULR, 31 (1982), 911–26.

[60] See D. Harris, *Cases and Materials on International Law* (London: Sweet & Maxwell, 5th edn, 1998), pp. 890–4.

[61] M. Dixon, *Textbook on International Law* (London: Blackstone, 3rd edn, 1996), p. 288, and see L. Doswald-Beck, 'The legal validity of military intervention by invitation of the government', BYIL, 56 (1985), 189–252.

[62] C. Greenwood, 'International humanitarian law and the Tadić case', n. 49 *supra*, p. 276.

whilst not explicitly stated, was the clear intention of the drafters, who accepted that grave breaches of the Geneva Conventions should be included in the Statute of the ICC prior to accepting the inclusion of jurisdiction over crimes in non-international armed conflicts.[63] Furthermore, this is also the clear meaning of the text as a whole, as is demonstrated by the expression '*[o]ther* serious violations of the laws and customs applicable in international armed conflict', used in Article 8(2)(b).[64] The Elements of Crimes confirm this interpretation, including in each element that the conduct 'took place in the context of . . . an international armed conflict'.[65]

Under Article 8(2)(a) an accused may be prosecuted for any of the listed grave breaches[66] if they are carried out against 'persons or property protected under the provisions of the relevant Geneva Convention'. The four Geneva Conventions protect the wounded and sick of the armed forces in the field, the wounded, sick and shipwrecked of the armed forces at sea, prisoners of war and civilians,[67] and according to Baxter 'are at their weakest in delineating the various categories of persons who benefit from the protection of each'.[68] Under Article 8(2)(a) of the ICC, however, the alleged victims must be protected against that particular crime under the grave breach provision of the relevant Geneva Convention.

Those entitled to protection under the First and Second Geneva Conventions are 'the wounded and sick' or the 'wounded, sick and shipwrecked at sea' belonging to the following categories: members of the armed forces, or militias or volunteer corps of the armed forces, of a Party to the conflict; members of militias or other volunteer corps who fulfil the four conditions laid down, including obeying the laws and customs of war; members of regular armed forces professing allegiance to an authority not recognised by a Detaining Power; persons accompanying armed forces without being members thereof; members of crews of the merchant marine and civil aircraft who do not benefit by more favourable treatment under international law, and inhabitants of a non-occupied territory who spontaneously take up arms to resist invading forces.[69]

[63] Report of the *Ad Hoc* Committee on the Establishment of an International Criminal Court, GAOR Supplement No. 22 (A/50/22) 1995, p. 16.

[64] Emphasis added, and see D. Sarooshi, 'The statute of the International Criminal Court', ICLQ, 48 (1999), 387–404, p. 399.

[65] EOC, pp. 125–30. See also K. Dörmann, 'The first and second sessions of the Preparatory Commission for the International Criminal Court', YIHL, 2 (1999), 283–306, p. 288.

[66] See J. Paust, 'The Preparatory Committee's "definition of crimes": war crimes', Crim LF, 8 (1997), 431–44, pp. 437–8.

[67] Geneva Conventions I, II, III and IV. For a brief description of persons protected under each Convention see T. Murphy, 'Sanctions and enforcement of the humanitarian law of the four Geneva Conventions of 1949 and Geneva Protocol I of 1977', Milit LR, 103 (1984), 3–77, pp. 23–4.

[68] R. Baxter, 'So-called "unprivileged belligerency": spies, guerrillas and saboteurs', BYIL, 27 (1951), 323–45, pp. 326–7.

[69] Article 13, Geneva Conventions I and II.

Those entitled to protection under the Third Geneva Convention are prisoners of war 'who have fallen into the power of the enemy'.[70] This expression is broader than the expression 'captured' and includes individuals who have become prisoners without fighting, such as those who have surrendered.[71] Prisoners of war must either belong to one of the categories described above in relation to the first two Geneva Conventions or belong, or have belonged, to the armed forces of an occupied territory if the Occupying Power finds it necessary to intern them, or belong to one of the categories above and be interned by neutral or non-belligerent Powers on their territory.[72]

Those entitled to protection under the Fourth Geneva Convention are persons, not protected by the first three Geneva Conventions,[73] 'who, at a given moment and in any manner whatsoever, find themselves, in the case of a conflict or occupation, in the hands of a Party to the conflict or Occupying Power of which they are not nationals'.[74] Particular difficulty has been encountered by the ICTY in interpreting the extent of protection for civilians under this Convention. This is owing to the fact that the definition causes problems in the case of an armed conflict on the territory of a single State which is 'internationalised' owing to the fact that 'some of the participants in the internal armed conflict act on behalf of that other [second] State'.[75] In such a situation all the active participants may hold the same formal nationality.[76]

There are three ways that the ICC could tackle this problem. First, the definition could be read strictly, resulting in no protection under the grave breach provisions in Article 8(2)(a) for civilians in an 'internationalised' conflict where all parties have the same nationality. This would be an undesirable outcome and arguably contrary to the object and purpose of the Conventions from which Article 8(2)(a) is drawn. Second, the expression 'in the hands of' could be interpreted more widely.[77] This was the approach of the ICTY in the Rule 61 hearing of *Rajić*. The Trial Chamber held that the Bosnian Croats were under the control of Croatia, and therefore the Bosnian Muslims in Stupni Do, which

[70] Article 4, Geneva Convention III.

[71] J. Pictet (ed.), *The Geneva Conventions of 12 August 1949: Commentary III Convention* (Geneva: ICRC, 1952–60; hereinafter: Pictet (ed.), *Commentary: I/II/III/IV Convention*), p. 50, but see comments on defectors in the *Manual of Military Law Part III: The Law of War on Land* (London: HMSO, 1958; hereinafter: *British Military Manual*), para. 126.

[72] Article 4, Geneva Convention III, and see Pictet (ed.), *Commentary: III Convention*, pp. 44–72, and G. Draper, *The Red Cross Conventions* (London: Stevens, 1958), pp. 52–4.

[73] According to the Commentary the result of this negative definition is that everyone is covered by one of the Conventions: '*there is no* intermediate status; nobody in enemy hands can be outside the law', original emphasis, Pictet (ed.), *Commentary: IV Convention*, p. 51.

[74] Article 4, Geneva Convention IV, and see Pictet (ed.), *Commentary: IV Convention*, pp. 45–51.

[75] *Tadić*, Appeal Judgement, para. 84.

[76] See Article 12, Geneva Conventions I and II, and comments by T. Meron, 'On the inadequate reach of humanitarian and human rights law and the need for a new instrument', AJIL, 77 (1983), 589–606, p. 595.

[77] See Pictet (ed.), *Commentary: IV Convention*, p. 47.

the Bosnian Croats controlled, were protected persons under the Fourth Geneva Convention, as they were 'constructively "in the hands of" Croatia, a country of which they were not nationals'.[78]

The shortcoming of this approach is that it offers somewhat one-sided protection. For example, if the rebels in State A are acting as agents for State B, then the civilians in areas controlled by the State A rebels will be protected by the Fourth Geneva Convention, as they will be constructively 'in the hands of' State B. However, if the State A government regains control over some State A rebel territory, then the State A rebels and supporters will not be constructively 'in the hands of' another State. This was essentially the *reductio ad absurdum* argument made by the Appeal Chamber in the Interlocutory Appeal on jurisdiction in the *Tadić* case.[79]

The third possible approach is more radical but rectifies the shortcomings of the other methods. It involves a flexible reading of the expression 'nationals', and was applied by the ICTY in the *Tadić* Appeal Judgement when interpreting Article 4 of the Fourth Geneva Convention.[80] The Appeal Chamber extrapolated from the protection for stateless persons and refugees in Article 4[81] that the legal bond of nationality was not crucial, even in 1949, and could be overridden by 'the lack of both allegiance to a State and diplomatic protection by this State'.[82] They stated that 'in modern inter-ethnic armed conflicts such as that in the former Yugoslavia, new States are often created during the conflict and *ethnicity rather than nationality may become the grounds for allegiance*'.[83] Therefore, the Appeal Chamber concluded, the primary purpose of Article 4 'is to ensure the safeguards afforded by the Convention to those civilians who do not enjoy the diplomatic protection, and correlatively are not subject to the allegiance and control, of the State in whose hands they may find themselves'.[84] This approach has since been consistently supported by the ICTY trial and appeal Chambers.[85]

This expansive interpretation of nationality for the purpose of determining protected person status under the Fourth Geneva Convention may be found persuasive

[78] *Rajić*, Rule 61 Review, para. 37, supported in *Blaškić*, Trial Judgement, paras 148–50.

[79] *Tadić*, Interlocutory Appeal Decision, para. 76, but see G. Aldrich, 'Jurisdiction of the International Criminal Tribunal for the former Yugoslavia', AJIL, 90 (1996), 64–9, pp. 66–7, and C. Greenwood, 'International humanitarian law and the Tadić case', n. 49 *supra*, pp. 272–3.

[80] *Tadić*, Appeal Judgement, paras 163–9.

[81] See Article 70, Geneva Convention IV, and Pictet (ed.), *Commentary: IV Convention*, pp. 46 and 350.

[82] *Tadić*, Appeal Judgement, para. 165.

[83] *Ibid.*, para. 166, emphasis added. See also W. Fenrick, 'The application of the Geneva Conventions by the International Criminal Tribunal for the former Yugoslavia', IRRC, 834 (1999), 317–29, p. 329.

[84] *Tadić*, Appeal Judgement, para. 168.

[85] *Blaškić*, Trial Judgement, para. 127, *Blaškić*, Appeal Judgement, paras 180–2, *Kordić and Čerkez*, Trial Judgement, para. 153, *Kordić and Čerkez*, Appeal Judgement, paras 328–30, *Aleksovski*, Appeal Judgement, paras 151–2, and *Čelebici*, Appeal Judgement, para. 84.

by the ICC.[86] It is a solution which provides protection for both parties to a conflict on the territory of one State in the situation where it is internationalised, by the fact that some of the participants are acting on behalf of another State, and when most of the active participants hold the same formal nationality, or when the issue of the participants' nationalities is unclear owing to the creation of new States in the territory of a former State.[87]

The EOC for the offences within Article 8(2)(a) reflect the requirement of the *chapeau* that in each case the persons or property must have been protected under one or more of the Geneva Conventions of 1949.[88] However, the elements impose an additional requirement that '[t]he perpetrator was aware of the factual circumstances that established that protected status',[89] although this does not appear to require a legal analysis on the part of the perpetrator.[90] A footnote to this element states that '[w]ith respect to nationality, it is understood that the perpetrator needs only to know that the victim belonged to an adverse party to the conflict',[91] thus leaving the way open for the ICC to adopt a *Tadić* approach with respect to protected persons under the Fourth Geneva Convention.[92]

## Article 8(2)(a)(i) Wilful killing

### Origins

Wilful killing is a grave breach under each of the Geneva Conventions and therefore the wounded and sick on land and at sea, the shipwrecked, prisoners of war and civilians are protected persons with respect to this offence. It is clear that the *actus reus* requires that the accused caused the death of another human being. However, the *mens rea* for this offence, described by the expression 'wilful', is not explained by the commentary to the Conventions.[93] The French translation of this offence as *l'homicide intentionnel* suggests that the killing must be done intentionally, not recklessly. However, this does not entirely clarify the issue, as, for example, under English law the *mens rea* for murder is intention to kill

[86] See T. Meron, 'The humanization of humanitarian law', AJIL, 94 (2000), 239–78, p. 257, and the same author, 'Classification of armed conflict in the former Yugoslavia', n. 48 *supra*, p. 239. See also K. Dörmann, 'Contributions by the *ad hoc* tribunals for the former Yugoslavia and Rwanda', n. 25 *supra*, pp. 285–6.

[87] For a criticism of this approach see M. Sassòli and L. Olson, 'International decisions', n. 41 *supra*, p. 576.

[88] EOC, pp. 125–30.

[89] *Ibid.*

[90] Compare with requirement of awareness of circumstances establishing the existence of an armed conflict, discussed *supra*, pp. 15–16.

[91] EOC, n. 33 on p. 125.

[92] See Lee (ed.), *ICC: Elements*, p. 117.

[93] Pictet (ed.), *Commentary: I Convention*, pp. 371–2.

or cause really serious harm,[94] whereas under French law only an intention to kill will suffice.[95]

The Geneva Conventions were concluded in the wake of the Second World War, and the precedent to 'wilful killing' was the offence of 'murder' under Article 6(b) of the Nuremberg Charter. The Judgement of the International Military Tribunal (IMT) at Nuremberg discussed examples of murder but did not expand on the *mens rea* required.[96] Equally many cases brought before national military tribunals under Control Council Law (CCL) No. 10 did not overly concern themselves with the mental element of murder.[97] However, the Dutch Special Court of Cassation in the case of *In re Ahlbrecht* (No. 2) considered on a policy basis that the mental element for murder in Article 6(b) should be construed in the broader Anglo-American sense rather than in the narrower Continental sense.[98]

The issue of whether wilful killing can be committed by omission has not been examined in the post-Second World War trials, but the commentaries to the Geneva Conventions stress that this is entirely possible, 'provided the omission was intended to cause death'.[99] An example of this would be 'letting wounded persons die for want of the care which would have saved them, or by allowing protected persons to starve to death'.[100] Therefore a person 'who gave instructions for the food rations of prisoners of war to be reduced to such a point that deficiency diseases causing death occurred would be held responsible'.[101]

## Development

The offence of 'wilful killing' was discussed in depth in the *Čelebici* case.[102] The Trial Chamber defined the *actus reus* of the offence as the 'death of the victim as a result of the actions of the accused', holding that 'the conduct of the accused must be a substantial cause of the death of the victim' and acknowledging that 'omissions as well as concrete actions' can satisfy this element.[103] However, the mental element of 'wilful killing' was more contentious.[104] The Trial Chamber found it unhelpful to rely on the meaning of 'wilful' in national

[94] *R. v. Moloney* [1985] AC 905, p. 917.

[95] C. Elliott, 'The French law of intent and its influence on the development of international criminal law', Crim LR, 11 (1999), 532–44, p. 38.

[96] 22 Trial of German Major War Criminals (1950, HMSO, London; hereinafter: '*IMT Judgement*'), p. 450.

[97] See the *Peleus* Trial, 1 LRTWC 1, p. 20.

[98] *In re Ahlbrecht* (No. 2), 16 AD 396, p. 397.

[99] Pictet (ed.), *Commentary: II Convention*, p. 267.

[100] Pictet (ed.), *Commentary: I Convention*, p. 371.

[101] Pictet (ed.), *Commentary: III Convention*, pp. 626–7.

[102] *Čelebici*, Trial Judgement, paras 420–39.

[103] *Ibid.*, para. 424, and *Kvočka et al.*, Appeal Judgement, para. 261. See R. Wolfrum, 'Enforcement of international humanitarian law', n. 9 *supra*, p. 12, and C. Rottensteiner, 'The denial of humanitarian assistance', n. 14 *supra*, p. 563.

[104] *Čelebici*, Trial Judgement, paras 426–30.

legal systems[105] and instead considered the definition of 'wilful' in the commentary to Articles 11 and 85 of AP I, which suggests that it includes the notions of intent and recklessness but excludes mere negligence.[106]

After lengthy consideration the *Čelebici* Trial Chamber concluded that the *mens rea* for murder or wilful killing under the Geneva Conventions was present 'where there is demonstrated an intention on the part of the accused to kill, or inflict serious injury in reckless disregard of human life'.[107] This was rephrased by the *Čelebici* Appeal Chamber as the intention 'to cause death or serious bodily injury which, as it is reasonable to assume, he had to understand was likely to lead to death'.[108] The Trial Chamber in *Stakić*, whilst agreeing that the standard of *mens rea* excludes negligence and gross negligence, has suggested that it includes the civil law concept of *dolus eventualis*, explaining that 'if the actor engages in life-endangering behaviour, his killing becomes intentional if he "reconciles himself" or "makes peace" with the likelihood of death' and that therefore 'if the killing is committed with "manifest indifference to the value of human life" even conduct of minimal risk can qualify as intentional homicide'.[109]

## The Rome Statute

Whilst there was agreement from an early stage that the Rome Statute should include grave breaches of the Geneva Conventions,[110] there is no amplification of the delegates' understanding of 'wilful killing' in the *travaux préparatoires*. The wording of Article 8(2)(a)(i), in both English and French, reflects exactly the wording of the Geneva Conventions' grave breach provisions.[111] The EOC for this offence, in addition to those related to the nature of the conflict and

[105] *Ibid.*, para. 431.

[106] *Ibid.*, paras 431–2, and see Y. Sandoz *et al.*, *Commentary on the Additional Protocols of 8 June 1977 to the Geneva Conventions of 12 August 1949* (Geneva: ICRC and Nijhoff, 1987), pp. 159 and 994.

[107] *Čelebici*, Trial Judgement, para. 439.

[108] *Čelebici*, Appeal Judgement, para. 422. A similarly worded approach has been followed in other ICTY judgements to substantially the same effect. See *Blaškić*, Trial Judgement, para. 153; *Kordić and Čerkez*, Trial Judgement, para. 229; *Kordić and Čerkez*, Appeal Judgement, para. 36, and *Krstić*, Trial Judgement, para. 485. Note that the *Martić* Trial Judgement, para. 60, accepts the criminal law concept of transferred malice, stating that '[i]n connection with the identity of victims, it is not required for the perpetrator to have intended to target a certain individual; indiscriminate intent to kill whoever is fatally injured as a result of his action is sufficient'. Murder contrary to Common Article 3 has been interpreted in the same manner as wilful killing in *Kvočka et al.*, Trial Judgement, para. 132, and *Krnojelac*, Trial Judgement, para. 324, but see the narrower interpretation of *Jelisic*, Trial Judgement, para. 35. See discussion of murder as a crime against humanity, *infra*, p. 207.

[109] *Stakić*, Trial Judgement, para. 587. The Appeal Chamber did not find it necessary to consider this issue, *Stakić*, Appeal Judgement, para. 152.

[110] *Ad Hoc* Committee on the Establishment of an International Criminal Court, 3–13 April 1995, UN Doc. A/AC.244/2, paras 32 and 34.

[111] Articles 50, 51, 130 and 147, Geneva Conventions I, II, III and IV, respectively.

protected status of the victim, simply require that the perpetrator must have killed one or more protected persons.[112]

Therefore, on a plain reading of the Statute and Elements, the *mens rea* of 'wilful killing' is still unclear. It is arguable that the 'default' *mens rea* of 'intent' and 'knowledge' in Article 30 applies,[113] but the expression 'wilful' could be interpreted as establishing a different standard of *mens rea* from that laid down in Article 30. Piragoff suggests that 'wilful' is synonymous with intent,[114] which would suggest that only an intention to cause death or an awareness that death will occur in the ordinary course of events as a result of the actions of the accused will suffice for 'wilful killing'. However, Fenrick maintains that the perpetrator of 'wilful killing' must act either intentionally or recklessly, in that they 'intended to cause bodily harm and was aware that death was a possible consequence of his or her actions'.[115]

This leaves the *mens rea* for 'wilful killing' before the ICC under some doubt. It is true that, when an element of an offence is uncertain, it should be construed in favour of the defendant, in this case restricting the *mens rea* to intention to kill alone.[116] However, in light of the jurisprudence and academic comment discussed above, it is arguable that the *mens rea* for 'wilful killing' or 'murder' under international customary law includes intention to cause serious injury, reckless as to the probability of death.

Another unresolved issue is whether 'wilful killing' under the Rome Statute may be committed by omission. The history and jurisprudence of this offence suggest that it may be committed in this way. The issue is clarified by a footnote to the EOC regarding the word 'killed', which states that '[t]he term "killed" is interchangeable with the term "caused death"'.[117] The use of this broader expression suggests that the ICC will accept that the offence of 'wilful killing' may be committed by omission.[118]

## Article 8(2)(a)(ii) Torture or inhuman treatment, including biological experiments

### Origins

There are two distinct offences under this article, one of torture and one of inhuman treatment, and the latter specifically includes biological experiments. Such

[112] EOC, p. 125. Dörmann states that there was some discussion of whether 'wilful' was identical with the standard in Article 30(2) of the Rome Statute, but the debate was not conclusive, K. Dörmann, *Elements of War Crimes*, n. 25 *supra*, p. 39.

[113] See Lee (ed.), *ICC: Elements*, p. 125.

[114] D. Piragoff, 'Article 30, mental element', pp. 527–35 in Triffterer (ed.), *Commentary on the Rome Statute*, p. 531, n. 32 *supra*.

[115] Cottier *et al.*, 'Article 8', p. 182.

[116] See Article 22(2), Rome Statute.

[117] EOC, n. 31 on p. 125.

[118] See discussion *supra*, p. 6.

acts are criminalised by the grave breach provisions of all four Conventions, and therefore the wounded and sick on land and at sea, the shipwrecked, prisoners of war and civilians are protected persons with respect to these offences.

Torture is explained by the commentaries to the Third and Fourth Geneva Conventions, which state that it refers 'especially to the infliction of suffering on a person in order to obtain from that person, or from another person, confessions or information'[119] and that it 'is more than a mere assault on the physical or moral integrity of a person' because the pain is not as important as 'the purpose behind its infliction'.[120] Therefore the *actus reus* of torture under the Geneva Conventions would appear to be the infliction of pain on the victim. The *mens rea* would seem to be intentionally inflicting pain for the purpose of obtaining information or confessions.

The notion of inhuman treatment is to a certain extent defined negatively by the commentaries to the Geneva Conventions as being treatment which is not 'humane'.[121] The commentaries therefore stress that not only does this provision protect individuals from physical abuse but, because the Conventions serve to preserve human dignity, this grave breach criminalises treatment which would bring individuals 'down to the level of animals'.[122] The expression 'treatment' is confirmed as being 'understood in its most general sense as applying to all aspects of life'.[123]

Article 27 of Geneva Convention IV lays down the requirement that civilians shall be humanely treated. The same sentence states that they 'shall be protected especially against all acts of violence or threats thereof and against insults and public curiosity' and, the following paragraph continues, women must be protected from 'rape, enforced prostitution, or any form of indecent assault'. It is therefore reasonable to argue that these are examples of actions incompatible with humane treatment,[124] and so would constitute a grave breach of inhuman treatment. A post-Second World War case, *Erich Killinger and Four Others*, which considered the 'ill treatment of British Prisoners of War' during their time at the Luftwaffe Interrogation Centre, could also be seen as an example of what would now be termed inhuman treatment.[125] In this case two of the accused were found guilty of ill treatment of the PoWs on the basis of excessive heating of the prisoners' cells, refusal of required medical attention and in some cases blows.[126] Therefore the *actus reus* of inhuman treatment would appear to be quite wide and to a certain extent subjective, including such things as violence, denial of requisite medical treatment, humiliating public display and sexual abuse. The *mens*

[119] Pictet (ed.), *Commentary: III Convention*, p. 627.
[120] Pictet (ed.), *Commentary: IV Convention*, p. 598.
[121] Pictet (ed.), *Commentary: II, III and IV Conventions*, pp. 268, 627 and 598 respectively.
[122] *Ibid.*
[123] Pictet (ed.), *Commentary: III Convention*, p. 140.
[124] Pictet (ed.), *Commentary: IV Convention*, p. 204.
[125] Trial of *Erich Killinger and Four Others*, 3 LRTWC 67.
[126] *Ibid.*

*rea* is unclear from the commentaries, but would certainly include intention to carry out acts such as those mentioned.

The grave breach provisions of each of the Geneva Conventions give biological experiments as an example of inhuman treatment. This example was specifically included as a result of some of the horrific practices of the Nazis in the Second World War.[127] However, as the commentary states, the prohibition prevents protected persons from being used as 'guinea-pigs'[128] but it does not 'deny a doctor the possibility of using new methods of treatment justified by medical reasons and based only on concern to improve the state of health of the patient'.[129] It should be noted that medical experiments may not be carried out even with consent, as protected persons under the Geneva Conventions cannot renounce their rights.[130]

## Development

### *The offence of torture*

The crime of torture has been developed in recent years by human rights law, particularly by the widely ratified Convention against Torture and other Cruel, Inhuman or Degrading Treatment or Punishment. This Convention defines torture as:

> any act by which severe pain or suffering, whether physical or mental, is intentionally inflicted on a person for such purposes as obtaining from him or a third person information or a confession, punishing him for an act he or a third person has committed or is suspected of having committed, or intimidating or coercing him or a third person, or for any reason based on discrimination of any kind, when such pain or suffering is inflicted by or at the instigation of or with the consent or acquiescence of a public official or other person acting in an official capacity.[131]

Therefore the main ingredients of the crime appear to be the infliction of severe pain, by an official or with official sanction, upon an individual for a particular purpose. This definition confirms that the offence must be carried out intentionally, that mental in addition to physical pain and suffering may amount to torture, and extends the purposes which may lie behind the torture. It also restricts the possible perpetrators of torture to those connected with public officials or acting in a public capacity.

[127] See the Trial of *Hoess*, 7 LRTWC 11, especially pp. 14–16.

[128] Pictet (ed.), *Commentary: I, III and IV Conventions*, pp. 139, 141 and 224 respectively.

[129] Pictet (ed.), *Commentary: II, III and IV Conventions*, pp. 269, 627–8 and 598–9 respectively.

[130] Articles 7, 7, 7 and 8, Geneva Conventions I, II, III and IV, respectively. This reverses the effect of *In re Brandt and Others*, 14 AD, 296, which suggested that medical experiments could take place in wartime if certain stringent conditions were fulfilled.

[131] Article 1, 1984 Torture Convention.

The ICTY has primarily considered the definition of torture in the cases of *Čelebici*, *Furundžija* and *Kunarać*.[132] Both the *Čelebici* and the *Furundžija* Trial Chambers drew upon the definition of torture contained in the Torture Convention and held that it was 'representative of customary international law'.[133] This was supported by the *Furundžija* Appeal Chamber.[134] However, it is notable that the Court in *Kunarać* emphasised the limited scope of the Torture Convention's definition of torture,[135] commenting that it was 'meant to apply at an inter-state level and was, for that reason, directed at the *state's* obligations',[136] and therefore it could serve only 'as an interpretational aid'.[137] All three judgements expanded upon the constituent elements of the crime of torture by drawing upon the jurisprudence of courts and monitoring bodies set up by treaties prohibiting torture.[138]

*Severity of the pain and suffering necessary for torture* The *Čelebici* Judgement referred first to the findings of the Human Rights Committee,[139] which considered that beating, electric shocks and mock executions amounted to torture in the case of *Muteba v. Zaire*,[140] and that *plantones* and beatings combined with lack of food constituted torture, in the case of *Setelich v. Uruguay*.[141] Second, the Chamber referred to the jurisprudence of the European Commission and Court of Human Rights.[142] In particular, the Court noted that the European Commission considered, in the *Greek* case,[143] that 'the practice of administering severe beatings to all parts of the body, known as *falanga*', was held to constitute torture and ill treatment.

The *Čelebici* Trial Chamber used the *Ireland v. United Kingdom* case,[144] heard before the European Commission and Court of Human Rights, to illustrate 'the

[132] *Čelebici*, Trial Judgement, paras 441–96, *Furundžija*, Trial Judgement, paras 137–64, and *Kunarać*, Trial Judgement, paras 468–97.

[133] *Čelebici*, Trial Judgement, para. 459, and *Furundžija*, Trial Judgement, para. 160.

[134] *Furundžija*, Appeal Judgement, para. 111.

[135] *Kunarać*, Trial Judgement, para. 473, upheld on appeal, *Kunarać*, Appeal Judgement, paras 147–8.

[136] *Kunarać*, Trial Judgement, para. 482, emphasis added.

[137] *Ibid.*

[138] The crime of torture is prohibited by Article 3, 1950 European Convention on Human Rights, Article 7, 1966 ICCPR, Article 5, 1969 American Convention on Human Rights, and Article 1, 1984 Torture Convention. See generally S. Sivakumaran, 'Torture in international human rights and international humanitarian law: the actor and the *ad hoc* tribunals', LJIL, 18 (2005), 541–56.

[139] *Čelebici*, Trial Judgement, para. 461.

[140] *Muteba v. Zaire* (124/1982), HRC Report, UNOR, GA Twenty-second Session, Supplement No. 40 (1984), para. 10.2.

[141] *Setelich v. Uruguay* (63/1979), HRC Report, UNOR, GA Fourteenth Session, para. 16.2. Note that *platones* involves forcing prisoners to remain standing for very long periods of time.

[142] *Čelebici*, Trial Judgement, paras 462–6.

[143] *Greek case*, 12 YB ECHR (1969) 1, p. 504.

[144] *Ireland v. United Kingdom*, Vol. 23-I, Series B, Pleadings, Oral Arguments and Documents (1976–78), Report of Commission, 8, and Vol. 25, Series A, Judgements and Decisions (1978), Judgement of 18 January 1978, 5.

inherent difficulties in determining a threshold level of severity beyond which inhuman treatment becomes torture'.[145] In this case, although the Commission found that the combination of 'wall-standing, hooding, subjection to noise, sleep deprivation and food and drink deprivation' amounted to torture,[146] the Court held that these acts constituted inhuman and degrading treatment, as they 'did not occasion suffering of the particular intensity and cruelty implied by the word torture as so understood'.[147]

The question of exactly how severe the pain must be to constitute torture was raised in the *Brđanin* Appeal Chamber.[148] The defendant argued that the current customary law on torture was best expressed by a memorandum from the US Department of Justice to the Counsel to the President[149] in which the US implementing legislation for the Convention against Torture was interpreted as requiring 'pain that is difficult to endure . . . equivalent in intensity to the pain accompanying serious physical injury, such as organ failure, impairment of bodily function, or even death' and that for mental pain or suffering to constitute torture under this legislation 'it must result in significant psychological harm of significant duration'.[150]

The Appeal Chamber responded by stating that '[n]o matter how powerful or influential a country is, its practice does not automatically become customary law'.[151] Further, it commented that the memorandum in question, the only evidence provided by the defence as to this new standard of the amount of harm required for a torture conviction, had in any case been withdrawn by the US Department of Justice.[152] The Court further explained that during the negotiations for the Convention against Torture a UK proposal to restrict the definition of torture to cases of infliction of 'extreme pain or suffering' was rejected and therefore the grave breach of torture could not be interpreted as requiring 'extreme pain or suffering' but something less severe would suffice.[153]

Whilst this 'less than *extreme* pain or suffering' still does not really assist in understanding the required suffering, the *Kvočka* and *Krnojelac* Trial Chambers

[145] *Čelebici*, Trial Judgement, para. 463.

[146] *Ireland* case, Report of Commission, n. 144 *supra*, pp. 410–1.

[147] *Ireland* case, Judgement of 18 January 1978, n. 144 *supra*, para. 167.

[148] *Brđanin*, Appeal Judgement, paras 244–52.

[149] *Ibid.*, 244.

[150] US Department of Justice, Office of Legal Counsel, Memorandum for Alberto R Gonzales, Counsel to the President, 1 August 2002, p. 1, available at: <http://news.findlaw.com/hdocs/docs/doj/bybee80101ltr.html>. This memo was written at a time when the United States had commenced interrogating individuals suspected of involvement in terrorism following the bombing of the World Trade Center in 2001.

[151] *Brđanin*, Appeal Judgement, para. 247.

[152] *Ibid.*, para. 248. See US Department of Justice, Office of Legal Counsel, Memorandum for James B. Comey, Deputy Attorney General, 30 December 2004, p. 2, available at: <http://www.usdoj.gov/olc/18usc23402340a2.htm>. For a discussion of the US approach to torture see O. Bekerman, 'Torture – the absolute prohibition of a relative term: does everyone know what is in room 101?', Am J Comp L, 53 (2005), 743–83.

[153] *Brđanin*, Appeal Judgement, para. 249.

both emphasised that although the Court must consider the objective severity of the harm inflicted, the gravity of the harm will also be affected by subjective criteria such as the effect of the treatment upon the particular individual, their state of health and their position of inferiority.[154] The *Krnojelac* Judgement also explained that 'to the extent that an individual has been mistreated over a prolonged period of time . . . the severity of the acts should be assessed as a whole' if it can be shown that they were interrelated or were directed towards the same prohibited goal.[155] This shows an understanding of the fact that severity of suffering is not simply made up of intensity of pain and that a lower level of intensity of suffering over time can still be severe enough to constitute torture. However, whilst the *Naletilić and Martinović* Appeal Chamber accepted that 'the duration over which suffering is inflicted may affect the determination whether it amounts to torture' they emphasised that 'no rigid durational requirement is built into the definition of . . . [the] crime'.[156]

Finally, further guidance on this issue can be found in the non-exhaustive list of actions severe enough to amount to torture given by Special Rapporteur Kooijmans in his 1986 report, approved of by the *Čelebici* Trial Chamber.[157] These included the extraction of fingernails or toenails and teeth, electric shocks, suffocation, prolonged denial of food, total isolation and sensory deprivation and simulated executions.[158]

*Official sanction or involvement in torture* The *Čelebici* Judgement held that '[i]n the context of international humanitarian law, this requirement must be interpreted to include officials of non-State parties to a conflict, in order for the prohibition to retain significance in situations of internal armed conflicts or international conflicts involving some non-State entities'.[159] The Trial Chamber also emphasised that the requirement of official sanction or involvement was very broad, and would 'extend to officials who take a passive attitude or turn a blind eye to torture'.[160] Nevertheless, the *Čelebici* Judgement did not question the requirement for official sanction, and the *Furundžija* Trial and Appeal Chambers both included the requirement for such sanction in their elements of this offence.[161]

[154] *Kvočka*, Trial Judgement, para. 143, and *Krnojelac*, Trial Judgement, para. 182.

[155] *Krnojelac*, Trial Judgement, para. 182.

[156] *Naletilić and Martinović*, Appeal Judgement, para. 300.

[157] *Čelebici*, Trial Judgement, para. 467.

[158] See the more recent Interim Report on torture by the Special Rapporteur, Sir Nigel Rodley, UN Doc. E/CN.4/1999/61, January 1999, and R. Bailey, 'Why do States violate the law of war? A comparison of Iraqi violations in two Gulf Wars', Sy J Intl L, 27 (2000), 103–29, p. 117. Note that the *Furundžija* and *Kunarać* Trial Chambers held that the *actus reus* of torture could be carried out by omission, *Furundžija*, Trial Judgement, para. 162, and *Kunarać*, Trial Judgement, para. 483(i) and (ii).

[159] *Čelebici*, Trial Judgement, para. 473.

[160] *Ibid.*, para. 474.

[161] *Furundžija*, Trial and Appeal Judgements, paras 162 and 111 respectively.

The *Kunarać* Judgement, however, held that, unlike human rights law, international criminal law was concerned with the criminal responsibility of the individual and that '[w]ith or without the involvement of the state, the crime committed remains of the same nature and bears the same consequences'[162] and furthermore that '[t]he characteristic trait of the offence in this context is to be found in the nature of the act committed rather than in the status of the person who committed it'.[163] Therefore, the Trial Chamber concluded, 'the presence of a state official or of any other authority-wielding person in the torture process is not necessary for the offence to be regarded as torture under international humanitarian law'.[164] This was upheld on appeal on the basis that 'the public official requirement is not a requirement under customary international law in relation to the criminal responsibility of an individual for torture outside of the framework of the Torture Convention'.[165]

*The mental element of torture* The *Furundžija* and *Kunarać* Judgements held that the torture must be carried out intentionally.[166] Regarding the forbidden purpose behind the imposition of suffering, such as to obtain information, to punish the person or to intimidate him or her, the Trial Chamber in *Čelebici* made it clear that the list given by Article 1 of the Torture Convention was not exhaustive.[167] This approach was supported by the Trial Chamber in *Furundžija*, which held that the purposes of torture must additionally include 'humiliating the victim'.[168] However, the *Kunarać* and *Krnojelac* Trial Judgements doubted whether the expansion of purposes beyond those listed in the Torture Convention was recognised under customary international law.[169]

Importantly, the *Čelebici* Judgement stated that 'there is no requirement that the conduct must be *solely* perpetrated for a prohibited purpose', or even that the prohibited purpose must predominate, provided that it was 'part of the motivation behind the conduct',[170] and this was supported by the *Kunarać* and *Krnojelac* Judgements.[171] The *Kunarać* Appeal Chamber, however, approached the crime of torture as requiring proof of intention, rather than one in which motives are relevant.[172] Therefore, 'even if the perpetrator's motivation is entirely sexual, it does not follow that the perpetrator does not have the intent to commit an act

[162] *Kunarać*, Trial Judgement, para. 493.

[163] *Ibid.*, para. 495.

[164] *Ibid.*, para. 496, and see *Kvočka et al.*, Trial Judgement, para. 139.

[165] *Kunarać*, Appeal Judgement, para. 148. This was supported by the *Kvočka et al.* Appeal Chamber, para. 284.

[166] *Furundžija*, Trial Judgement, para. 162, and *Kunarać*, Trial Judgement, para. 483(i).

[167] *Čelebici*, Trial Judgement, para. 470.

[168] *Furundžija*, Trial Judgement, para. 162, and see *Kvočka et al.*, Trial Judgement, para. 140.

[169] *Kunarać*, Trial Judgement, para. 485, and *Krnojelac*, Trial Judgement, para. 186.

[170] *Čelebici*, Trial Judgement, para. 470, emphasis added.

[171] *Kunarać*, Trial Judgement, para. 486, and *Krnojelac*, Trial Judgement, para. 184.

[172] *Kunarać*, Appeal Judgement, para. 153.

of torture . . . [if] such pain or suffering is a likely and logical consequence of his conduct'.[173]

*Rape or sexual violence as torture*[174] The Yugoslavia Commission of Experts determined that rape and sexual assaults could amount to the grave breach of torture or inhuman treatment,[175] and this approach was supported by Gay McDougall, the Special Rapporteur on contemporary forms of slavery, in her report on rape and sexual slavery in armed conflict.[176] A previous Special Rapporteur on the question of torture and other cruel, inhuman or degrading treatment or punishment, Sir Nigel Rodley, has also referred to 'gender-specific forms of torture' as an issue of special concern, and stated that this includes 'rape, sexual abuse and harassment, virginity testing, forced abortion or forced miscarriage'.[177]

The first international criminal tribunal to hold that rape could constitute torture, albeit in the context of crimes against humanity, was the International Criminal Tribunal on Rwanda (ICTR) in the case of *Akayesu*.[178] The Judgement stated that '[l]ike torture, rape is a violation of personal dignity and rape in fact constitutes torture when inflicted by or at the instigation of or with the consent or acquiescence of a public official or other person acting in an official capacity'.[179] The ICTY in the case of *Čelebici* later confirmed that rape could amount to the grave breach of torture[180] and in *Furundžija* held that rape could constitute torture under Common Article 3 of the Geneva Conventions.[181]

The *Čelebici* Trial Chamber considered the issue of rape as torture in some depth and held that, in order to constitute torture, the crime of rape must meet each of the elements of the offence of torture.[182] The court examined cases of rape as torture from human rights jurisprudence,[183] including the case of *Raquel*

[173] *Ibid.*

[174] For the definition of rape under international law see *infra*, pp. 146–9 and 151–2.

[175] Final Report of the Commission of Experts established pursuant to Security Council Resolution (SC Res.) 780 (1992), UN Doc. S/1994/674, 27 May 1994 (hereinafter: Yugoslavia Commission of Experts Report), para. 105.

[176] G. McDougall, 'Contemporary forms of slavery: systematic rape, sexual slavery and slavery-like practices during armed conflict', Commission on Human Rights, Sub-commission on Prevention of Discrimination and Protection of Minorities, UN Doc. E/CN.4/Sub.2/1998/12, 22 June 1998, paras 53–5.

[177] N. Rodley, 'Interim Report on the question of torture and other cruel, inhuman or degrading treatment or punishment', Commission of Human Rights, UN Doc. A/55/290, 11 August 2000, para. 5.

[178] *Akayesu*, Trial Judgement, para. 597.

[179] *Ibid.*, and see *Nikolić*, Rule 61 Review, at para. 33.

[180] *Čelebici*, Trial Judgement, para. 496.

[181] *Furundžija*, Trial Judgement, para. 163.

[182] *Čelebici*, Trial Judgement, para. 480.

[183] *Ibid.*, paras 480–9.

*Martín de Mejía v. Peru*,[184] where the Inter-American Commission of Human Rights held that the act of rape causes sufficient physical suffering from the violence of the act itself to constitute torture, but also constitutes mental torture by causing 'a psychological trauma that results, on the one hand, from having been humiliated and victimized, and on the other, from suffering the condemnation of the members of their community if they report what has been done to them'.[185]

After reviewing human rights jurisprudence the *Čelebici* Judgement held that '[r]ape causes severe pain and suffering, both physical and psychological'.[186] Indeed, the *Kunarać* Appeal Chamber commented in respect of the suffering caused by rape that '[s]evere pain or suffering, as required by the definition of the crime of torture, can thus be said to be established once rape has been proved, since the act of rape necessarily implies such pain or suffering'.[187] Further, the *Kvočka* Judgement held that in some circumstances the *threat* of rape and sexual violence could amount to torture.[188]

The *Čelebici* Trial Chamber found that the offence of torture had been committed in respect of one of Delic's rape victims, as 'the violence suffered by Ms. Antic in the form of rape was inflicted upon her by Delic because she is a woman . . . this represents a form of discrimination which constitutes a prohibited purpose for the offence of torture'.[189] This suggests, rather progressively, that the prohibited purpose of torture will always be met in the case of rape. In any event, Askin stresses, '[i]t is paramount that when the requisite elements for torture are met, the international legal arena must formally prosecute sexual assault as torture', thus confirming that sexual assault often amounts to that offence.[190]

### *Inhuman treatment*[191]

The *Čelebici* case in particular considered the meaning of inhuman treatment as a grave breach in depth.[192] The Trial Chamber stated that 'humane treatment is the cornerstone of all four Conventions, and is defined in the negative in relation to a general, non-exhaustive catalogue of deplorable acts which are inconsistent

[184] *Raquel Martín de Mejía v. Peru*, Inter-American Commission on Human Rights, Case No. 10.970, Report No. 5/96, 1 March 1996, reprinted in 4 IHRR (1997), 609.

[185] *Ibid.*, p. 632.

[186] *Čelebici*, Trial Judgement, para. 495.

[187] *Kunarać*, Appeal Judgement, para. 151.

[188] *Kvočka et al.*, Trial Judgement, para. 561.

[189] *Čelebici*, Trial Judgement, para. 963, and see K. Askin, *War Crimes against Women, Prosecution in International War Crimes Tribunals* (The Hague: Nijhoff, 1997), p. 319.

[190] K. Askin, *War Crimes against Women*, pp. 320–1.

[191] The development of the offence of biological experiments will not be covered, as there have been no prosecutions of this offence in recent years.

[192] *Čelebici*, Trial Judgement, paras 521–32 (considering Article 12 of Geneva Conventions I and II, Articles 13 and 20 of Geneva Convention III and Articles 27 and 32 of Geneva Convention IV and Common Article 3).

with it, these constituting inhuman treatment'.[193] The tribunal reviewed human rights jurisprudence and,[194] among others, referred to the case of *A. v. United Kingdom* before the European Court on Human Rights (ECHR), which found that the minimum level of severity for inhuman treatment was relative and depended upon 'all the circumstances of the case, such as the nature and context of the treatment, its duration, its physical and mental effects and, in some instances, the sex, age and state of health of the victim'.[195] However, the Judgement held the 'most coherent framing of the concept'[196] to be the definition of inhuman treatment given by the European Commission in *Yagiz v. Turkey*, which was treatment which 'deliberately causes serious mental and physical suffering'.[197]

The *Čelebici* Judgement concluded that inhuman treatment 'is an intentional act or omission . . . which causes serious mental or physical suffering or injury or constitutes a serious attack on human dignity'.[198] The Trial Chamber further described this as 'treatment which does not conform with the fundamental principle of humanity . . . [h]ence, acts characterised in the Conventions and Commentaries as inhuman, or which are inconsistent with the principle of humanity, constitute examples of actions that can be characterised as inhuman treatment'.[199] This finding was approved by the Trial Chamber in *Blaškić*,[200] which further held that the infliction of physical and mental violence upon detainees whilst forcing them to dig trenches in a life-threatening situation at the battlefront amounted to inhuman treatment.[201]

Inhuman treatment, as opposed to torture, during interrogation has not been considered by the ICTY cases but it has become clear that detainees undergoing interrogation are particularly vulnerable to all sorts of ill treatment following the Abu Ghraib scandal, when Iraqi prisoners were abused by US forces.[202] This concern is discussed by the new British *Manual on the Law of Armed Conflict* in the light of the prohibition of inhuman treatment.[203] The *Manual* emphasises that those who refuse to answer questions may not be 'threatened, insulted or exposed to any unpleasant or disadvantageous treatment of any kind'.[204] Whilst

[193] *Ibid.*, para. 532.

[194] *Ibid.*, paras 534–41.

[195] *A. v. United Kingdom*, ECHR Judgement, 23 September 1998, 90 Reports of Judgements and Decisions, 1998-V, 2692.

[196] *Čelebici*, Trial Judgement, para. 538.

[197] *Yagiz v. Turkey*, ECHR Judgement, 7 August 1996, 22 EHRR (1996), 573.

[198] *Čelebici*, Trial Judgement, para. 543, supported by the *Kordić and Čerkez* Appeal Judgement, para. 39.

[199] *Čelebici*, Trial Judgement, para. 543.

[200] *Blaškić*, Trial Judgement, para. 154, supported by the *Kordić and Čerkez* Trial Judgement, para. 256.

[201] *Blaškić*, Trial Judgement, para. 700. Note the Judgement also classified this as cruel treatment.

[202] See also discussion *infra*, pp. 39–40 and 143.

[203] UK Ministry of Defence, *The Manual of the Law of Armed Conflict* (Oxford: Oxford University Press, 2004), para. 8.34.

[204] *Ibid.*

the *Manual* allows blindfolding and segregation of prisoners in the interests of security or in order to prevent collaboration prior to interrogation, it stresses that 'these discomforts must be truly justified and be for as short a period as possible'.[205]

## The Rome Statute

The offences of torture and inhuman treatment before the ICC would appear to require the default *mens rea* of intention and knowledge under Article 30 of the Rome Statute. No alternative *mens rea* is suggested by the wording of Article 8(2)(a)(ii) or the EOC. It is unclear from the *travaux préparatoires* whether these offences may be committed by omission, and, whilst there are *dicta* to this effect in the judgements of the ICTY, it is easier to comprehend the concept of inhuman treatment by omission than by torture.

### *The offence of torture*

The EOC state that the perpetrator must have 'inflicted severe physical or mental pain or suffering upon one or more persons' and have done so 'for such purposes as obtaining information or a confession, punishment, intimidation or coercion or for any reason based on discrimination of any kind'.[206] Whilst this does not elucidate the level of pain necessary to constitute torture, it is likely that the ICC will take into consideration the jurisprudence of the ICTY and human rights bodies which have considered the issue.

The elements require a specific purpose for the torture, although the expression 'such as' demonstrates that other similar purposes, such as humiliation of the victim proposed by the ICTY in *Furundžija*, could also amount to a prohibited purpose.[207] It is submitted that the ICC should follow the *Čelebici* and *Kunarać* Judgements in holding that the prohibited purpose need not be the sole purpose of the accused.[208] Nevertheless, this requirement of a prohibited purpose requires an additional mental element, above the *mens rea* of intention to commit the act causing the pain and suffering.

It is notable that the requirement of official sanction has been dropped from the Elements. This omission was supported by the Women's Caucus for Gender Justice, which argued that official involvement has never, in any case, been part of the offence of torture in armed conflict,[209] an approach taken by the ICTY

[205] *Ibid.*, para. 8.34.2.

[206] EOC, p. 126.

[207] *Furundžija*, Trial Judgement, para. 162, and see K. Dörmann, 'Preparatory Commission for the International Criminal Court: the elements of war crimes', IRRC, 839, 771–95, p. 786.

[208] *Čelebici*, Trial Judgement, para. 470, and *Kunarać* Trial Judgement, para. 486.

[209] Women's Caucus for Gender Justice, 'Suggestions for the Elements', submitted to the 16–26 February 1999 Preparatory Commission for the International Criminal Court, available at <http://www.iccwomen.addr.com/icc/pc199902/torture.htm>.

Trial Chamber in the *Kunarać* case.[210] Dörmann states that this element was omitted in order to ensure that acts of torture committed by irregular forces would not be excluded from the grave breach of torture.[211]

A notorious example of ill treatment of detainees involved the abuse of prisoners held by the United States in the Abu Ghraib prison in Iraq. This scandal shocked the world in April 2004, when explicit photographs of the abuse were released by the media.[212] Whilst the ICC did not have jurisdiction in this case, as neither Iraq nor the United States was a Party to the Rome Statute, it is interesting to question whether the elements of the offence of torture were present with respect to some of the more severe abuse.[213]

According to the US army investigation, detainees were punched, slapped and kicked; working dogs were used to intimidate them, in at least one case biting and severely injuring a detainee; detainees were threatened with a pistol, detainees were threatened with rape and in one case '[s]odomiz[ed] . . . with a chemical light and perhaps a broomstick'.[214] The leaked report of the International Committee of the Red Cross (ICRC) on the conditions at Abu Ghraib also stated that detainees faced threats of ill treatment, reprisals against family members and imminent execution.[215] The ICRC report also stated that persons deemed to have an 'intelligence' value 'were subjected to a variety of ill-treatments ranging from insults and humiliation to both physical and psychological coercion that in some cases might amount to torture in order to force them to cooperate with their interrogators'.[216]

If the ICC bases its decisions on the severity of pain and suffering necessary on the ICTY jurisprudence it is clear that at least some of this treatment would be considered severe enough to constitute torture. With respect to the prohibited purpose it is clear that at least some of the detainees were being ill treated for a prohibited purpose, that of obtaining information or a confession.[217] However,

[210] *Kunarać*, Trial and Appeal Judgements, paras 496 and 148 respectively.

[211] K. Dörmann, 'The first and second sessions of the Preparatory Commission', n. 65 *supra*, p. 290.

[212] The scandal broke when photographs of Iraqi detainees being abused were broadcast on CBS television in the United States, see details on website: <http://www.cbsnews.com/stories/2004/04/27/60II/main614063.shtml>. Subsequently the photographs appeared in newspapers all over the world.

[213] Other incidents reported to have taken place at Abu Ghraib will be considered under the heading of inhuman treatment and outrages upon personal dignity, *infra*, pp. 39–40 and 143.

[214] Article 15-6, Investigation of the 800th Military Police Brigade, findings of fact following Part 1 of investigation, March 2004, paras 6–8, available at: <http://news.findlaw.com/usatoday/docs/iraq/tagubarpt.html>.

[215] Report of the International Committee of the Red Cross (ICRC) on the treatment by coalition forces of prisoners of war and other protected persons by the Geneva Conventions in Iraq during arrest, internment and interrogation, February 2004 (hereinafter: ICRC Report), para. 25, available at: <http://www.globalsecurity.org/military/library/report/2004/icrc_report_iraq_Feb2004.pdf>.

[216] *Ibid.*, para. 24.

[217] Final Report of the Independent Panel to Review DoD Detention Operations, August 2004 (hereinafter the Schlesinger Report), pp. 69–70, available at: <http://www.humanrightsfirst.org/us_law/PDF/abuse/Schlesinger_report.pdf>.

the Schlesinger Report on Department of Defense Detention Operations (which looked at mistreatment of prisoners in US custody generally) suggested that some mistreatment was carried out by some members of the military police 'just for the fun of it'.[218] Therefore, if the ICC had been able to take jurisdiction over the case, it would have had to consider each incident on its merits. Arguably, the abuse carried out for the 'fun of it' would amount to an action based on discrimination against the detainees as Iraqis and would therefore still constitute a prohibited purpose. Those incidents not amounting to torture, whether through an insufficient amount of pain or suffering or carried out without a prohibited purpose, could still be considered as the offences of inhuman treatment, outrages upon personal dignity or as sexual violence.[219]

### *Inhuman treatment*

The EOC for inhuman treatment simply require that the accused has 'inflicted severe physical or mental pain or suffering upon one or more persons'.[220] This omits a 'serious attack on human dignity', which the ICTY case of *Čelebici* included in the offence of inhuman treatment.[221] Dörmann comments that this omission was controversial at the Preparatory Commission, but it was decided that such behaviour would instead constitute a crime under 8(2)(c)(ii) as an outrage upon personal dignity.[222] Nevertheless, if an attack on human dignity caused serious mental pain or suffering, an accused could still be prosecuted under this section.

### *Biological experiments*

The EOC list biological experiments as a separate crime. The accused must have subjected one or more persons to a particular biological experiment which 'seriously endangered the physical or mental health or integrity' of the victim.[223] Additionally, the experiment must have had no therapeutic intent, and must have been 'neither justified by medical reasons nor carried out' in the victim's interest.[224] This offence is more difficult to prove than inhuman treatment, as, for the latter, it is sufficient to inflict severe pain or suffering, but in the case of biological experiments it must be shown that the health or integrity of the victim was actually seriously endangered. Presumably an experiment which caused severe pain, but did not actually endanger the victim in this way, could be charged as inhuman treatment.

The *mens rea* for this offence requires that the accused had a 'non-therapeutic intent' in conducting the experiment, and that the experiment was not justified

[218] *Ibid.*, p. 13.

[219] See discussion *infra*, pp. 40, 139–43 and 149–50.

[220] EOC, p. 126.

[221] *Čelebici*, Trial Judgement, para. 543.

[222] K. Dörmann, 'Preparatory Commission for the International Criminal Court', n. 207 *supra*, pp. 786–7.

[223] EOC, p. 127.

[224] *Ibid.*

by medical reasons, nor in the person's interest.[225] Therefore a well intentioned but incompetent doctor who carried out a procedure which was not objectively justified by medical reasons or in the patient's interests would not fulfil the *mens rea* of this offence, as he would have had a 'therapeutic' intent. This also means that an experiment aimed to assist the patient's recovery from an illness or disease, carried out in less than ideal circumstances owing to the armed conflict, would not constitute the offence of biological experiments.[226]

## Article 8(2)(a)(iii) Wilfully causing great suffering, or serious injury to body or health

### Origins

This offence is prohibited in the grave breaches of all four Geneva Conventions, and so all those protected under those Conventions are protected persons for the purposes of the offence. The commentary to the Conventions states that wilfully causing great suffering includes 'moral suffering' in addition to physical suffering.[227] Therefore the *actus reus* of this offence is causing great physical or mental suffering, or seriously injuring a person's body or health. The *mens rea* is contained in the expression 'wilfully', which is not defined or explained by the commentaries to the Geneva Conventions.[228] However, the commentaries do stress that there is no requirement that the accused must have had a prohibited purpose behind the infliction of suffering or serious injury, and indeed may have committed the *actus reus* of the offence 'out of pure sadism'.[229]

### Development

The international criminal case which has considered the meaning of this offence in most detail is *Čelebici* before the ICTY.[230] The Trial Chamber held that 'wilfully causing great suffering or serious injury to body or health' was one offence, the elements of which are framed in the alternative.[231] On the definition of 'great suffering' the Court concurred with the commentaries that this encompasses 'moral' or mental suffering.[232] However, the Judgement drew support for this interpretation from the omission to qualify 'great suffering' by 'to body or

[225] *Ibid.*

[226] See comments by M. Gunn and H. McCoubrey, 'Medical ethics and the laws of armed conflict', JACL, 3 (1998), 133–61, p. 140.

[227] Pictet (ed.), *Commentary: II, III and IV Conventions*, pp. 269, 628 and 599 respectively.

[228] See discussion *supra*, p. 25.

[229] Pictet (ed.), *Commentary: III and IV Convention*, pp. 628 and 599 respectively.

[230] *Čelebici*, Trial Judgement, paras 506–11.

[231] *Ibid.*, para. 506, supported by *Blaškić*, Trial Judgement, para. 156.

[232] *Čelebici*, Trial Judgement, para. 509, supported by *Kordić and Čerkez*, Trial Judgement, para. 244.

health', which suggests that 'serious injury to body or health' cannot include serious psychiatric injury.[233] The Judgement of *Blaškić*, on the other hand, stated clearly that this part of the offence consists of 'causing great suffering or serious injury to body or health, *including mental health*'.[234]

In order to interpret the expressions 'great' and 'serious' the *Čelebici* Judgement applied the ordinary meaning of the words from the *Oxford English Dictionary*.[235] 'Great' was defined as 'much above average in size, amount or intensity', and 'serious' defined as 'not slight or negligible', and the Trial Chamber stated that it viewed 'these quantitative expressions as providing for the basic requirement that a particular act of mistreatment results in a requisite level of serious suffering or injury'.[236] Additionally the *Čelebici*, *Blaškić* and *Kordić and Čerkez* Trial Chambers emphasised that this offence could be committed by omission.[237]

The *mens rea* of the offence is governed by the expression 'wilfully', which has already been discussed with respect to the offence of 'wilful killing'.[238] However, the *Čelebici* Judgement stated that for this offence the act or omission must be 'intentional, being an act which, judged objectively, is deliberate and not accidental'.[239] This suggests nothing more than that the offence must be committed voluntarily, and does not really explain whether the accused must intend to cause great suffering or serious injury when he carries out a deliberate act or omission, or whether he may be reckless as to causing such suffering or injury. The Trial Chamber in *Blaškić* does not really amplify the *mens rea*, and simply confirms that the act or omission must be done intentionally.[240]

### *Rape or sexual violence as great suffering or serious injury to body or health*

The Yugoslavia Commission of Experts asserted that rape or sexual assault could amount to this offence.[241] Additionally, it has already been seen that rape and sexual violence can constitute the crime of torture and inhuman treatment, and the Judgement in *Čelebici* acknowledged that 'all acts constituting torture could also fall within the ambit' of the offence of wilfully causing great suffering or serious injury to body or health.[242] Indeed, Landzo, a defendant in *Čelebici*, was found to have committed this offence in a case of sexual violence when he 'placed

[233] *Čelebici*, Trial Judgement, para. 509.

[234] *Blaškić*, Trial Judgement, para. 156, emphasis added.

[235] *Čelebici*, Trial Judgement, para. 510.

[236] *Ibid.*, para. 510.

[237] *Ibid.*, para. 511, and *Blaškić*, Trial Judgement, para. 156, and *Kordić and Čerkez*, Trial Judgement, para. 245.

[238] Discussed *supra*, pp. 26–7.

[239] *Čelebici*, Trial Judgement, para. 511.

[240] *Blaškić*, Trial Judgement, para. 156.

[241] Yugoslavia Commission of Experts Report, para. 105.

[242] *Čelebici*, Trial Judgement, para. 511.

a burning fuse-cord directly against . . . [the victim's] bare skin in the genital area, thereby inflicting serious pain and injury upon him'.[243] This recognition that rape and sexual violence may constitute the grave breach of wilfully causing great suffering or serious injury to body or health has also been supported by many commentators.[244]

## The Rome Statute

The EOC state that the perpetrator must have 'caused great physical or mental pain or suffering to, or serious injury to body or health of' one or more persons.[245] This really does not elucidate the *actus reus* of this offence, and in particular does not clarify whether the serious injury to body or health can include injury to mental health.[246] The ICTY jurisprudence is unhelpful on this issue, as the Judgements of *Blaškić* and *Čelebici* appear to contradict each other.[247] Furthermore, academic comment is not in agreement on the issue, with Fenrick asserting that '[d]amage to mental health is also prohibited by this provision'[248] and Dörmann stating that in the Elements '[t]he term "physical or mental" is linked only to pain and suffering . . . [d]elegations felt it would be difficult to conceive of "mental injury"'.[249] However, whilst the Elements have clearly separated this offence into two alternatives, it is still not entirely clear that health cannot be broadly interpreted to include mental health. There is surely a difference between mental suffering, which may disappear as soon as the cause of the suffering is removed, and damage to mental health such as post-traumatic stress, which may require medical intervention for some time after the causal events. Finally, although rape and sexual violence are not explicitly mentioned in the Elements, von Hebel and Robinson report that most States at the Rome Conference were of the view that the language covered sexual crimes in any case.[250]

The *mens rea* of this offence is not further explained by the EOC. The expression 'wilfully', by analogy to 'wilful killing', suggests that the offence has a specified *mens rea*, rather than the 'default' mental element of Article 30. It

[243] *Ibid.*, paras 1,039–40.

[244] See T. Meron, 'Rape as a crime under international humanitarian law', AJIL, 87 (1993), 424–8, p. 426; V. Morris and P. Scharf, *An Insider's Guide to the International Criminal Tribunal for the Former Yugoslavia*, n. 7 *supra*, p. 67, and C. Cleiren and M. Tijssen, 'Rape and other forms of sexual assault in the armed conflict in the former Yugoslavia: legal, procedural and evidentiary issues', pp. 257–92, in R. Clark and M. Sann (eds), *The Prosecution of International Crimes*, n. 7 *supra*, p. 277.

[245] EOC, p. 127.

[246] Lee (ed.), *ICC: Elements*, p. 130, suggests that 'mental injury' is not included.

[247] Discussed *supra*, pp. 41–2.

[248] Cottier *et al.*, 'Article 8', p. 183.

[249] K. Dörmann, *Elements of War Crimes*, n. 25 *supra*, p. 76.

[250] H. von Hebel and D. Robinson, 'Crimes within the jurisdiction of the Court', n. 28 *supra*, pp. 108–9. See also J. Paust, 'Commentary on Parts 1 and 2 of the Zutphen Intersessional Draft', pp. 27–42 in L. Sadat Wexler (ed.), *Observations on the Consolidated ICC Text before the Final Session of the Preparatory Committee*, 13 *bis* Nouvelles Études Pénales (1998), p. 29.

certainly includes committing the act or omission with the intention to cause such suffering or injury, but may also include carrying out an action or omission with reckless foresight such that it *may* cause great suffering or serious injury.[251] Unfortunately the ambit of the mental element of this offence will remain unclear until ruled upon by the ICC.

## Article 8(2)(a)(iv) Extensive destruction and appropriation of property, not justified by military necessity and carried out unlawfully and wantonly

### Origins

Property is protected against destruction and appropriation only under the First, Second and Fourth Geneva Conventions. Therefore this provision essentially criminalises extensive destruction of civilian property and property associated with the sick, wounded and shipwrecked. The property protected under the Conventions from wanton destruction or appropriation is dependent upon the provisions in each Convention, which set out different types of protection for different types of property.

The property protected by the first two Geneva Conventions includes the buildings, materials and stores of fixed and mobile medical establishments, transports for the sick and wounded, hospital ships, sick bays of warships, lifeboats and medical aircraft.[252] Two types of property are protected under the Fourth Convention. Protected property similar to that under the first two Conventions includes civilian hospitals, convoys of vehicles or hospital trains carrying sick and wounded civilians and aircraft employed in the removal of sick and wounded civilians.[253] The medical associated property described above would appear to be protected everywhere, extending 'not only to the fighting zones and occupied territories, but also to the territories of the belligerents themselves'.[254]

In addition, the Fourth Geneva Convention protects certain categories of civilian property in occupied territory. The destruction of real or personal property belonging to individuals or the State is prohibited under Article 53 in occupied territory unless 'rendered absolutely necessary by military operations'.[255] Therefore, whilst the destruction of munition factories in the adverse party's territory would be permissible, such destruction would be prohibited within occupied territory, unless, for example, a ground attack was imminent and the occupier needed a clear field of fire in order to protect his troops and retain the

[251] See discussion *supra*, p. 28.

[252] Articles 33–6, Geneva Convention I, and Articles 22–5, 27–8 and 38–9, Geneva Convention II.

[253] Articles 18–19 and 21–3, 1949 Geneva Convention IV.

[254] G. Schwarzenberger, *International Law as applied by International Courts and Tribunals*, n. 4 *supra*, p. 253.

[255] Article 53, 1949 Geneva Convention IV.

territory.[256] There are also limits on the property which may be appropriated or requisitioned by an Occupying Power. Civilian hospitals and their stores are particularly protected, as are civilian foodstuffs and supplies, and may be requisitioned only subject to restrictive conditions.[257]

The wording of this grave breach establishes that an accused may be prosecuted for the offence only if the destruction or appropriation is both extensive and unlawful.[258] These terms are not defined by the commentary to the Conventions, but the ordinary meaning of the expression 'extensive' is 'covering a large area' or 'having a wide scope'.[259] Therefore, whether the destruction or appropriation was extensive would have to be decided on an individual basis as a matter of fact and degree. The articles referred to in the First, Second and Fourth Geneva Conventions describe the protected property and also lay down the limited circumstances in which such property may be destroyed or appropriated lawfully. If property protected by these Conventions were destroyed or appropriated in circumstances other than those laid down in the relevant Articles, then it would be done 'unlawfully'.

Destruction or appropriation of property on grounds of military necessity does not amount to this offence.[260] One of the earliest legal formulations of military necessity was set out in the Lieber Code,[261] Article 14 of which stated that it 'consists in the necessity of those measures which are indispensable for securing the ends of the war, *and which are lawful according to the modern law and usages of war*'.[262] Green also stresses that a plea of military necessity 'is not sufficient to evade compliance with the laws of war', as otherwise the law of armed conflict would be nothing more than a code to apply when convenient.[263]

Military necessity as a plea in defence of the destruction of property was raised in post-Second World War cases, where the charge was 'wanton destruction of cities, towns, or villages, or devastation not justified by military necessity', under Article 6(b) of the Nuremberg Charter and Article 2(1)(b) of CCL No. 10.[264] In the case of *von Manstein*, the accused was charged *inter alia* with wanton destruction and devastation of public and private buildings in the course of a forced

[256] Pictet (ed.), *Commentary: IV Convention*, p. 601.

[257] Articles 55, 57 and 60, Geneva Convention IV.

[258] Articles 50, 51 and 147, Geneva Conventions I, II and IV respectively.

[259] *Concise Oxford Dictionary* (Oxford: Clarendon Press, 9th edn, 1995).

[260] See generally N. Dunbar, 'The significance of military necessity in the law of war', Jur Rev 67 (1955), 201–12, H. McCoubrey, 'The nature of the modern doctrine of military necessity', Rev Dr Milit, 30 (1991), 215–42, and Y. Dinstein, 'Military necessity', pp. 274–6 in R. Bernhardt (ed.), *Encyclopaedia of Public International Law*, Vol. III (Amsterdam: North-Holland, 1982).

[261] Articles 14–16, Lieber Code, and B. Carnahan, 'Lincoln, Lieber and the laws of war: the origins and limits of the principle of military necessity', AJIL, 92 (1998), 213–31.

[262] *Ibid.*, emphasis added.

[263] Green, *Contemporary Law of Armed Conflict*, n. 2 *supra*, p. 123; I. Detter, *The Law of War* (Cambridge, Cambridge University Press, 2nd edn, 2000), pp. 393–8, and the summing up of the Judge Advocate *in re von Manstein*, 16 AD (1949), 509, p. 512.

[264] Article 6, Nuremberg Charter, and Article 2, CCL No. 10.

retreat from occupied territory in Russia.[265] The Judge Advocate emphasised that the accused is required to demonstrate military 'necessity' and not merely military 'advantage'.[266] However, he instructed the tribunal to assess whether the devastation was justified 'through the eyes of the accused . . . at the time when the events were actually occurring' and without hindsight.[267]

The *Hostages* Trial also considered the defence of military necessity to a charge of wanton destruction of private and public property.[268] The defendant had devastated public and private property pursuant to a 'scorched earth' policy in Finnmark, Norway, when retreating from the Russian attacks. The Judgement stated that military necessity in occupied territory generally 'sanctions measures by an occupant necessary to protect the safety of his forces and to facilitate the success of his operations'.[269] The Court found the defendant not guilty on this count, as 'the conditions as they appeared to the defendant at the time were sufficient, upon which he could honestly conclude that urgent military necessity warranted the decision made' as a result of his fear of further Russian attacks.[270]

The *German High Command* Trial considered the case of von Leeb and other high-ranking officers who were accused, *inter alia*, of wanton destruction when retreating from Russian territory under attack and in danger of being cut off.[271] The Court held that in such circumstances a commander would need to make quick decisions, and hence must be accorded 'a great deal of latitude',[272] but appeared to accept the difference between 'military necessity' and 'military expediency', the latter being no defence.[273]

The *mens rea* required for this offence is governed by the expression 'wantonly'. The post-Second World War cases discussed did not really consider the *mens rea* necessary for the analogous Charter crime of 'wanton destruction',[274] although it appears that for the most part the destruction alleged was carried out intentionally. A dictionary definition of 'wanton' as 'capricious; random; arbitrary; motiveless'[275] suggests that specific motives are not an element of this offence but does not really assist in explaining whether reckless destruction, as opposed to intentional destruction, would suffice for this offence.

265 *In re von Manstein*, 16 AD (1949), 509.

266 *Ibid.*, p. 522.

267 *Ibid.* Von Manstein was found not guilty on this charge but the *British Military Manual* cast doubt upon the last direction, para. 616.

268 *Hostages* Trial, 8 LRTWC 34.

269 *Ibid.*, p. 66.

270 *Ibid.*, pp. 68–9.

271 *German High Command* Trial, 12 LRTWC 1.

272 *Ibid.*, p. 125, and see M. McDougal and F. Feliciano, *The International Law of War, Transnational Coercion and World Public Order* (New Haven CT: New Haven Press, 1994), p. 604.

273 *German High Command* Trial, 12 LRTWC 1, p. 125.

274 See E. Rosenblad, 'Area bombing and international law', Rev dr milit, 15 (1976), 53–104, p. 79.

275 *Concise Oxford Dictionary*, n. 259 *supra*.

Development

The case of *Blaškić* was the first ICTY Judgement to consider the elements of this offence, but it did so very briefly, and only with respect to the destruction of property by an Occupying Power.[276] The Judgement simply stated that the Occupying Power may destroy such property only where it is made 'absolutely necessary by military operations'.[277] Furthermore, the Trial Chamber held that to constitute a grave breach such destruction must be 'extensive, unlawful and wanton'[278] and emphasised that '[t]he notion of "extensive" is evaluated according to the facts of the case – a single act, such as the destruction of a hospital, may suffice to characterise an offence under this count'.[279]

The Trial Chamber in *Kordić and Čerkez* discussed the elements of this offence in more depth.[280] It held that the crime is committed either where property protected under the Geneva Conventions is destroyed, whether or not in occupied territory, or where property is protected under the Geneva Conventions because of its location in occupied territory and the destruction occurs on a large scale and is not justified by military necessity. In each case the tribunal defined the *mens rea* of the offence as acting with 'the intent to destroy the property in question or in reckless disregard of the likelihood of its destruction'.[281] This shows that military necessity is not a defence to the destruction of property specifically protected by the Geneva Conventions such as hospitals and suggests that recklessness is a sufficient *mens rea* for the offence.

The possible criminality of the destruction carried out by Iraq during its occupation of and withdrawal from Kuwait in 1990–91 has been discussed by a report of the US Department of Defense. The report contends that the actions of Iraq in setting fire to oil wells and releasing oil into the Persian Gulf constituted the grave breach of extensive destruction of property.[282] It emphasises that setting fire to oil wells 'had no military purpose, but was simply punitive destruction at its worst'.[283] Had the Iraqi forces intended simply to obscure visibility they could have opened valves, as opposed to setting explosive charges on each well for maximum destruction.[284] Additionally, the report comments that the Iraqi forces, when retreating from Kuwait, failed to set ablaze wells on their side of the border, whereas had there been a military necessity for an obscurant they

[276] *Blaškić*, Trial Judgement, para. 157.

[277] *Ibid.*

[278] *Ibid.*

[279] *Ibid.* Both the *Naletilić and Martinović* Trial Judgement, para. 576, and the *Brđanin* Trial Judgement, para. 587, supported the view that this may be the case in exceptional circumstances.

[280] *Kordić and Čerkez*, Trial Judgement, paras 340–1.

[281] *Ibid.*, para. 341.

[282] US Department of Defense, 'Conduct of the Persian Gulf War', Final Report to Congress, Washington DC, 1992, Appendix O, 'The role of the law of war', ILM, 31 (1992), 615–44, p. 636.

[283] *Ibid.*, p. 637.

[284] *Ibid.*

undoubtedly would have done so.[285] White and McCoubrey also comment that there was no justification of military necessity regarding the destruction of buildings in Kuwait City prior to the Iraqi retreat.[286]

The evaluation of the Department of Defense report with respect to the Iraqi release of oil into the Persian Gulf is less convincing. The report simply states that 'this aspect of Iraq's wanton destruction of Kuwaiti property had little effect on Coalition offensive combat operations'.[287] However, the issue is not whether the actions of the accused were militarily effective but whether the accused took such action because, at the time, he believed it to be a military necessity. Hampson suggests that Iraq could argue that 'the oil spillages into the Gulf were intentional and designed to inhibit a feared amphibious landing'.[288] Furthermore, she explains that '[t]he American forces were apparently deployed in such a way as to make that threat a real one'.[289]

## The Rome Statute

The EOC state that the accused must have destroyed or appropriated property, that such destruction or appropriation could not be justified by military necessity, and finally that '[t]he destruction or appropriation was extensive and carried out wantonly'.[290] 'Appropriation' is not defined in the Elements, as the majority of delegates in the Preparatory Commission felt that it should be defined on a case-by-case basis.[291] However, the word order of the EOC confirms that both destruction and appropriation must be 'extensive' before the *actus reus* of this offence is committed.[292]

In the commentary to the Rome Statute, Fenrick suggests that '[t]he expression "and carried out unlawfully and wantonly" is surplusage',[293] and it is true that the expression 'unlawfully' is not repeated in the Elements. However the expression does serve as a reminder that if the stringent conditions of the articles of the Geneva Conventions concerned with property are followed, then not all destruction and appropriation constitutes a crime under this section.[294]

The expression 'wantonly', however, is repeated in the Elements and, although it is not explained, the repetition suggests that the word is not mere 'surplusage'. Piragoff suggests that the expression 'wantonly' connotes a different

[285] *Ibid.*

[286] N. White and H. McCoubrey, 'International law and the use of force in the Gulf', Int Rel, 10 (1991), 347–73, pp. 369–70.

[287] US Department of Defense report, n. 282 *supra*, p. 637.

[288] F. Hampson, 'Liability for war crimes', pp. 241–60 in P. Rowe (ed.), *The Gulf War, 1990–1991, in International and English Law* (London: Routledge, 1993), p. 250.

[289] *Ibid.*

[290] EOC, p. 127.

[291] Lee (ed.), *ICC: Elements*, p. 133.

[292] *Ibid.*

[293] Cottier *et al.*, 'Article 8', p. 183.

[294] Discussed *supra*, p. 45.

mental element from the default one provided for in Article 30.[295] Therefore it seems likely that 'wantonly' is an expression of *mens rea*, rather than merely an indication that specific motives need not be proved for this offence. The question remains as to what standard of *mens rea* 'wantonly' imposes. Paust asserts that the *mens rea* imported by the expression 'wantonly' is 'recklessly'.[296] However, there is insufficient evidence to accept this as the definitive answer.

Dörmann explains that the expression 'not justified by military necessity', used in this section, does not provide a defence unless one has been laid down in the Geneva Conventions with regard to that type of property.[297] It must be borne in mind that 'a rule of the law of armed conflict cannot be derogated from by invoking military necessity unless this possibility is explicitly provided for by the rule in question'.[298] Dörmann gives the example of Article 18 of the Fourth Geneva Convention, which states that '[c]ivilian hospitals . . . may in no circumstances be the object of the attack'.[299] The strict circumstances in which such a hospital may be attacked are laid down in Article 19 but do not include a defence of military necessity, and therefore an accused could not rely on such a defence if accused of attacking a civilian hospital.[300]

## Article 8(2)(a)(v) Compelling a prisoner of war or other protected person to serve in the forces of a hostile power

### Origins

This offence is prohibited by the Third and Fourth Geneva Conventions, and therefore prisoners of war and civilians are protected from being compelled to serve in the forces of a hostile power. Even during the American Civil War the Lieber Code prohibited forcing 'the subjects of the enemy into the service of the victorious government'[301] but did allow the army to use 'guides' and to obtain their services by force if necessary.[302] The Hague Regulations, whilst confirming that nationals of the hostile party could not be compelled to take part in operations of war against their own country, forbade the practice of forcing the inhabitants of occupied territory to give information about their government's army or defence.[303] Furthermore, under the Geneva Conventions all compelled enlistment

[295] D. Piragoff, 'Article 30, mental element', n. 114 *supra*, p. 531.

[296] J. Paust, 'Commentary on Parts 1 and 2 of the Zutphen Intersessional Draft', n. 250 *supra*, pp. 31–3.

[297] K. Dörmann, 'The first and second sessions of the Preparatory Commission', n. 65 *supra*, pp. 297–8.

[298] *Ibid*., p. 298.

[299] *Ibid*., p. 297.

[300] *Ibid*.

[301] Article 33, Lieber Code.

[302] Article 93, *ibid*.

[303] Article 23 and 44, 1907 Hague Regulations, and see Trial of *Rath and Schutz*, referred to in 15 LRTWC, p. 122. See also *infra*, p. 125.

in the armed forces of the hostile power is prohibited, 'whatever the theatre of operations and whoever the opposing forces might be'.[304]

## Development

To date the ICTY has not dealt with the grave breach of compelling protected persons to serve in the armed forces of a hostile power. Furthermore, despite '[p]ersistent evidence [which] emerged from Kuwait that attempts were being made to force Kuwaiti men of military age into service in the Iraqi forces' during the Gulf War,[305] there have been as yet no prosecutions at all for war crimes during that conflict.

## The Rome Statute

The EOC state that the perpetrator must have 'coerced one or more persons, by act or threat, to take part in military operations against that person's own country or forces or otherwise serve in the forces of a hostile power'.[306] Therefore, to coerce a person by an act or a threat, presumably of physical violence or of another severely prejudicial act,[307] to serve in the forces of the hostile power is forbidden. Fenrick states that 'forces' should be interpreted as including 'at a minimum, all entities encompassed by article 43 of the [AP I], which defines "armed forces" as "all organized armed forces, groups and units which are under a command responsible to that party for the conduct of its subordinates"'.[308]

Coercion to take part in military operations against one's own country or forces, other than as part of the forces of the hostile power, is also forbidden. Additionally, it is clear that coercion to serve in the forces of a hostile power against allied powers, resistance movements, or even such service not directly connected with the actual fighting, is also prohibited.[309] In respect of the mental element of this offence, the default *mens rea* of intention and knowledge under Article 30 of the Rome Statute applies, as no alternative *mens rea* is suggested by the EOC or Article 8(2)(a)(v). Therefore the accused would have to know that he was pressuring or coercing the victim and intended the victim to serve in forces hostile to him, or take part in military operations against his own country or forces.

[304] Pictet (ed.), *Commentary: IV Convention*, p. 293. See also Trial of *Wagner*, 3 LRTWC 23, p. 41.

[305] H. McCoubrey, 'Civilians in occupied territory', pp. 205–23 in P. Rowe (ed.), *The Gulf War*, n. 288 *supra*, p. 221, and A. DeSaussure, 'The role of the law of armed conflict during the Persian Gulf War: an overview', AFLR, 37 (1994), 41–68, p. 54. See also US Department of Defense report, n. 282 *supra*, p. 618.

[306] EOC, p. 128.

[307] A threat short of violence, such as threatening to take a person's children away to be adopted by another couple, would presumably be a sufficient threat to constitute coercion.

[308] Cottier *et al.*, 'Article 8', p. 183.

[309] Pictet (ed.), *Commentary: IV Convention*, p. 293.

## Article 8(2)(a)(vi) Wilfully depriving a prisoner of war or other protected person of the right to a fair and regular trial

### Origins

This offence is prohibited by the Third and Fourth Geneva Conventions and therefore it is an offence to deprive prisoners of war or civilians of fair and regular trial. The right to a fair and regular trial was also asserted during the post-Second World War war crimes trials.[310] In particular, the *Justice* Trial considered the character of the trials under the *Nacht und Nebel* decree.[311] It found that they 'did not approach even a semblance of a fair trial or justice', citing the fact that the defendants were held incommunicado, were in many cases 'denied the right to introduce evidence, to be confronted by witnesses against them, or to present witnesses on their own behalf'.[312] They were not allowed counsel of their choice and were occasionally denied the aid of counsel. Frequently no indictment was served and 'the accused learned only a few moments before the trial of the nature of the alleged crime for which he was to be tried'.[313]

Whilst the elements of a fair trial can be deduced from this negative phrasing, the Judge Advocate in the Trial of *Ohashi* set out the fundamental principles of justice necessary for a 'fair and reasonable' trial.[314] He stated that, first, the tribunal must be 'comprised of one or more men who will endeavour to judge the accused fairly upon the evidence . . . endeavouring to discard any preconceived belief in the guilt of the accused or any prejudice against him'.[315] Second, the accused must know the exact nature of the charge and the evidence against him and 'should have full opportunity to give his own version of the case and produce evidence to support it'.[316] Finally, the court should satisfy itself that the accused is guilty before awarding punishment and should not award a punishment which 'outrages the sentiments of humanity'.[317] However, in the Trial of *Latza* the Supreme Court of Norway emphasised that the denial of one right alone may not amount to the denial of a fair trial, and it should be considered whether a sufficient number of such rights have been breached seriously enough to constitute an unfair trial.[318]

[310] See G. Draper, *The Red Cross Conventions*, n. 72 *supra*, pp. 71–2.

[311] *Justice* Trial, 6 LRTWC 1, p. 97. (The *Nacht und Nebel* Decree translates as the Night and Fog Decree. Under it persons who were suspected of committing an offence against the German forces in occupied territories were taken secretly to Germany for trial and punishment, *IMT Judgement*, p. 453.)

[312] *Ibid.*

[313] *Ibid.*

[314] Trial of *Ohashi and Others*, 5 LRTWC 25, p. 30.

[315] *Ibid.*

[316] *Ibid.*

[317] *Ibid.*

[318] Trial of *Latza and Two Others*, 14 LRTWC 49, p. 85.

The commentaries to the Third and Fourth Geneva Conventions discuss the requirements of a fair and regular trial.[319] Together they include the right to notification of the charges, to appoint defence counsel, to have time to prepare a case, to bring witnesses, to have an interpreter and to appeal.[320] The commentary to the Fourth Geneva Convention confirms that the safeguard of a fair and regular trial applies 'to all accused persons, even those who are charged with having contravened the Geneva Conventions themselves'.[321]

### Development

There have been no recent prosecutions of this offence before international criminal tribunals.

### The Rome Statute

The elements of denying a fair trial require that the perpetrator 'deprived one or more persons of a fair and regular trial by denying judicial guarantees as defined, in particular, in the Third and Fourth Geneva Conventions of 1949'.[322] Therefore the prosecution must prove that the denial of the judicial guarantee or guarantees was sufficient to deprive the victim of a fair and regular trial. It is likely that the ICC will look at the trial procedure in totality when deciding whether the denial of guarantees was sufficient to amount to depriving the individual of a fair and regular trial.[323] Whilst the judicial guarantees in the Geneva Conventions have been discussed above,[324] the expression 'in particular' leaves the door open for the ICC to find that other judicial guarantees are essential for a fair and regular trial, and Dörmann comments that a denial of the presumption of innocence at the victim's trial may also constitute this offence.[325]

The mental element accompanying the deprivation of a fair and regular trial is described as 'wilfully' in Article 8(2)(a)(vi) but is not further elucidated in the EOC. By analogy with 'wilful killing', this expression denotes a specific *mens rea* for the offence, which may include recklessly as well as intentionally carrying out an action or omission which results in depriving an individual of a fair and regular trial.[326]

[319] Pictet (ed.), *Commentary: III and IV Conventions*, pp. 412, 484–95 and 352–9 respectively.

[320] *Ibid.* See Articles 84–8, 99, 103 and 105–6, Geneva Convention III and Articles 70–3, Geneva Convention IV.

[321] Pictet (ed.), *Commentary: IV Convention*, p. 354, and see Article 85 of Geneva Convention III.

[322] EOC, p. 128.

[323] See Trial of *Latza and Two Others*, 14 LRTWC 49, p. 85.

[324] Discussion *supra*, pp. 51–2.

[325] K. Dörmann, 'Preparatory Commission for the International Criminal Court', n. 207 *supra*, p. 789. See also Cottier *et al.*, 'Article 8', p. 184, and Lee (ed.), *ICC: Elements*, pp. 134–5.

[326] See discussion *supra*, pp. 26–8.

## Article 8(2)(a)(vii) Unlawful deportation or transfer or unlawful confinement

### Origins

Under Geneva Convention IV civilians are protected against the grave breach of unlawful deportation or transfer or unlawful confinement.[327] Whilst the prohibitions on deportation or transfer restrict the actions of an Occupying Power,[328] the offence of unlawful confinement can be committed either by an Occupying Power or by a party to the conflict in respect of alien civilians on its territory.[329]

*Unlawful deportation or transfer*

Article 49 of the Fourth Geneva Convention forbids both individual and mass forcible transfers of the civilian population by the Occupying Power and forbids deportation to any other country, including that of the Occupying Power, regardless of motive. The expressions 'transfer' and 'deportation' are not defined by the commentary to the Conventions, but presumably 'a transfer is a relocation within the occupied territory and a deportation is a relocation outside the occupied territory'.[330]

The prohibition is limited to *forcible* transfers of the civilian population, as individuals belonging to ethnic or political minorities 'might have suffered discrimination or persecution on that account and might therefore [voluntarily] wish to leave the country'.[331] However, the wording of Article 49 suggests that, whilst only forcible transfers are prohibited, all deportations are forbidden. Nevertheless, it is arguable that voluntary deportations would not be considered 'unlawful' and would therefore not constitute a grave breach of the Geneva Conventions.[332]

In certain strictly limited situations Article 49 provides for lawful transfers and deportations if either the security of the population or 'imperative military reasons so demand'. The commentary emphasises that an evacuation under these conditions 'is a provisional measure . . . often taken in the interests of the protected persons themselves' and gives the example of the population of an area which is suffering intense bombing being removed for their own safety and security.[333] According to Yingling and Ginnane an area could be evacuated for

[327] Article 147, Geneva Convention IV.

[328] For the definition of an Occupying Power see *infra*, pp. 104–5.

[329] Articles 49, 78 and 42, respectively, Geneva Convention IV.

[330] J. Henckaerts, *Mass Expulsion in Modern International Law and Practice* (Dordrecht: Nijhoff, 1995), p. 144.

[331] Pictet (ed.), *Commentary: IV Convention*, p. 279. However, if the discrimination is aimed at 'encouraging' the group to leave the country it may still constitute forcible transfer.

[332] J. Henckaerts, *Mass Expulsion*, n. 330 *supra*, pp. 144–5.

[333] Pictet (ed.), *Commentary: IV Convention*, p. 280.

imperative military reasons if illegal combatant activities were rife.[334] Such evacuations would be lawful, possibly even if carried out using reasonable force, but they may not displace the population outside the bounds of the occupied territory unless it is physically impossible to avoid doing so, and the population must be evacuated under humane conditions and returned to their homes as soon as feasible.[335]

Interpretation of this provision is also reliant upon jurisprudence from post-Second World war cases. Although deportations were not specifically prohibited by the 1907 Hague Regulations, it is thought that the omission was simply due to 'the fact that deportation of civilians was no longer practised . . . at the beginning of the twentieth century'.[336] However, Article 6(b) of the Nuremberg Charter recognised the war crime of 'deportation to slave labor or for any other purpose of the civilian population of or in occupied territory'.[337] The Nuremberg Judgement recounts that at least 5 million workers were deported to Germany by such methods as 'withdrawing the ration cards of laborers . . . or by discharging them from their jobs and denying them unemployment benefit or an opportunity to work elsewhere'.[338]

### *Unlawful confinement*

The Fourth Geneva Convention discusses two types of 'confinement' of civilians. The first is the internment or placing in assigned residence of civilian aliens in the territory of one of the Parties to the conflict and the second is the internment or placing in assigned residence of civilians in occupied territory by the Occupying Power.[339] The grave breach of unlawful confinement is committed if the internment or assigned residence of civilians in either of these situations is not in accordance with the restrictions laid down within the relevant articles of the Fourth Geneva Convention. The commentary to the Geneva Conventions defines assigned residence as moving persons from their domicile and forcing them to live 'in a locality which is generally out of the way and where supervision is more easily exercised'.[340] Internment is defined as 'a form of assigned residence' but a more severe one, 'as it generally implies an obligation to live in a camp with other internees'.[341]

According to Article 42 of the Fourth Geneva Convention, aliens in the territory of a Party to the conflict may be interned 'only if the security of the Detaining

[334] R. Yingling and R. Ginnane, 'The Geneva Conventions of 1949', AJIL, 46 (1952), 393–427, p. 419.

[335] Pictet (ed.), *Commentary: IV Convention*, p. 280. See the *British Military Manual*, para. 560.

[336] T. Meron, *War Crimes Law Comes of Age* (Oxford: Clarendon Press, 1998), p. 143.

[337] Article 6(c), Nuremberg Charter, also recognised deportation as a crime against humanity.

[338] *IMT Judgement*, p. 461, and see Trial of *Milch*, 7 LRTWC 27, p. 46, and *In re Lippert*, 17 ILR (1950), 432, p. 433.

[339] Articles 41–3 and 78, Geneva Convention IV.

[340] Pictet (ed.), *Commentary: IV Convention*, p. 256.

[341] *Ibid.*

Power makes it absolutely necessary', whereas under Article 78 only 'imperative reasons of security' will suffice to confine civilians in occupied territory. The commentary stresses with regard to both articles that the belligerent must have 'serious and legitimate reason[s]' to confine enemy alien civilians in its territory and may not take collective action against particular classes of people.[342] The State must 'have good reason to think that the person concerned, by his activities, knowledge or qualifications, represents a real threat to its present or future security'.[343] Articles 43 and 78 lay down procedural rules connected with any confinement, giving individuals the right to have their cases reconsidered by a court or administrative board as soon as possible and setting down a procedure for the automatic biannual reconsideration of confinements.

## Development

### *Unlawful deportation or transfer*

This offence has been discussed with respect to the actions of Iraq against Kuwaiti citizens during the Gulf conflict in 1990 and the actions of Israel against the Palestinians from the occupied territories in 1992. During the Gulf conflict Iraq allegedly deported large numbers of Kuwaiti citizens from Kuwait to Iraq.[344] The Security Council condemned the 'forced departure of Kuwaitis' and stated that Iraq was attempting to 'alter the demographic composition of the population of Kuwait'.[345] Such actions would clearly amount to the grave breach of unlawful deportation.

In 1992 Israel deported 415 Palestinians, who were allegedly members of Hamas and Islamic Jihad, from the West Bank and the Gaza Strip into no-man's-land between Israeli controlled territory and Lebanon.[346] According to Machover and Cragg, Israel argued that Article 49 prohibits only mass deportations and that the Palestinians were not in fact truly deported but only 'temporarily removed' for a period up to two years.[347] However, it is clear on the face of Article 49 that it is not so restricted and as neither the Convention nor the commentary makes any mention of a minimum length of time necessary to constitute a deportation it would seem that even the shortest expulsion from the occupied area could amount

[342] *Ibid.*, p. 258 and p. 367.

[343] *Ibid.*

[344] J. Henckaerts, *Mass Expulsion*, n. 330 *supra*, pp. 158–62.

[345] SC Res. 674, 29 October 1990, and SC Res. 677, 28 November 1990.

[346] See D. Machover and S. Cragg, 'The deportation of Palestinians', NLJ, 6583:143 (1993), 59–60, and C. Foster, 'Jerusalem, Geneva and the hills of Lebanon', NLJ, 6589:143 (1993), 282 and 297–8. Israel contests the applicability of the Geneva Conventions, but this is not accepted by most academics or the Security Council, see J. Henckaerts, *Mass Expulsion*, n. 330 *supra*, pp. 166–9, and SC Res. 799, 18 December 1992, para. 2.

[347] D. Machover and S. Cragg, 'The deportation of Palestinians', n. 346 *supra*, p. 60.

to that offence.[348] Had the Palestinians on an individual basis represented a real threat to Israeli security they should have been interned in accordance with the procedures laid down in Article 78.

A judicial decision on the offence of unlawful transfer of protected persons as a war crime was given in the ICTY case of *Nikolić*.[349] The original indictment in 1994 accused Nikolić of a grave breach of the Geneva Convention by participating in the unlawful transfer of civilians from Susica camp to Batkovic camp.[350] The Trial Chamber in the Rule 61 hearing commented that this set of facts could also have been characterised as deportation and charged as a crime against humanity.[351] This leaves the difference between transfer and deportation somewhat confused, given that both the camps were situated in Bosnia, and in any case omits the consideration that deportation could also have been charged as a war crime. In the event the indictment was amended in 1999 and omitted any reference to unlawful transfer or deportation.[352]

### *Unlawful confinement*

The ICTY has primarily considered the crime of unlawful confinement as a crime against humanity.[353] However, the grave breach of unlawful confinement was considered in the Rule 61 hearing of *Nikolić*, which held that internment in the Susica camp was unlawful, as the establishment of the camp 'was aimed at detaining a defenceless civilian population which was not organised into a resistance movement'.[354] In *Čelebici* the Trial Chamber emphasised that '[t]he fact that an individual is male and of military age should not necessarily be considered as justifying the application of [internment]' and stated that an 'initially lawful internment clearly becomes unlawful if the detaining party does not respect the basic procedural rights of the detained persons'.[355] This approach was upheld by the Appeal Judgement in *Čelebici*,[356] which emphasised that 'there is no such blanket power to detain the entire civilian population of a party to the conflict . . . but . . . there must be an assessment that each civilian taken into detention poses a *particular risk* to the security of the State'.[357]

[348] *Ibid.*

[349] *Nikolić*, Rule 61 Review, and see *Naletilić and Martinović*, Trial Judgement, which also considered this crime, see *infra*, pp. 106–7, discussion under Article 8(2)(b)(viii).

[350] Indictment of *Nikolić*, 4 November 1994, para. 22.1.

[351] *Nikolić*, Rule 61 Review, para. 23. This has been the approach of the ICTY in *Krstić* and *Krnojelac*, see *infra*, pp. 218–19.

[352] First Amended Indictment, 12 February 1999.

[353] See *infra*, pp. 221–2.

[354] *Nikolić*, Rule 61 Review, para. 20.

[355] *Čelebici*, Trial Judgement, paras 577 and 583, and see F. Hampson, 'The Geneva Conventions and the detention of civilians and alleged prisoners of war', Public Law (1991), 507–22.

[356] *Čelebici*, Appeal Judgement, paras 322 and 327, and see *Kordić and Čerkez*, Trial Judgement, paras 289 and 291.

[357] *Čelebici*, Appeal Judgement, para. 327, original emphasis. The *Kordić and Čerkez* Appeal Judgement, paras 70–3, upheld this approach.

### The Rome Statute

The EOC for both unlawful deportation or transfer and unlawful confinement are brief. The former merely states that the perpetrator 'deported or transferred one or more persons to another State or to another location',[358] whereas the latter states that the perpetrator 'confined or continued to confine one or more persons to a certain location'.[359] This has the effect of confirming the findings of the ICTY in *Čelebici* when it stated that a lawful confinement could become unlawful if the correct procedures such as appeal and review were not carried out.[360] In respect of the mental element of this offence, the default *mens rea* of intention and knowledge under Article 30 of the Rome Statute applies, as no alternative *mens rea* is suggested in the EOC or in Article 8(2)(a)(vii). Therefore the perpetrator would have to intend to deport, transfer or confine the victims and to know of the factual circumstances which made this act unlawful.[361]

## Article 8(2)(a)(viii) Taking of hostages

### Origins

The Fourth Geneva Convention prohibits the taking of hostages, and so civilians are protected persons in respect of this grave breach. Prior to the conclusion of the 1949 Geneva Conventions it had been accepted practice to take hostages 'as a means of securing legitimate warfare'.[362] Whilst the offence of 'killing of hostages' was prosecuted as a war crime before post-Second World War tribunals,[363] no offence was committed at that time by *taking* hostages, and there was even debate over whether hostages could be killed legitimately in certain circumstances.[364]

The commentary to the Fourth Geneva Convention gave a definition of hostages as 'nationals of a belligerent State who of their own free will or through compulsion are in the hands of the enemy and are answerable with their freedom or their life for the execution of his orders and the security of his armed forces'.[365] Examples of hostage taking include taking prominent persons from a district in order to prevent attacks on occupation troops, or taking hostages from a district after such attacks so that the attackers will be given up and 'the

[358] EOC, p. 129.

[359] *Ibid.*

[360] *Čelebici*, Trial Judgement, para. 583, and see Lee (ed.), *ICC: Elements*, pp. 137–8.

[361] For example, the perpetrator may be aware that the civilians he intends to confine pose no security risk but would not have to know that such confinement was illegal.

[362] *British Military Manual*, para. 650. See also Articles 54 and 55, Lieber Code 1863.

[363] Article 6(b), Nuremberg Charter, *IMT Judgement*, p. 454, *Hostages* Trial, 8 LRTWC 34, *German High Command* Trial, 12 LRTWC 1, and Trial of *Rauter*, 14 LRTWC 89.

[364] See M. Greenspan, *The Modern Law of Land Warfare*, n. 46 *supra*, pp. 414–17; G. Schwarzenberger, *International Law as applied by International Courts and Tribunals*, n. 4 *supra*, pp. 237–41, and Lord Wright, 'The killing of hostages as a war crime', BYIL, 25 (1948), 296–310.

[365] Pictet (ed.), *Commentary: IV Geneva Convention*, p. 229.

practice of taking so-called accompanying hostages [which] consists of placing inhabitants of occupied territory on board lorry convoys or trains in order to prevent attacks by their compatriots'.[366] The commentary explained that hostage taking would be accompanied by 'the threat either to prolong the hostage's detention or to put him to death'.[367]

## Development

The offence of taking civilians hostage was considered in the case of *Blaškić*.[368] The Trial Chamber stated that the elements of the taking of hostages as a grave breach were similar to those of the taking of hostages as a breach of Common Article 3 of the Geneva Conventions, and held that '[t]he Prosecution must establish that, at the time of the supposed detention, the allegedly censurable act was perpetrated in order to obtain a concession or gain an advantage'.[369] Blaškić was found guilty of taking hostages, both as a grave breach and as a breach of Common Article 3, for detaining civilians and other persons *hors de combat* at the Vitez cultural centre in order 'to compel the ABiH [Muslim army of Bosnia-Herzegovina] to halt its advance'.[370]

## The Rome Statute

The elements of taking hostages under Article 8(2)(a)(viii) consist of three specific parts. The perpetrator must have 'seized, detained or otherwise held hostage one or more persons' and 'threatened to kill, injure or continue to detain such person or persons'.[371] In addition he or she must intend 'to compel a State, an international organization, a natural or legal person or a group of persons to act or refrain from acting as an explicit or implicit condition for the safety or the release of such person or persons'.[372]

These elements are based, with some alterations, on the definition of hostage taking under Article 1 of the 1979 International Convention against the Taking of Hostages.[373] The element of taking the hostage is made broader than that of the Hostage Convention by the use of the all-inclusive expression 'or otherwise held hostage'. Fenrick comments that the offence of hostage taking may be

[366] *Ibid.*, p. 230.

[367] *Ibid.*, p. 600.

[368] *Blaškić*, Trial Judgement, paras 158 and 187.

[369] *Ibid.*, para. 158, followed in *Kordić and Čerkez*, Trial Judgement, para. 313.

[370] *Blaškić*, Trial Judgement, para. 708, and 'Disposition'. See also the detention of Hizbullah hostages in Lebanon by Israeli forces, discussed in Green, *The Contemporary Law of Armed Conflict*, n. 2 *supra*, pp. 214–15.

[371] EOC, p. 129.

[372] *Ibid.*

[373] K. Dörmann, 'The first and second sessions of the Preparatory Commission', n. 65 *supra*, p. 298.

committed irrespective of whether the initial detention was lawful or unlawful and that the threat issued by the hostage taker to kill, injure or continue to detain may be implicit or explicit.[374] Although on the face of it the second element, 'threatened to kill . . .', appears to require an explicit threat, it is submitted that it should be interpreted in a broad sense and should include an implicit threat, or an unacceptable loophole in this offence would be created.

The mental element of this offence requires that the hostage taker should have *intended* to compel one of the listed entities to 'act or refrain from acting' as an explicit or implicit condition of the 'safety or release' of the hostages.[375] Dörmann comments that the expression 'safety' was inserted into this element in addition to the word 'release' in the Hostages Convention as a result of Second World War experience.[376] Therefore, it appears that the accused must intend to take the victim into captivity, or extend previously lawful captivity and then threaten to kill, injure or continue to detain that person. Furthermore the accused must intend to compel specified entities to modify their behaviour in return for the safety or release of the hostages.

[374] Cottier *et al*., 'Article 8', p. 185.

[375] EOC, p. 129.

[376] K. Dörmann, 'The first and second sessions of the Preparatory Commission', n. 65 *supra*, p. 298.

# 3

# War crimes (II): other offences in international armed conflicts

## Article 8(2)(b) of the Rome Statute

### The *chapeau* to Article 8(2)(b) Other serious violations of the laws and customs applicable in international armed conflict, within the established framework of international law, namely, any of the following acts . . .

The *chapeau* explains that the offences under Article 8(2)(b) must be committed in an international armed conflict,[1] but the meaning of 'serious violations' is unclear. The International Criminal Tribunal for the former Yugoslavia (ICTY) Trial Chamber in the case of *Čelebici* stated that, in order to be considered as a serious violation of international humanitarian law, an offence must 'be one which constitutes a breach of a rule protecting important values' and 'also be one which involves grave consequences for the victim'.[2] Fenrick suggests that '[a]ll of the acts listed in article 8 para. 2 (b) may be regarded as meeting an appropriate level of seriousness',[3] an interpretation which is supported by the phrase 'namely, any of the following acts' in the *chapeau*, prior to the enunciation of the various offences.

The phrase 'within the established framework of international law' has been described as 'unnecessary and confusing' by Paust.[4] Despite the uncertainty surrounding this expression, Fenrick's explanation that it 'is merely intended to confirm that the listed acts are serious violations bearing in mind the existing framework of international law' seems likely.[5] Nevertheless, it should be noted that the United

[1] See discussion *supra*, pp. 17–21.

[2] *Čelebici*, Trial Judgement, para. 1154.

[3] M. Cottier, W. Fenrick, P. Viseur Sellers and A. Zimmermann, 'Article 8, war crimes', pp. 173–288 in O. Triffterer (ed.), *Commentary on the Rome Statute of the International Criminal Court* (Baden-Baden: Nomos, 1999; hereinafter: Cottier *et al.*, 'Article 8'), p. 185.

[4] J. Paust, 'Commentary on parts 1 and 2 of the Zutphen Intersessional Draft', pp. 27–42 in L. Sadat Wexler (ed.), *Observations on the Consolidated ICC Text before the Final Session of the Preparatory Committee*, 13 *bis* Nouvelles études pénales (1998), p. 29.

[5] Cottier *et al.*, 'Article 8', pp. 185–6.

Kingdom's interpretative declaration to the Rome Statute explains its understanding that the phrase was used 'to include customary international law as established by State practice and *opinio iuris*', and consequently drew attention to its understandings with respect to Additional Protocol (AP) I and other relevant international law instruments.[6]

A notable absence from the *chapeau* of this article is any reference to protected persons. This suggests that, contrary to the grave breach offences, protected person status under the Geneva Conventions is not a requirement for the victims of Article 8(2)(b), and indeed the Elements of Crimes (EOC) to this section make no reference to protected person status.[7] With respect to the Hague law, from which much of Article 8(2)(b) is derived, the focus is on combatants and so the concept of protected persons is not relevant.[8] However, this section of Article 8 also draws upon AP I, including articles providing jurisdiction over various acts against 'civilians', and so the scope of such articles is clearly restricted despite the lack of reference to 'protected persons' as such.[9]

## Article 8(2)(b)(i) Intentionally directing attacks against the civilian population as such or against individual civilians not taking direct part in hostilities

### Origins

The prohibition of attacks upon civilians has been recognised as far back as the Lieber Code.[10] However, during the Second World War the practice of 'carpet bombing', which led to the deaths of hundreds of thousands of civilians, brought this proscription into question.[11] The modern prohibition against attacks upon civilians is contained within Article 51(2) of AP I and states, in language similar to that of Article 8(2)(b)(i), that '[t]he civilian population as such, as well as individual civilians, shall not be the object of attack'.[12] AP I defines 'civilians'

[6] UK interpretive declaration to the Rome Statute of the International Criminal Court, made on ratification of the Statute on 4 October 2001, available on the ICRC website at: <http://www.icrc.org>.

[7] See W. Schabas, *An Introduction to the International Criminal Court* (Cambridge: Cambridge University Press, 2nd edn, 2001), p. 123.

[8] *Ibid.*

[9] It is suggested that a decision on the extent of the protection of the section concerned should be made in the light of the source of the provision concerned.

[10] Article 22, Lieber Code.

[11] The Hague Regulations did not expressly prohibit attacks against civilians and Article 22 of the 1923 Hague Rules of Aerial Warfare was not legally binding. On 30 September 1938 the League of Nations GA adopted a resolution acknowledging that '[t]he intentional bombing of civilian populations is illegal', but that did not prevent indiscriminate bombing during the Second World War, see D. Schindler and J. Toman (eds), *The Laws of Armed Conflicts: A Collection of Conventions, Resolutions and other Documents* (Dordrecht: Nijhoff, 1988), pp. 221–2.

[12] See also Article 85(3), AP I.

negatively, by excluding those defined as combatants in the Geneva Convention and Protocols.[13] The Bothe *et al.* commentary emphasises that the definition of civilians also includes individuals linked to the armed forces without being members thereof, such as civilians accompanying, serving and transporting the military or employed in munitions work, as well as civilians who have previously taken part in hostilities without combatant status.[14]

AP I defines the 'civilian population' as comprising all those who are civilians. However, it confirms that '[t]he presence within the civilian population of individuals who do not come within the definition of civilians does not deprive the population of its civilian character'.[15] The commentary of the International Committee of the Red Cross (ICRC) to AP I suggests that such intermingling of combatants with civilians as soldiers on leave visiting families would not alter the civilian nature of a population.[16] The expression 'civilian population as such' 'implies that there can be no assurance that attacks against combatants and other military objectives will not result in civilian casualties'.[17]

Article 51(3) of AP I provides that civilians are only protected 'unless and for such time as they take a direct part in hostilities'. The expression 'direct part in hostilities' is explained by the Bothe *et al.* and the ICRC commentaries as essentially participation in combatant activities,[18] although Bothe *et al.* propose that the expression is broader than 'attacks' and includes preparation for and return from combat.[19] Both commentaries agree, however, that civilians participating in the war effort, such as workers in defence plants, do not lose their protected status.[20] Finally, the expression 'attacks' has also been defined by AP I in Article 49(1) as 'acts of violence against the adversary, whether in offence or

[13] Article 50(1), AP I, excludes those persons referred to in Article 4(a)(1) (2) (3) and (6) of Geneva Convention III and those persons referred to in Article 43 of AP I. On combatant status see generally M. Clarke, T. Glynn and A. Rogers, 'Combatant and prisoner-of-war status', pp. 107–35 in M. Meyer (ed.), *Armed Conflict and the New Law: Aspects of the 1977 Geneva Protocols and the 1981 Weapons Convention* (London: British Institute of International and Comparative Law, 1989).

[14] M. Bothe, K. Partsch and W. Solf, *New Rules for Victims of Armed Conflicts* (The Hague: Nijhoff, 1982, hereinafter: Bothe *et al.*, *New Rules for Victims*), pp. 293–4, and see A. Rogers, *Law on the Battlefield* (Manchester: Manchester University Press, 2nd edn, 2004), pp. 8–9.

[15] Article 50(3), AP I.

[16] Y. Sandoz, C. Swinarski and B. Zimmermann (eds), *Commentary on the Additional Protocols of 8 June 1977 to the Geneva Conventions of 12 August 1949* (Geneva: ICRC and Nijhoff, 1987, hereinafter: Sandoz *et al.*, *Commentary on the Additional Protocols*), p. 612.

[17] Bothe *et al.*, *New Rules for Victims*, p. 300, and see H. Blix, 'Area bombardment: rules and reasons', BYIL, 49 (1978), 31–69, p. 42. See discussion *infra*, pp. 81–9.

[18] Bothe *et al.*, *New Rules for Victims*, p. 303, and Sandoz *et al.*, *Commentary on the Additional Protocols*, p. 619.

[19] Bothe *et al.*, *New Rules for Victims*, p. 303, and see comments of A. Rogers, *Law on the Battlefield*, n. 14 *supra*, pp. 10–12.

[20] Bothe *et al.*, *New Rules for Victims*, p. 303, and Sandoz *et al.*, *Commentary on the Additional Protocols*, p. 619. Although see Spaight's arguments that such people are 'quasi-combatants', J. Spaight, 'Legitimate objectives in air warfare', BYIL, 21 (1944), 158–64, p. 162.

in defence'. The ICRC commentary explains that this definition essentially equates the word 'attack' with 'combat action'.[21]

## Development

The definition of 'attacks' in AP I has been the subject of much discussion. Whilst conceding that the definition of 'attacks' as 'acts of violence' is broad enough to cover the actions of individual soldiers, Fenrick argues that in the context of Articles 51 and 57 'it would normally be inappropriate and impractical to classify an operation below divisional or equivalent level as an "attack"' because of the planning process envisaged.[22] Support for this approach can be found in the Swiss reservation to Article 57(2), which states that the article only creates obligations for commanders at the battalion or group level and above to ensure that civilian objects are not attacked.[23]

However, this interpretation has been disputed by Rogers, who contends, more in line with the AP I commentaries, that '[t]he definition of attack is wide enough to include a whole range of attacks, from that of a single soldier opening fire with his rifle to that of an army group's major offensive'.[24] He proposes that the United Kingdom's interpretative declaration to AP I, that those responsible for deciding upon or executing attacks must be judged in light of the information available to them at that time, takes account of the knowledge and situation of the accused in respect of the standard required of him.[25] This approach has the benefit of accepting that individual soldiers must rely upon the military intelligence and analysis of those who designate a particular target, whilst holding them responsible if they become aware upon approach that the target is in fact civilian and nevertheless proceed to attack.

The question of the definition of 'civilians' was considered by the *Kordić and Čerkez* Appeal Chamber, which described civilians negatively, explaining that whilst it clearly excluded members of the armed forces, it also excluded 'members of organised resistance groups' which fulfilled the requirements set out in Article 4(2) of the Third Geneva Convention.[26] Therefore, the court

[21] Sandoz *et al.*, *Commentary on the Additional Protocols*, p. 603, and see S. Oeter, 'Methods and means of combat', pp. 105–207 in D. Fleck (ed.), *Handbook of Humanitarian Law in Armed Conflicts* (Oxford: Oxford University Press, 1999), para. 441(3).

[22] W. Fenrick, 'The rule of proportionality and Protocol 1 in conventional warfare', Milit LR, 98 (1982), 91–127, p. 102.

[23] See Switzerland's reservation to AP I, available from the ICRC website: <http://www.icrc.org/>.

[24] A. Rogers, *Law on the Battlefield*, n. 14 *supra*, p. 28, and see Bothe *et al.*, *New Rules for Victims*, p. 288.

[25] A. Rogers, *Law on the Battlefield*, n. 14 *supra*, pp. 28–9. UK reservations and understandings in relation to AP I available from the ICRC website: <http://www.icrc.org/>.

[26] *Kordić and Čerkez*, Appeal Judgement, para. 50.

essentially excluded from the notion of 'civilian' anyone who would have prisoner-of-war status if captured. The *Galić* Trial Chamber suggested that 'the clothing, activity, age, or sex of a person' are factors which should be considered in deciding whether an individual is a civilian.[27]

With respect to the definition of a 'civilian population' the *Galić* Appeal Chamber found that the ICTY jurisprudence is clear on the fact that 'the presence of individual combatants within the population attacked does not *necessarily* change the fact that the ultimate character of the population remains, for legal purposes, a civilian one'.[28] In this context, the *Blaškić* Appeal Chamber explained that 'in order to determine whether the presence of soldiers within a civilian population deprives the population of its civilian character, the number of soldiers, as well as whether they are on leave, must be examined'.[29] This treatment of the effect of the presence of soldiers on a civilian population is interesting, given that members of the armed forces can lawfully be attacked at any time, whether they are on duty or off.

The ICTY, in *Blaškić*, considered attacks upon civilians in the village of Ahmici.[30] The Trial Chamber stated that in order to constitute an offence the attack must have caused deaths or serious bodily injury, not have been justified by military necessity and have been conducted intentionally in the knowledge that the target was civilian.[31] A similar definition was also given in the *Kordić and Čerkez* case.[32] The proposition that death or serious injury of civilians must result from the incident appears to have been based on Article 85 of AP I, which confines the grave breach of attacking civilians to situations where death or serious injury has been caused.[33] The defence of military necessity, read into this offence by the tribunal, is questionable and was in fact rectified on appeal.[34] The correction was necessary as the relevant articles of AP I do not suggest that there is any defence of military necessity in respect of the killing of civilians.[35] Indeed, under AP I even reprisal attacks against civilians are prohibited.[36]

An important issue which has been discussed by academic commentators and has been the subject of Expert meetings organised by the ICRC and the T. M. C. Asser Institute, is the meaning of the phrase 'direct part in hostilities'

[27] *Galić*, Trial Judgement, para. 50.

[28] *Galić*, Appeal Judgement, para. 136, original emphasis.

[29] *Blaškić*, Appeal Judgement, para. 115.

[30] *Blaškić*, Trial Judgement, paras 180 and 414–17.

[31] *Ibid.*, para. 180.

[32] *Kordić and Čerkez*, Trial Judgement, para. 328.

[33] This was confirmed by the Appeal Chamber, *Kordić and Čerkez*, Appeal Judgement, paras 63–7.

[34] *Blaškić*, Appeal Judgement, para. 109.

[35] Although civilians may be killed or injured as an incidental result of an attack upon a legitimate military object, see *infra*, pp. 81–9.

[36] Article 51(6), AP I, and see G. Aldrich, 'New life for the laws of war', AJIL, 75 (1981), 764–83, pp. 781–2.

as civilians who take such a direct part may exceptionally be lawfully attacked.[37] The explanation by the ICRC commentary that the phrase 'direct part in hostilities' means 'acts of war which by their nature or purpose are likely to cause actual harm to the personnel and equipment of the enemy armed force' is a good starting point for a complex issue.[38]

First, it must be noted that the fact that civilians are armed does not necessarily indicate that they are taking a direct part in hostilities. Schmitt comments that in some countries the possession of weapons is a cultural feature and that additionally civilians may possess arms to protect themselves from lawlessness.[39] McDonald suggests that the civilians' action must have some sort of link with the armed conflict in order for them to be considered as taking a direct part in hostilities and so lose their immunity from attack.[40] She gives the example of a civilian who shoots a neighbour in order to take their money during an armed conflict and states that, whilst this would be a criminal act, if there were link with the conflict the civilian would not lose their immunity from attack.[41]

This interpretation was supported and developed by the Third Expert Meeting in Geneva, where some of the experts commented that conduct with a nexus to the armed conflict required that the civilian was engaged in military activity against the enemy and that civilians could not be targeted 'simply because they provided some indirect or causal contribution to hostilities'.[42] Nevertheless, McDonald comments that some civilians at a geographical remove from the zone of hostilities can still be considered as directly participating, such as 'civilians manning computers which remotely control drones flying over foreign territory, gathering intelligence, selecting targets, or engaging in attacks'.[43]

The experts were agreed that the meaning of 'hostilities' had to be clearly distinguished from the general 'war effort' and differentiated between activities that were actually intended to cause harm from activities that merely built up

[37] References to the ICRC/Asser Institute Expert Meeting will be to the Third Expert Meeting on the Notion of Direct Participation in Hostilities, Summary Report, Geneva, 23–25 October (hereinafter: ICRC Expert Meeting) available at: <http://www.icrc.org/web/eng/siteeng0.nsf/htmlall/participation-hostilities-ihl-311205>.

[38] Sandoz *et al.*, *Commentary on the Additional Protocols*, p. 619.

[39] M. Schmitt, '"Direct participation in hostilities" and twenty-first-century armed conflict', pp. 505–29 in H. Fischer, U. Froissart, W. Heintschel von Heinegg and C. Raap (eds), *Crisis Management and Humanitarian Protection: In Honour of Dieter Fleck* (Berlin: Berliner Wissenschafts-Verlag, 2004), p. 519.

[40] A. McDonald, 'The challenges to international humanitarian law and the principles of distinction and protection from the increased participation of civilians in hostilities', in Spotlight on Issues of Contemporary Concern in International Humanitarian Law and International Criminal Law, p. 27, available at: <http://www.wihl.nl>.

[41] *Ibid.*

[42] ICRC Expert Meeting, p. 27.

[43] A. McDonald, 'The challenges to international humanitarian law', n. 40 *supra*, p. 18, and see M. Schmitt, 'Direct participation in hostilities', n. 39 *supra*, pp. 511–12. This issue was also raised at the ICRC Expert Meeting, p. 35.

the capacity to do so.[44] Schmitt's approach to this distinction is to assess 'the criticality of the act to the direct application of violence against the enemy'.[45] This sensible interpretation avoids defining all civilians working in munition factories or the manufacture of military hardware as lawful targets whilst accepting that some other civilians working at a remove from the war zone might be taking a direct part in hostilities.[46]

The final question is a temporal one and asks for how long civilians who have taken a direct part in hostilities lose their immunity? Do they lose it only when they are actually carrying out hostile acts or can they be legitimately targeted as they sleep in their beds in the same way as members of the armed forces? This question caused much discussion and disagreement at the Third Expert Meeting in Geneva.[47] With respect to individual civilians who were not part of organised groups and lost immunity because of a specific act, some experts stated that such civilians could be targeted during measures preparatory to attack, deployment, attack and during return from engaging in hostilities.[48] However, it was accepted that situations where civilians who are not part of organised groups attack the armed forces directly are very rare.[49]

In the case of civilians who have joined an organised armed group most experts felt that the approach detailed above was 'too narrow for a realistic interpretation of the notion of "direct participation in hostilities"'.[50] However, there was a split between two approaches, termed the 'affirmative disengagement approach', whereby such individuals could be lawfully targeted until they declared their disengagement, and the 'membership' approach, whereby civilians could be attacked whilst remaining members of organised armed groups.[51] Neither proposal is without problems; the 'affirmative disengagement approach' would not work well if there were thousands of civilians involved in the conflict and it was agreed 'would be more realistic where an entire group wanted to disengage, rather than where the disengagement concerned only individual members'.[52] The 'membership' approach if applied literally would treat civilians of organised armed groups in exactly the same way as members of the armed forces but there is really no authority to do this under the Geneva Conventions and Additional Protocols.

A limited 'membership' approach was proposed which would allow the targeting of fighting members of such organised groups who were regularly

[44] ICRC Expert Meeting, p. 21.

[45] M. Schmitt, 'Direct participation in hostilities', n. 39 *supra*, p. 509.

[46] This does not mean that the factory would not be a legitimate military objective and that civilians might not be killed or injured collaterally, see *infra*, p. 82.

[47] ICRC Expert Meeting, pp. 59–68.

[48] *Ibid.*, p. 60.

[49] *Ibid.*

[50] *Ibid.*, p. 62.

[51] *Ibid.*, pp. 62–5. This approach is supported by M. Schmitt, 'Direct participation in hostilities', n. 39 *supra*, p. 510.

[52] ICRC Expert Meeting, p. 62.

conducting or commanding hostilities.[53] This would exclude members who had separated geographically by returning home 'on leave', although such individuals could be arrested and prosecuted,[54] but would not prohibit targeting the organised camp from which the civilians were regularly carrying out attacks if it was situated in a position which made capture impossible. This approach is perhaps a good compromise, sticking fairly closely to the spirit of Article 51(3) of AP I whilst acknowledging the reality that civilians who continuously engage in hostilities cannot be allowed complete immunity from attack whilst resting between hostilities if it is impossible to arrest and detain them during that time.

## The Rome Statute

The definition of the offence of attacking civilians in the Rome Statute follows closely the definitions of attacking civilians as a grave breach in AP I and as an offence in the Draft Code of Crimes of the International Law Commission (ILC).[55] The EOC, other than those related to the nature of the conflict, require that the perpetrator 'directed an attack', that the 'object of the attack was a civilian population as such or individual civilians not taking direct part in hostilities' and that the perpetrator intended such persons to be the object of the attack.[56]

The element of 'directing an attack' is somewhat unclear. This is due, in part, to debate over the meaning of 'attack' in AP I, but also to the choice of the phrase 'directing attacks' in Article 8(2)(b)(i)–(iii), (ix) and (xxiv), as opposed to 'launching an attack' in Article 8(2)(b)(iv) and 'attacking' in article 8(2)(b)(v) of the Rome Statute. These terms are not defined in the Statute and the EOC do not assist in understanding them. In light of the discussion above, the ICC may well interpret attack broadly as including any combat action either by an individual combatant or by a formation or group of combatants. Fenrick suggests that the use of the expression 'launching' rather than 'directing' when referring to attacks where proportionality is a relevant issue implies that such decisions are usually made at a higher level and involve a formal planning process.[57] This would support the argument that the offence of 'directing attacks' at civilians in the Rome Statute envisages attacks committed by a single combatant acting alone.

The object of the attack must be civilians or the civilian population, clearly defined by AP I and its commentaries.[58] In particular, it must be noted that the presence of combatants does not necessarily transform a civilian population into a legitimate objective. When the level of combatants within a civilian population has increased to the point where they could be considered a military

[53] *Ibid.*, p. 64.

[54] *Ibid.*, p. 65.

[55] Article 85(3), AP I, and Article 20(b)(i), 1996 ILC Draft Code.

[56] Elements of Crimes, Assembly of States Parties to the Rome Statute of the ICC, Official Records, First Session, ICC-ASP/1/3, 3–10 September 2002 (hereinafter: EOC), p. 130.

[57] Cottier *et al.*, 'Article 8', p. 197.

[58] See *supra*, pp. 61–2.

objective, the legitimacy of the attack would depend upon the question of proportionality dealt with under Article 8(2)(b)(iv).[59]

The EOC confirm that it is not an offence to attack civilians who are taking a 'direct part in hostilities'.[60] This proviso was inserted during the fifth Preparatory Committee prior to the Rome Conference,[61] to reflect the same phrase in Article 51(3) of AP I, but its scope is still uncertain, as has been seen above. Whilst participation in combat activities would clearly deprive civilians of the protection of this section and working in a munitions factory would clearly not,[62] what of civilian engineers working to mend tanks near the front line or civilian computer operators controlling unmanned drones to assist remote attacks? In the 'grey' areas between direct participation and indirect participation in hostilities the ICC will have to take each case on its merits.

Importantly, the EOC do not include a result element for this offence, so it need not be proved that civilians were actually killed or injured because of the attack. Dörmann comments that this was a controversial issue in the Preparatory Commission, as the AP I grave breach provision on attacks against civilians or the civilian population requires that death or serious injury to body or health must have resulted from the attack.[63] The consensus of the Preparatory Commission, however, was that the result requirement had been consciously left out of this article in the Rome Statute and therefore the EOC should not reintroduce the limitation.[64]

The *mens rea* of this offence is set out in the element requiring that the perpetrator 'intended' the civilians to be the object of the attack. It appears that recklessness as to civilian injury would not suffice.[65] Therefore, although the Iraqi use of Scuds against Israeli and Saudi cities during the Gulf conflict was indiscriminate, as the missiles were not capable of being targeted at specific military objects,[66] it would not have breached this article of the Rome Statute unless it could be proved that an accused Iraqi had *intended* to make civilians the object

[59] See *infra*, pp. 81–9.

[60] EOC, p. 130.

[61] Preparatory Committee on the Establishment of an ICC, UN Doc. A/AC.249/1997/L.9/Rev.1, 18 December 1997, p. 3.

[62] Although a munitions factory itself would be a legitimate military target, and thus the civilian workers could be considered as collateral damage in such an attack provided that the rule on proportionality under Article 8(2)(b)(iv) was not breached.

[63] Article 85(3), AP I, and K. Dörmann, 'Preparatory Commission for the International Criminal Court: the Elements of War Crimes, Part II: Other serious violations of the laws and customs applicable in international and non-international armed conflicts', IRRC, 842 (2001), 461–87, pp. 466–7.

[64] *Ibid.*, p. 467.

[65] Fenrick argues that recklessness is sufficient, but that was prior to the conclusion of the EOC, Cottier *et al.*, 'Article 8', p. 186.

[66] Such attacks would breach Article 51(4) of AP I, although Iraq is not a party to AP I, see M. Schmitt, 'Future war and the principle of discrimination', Israel Yrbk Hum Rts, 28 (1998), 51–90, p. 55, and A. Rogers, *Law on the Battlefield*, n. 14 *supra*, p. 24.

of the attack, as opposed to simply being reckless.[67] The argument that the accused must have foreseen that such an attack would amount to an attack against civilians, or that the requisite intention could be inferred from his failure to take precautionary measures (such as more precisely targeted weapons) in the attack, is not a watertight argument.[68] This appears to leave an unfortunate loophole in the Rome Statute, which defendants will no doubt attempt to exploit.

## Article 8(2)(b)(ii) Intentionally directing attacks against civilian objects, that is, objects which are not military objectives

### Origins

Whilst specific civilian objects have been protected by international conventions since the Hague Regulations,[69] the first treaty to set out the absolute prohibition that '[c]ivilian objects shall not be the object of attack or of reprisals' was Article 52 of AP I, the basis of this article in the Rome Statute.[70] AP I defines civilian objects negatively, as 'objects which are not military objectives'. However, it is restricted to dealing with attacks against civilian objects *per se* and not collateral damage or 'unintentional or unavoidable but necessary destruction of civilian objects incidental to military operations such as destruction to delay pursuit, [or] clearing fields of fire'.[71]

When analysing this offence, because of the negative definition of 'civilian objects', the real question becomes: what are military objectives?[72] AP I defines military objectives as 'those objects which by their nature, location, purpose or use make an effective contribution to military action and whose total or partial destruction, capture or neutralization, in the circumstances ruling at the time, offers a definite military advantage'.[73] Bothe *et al.* comment that this definition provides a 'two-pronged test'.[74] The objects must 'make an effective contribution

[67] The Rome Statute does not include jurisdiction over indiscriminate attacks *per se*.

[68] See comments of K. Dörmann, 'Preparatory Commission for the International Criminal Court', n. 63 *supra*, p. 469. The *Galić* Trial Judgement, para. 57, comments that indiscriminate attacks 'may qualify as direct attacks against civilians' but the *Galić* Appeal Judgement, para. 132, emphasises that evidence of the use of indiscriminate weapons would merely be evidence from which a direct attack could be inferred. The use of such weapons could also be considered under the rule of proportionality of Article 8(2)(b)(iv), see *infra*, pp. 81–9.

[69] See Article 27, 1907 Hague Regulations.

[70] See A. Randelzhofer, 'Civilian objects', pp. 93–6 in R. Bernhardt (ed.), *Encyclopaedia of Public International Law*, Vol. III (Amsterdam: North-Holland, 1982, hereinafter: Bernhardt (ed.), *Encyclopaedia Vol. 3/4*), p. 94.

[71] Bothe *et al.*, *New Rules for Victims*, p. 321.

[72] See F. von der Heydte, 'Military objectives', pp. 276–9, in Bernhardt (ed.), *Encyclopaedia Vol. 3*.

[73] Article 52, AP I.

[74] Bothe *et al.*, *New Rules for Victims*, p. 323.

to military action' and their neutralisation 'in the circumstances ruling at the time' must offer a 'definite military advantage'.[75]

With respect to the first part of this test, the ICRC commentary suggests that objects which by 'nature' make an effective contribution to military action are 'all objects directly used by the armed forces', such as weapons, equipment, fortifications, staff headquarters and communications centres.[76] 'Location' refers to objects such as a construction or a site that it is strategically important to seize, withhold from enemy possession or force the enemy to retreat from.[77] Indeed, the United Kingdom's understanding to Article 52 of AP I confirms that 'a specific area of land may be a military objective if, because of its *location* . . . its total or partial destruction . . . offers definite military advantage'.[78] Finally the commentary states that '[t]he criterion of *purpose* is concerned with the intended future use of an object, while that of *use* is concerned with its present function'.[79] However, the Bothe *et al.* commentary to AP I emphasises that the object's 'nature, location, purpose or use' need not have a direct connection with combat operations in order to constitute an effective contribution to military action.[80]

With respect to the second part of the test, the terms 'total or partial destruction' and 'capture' are relatively clear. 'Neutralisation' is explained by the Bothe *et al.* commentary as denying a location or object to the enemy without necessarily destroying it, perhaps by a temporary bombardment or by setting land mines.[81] The definite military advantage from this destruction, capture or neutralisation must be offered 'in the circumstances ruling at the time' and 'not at some hypothetical future time',[82] and this phrase also emphasises that 'objects which may have been military objectives yesterday may no longer be such today, and vice versa'.[83]

The expression 'military advantage' 'involves a variety of considerations, including the security of the attacking force'[84] and must be judged 'in the context of the military advantage anticipated from the specific military operation of which

[75] *Ibid.*

[76] Sandoz *et al.*, *Commentary on the Additional Protocols*, p. 636.

[77] *Ibid.*

[78] UK reservations and understandings to AP I, emphasis added, available at the ICRC website: <http://www.icrc.org/>. Canada, Germany, Italy, New Zealand and the Netherlands made similarly worded understandings also available at the ICRC website, *ibid.*

[79] Sandoz *et al.*, *Commentary on the Additional Protocols*, p. 636, original emphasis.

[80] Bothe *et al.*, *New Rules for Victims*, p. 324.

[81] *Ibid.*, p. 325. Neutralisation by land mines would be restricted for parties to the 1997 Ottawa Convention or the 1980 Convention on Conventional Weapons and its 1980 Protocol II or 1996 Amended Protocol II.

[82] Bothe *et al.*, *New Rules for Victims*, pp. 323–4.

[83] *Ibid.*, p. 326.

[84] See the understandings to AP I on this issue made by Australia and New Zealand, available at the ICRC website: <http://www.icrc.org/>. See also M. Schmitt, 'The law of targeting', pp. 131–68 in E. Wilmshurst and S. Breau (eds), *Perspectives on the ICRC Study on Customary International Humanitarian Law* (Cambridge: Cambridge University Press, 2007), p. 146.

the attack is a part considered as a whole, and not only from isolated or particular parts of that operation'.[85] The military advantage must be definite, that is, 'a concrete and perceptible military advantage rather than a hypothetical and speculative one',[86] although it need not be related to 'the advantage anticipated by the attacker from the destruction, capture or neutralization of the object' as would be the case in a diversionary attack.[87]

## Development

The Iraq–Kuwait Gulf conflict and the NATO air campaign against the Federal Republic of Yugoslavia (FRY), have raised interesting issues in respect of the prohibition against attacking civilian targets. In particular, the air bombardment of Iraq during the Gulf conflict raised the difficult issue of dual-use objects, that is, objects which are contributing to the military campaign as well as supporting ordinary civilian life. As Schachter comments, 'the hostilities revealed how difficult it can be to make a sharp separation between the military targets and civilian objects, especially in an industrial society where their commingling is widespread'.[88]

On this issue the US Department of Defense report simply stated that '[w]hen objects are used concurrently for civilian and military purposes, they are liable to attack if there is a military advantage to be gained in their attack'.[89] Greenwood sums up that 'there is no intermediate category of "dual use" objects: either something is a military object or it is not'.[90] This harsh approach reflects the basic problem of modern conflicts, where many of the necessities of civilian life, such as power and communication lines, are also being used to support the military machine. However, with regard to dual-use bombardment during the Kosovo crisis, Rowe emphasised the limiting effect of the words *effective* contribution to military action and *definite* military advantage in

[85] Bothe *et al.*, *New Rules for Victims*, pp. 324–5, and the understandings to AP I of the United Kingdom, Australia, Belgium, Canada, Germany, Italy, New Zealand, the Netherlands and Spain, available at the ICRC website: <http://www.icrc.org/>.

[86] Bothe *et al.*, *New Rules for Victims*, pp. 325–6.

[87] *Ibid.*, p. 325. Although AP I does not provide a list of military objectives, for examples see Draft Article 24 of the 1923 Hague Rules of Aerial Warfare and Article 8 of the 1954 Hague Convention.

[88] O. Schachter, 'United Nations law in the Gulf conflict', AJIL, 85 (1991), 452–73, p. 466. In this respect see discussion of the targeting of the national power grid of Iraq in A. Rogers, *Law on the Battlefield*, n. 14 *supra*, p. 71, and A. DeSaussure, 'The role of the law of armed conflict during the Persian Gulf War: an overview', AFLR, 37 (1994), 41–68, pp. 62–3.

[89] US Department of Defense Report, Department of Defense, 'Conduct of the Persian Gulf War', Final Report to Congress, Washington DC, 1992, Appendix O, 'The role of the law of war', reprinted in ILM, 31 (1992), 615–44 (hereinafter: US Department of Defense Report), p. 623.

[90] C. Greenwood, 'Customary international law and the first Geneva Protocol of 1977 in the Gulf conflict', pp. 63–88 in P. Rowe (ed.), *The Gulf War, 1990–1991, in International and English Law* (London: Routledge, 1993), p. 73. However, attack against dual use objects is subject to the laws of proportionality, see *infra*, pp. 81–9.

respect of dual-use objects.[91] The fact that an object is of some use to the military is not alone sufficient to justify its being targeted as a military objective.[92]

Another controversial issue raised by the Gulf conflict and NATO's bombardment of FRY was the targeting of communications. The US Department of Defense report stated that 'microwave towers for everyday, peacetime civilian communications can constitute a vital part of a military command and control system'.[93] Indeed, Oeter observes that '[i]n the case of modern densely interlinked infrastructures of telecommunication, it may be doubted whether any "unimportant" installation still exists'.[94] Furthermore, he contends that the Gulf conflict demonstrated that 'an attacker nowadays must probably destroy a network of telecommunication *in toto* (or at least its central connection points) in order to paralyse the command and control structures of the enemy armed force, which in themselves clearly constitute a legitimate military objective'.[95]

NATO's bombardment of FRY during the Kosovo crisis led to an assessment by the Office of the Prosecutor (OTP) at the ICTY of possible breaches of international humanitarian law.[96] The OTP then issued a report on the bombing campaign which included reasoning for the decision not to open a full criminal investigation.[97] The report examined the AP I definition of a military objective and found that this definition is 'generally accepted as part of customary law'.[98] Whilst most of NATO's bombardment was against 'military facilities, fielded forces, heavy weapons and military vehicles and formations',[99] great controversy arose after the NATO bombardment of a State-owned television and radio station in Belgrade.

The OTP report found that whether the media could be a legitimate target was debatable[100] but, importantly, confirmed that 'civilian morale as such' is not

[91] P. Rowe, 'Kosovo 1999: the air campaign – have the provisions of Additional Protocol I withstood the test?', IRRC, 837 (2000), 147–64, pp. 151–2.

[92] *Ibid.* However, the US definition of military advantage is broader than the definition in Article 52(2), AP I, see US Department of Defense Report, p. 623.

[93] US Department of Defense Report, p. 623.

[94] S. Oeter, 'Methods and means of combat', n. 21 *supra*, p. 161.

[95] *Ibid.*

[96] On the NATO action see generally Lord Robertson, 'Kosovo: An Account of the Crisis', 7 October 1999, available at: <http://www.fas.org/man/dod-101/ops/docs99/account/> and D. Kritsiotis, 'The Kosovo crisis and NATO's application of armed force against the Federal Republic of Yugoslavia', ICLQ, 49 (2000), 330–59.

[97] See N. Ronzitti, 'Is the *non liquet* of the final report by the committee established to review the NATO bombing campaign against the Federal Republic of Yugoslavia acceptable?', IRRC, 840 (2000), 1017–28.

[98] Final report to the prosecutor by the committee established to review the NATO bombing campaign against the Federal Republic of Yugoslavia, 13 June 2000, ILM, 39 (2000), 1257–83 (hereinafter: OTP Report), para. 42.

[99] Lord Robertson, 'Kosovo one year on: achievement and challenge', 13 April 2000, available at: <http://www.nato.int/kosovo/repo2000/index.htm>.

[100] OTP Report, para. 47.

a legitimate military objective[101] and that 'merely disseminating propaganda to generate support for the war effort' would not convert the media into a military objective.[102] However, the report contended that 'if the media is used to incite crimes, as in Rwanda, it can become a legitimate military objective'.[103] This latter statement, however, was criticised as somewhat dubious by Cottier, who asserted that 'the prevention or repression of international crimes may often not present a definite military advantage'.[104] In the event, NATO never claimed that the radio and television centre was being used to incite crimes, but primarily supported its targeting as 'part of a more general attack aimed at disrupting the FRY Command, Control and Communications network'.[105]

Whilst the OTP report accepted that the targeting of the station on a propaganda basis was an incidental, albeit complementary, aim to the legitimate targeting of the station on that basis, it also claimed that '[i]f the media is the nerve system that keeps a warmonger in power and thus perpetuates the war effort, it may fall within the definition of a legitimate military objective'.[106] However, although the media of dictatorial regimes are often used as part of the control mechanism to sustain the ruling party in power, during a conflict practically all media display bias in supporting their country. Therefore the OTP approach could risk opening the way to the bombardment of the media during conflicts as a matter of course.[107] Additionally, as the OTP acknowledged, '[w]hilst stopping such propaganda may serve to demoralize the Yugoslav population and undermine the government's political support, it is unlikely that either of these purposes would offer the "concrete and direct" military advantage necessary to make them a legitimate military objective'.[108]

[101] *Ibid.*, para. 55. This is supported by G. Aldrich, 'Yugoslavia's television studios as military objectives', ILF, 1 (1999), 149–50, p. 150, but see comments by O. Medenica, 'Protocol 1 and Operation Allied Force: did NATO abide by principles of proportionality?', Loy LA Int & Comp LR, 23 (2001), 329–426, p. 423.

[102] OTP Report, para. 47.

[103] *Ibid.*, para. 55.

[104] M. Cottier, 'Did NATO forces commit war crimes during the Kosovo conflict? Reflections on the prosecutor's report of 13 June 2000', pp. 505–37, in H. Fischer, C. Kreß and S. Lüder (eds), *International and National Prosecution of Crimes under International Law: Current Developments* (Berlin: Berlin Verlag, 2001), pp. 521–2.

[105] OTP Report, para. 75.

[106] *Ibid.*, para. 76, and see W. Fenrick, 'Targeting and proportionality during the NATO bombing campaign against Yugoslavia', EJIL, 12 (2001), 489–502, p. 497.

[107] Note that in the 2003 Iraq conflict Iraqi television stations were bombed and the Baghdad offices of Al Jazeera were hit by a bomb, see B. Rooney, 'TV stations bombed to silence Saddam', *Electronic Telegraph*, 27 March 2003 (<http://www.telegraph.co.uk/news/main.jhtml?xml=/news/2003/03/27/wbag127.xml>, visited 24 August 2007); R. Fisk, 'Is there some element in the US military that wants to take out journalists?', and P. Vallely, 'Journalists perish, looters flourish and medics despair in the chaotic jigsaw of war', both *The Independent*, 9 April 2003 (<http://news.independent.co.uk/fisk/article114390ece> and <http://news.independent.co.uk/world/middle_east/article114393.ece> respectively, visited 24 August 2007).

[108] OTP Report, para. 76, and see G. Aldrich, 'Yugoslavia's television studios as military objectives', n. 101 *supra*, p. 150.

Another important issue raised by the prohibition against attacking civilian objects is whether those involved in conflicts at sea are also bound by the rule in AP I to attack only military objectives. Article 49 of AP I states that the provisions of that section apply to any warfare which may affect objects on land. This suggests that ship-to-ship warfare would not be bound by the prohibition against attacking civilian objects, but Heintschel von Heinegg argues that the basic rule of distinction between civilian objects and military objectives is customary in character and thus binding in naval warfare.[109] This proposition is supported by the San Remo Manual on International Law applicable to Armed Conflicts at Sea, which, whilst not legally binding, was prepared by experts as a restatement of international humanitarian law at sea.[110]

An important question is whether a country's economic and financial systems could amount to military objectives. Fleck suggests that whether economic objectives could be viewed as constituting military objectives would be influenced by the 'means available and by existing options for successful operations'.[111] Schmitt also warns that '[d]isparity also provides an incentive for "have nots" to define the concept of military objective broadly . . . [s]ince economic facilities undergird the "haves"' superiority, they will seem particularly lucrative targets'.[112] Surprisingly, the ICRC study on customary international humanitarian law (ICRC Study) appears to support the theory that, in certain circumstances '[e]conomic targets that effectively support military operations' may amount to a military objective.[113] However, a review of Part 2 of the study shows that the State practice relied upon mainly includes uncontroversial examples such as industrial installations producing material for armed forces, which are clearly closely connected with the prosecution of the armed conflict.[114]

Rogers argues that the general financial system of a country or particular exports upon which a country greatly relied could not constitute a legitimate military objective, as they could not be described as making 'an *effective* contribution to *military* action'.[115] This would seem correct, as the definition of military objectives in Article 52 would be stretched to breaking point by the inclusion of financial institutions and banks and other industries whose only link with the conflict

[109] W. Heintschel von Heinegg, 'The law of armed conflicts at sea', pp. 405–83, in D. Fleck (ed.), *Handbook of Humanitarian Law*, n. 21 *supra*, p. 420.

[110] See Articles 39–41, 1994 San Remo Manual.

[111] D. Fleck, 'Strategic bombing and the definition of military objectives', Israel Yrbk Hum Rts, 27 (1997), 41–64, p. 52.

[112] M. Schmitt, 'Future war', n. 66 *supra*, p. 65.

[113] J. Henckaerts and L. Doswald-Beck, *Customary International Humanitarian Law* (commonly referred to as the ICRC Study) (Cambridge: ICRC and Cambridge University Press, 2005), p. 32. See analysis in M. Schmitt, 'The law of targeting', n. 84 *supra*, pp. 148–9.

[114] ICRC Study *ibid.*, Vol. II, Part 1, paras 565–72.

[115] A. Rogers, *Law on the Battlefield*, n. 14 *supra*, pp. 70–1, original emphasis. See also H. Robertson, 'The principle of the military objective in the law of armed conflict', pp. 197–223 in M. Schmitt (ed), *The Law of Military Operations: Liber Amicorum Professor Jack Grunawalt*, 72 US Naval War College International Law Studies (Newport RI: Naval War College Press, 1998), pp. 209–11.

is that the government derives income from them which may assist in the financing of the military campaign. Furthermore, if the expression 'military action' was interpreted so broadly as to cover any type of contribution to the war effort, then the principle of distinction would become totally illusory.

The ICTY has considered attacks upon civilian property in the cases of *Blaškić* and *Kordić and Čerkez*.[116] The Judgements in both cases demand that there must be intentional targeting of civilian property which is not justified by military necessity.[117] Additionally, the Trial Chamber in *Kordić and Čerkez* added that the attack must result in 'extensive damage to civilian objects'.[118] The restriction of this offence to damage to civilian objects not justified by military necessity is in line with the commentary to Article 52 of AP I.[119] However, the requirement that the destruction of civilian property must be extensive appears to confuse the offence of attacking civilian objects under Article 52 of AP I with the grave breach of extensive destruction and appropriation of property.[120] Evidence of extensive destruction of civilian objects would, of course, support a finding that the defendant intended to make such objects the target of his attack.[121]

### The Rome Statute

The EOC in respect of attacking civilian objects are very similar to those of attacking the civilian population.[122] First, the perpetrator must have 'directed an attack'. This element has been discussed in respect of attacking the civilian population and should be defined similarly for this offence, as combat action by one or more combatants.[123] Second, the target of the attack must have been civilian objects, 'that is, objects which are not military objectives'. Although the Rome Statute and Elements do not refer directly to Article 52 of AP I and its definition of military objectives, it is likely that the ICC will apply this definition as customary law.[124] Finally it must be shown that the perpetrator 'intended such civilian objects to be the object of the attack', as opposed to being reckless thereto.[125] As with Article 8(2)(b)(i), the EOC do not require a result for this

[116] *Blaškić*, Trial Judgement, para. 180, and *Kordić and Čerkez*, Trial Judgement, para. 328.

[117] *Ibid.*

[118] *Kordić and Čerkez*, Trial Judgement, para. 328.

[119] Bothe *et al.*, *New Rules for Victims*, p. 321.

[120] *Kordić and Čerkez*, Appeal Judgement, para. 67 upheld the requirement of a result of damage to property as part of this crime, but they did not clearly state whether they agreed with the Trial Chamber that such damage must be extensive. See also comments in *Strugar*, Trial Judgement, para. 280.

[121] Although very minor damage would not be sufficiently 'serious' for prosecution before the ICC, see Article 17(1)(d), Rome Statute, on admissibility.

[122] EOC, p. 130.

[123] *Supra*, p. 67.

[124] See discussion *supra*, p. 72. This is supported by para. 5 of the French understanding to the Rome Statute, which defines military objective using a very similar formula to AP I.

[125] See discussion *supra*, pp. 68–9.

offence and therefore if a weapon is directed at a civilian object, yet fails to hit its target, the offence of intentionally directing attacks against civilian objects would still be committed.[126]

Some objects, such as military vehicles and weapons, are clearly military objectives, and others, such as schools and hospitals (when being used for those purposes) are clearly not. AP I in Article 52(3) imposes a presumption that 'in cases of doubt whether an object which is normally dedicated to civilian purposes . . . is being used to make an effective contribution to military action, it shall be presumed not to be so used'. Whilst this presumption is not mentioned in the Rome Statute or Elements, it would be open to the ICC to hold that the presumption represented customary law.[127] However, the real legal difficulty for the ICC will probably arise in drawing the line between military objectives and civilian objects in the grey areas of dual-use objects. Here it must be remembered that not every object which contributes to the war effort is immediately a legitimate military objective; the contribution must be *effective* and destruction must produce a *definite* military advantage.[128] Additionally, even if an object constitutes a military objective under this test, action against it must still be considered under the test of proportionality of Article 8(2)(b)(iv).[129]

## Article 8(2)(b)(iii) Intentionally directing attacks against personnel, installations, material, units or vehicles involved in a humanitarian assistance or peacekeeping mission in accordance with the Charter of the United Nations, as long as they are entitled to the protection given to civilians or civilian objects under the international law of armed conflict

### Origins

The origins of the prohibition against attacking persons involved in humanitarian assistance or peacekeeping missions has its roots in the 1994 Convention on the Safety of United Nations and Associated Personnel. This Convention obliges States to criminalise crimes of murder, kidnapping or other attack upon UN and Associated Personnel, or attacks against their official premises, private accommodation or means of transportation.[130]

[126] K. Dörmann, 'Preparatory Commission for the International Criminal Court', n. 63 *supra*, p. 467.

[127] See Cottier *et al.*, 'Article 8', p. 187.

[128] See P. Rowe, 'Kosovo 1999', n. 91 *supra*, pp. 151–2.

[129] *Infra*, pp. 81–9.

[130] There was support for inclusion of this Convention in the Rome Statute at the Preparatory Committee but it was not at that time in force, M. Arsanjani, 'The Rome Statute of the International Criminal Court', AJIL 93 (1999), 22–43, p. 29.

## Development

There have yet to be any prosecutions under the UN Convention, which entered into force only in January 1999. However, the offence was contained in similar wording in Article 19 of the ILC's Draft Code of Crimes, and the ILC's commentary states that:

> [a]ttacks against United Nations and associated personnel constitute violent crimes of exceptionally serious gravity which have serious consequences not only for the victims, but also for the international community . . . [as] they are committed against persons who represent the international community and risk their lives to protect its fundamental interest in maintaining the international peace and security of mankind.[131]

The Statute for the Special Court for Sierra Leone includes in Article 4(b) an offence identical to Article 8(2)(b)(iii) of the Rome Statute. The only accused undergoing trial on this charge at the Special Court are Sesay, Kallon and Gbao of the Revolutionary United Front, but their trial is still under way.[132] The commentary to this offence in the Secretary General's report acknowledges that '[a]ttacks against peacekeeping personnel, to the extent that they are entitled to protection recognized under international law to civilians in armed conflict, do not represent a new crime', but explains that persons with a humanitarian or peacekeeping mission were felt to deserve special protection.[133] Notwithstanding this, the commentary emphasises that '[t]he specification of the crime of attacks against peacekeepers, however, does not imply a more serious crime than attacks against civilians in similar circumstances and should not entail, therefore, a heavier penalty'.[134]

## The Rome Statute

In addition to the requirements relating to the international status of the conflict the EOC lay down five points that must be proved for this offence.[135] The perpetrator must have directed an attack, the object of the attack must have been

[131] 1996 ILC Commentary, available at <http://un.org/law/ilc/texts/dccomfra.htm>.

[132] *Sesay, Kallon and Gbao* (known as the RUF Trial), count 15 of the indictment. Note that Johnny Paul Koroma was also charged with this under count 14 of his indictment but despite reports of his death in Liberia (see 'War crime court probes death reports', BBC News report on 16 June 2003, available at: http://news.bbc.co.uk/go/pr/fr/-/1/hi/world/africa/2992462.stm) the indictment has not been withdrawn and the website of the Special Court still states that Koroma's whereabouts are unknown.

[133] Report of the Secretary General on the Establishment of a Special Court for Sierra Leone, 4 October 2000, UN Doc. S/2000/915, p. 4. See also C. Greenwood, 'International humanitarian law and United Nations military operations', YIHL, 1 (1998) 3–34, pp. 30–1.

[134] Report of the Secretary General on the Establishment of a Special Court for Sierra Leone, n. 133 *supra*, p. 4.

[135] EOC, p. 131.

'personnel, installations, material, units or vehicles involved in a humanitarian assistance or peacekeeping mission in accordance with the Charter of the United Nations' and the perpetrator must have intended these to be the object of the attack.[136] The personnel and associated objects must have been 'entitled to that protection given to civilians or civilian objects under the international law of armed conflict' and the perpetrator must be 'aware of the factual circumstances that established that protection'.[137] Once again, there is no requirement in the Elements for a particular result to occur, so provided that humanitarian or peacekeeping personnel or objects are attacked there is no need to show that such personnel or objects have actually been killed, injured or destroyed.[138]

The element of directing an attack has been discussed in respect of attacking the civilian population and civilian objects and so should be defined similarly to combat action by one or more combatants.[139] In respect of the object of the attack, the difficulty lies in ascertaining how the ICC will interpret the phrases 'humanitarian assistance', 'peacekeeping mission' and 'in accordance with the Charter of the United Nations'. This expression suggests that such missions must be in accordance with the purposes of the United Nations and not contrary to any articles of the UN Charter. The purposes of the United Nations are laid down in Article 1 of the Charter, and include the maintenance of international peace and security, peaceful settlement of international disputes, and co-operation in solving international problems of an economic, social, cultural or humanitarian character. The Charter prohibits under Article 2(4) the threat or use of force against the territorial integrity or political independence of any State, and under Article 2(7) intervention in matters within the domestic jurisdiction of a State.

Although '[t]here is no generally accepted definition of what constitutes a "humanitarian assistance mission" ',[140] assistance to a State of a humanitarian nature would appear, in principle, to be in accordance with the purposes of the UN Charter. In order to avoid breaching Article 2 of the Charter such assistance must have the consent of the State involved. Cottier suggests that 'humanitarian assistance' in connection with an armed conflict would primarily consist of 'relief assistance, that is, assistance to prevent or alleviate human suffering of victims of armed conflicts and other individuals with immediate and basic needs' and that their personnel may include 'administrative staff, coordinators and logistic experts, doctors, nurses and other specialists and relief workers'.[141]

Assistance by the Red Cross, an independent humanitarian organisation,[142] or by UN agencies would clearly come under the heading of humanitarian

[136] *Ibid.*

[137] *Ibid.*

[138] K. Dörmann, 'Preparatory Commission for the International Criminal Court', n. 63 *supra*, p. 467.

[139] See discussion *supra*, p. 67.

[140] Cottier *et al.*, 'Article 8', p. 189.

[141] *Ibid.*, pp. 189–90.

[142] Article 1, 1998 ICRC Statute (revised).

assistance. The aid should be given impartially to all in need.[143] Cottier casts doubt as to whether humanitarian action by a State would also constitute humanitarian assistance for the purposes of this offence,[144] but it is submitted that Article 8(2)(b)(iii) does not rule out such assistance if it is given with consent of the State involved and on an impartial and neutral basis.

The expression 'peacekeeping mission' has primarily been used with respect to UN operations. The former Secretary General of the United Nations, Boutros-Ghali, defined peacekeeping as 'the deployment of a United Nations presence in the field, hitherto with the consent of all the parties concerned, normally involving United Nations military and/or police personnel and frequently civilians as well'.[145] Peacekeepers carry out tasks such as 'monitoring and enforcement of cease-fires, observation of frontier lines, interposition between belligerents, election monitoring, protection and delivery of humanitarian aid, and the maintenance of government and public order'.[146] Indeed, Boutros-Ghali commented that the personnel involved in peacekeeping could include 'civilian police officers, human rights monitors, electoral officials, refugee and humanitarian aid specialists'.[147]

The three basic principles of peacekeeping were laid down by Boutros-Ghali as 'consent of the parties, impartiality and the non-use of force except in self-defence'[148] and these were referred to as 'bedrock principles' by the Brahimi Report on UN Peace Operations.[149] The legality of such operations within the UN system was confirmed by the International Court of Justice (ICJ) in the *Certain Expenses of the United Nations* case, which confirmed that the peacekeeping forces in the Middle East and the Congo, which had been established with the consent of the States involved, were 'undertaken to fulfil a prime purpose of the United Nations, that is, to promote and to maintain a peaceful settlement of the situation'.[150]

The Elements do not clarify whether peacekeeping missions protected by Article 8(2)(b)(iii) are only those under the UN banner or include regional

[143] See Article 4(1), 1998 ICRC Statute (revised).

[144] Cottier *et al.*, 'Article 8', p. 191.

[145] Report of the Secretary General, 'An agenda for peace: preventative diplomacy, peacemaking and peacekeeping', UN Doc. A/47/277-S/24111, 17 June 1992, para. 20.

[146] A. Roberts and B. Kingsbury, 'Introduction: the UN's roles in international society since 1945', pp. 1–62 in B. Kingsbury and A. Roberts, *United Nations, Divided World: the United Nations Roles in International Relations* (Oxford: Oxford University Press, 2nd edn, 1993), p. 32. For other peacekeeping activities see M. Shaw, *International Law* (Cambridge: Cambridge University Press, 4th edn, 1997), p. 853.

[147] Report of the Secretary General, 'An agenda for peace', n. 145 *supra*, para. 52.

[148] Report of the Secretary General, 'Supplement to an agenda for peace', UN Doc. A/50/60-S/1995/1, 3 January 1995, para. 33.

[149] Report of the Panel on United Nations Peace Operations, Brahimi Report, UN Doc. A/55/305-S/2000/809, 21 August 2000, para. 48.

[150] *Certain Expenses of the United Nations Case*, Advisory Opinion, ICJ Rep (1962), 151, pp. 24–5.

peacekeeping operations. Cottier comments that 'regional organizations such as the OSCE, EU or ECOWAS have been establishing or authorizing peacekeeping and observer missions'[151] and Miyet, the UN Under-Secretary General for Peacekeeping Operations, has spoken of the work of regional peacekeeping NATO forces in Bosnia.[152] Therefore, it would appear that such peacekeeping forces would be protected by Article 8(2)(b)(iii) of the Rome Statute, provided that they abide by the UN standard of consent, impartiality and non-use of force.

The EOC state that the persons and objects protected under this article must be 'entitled to that protection given to civilians or civilian objects under the international law of armed conflict'.[153] As a result, from a technical viewpoint, this provision is superfluous,[154] given that those on humanitarian assistance or peacekeeping missions would in any case be protected under Article 8(2)(b)(i) and (ii). However, von Hebel and Robinson stress this article's 'symbolic importance as a clear signal by the world community that it attaches great importance to the work and protection of such personnel and considers attacks against them as a serious crime of international concern'.[155]

The limitation of protection to civilians and civilian objects raises the question of whether those giving humanitarian assistance and peacekeepers remain protected if they carry or use weapons for self-defence. Cottier suggests plausibly that such persons should be entitled to self-defence to the same extent as protected persons are so entitled without losing their status under the Geneva Conventions.[156] An example of this is found in Article 22 of the First Geneva Convention, which states that medical units shall not be deprived of their protection because the personnel of the unit are armed and use the arms in their own defence.[157] However, it is more doubtful whether an expanded notion of self-defence, which includes defence of the mission objectives in addition to defence of the peacekeepers themselves, would allow such personnel to retain the protection of this article.[158]

The mental element of this offence is an intention to make the humanitarian or peacekeeping personnel or their material objects of the attack and awareness of the factual circumstances that established their protection under the international law of armed conflict. It therefore would seem that the perpetrator must

[151] Cottier *et al.*, 'Article 8', p. 192.

[152] B. Miyet, Under Secretary General for Peacekeeping Operations, Press Conference, United Nations Headquarters, 29 May 1998, available at: <http://www.un.org/Depts/dpko/dpko/50web/50years.htm>.

[153] EOC, p. 131.

[154] H. von Hebel and D. Robinson, 'Crimes within the jurisdiction of the court', pp. 79–126 in R. Lee (ed.), *The International Criminal Court: The Making of the Rome Statute: Issues, Negotiations, Results* (The Hague: Kluwer, 1999), p. 110.

[155] *Ibid.*

[156] Cottier *et al.*, 'Article 8', pp. 193 and 195.

[157] See also Article 35, Geneva Convention II, and Article 13, AP I.

[158] See Cottier *et al.*, 'Article 8', p. 195.

intentionally, rather than recklessly, attack the relevant personnel or objects, and additionally he must be aware of the factual circumstances establishing the civilian nature of the personnel and their material.

## Article 8(2)(b)(iv) Intentionally launching an attack in the knowledge that such attack will cause incidental loss of life or injury to civilians or damage to civilian objects or widespread, long-term and severe damage to the natural environment which would be clearly excessive in relation to the concrete and direct overall military advantage anticipated

### Origins

Although the rule of proportionality in the use of force has been acknowledged at least since the Caroline case of 1837,[159] the modern rule of proportionality within international humanitarian law is contained in Article 85(3)(b) of AP I, 'launching an indiscriminate attack . . . in the knowledge that such attack will cause excessive loss of life, injury to civilians or damage to civilian objects'.[160] Article 57(2)(a)(iii) of AP I explains that any collateral damage must not be 'excessive in relation to the concrete and direct military advantage anticipated'. In addition, the prohibition against excessive damage to the environment is contained in Articles 35(3) and 55(1) of AP I, the former stating that '[i]t is prohibited to employ methods or means of warfare which are intended, or may be expected, to cause widespread, long-term and severe damage to the natural environment'.

Declarations made upon ratification of AP I have made it clear that the decision on proportionality must be made on the basis of an assessment of the information 'from all sources which is reasonably available to them at the relevant time'.[161] It is clear that the decision of a commander or other person to attack a particular object with a particular weapon may not be judged with hindsight. In this respect, McCoubrey comments that the proportionality decision must 'clearly be undertaken in good faith in the light of the possibly limited information available'.[162]

[159] See D. Harris, *Cases and Materials on International Law* (London: Sweet & Maxwell, 5th edn, 1998), pp. 894–6.

[160] On State practice on proportionality between these two dates see W. Fenrick, 'The rule of proportionality', n. 22 *supra*, pp. 124–5, and, for proportionality in naval warfare, E. Roucounas, 'Some issues relating to war crimes in air and sea warfare', pp. 275–92 in Y. Dinstein and M. Tabory (eds), *War Crimes in International Law* (The Hague: Kluwer, 1996), pp. 288–9.

[161] United Kingdom's declaration, para. (c), in respect of AP I, available from the ICRC website: <http://www.icrc.org/>. Similar declarations were made by Australia, Austria, Belgium, Canada, Germany, Ireland, Italy, New Zealand, Spain and the Netherlands.

[162] H. McCoubrey, *International Humanitarian Law: the Regulation of Armed Conflicts* (Aldershot: Dartmouth, 1990), p. 116.

Dinstein comments that when postulating collateral casualties planners must take into account several ways in which civilians could be hit.[163] First, they may be inside the target, for example workers in a munitions factory; second, they may 'live, work or even pass by near a military target' and, third, a bomb can fall short of its target or a missile may go off-course.[164] Fenrick also adds the risk of collateral casualties resulting from the actions of the responding defence forces but suggests that such possible casualties should not be taken into account in the proportionality balance.[165] In addition, there are suggestions that collateral casualties among civilians working for the armed forces would carry less weight in the proportionality balance than such casualties among 'innocent' civilians.[166]

A common declaration on the issue of proportionality in AP I is that 'the military advantage anticipated from an attack is intended to refer to the advantage anticipated from the attack considered as a whole and not only from isolated or particular parts of the attack'.[167] Doswald-Beck suggests that this approach is acceptable 'if seen within the context of a given tactical operation'.[168] She gives the example of an operation necessitating the destruction of six military objectives, one of which would involve more casualties than the others but within the context of the operation was an essential objective: '[t]he yardstick, in this example, would be the number of casualties overall in relation to the value of the operation as a whole'.[169] However, as Fenrick warns, '[i]f military benefit is assessed on too broad a basis . . . then it may well be extremely difficult to apply the proportionality equation until the war has ended'.[170]

The proportionality equation is based on the premise that collateral damage must not be *excessive* compared with the military advantage expected. Factors which must be weighed in this balance include 'the military importance of the target or objective, the density of the civilian population in the target area, the likely incidental effects of the attack, including the possible release of hazardous substances, the types of weapon available to attack the target and their accuracy

[163] Y. Dinstein, 'The laws of air, missile and nuclear warfare', Israel Yrbk Hum Rts, 27 (1997) 1–16, p. 6.

[164] *Ibid.*

[165] W. Fenrick, 'Attacking the enemy civilian as a punishable offence', Duke J Comp & Int'l L, 7 (1997), 539–59, p. 547.

[166] Bothe *et al.*, *New Rules for Victims*, p. 295, and S. Oeter, 'Methods and means of combat', n. 21 *supra*, para. 445(3).

[167] United Kingdom's declaration, para. (i), in respect of AP I, available from the ICRC website: <http://www.icrc.org/>. Similar declarations were made by Australia, Belgium, Canada, Germany, Italy, New Zealand, Spain and the Netherlands. See S. Oeter, 'Methods and means of combat', n. 21 *supra*, para. 444.

[168] L. Doswald-Beck, 'The value of the 1977 Geneva Protocols for the Protection of Civilians', pp. 137–72, in M. Meyer (ed.), *Armed Conflict and the New Law*, n. 13 *supra*, pp. 156–7.

[169] *Ibid.*

[170] W. Fenrick, 'The rule of proportionality', n. 22 *supra*, p. 107, and see J. Gardam, 'Proportionality and force in international law', AJIL, 87 (1993), 391–413, p. 407.

. . . and the timing of the attack'.[171] Schmitt comments upon the difficulty of applying this equation, as, although jurisprudential balancing tests should compare like values, 'proportionality calculations are heterogeneous, for dissimilar value genres – military and humanitarian – are being weighed against each other'.[172]

The ICRC commentary to AP I explains that the expression 'concrete and direct military advantage' shows that 'the advantage concerned should be substantial and relatively close'.[173] On this point New Zealand and Australia entered declarations upon ratification of AP I that this expression 'means a *bona fide* expectation that the attack will make a relevant and proportional contribution to the objective of the military attack involved'.[174] The ICRC commentary explains that a 'concrete and direct' military advantage imposes stricter conditions upon the attacker than the 'definite' military advantage required by Article 52(2) of AP I in its definition of military objectives.[175]

The meaning of 'widespread, long-term and severe damage to the natural environment' has also been the subject of much debate.[176] Within the *travaux préparatoires* to AP I the expression 'long-term' was explained in terms of decades, with First World War battlefield damage to France being treated as outside that range.[177] Whilst the expression used in AP I is similar to that used in the Convention on the Prohibition of Military or any other Hostile Use of Environmental Modification Techniques, it is clear from the *travaux préparatoires* that States did not accept that the words had the same meaning in the two treaties.[178]

[171] A. Rogers, *Law on the Battlefield*, n. 14 *supra*, p. 23. With respect to accuracy of weapons available see S. Belt, 'Missiles over Kosovo: emergence, *lex lata*, of a customary norm requiring the use of precision guided munitions in urban areas', Nav LR, 47 (2000), 115–75, p. 150, and D. Infeld, 'Precision-guided munitions demonstrated their pinpoint accuracy in Desert Storm; but is a country obligated to use precision technology to minimize collateral civilian injury and damage?', Geo Wash JIL & Econ, 26 (1992), 109–41, pp. 130–1.

[172] M. Schmitt, 'Future war', n. 66 *supra*, p. 59.

[173] Sandoz *et al.*, *Commentary on the Additional Protocols*, p. 684.

[174] New Zealand's declaration in respect of AP I, para. 3, available from the ICRC website: <http://www.icrc.org/>. A similar declaration was made by Australia.

[175] Sandoz *et al.*, *Commentary on the Additional Protocols*, p. 685.

[176] See generally B. Baker, 'Legal protection for the environment in times of armed conflict', Va JIL, 33 (1993), 351–83; A. Bouvier, 'Protection of the natural environment in time of armed conflict', IRRC, 285 (1991), 567–78; G. Plant (ed.), *Environmental Protection and the Law of War* (London: Belhaven Press, 1992), and M. Schmitt, 'Green war: an assessment of the environmental law of international armed conflict', Yale J Int'l L, 22 (1997), 1–109.

[177] *Official Records of the Diplomatic Conference on the Reaffirmation and Development of International Humanitarian Law applicable in Armed Conflict* (1974–77), Geneva (hereinafter: 'OR 1977 Diplomatic Conference') Vol. XV, pp. 268–9, CDDH/215/Rev.1, para. 27. See also Henckaerts's criticism of the expression 'long-term', J. Henckaerts, 'Towards better protection for the environment in armed conflict: recent developments in international humanitarian law', RECIEL, 9 (2000), 13–19, p. 16.

[178] OR 1977 Diplomatic Conference, Vol. VI, p. 100, CDDH/SR.39, paras 49 and 53, and pp. 208–9, CDDH/SR.42, paras 21 and 25–7.

Leibler suggests that 'widespread' would encompass 'at least an entire region of several hundred square kilometres' and that 'severe' could be interpreted as 'causing death, ill-health or loss of sustenance to thousands of people, at present or in the future'.[179] Rogers interprets 'widespread' similarly and suggests that 'severe' would entail 'prejudicing the continued survival of the civilian population or involving the risk of major health problems'.[180] This appears to give a great deal of leeway to those fighting in a conflict. Indeed, Bothe *et al.* comment that Articles 35(3) and 55 of AP I 'will not impose any significant limitation on combatants waging conventional warfare'[181] and Leibler suggests from his analysis that 'any broader interpretation could not be said to reflect international consensus'.[182]

## Development

The offence of disproportionate collateral damage and damage to the environment has been developed by debate and discussion following the 1991 Gulf and Kosovo conflicts and by Judgements of the ICTY.[183] In particular, after the Gulf conflict the question arose in respect of whether the proportionality equation should take into account longer-term collateral damage. Greenwood comments that previously the tendency had been to apply the proportionality principle by 'comparing the immediate military advantage resulting from an attack with the immediate civilian losses'.[184] However, during the Gulf conflict there were many more civilian deaths from the longer-term results of the destruction of the power grids 'as hospitals, sewerage plants, water purification facilities and the like ceased to be able to operate' than there were during the actual attacks themselves.[185]

Greenwood argues that these longer-term effects must be taken into account when calculating the proportionality equation, but concedes that such side effects may be difficult to predict and may be due to a combination of factors, such as the priority given to military over civilian needs by the opposing

[179] A. Leibler, 'Deliberate wartime environmental damage: new challenges for international law', Calif West ILJ, 23 (1992), 67–137, p. 111.

[180] A. Rogers, *Law on the Battlefield*, n. 14 *supra*, p. 171.

[181] Bothe *et al.*, *New Rules for Victims*, p. 348, and see M. Bothe, 'The protection of the environment in times of armed conflict', Germ Yrbk Int'l L, 34 (1991), 54–62, pp. 56–7.

[182] A. Leibler, 'Deliberate wartime environmental damage', n. 179 *supra*, p. 111.

[183] On the Kosovo conflict see the UN Environment Programme/UN Centre for Human Settlements report 'The Kosovo Conflict: Consequences for the Environment and Human Settlements' (1999), available at: <http://www.grida.no/inf/news/news99/finalreport.pdf>, especially p. 10.

[184] C. Greenwood, 'A critique of the additional protocols to the Geneva Conventions of 1949', pp. 3–20 in H. Durham and T. McCormack (eds), *The Changing Face of Conflict and the Efficacy of International Humanitarian Law* (The Hague: Kluwer, 1999), p. 13.

[185] *Ibid.*, p. 12, and R. Normand and C. af Jochnick, 'The legitimation of violence: a critical analysis of the Gulf War', Harv ILJ, 35 (1994), 387–416, pp. 400–1 and 404–5.

power.[186] Nevertheless, whilst the lessons of the Gulf show that the proportionality equation should not be restricted to the immediate effects of an attack,[187] it is clear that commanders and those planning an attack do not operate with hindsight and can be expected to take into account only the potential side effects which would be apparent at the time. In this respect the Trial Chamber in *Galić* stated that in determining whether an attack was proportionate 'it is necessary to examine whether a reasonably well informed person in the circumstances of the actual perpetrator, making reasonable use of the information available to him or her, could have expected excessive civilian casualties to result from the attack'.[188]

The ICTY discussed the proportionality requirement in the *Blaškić* Judgement, which considered the possible breach of this rule by the defendant during an attack against some villages in central Bosnia.[189] The Trial Chamber held that '[b]y advocating the vigorous use of heavy weapons to seize villages inhabited mainly by civilians, General Blaškić gave orders which had consequences out of all proportion to military necessity and knew that many civilians would inevitably be killed and their homes destroyed'.[190] This confirms that, by using inappropriate and indiscriminate weapons for the target selected, the proportionality rule may be breached.[191] It also demonstrates that the proportionality rule may be breached through excessive damage to civilian objects as well as by wounding or killing civilians.[192] The Trial Chamber in *Galić* also maintained that whilst the parties to the conflict are under a duty to site military objectives away from civilians and civilian objects, 'the failure of a party to abide by this obligation does not relieve the attacking side of its duty' to comply with the proportionality rule when launching an attack.[193]

The Trial Chamber in the *Kupreškić* Judgement also considered the issue of proportionality and suggested that whereas a single attack falling in the grey area of legitimacy regarding proportionality may not contravene AP I *per se*, in the case of repeated attacks almost all of which fall within this grey area 'it might be warranted to conclude that the cumulative effect of such acts entails that they may not be in keeping with international law'.[194] This appears to suggest that a number of attacks, legitimate in themselves, may breach the proportionality

[186] C. Greenwood, 'A critique of the additional protocols', n. 184 *supra*, p. 13, and C. Greenwood, 'Customary international law and the first Geneva Protocol', n. 90 *supra*, p. 79.

[187] J. Crawford, 'The law of noncombatant immunity and the targeting of national electrical power systems', Fletcher F World Aff, 21 (1997), 101–15, p. 114.

[188] *Galić*, Trial Judgement, para. 58.

[189] *Blaškić*, Trial Judgement, paras 650–1.

[190] *Ibid.*, para. 651.

[191] Voon argues that flying at a high altitude when carrying out aerial bombardment could prevent compliance with the proportionality rule, T. Voon, 'Pointing the finger: civilian casualties of NATO bombing in the Kosovo conflict', Am U Int LR, 16 (2001), 1083–113, pp. 1104–5.

[192] See P. Benvenuti, 'The ICTY prosecutor and the review of the NATO bombing campaign against the Federal Republic of Yugoslavia', EJIL, 12 (2001), 503–29, pp. 508–9.

[193] *Galić*, Trial Judgement, para. 61, approved by the *Galić* Appeal Judgement, para. 194.

[194] *Kupreškić*, Trial Judgement, para. 526.

requirement when considered together, but it is difficult to see how a number of legal actions could add up to an illegal action. However, the OTP report on the NATO bombing of Serbia acknowledged that this 'progressive statement of the applicable law' was somewhat ambiguous and proposed an understanding of the formulation as referring to 'an *overall* assessment of the totality of civilian victims as against the goals of the military campaign'.[195]

The OTP Report also considered the problem of how to evaluate the proportionality calculation between the military advantage to be gained by an attack and the collateral damage and held that 'the determination of relative values must be that of the "reasonable military commander" '.[196] However, Schmitt points out that such a value judgement would be affected by the social or cultural background of the commander and whether his side was currently winning or losing the conflict.[197] Bothe has also questioned the OTP solution, arguing that '[i]n a democratic system, the order of values determining military behaviour must not be too far apart from the order of values which prevail in society at large'.[198]

The OTP report also considered the prohibition on excessive environmental damage and concluded that Articles 35(3) and 55 of AP I 'have a very high threshold of application' and are widely believed to cover only 'very significant damage'.[199] This opinion of the restricted nature of these articles is shared by many commentators on the environmental damage caused by Iraq during the Gulf conflict.[200] In February 1991 Iraq sabotaged hundreds of Kuwaiti oil wells, setting many on fire, which caused huge emissions of noxious gases and deposited soot over half of Kuwait, damaging agriculture and causing risks to the health of the local population.[201] Although Iraq was not a party to AP I, Rogers speculated as to whether Iraq's actions would have breached the 'widespread,

[195] OTP Report, para. 52, original emphasis.

[196] OTP Report, para. 50. This phrase is also used by W. Fenrick, 'Attacking the enemy civilian', n. 165 *supra*, p. 546.

[197] M. Schmitt, 'The principle of discrimination in twenty-first century warfare', Yale HR & Dev LJ, 2 (1999), 143–82, pp. 152 and 157, and see M. Bothe, 'The protection of the civilian population and NATO bombing on Yugoslavia: comments on a report to the prosecutor of the ICTY', EJIL, 12 (2001), 531–5, p. 535.

[198] M. Bothe, 'War crimes', pp. 379–426 in A. Cassese, P. Gaeta and J. Jones (eds), *The Rome Statute of the International Criminal Court: A Commentary*, Vol. I (Oxford: Oxford University Press, 2002), p. 399.

[199] OTP Report, para. 15. This interpretation is challenged by T. Marauhn in 'Environmental damage in times of armed conflict – not "really" a matter of criminal responsibility', IRRC, 840 (2000), 1029–36, para. 3.

[200] L. Green, 'The environment and the law of conventional warfare', Can.YBIL, 29 (1991), 222–37, pp. 233–4 and A. Rogers, *Law on the Battlefield*, n. 14 *supra*, pp. 181–2. See generally, C. York, 'International law and the collateral effects of war on the environment: the Persian Gulf', SAJHR, 7 (1991) 269–90 and R. Falk, 'The environmental law of war: an introduction', pp. 78–95, in G. Plant (ed), *Environmental Protection and the Law of War*, n. 176 *supra*.

[201] A. Rogers, *Law on the Battlefield*, n. 14 *supra*, pp. 178–9.

long-term and severe' tests and suggested that the 'long-term' test might not have been satisfied.[202]

## The Rome Statute

The EOC, in addition to those related to the nature of the conflict, require that the perpetrator 'launched an attack'.[203] The attack must have been such to cause 'incidental death or injury to civilians or damage to civilian objects or widespread, long-term and severe damage to the natural environment and that such death, injury or damage would be of such an extent as to be clearly excessive in relation to the concrete and direct overall military advantage anticipated'.[204] The perpetrator must have known that this incidental death, injury or damage would occur and that it would be clearly excessive in relation to the concrete and direct overall military advantage anticipated.[205]

The first element, that the perpetrator 'launched an attack', differs from the EOC for Article 8(2)(b)(i)–(iii), which use the expression 'directed an attack' and rather follows the wording of the grave breach of excessive loss of civilian life in Article 85(3)(b) of AP I.[206] Fenrick proposes that this evidences an understanding on the part of those drafting the Rome Statute that offences involving proportionality are usually made at a higher level and involve a planning process.[207] This is a reasonable approach, as, for example, the selection of targets, type of weapons and timing of an attack would be made by commanders and planners who would have access to information about the likely effects upon civilians.

However, it is also feasible that an individual soldier may have to make a proportionality assessment in the field. For example, a soldier may have been ordered to destroy a series of strategically important bridges, but he would surely breach Article 8(2)(b)(iv) if he chose to open fire upon one of them at the time a large convoy of refugees was crossing.[208] Equally he would not be expected

[202] *Ibid.*, pp. 181–2 and see J. Sills, J. Glenn, E. Florescu and T. Gordon, 'Environmental crimes in military actions and the International Criminal Court (ICC): United Nations perspectives' (April 2001, Army Environmental Policy Institute, AEPI-IFP-0502A), p. 22, although Sharp disagrees, P. Sharp, 'Prospects for environmental liability in the International Criminal Court', Va Envt'l LJ, 18 (1999), 217–43, p. 242.

[203] EOC, pp. 131–2.

[204] *Ibid.*

[205] *Ibid.*

[206] See *supra*, p. 67.

[207] Cottier *et al.*, 'Article 8', p. 197. This appears to have been the uncontested view of one of the delegates present at the Preparatory Commission, K. Dörmann, *Elements of War Crimes under the Rome Statute of the International Criminal Court: Sources and Commentary* (Cambridge: Cambridge University Press and ICRC, 2002), p. 162.

[208] Alternatively it could be found that this evidenced an intention to kill the civilians and the soldier could be charged under Article 8(2)(b)(i).

to desist from firing upon each target because a single car or person was crossing the bridge at the time.[209]

The EOC for this offence follow the wording of Article 8(2)(b)(iv) closely, and whilst 'death or injury to civilians or damage to civilian objects' is quite clear,[210] the Elements do not expand upon the meaning of 'widespread, long-term and severe damage to the natural environment'. First, it is clear from the construction of this offence that the proportionality equation applies to the environmental damage as well as to the collateral damage to civilians.[211] This has been criticised by Bothe, as API prohibited 'widespread, long-term and severe damage to the environment' in absolute terms rather than subject to a proportionality equation.[212] He further criticises the internal logic of this conflation of Article 35(3) and Article 55, as, to the extent to which the elements of the environment are civilian, damage caused to them would be prohibited under Article 8(2)(b)(iv), irrespective of whether it was widespread, long-term or severe.[213] He suggests that this article makes sense in only two situations, 'first, if the element of the environment has a military value of its own, secondly, to indicate a level of environmental damage which would in all cases be "excessive"', and, as the wording of the article does not quite cover these situations, Bothe describes the situation as 'confusing'.[214]

Second, the environmental criteria are clearly intended to be cumulative, as in AP I, and, given that there is no suggestion to the contrary, should be given a similar meaning. Finally, although France declared upon ratification of the Rome Statute that Article 8(2)(b) neither regulates nor prohibits the possible use of nuclear weapons,[215] it is clear that nuclear weapons must be used, as must conventional weapons, in accordance with the rule of proportionality.[216]

The EOC require that the collateral damage must be 'clearly excessive in relation to the concrete and direct overall military advantage anticipated' and

[209] See the controversy surrounding the NATO pilot who attacked a bridge when a civilian train was crossing it, OTP Report, paras 58–62, although this was primarily discussed in the context of whether the pilot intentionally attacked the civilians.

[210] For the meaning of 'civilians' and 'civilian objects' see discussion *supra*, pp. 61–2 and 69–71.

[211] H. von Hebel and D. Robinson, 'Crimes within the jurisdiction of the court', n. 154 *supra*, pp. 111–12. For a definition of 'the natural environment' see G. Plant, 'Environmental damage and the laws of war: points addressed to military lawyers', pp. 159–74 in H. Fox and M. Meyer (eds), *Armed Conflict and the New Law*, Vol. II, *Effecting Compliance* (London: British Institute of International and Comparative Law, 1993), pp. 169–70.

[212] M. Bothe, 'War crimes', n. 198 *supra*, p. 400.

[213] *Ibid.*, pp. 400–1.

[214] *Ibid.*, p. 401.

[215] See France's interpretative declaration to the Rome Statute, para. 2, available from the ICRC website: <http://www.icrc.org/>.

[216] See Ireland's understanding of Article 55, AP I, available from the ICRC website: <http://www.icrc.org/>, and J. Burroughs, of the Lawyers' Committee on Nuclear Policy, 'The French "interpretative declaration" regarding nuclear weapons', available at: <http://www.lcnp.org/global/french/htm>. See also *Legality of the Threat or Use of Nuclear Weapons*, Advisory Opinion, ICJ Rep (1996) 226, paras 31 and 33.

according to the OTP report the expression 'clearly' 'ensures that criminal responsibility would be entailed only in cases where the excessiveness of the incidental damage was obvious'.[217] This approach is supported by academic commentary, which confirms that, as the Rome Statute was not intended to be used to prosecute 'mere errors of judgement by commanders in the field', only serious criminal conduct will contravene this article.[218] A footnote to the EOC explains that the expression 'concrete and direct overall military advantage' 'refers to a military advantage that is foreseeable by the perpetrator at the relevant time'.[219] This ensures that the accused will be judged in the light of the information available to him at the time of the decision to attack.[220]

The mental element of this offence is that the perpetrator knew the attack would cause collateral damage which would be clearly excessive in relation to military advantage anticipated.[221] Therefore, the prosecution must prove that the attack was objectively likely to cause the disproportionate collateral damage and show that the perpetrator knew this. A footnote to the EOC explains that this element requires a value judgement on the part of the perpetrator.[222] Consequently, it must be shown that the perpetrator was aware, as a result of the information available to him at the time, that the collateral damage would be excessive in relation to the military advantage anticipated. The mental element of this offence will doubtless be difficult to prove in all but the clearest of cases and is criticised by Bothe as making the perpetrator 'the judge in his own cause'.[223]

Nevertheless, Dörmann states that the members of the Preparatory Commission accepted that the content of the footnote 'should not benefit a reckless perpetrator who knows perfectly well the anticipated military advantage and the expected incidental injury or damage, but gives no thought to evaluating the latter's possible excessiveness'.[224] Furthermore, he suggests that in any case 'an unreasonable judgement or an allegation that no judgement was made would, in a case of death, injury or damage clearly excessive to the military advantage anticipated, simply not be credible'.[225]

[217] OTP report, para. 21, and R. Lee (ed.), *The International Criminal Court: Elements of Crimes and Rules of Procedure and Evidence* (New York: Transnational, 2001) (hereinafter: Lee (ed.), *ICC: Elements*), p. 148.

[218] H. von Hebel and D. Robinson, 'Crimes within the jurisdiction of the court', n. 154 *supra*, p. 111, and A. Rogers, 'Zero-casualty warfare', IRRC, 837 (2000), 165–81, p. 180.

[219] EOC, fn. 36 on p. 131.

[220] See France's interpretative declaration to the Rome Statute, para. 7, available from the ICRC website: <http://www.icrc.org/>.

[221] EOC, pp. 131–2.

[222] EOC, fn. 37 on p. 132. The contentious nature of this footnote is discussed by D. Pfirter in Lee (ed.), *ICC: Elements*, pp. 150–1.

[223] M. Bothe, 'War crimes', n. 198 *supra*, p. 400, and see J. Pejic, 'The International Criminal Court Statute: an appraisal of the Rome package', Int Law, 34 (2000), 65–84, p. 71 and fn. 35.

[224] K. Dörmann, 'Preparatory Commission for the International Criminal Court', n. 63 *supra*, p. 474.

[225] *Ibid.*, p. 475.

## Article 8(2)(b)(v) Attacking or bombarding, by whatever means, towns, villages, dwellings or buildings which are undefended and which are not military objectives

### Origins

The concept of an open or undefended town dates back centuries to the time when land armies would lay siege to walled cities. A practice arose of declaring a city or town open to the invading forces and therefore avoiding destruction and pillage.[226] In 1899 the Hague Regulations codified this rule,[227] in wording similar to Article 8(2)(b)(v), that 'the attack or bombardment of towns, villages, habitations or buildings which are not defended, is forbidden'.[228] This was amended in 1907 by the addition of the words 'bombardment, by whatever means',[229] and it is widely accepted that this phrase was introduced to cover bombardment from the air.[230]

The prohibition against attacks upon undefended towns was also provided for in Article 1 of the 1907 Hague Convention IX, but Article 2 stated that '[m]ilitary works, military or naval establishments, depots of arms or war *matériel*' were excluded from the prohibition unless destroyed by the local authorities when so commanded. This exception supports a reading of Article 25 of the IV Hague Regulations as prohibiting only the destruction of undefended towns near the conflict zone, where the army is in a position to take possession of them and thus deny their military resources to the enemy. Since the navy would not be able to take possession of a place in order to deny its use to the opposing power, they were permitted to destroy military resources even when sited in undefended towns.[231] Jennings explains that '[t]he quality of being open to entry by the enemy is the essence of the rule', otherwise 'a belligerent could secure the immunity of his production centres and lines of communication from lawful bombardment simply by omitting to defend them'.[232]

[226] See A. de Zayas, 'Open towns', pp. 69–71 in Bernhardt (ed.), *Encyclopaedia Vol. 4*.

[227] W. Hays Parks, 'Air war and the law of war', AFLR, 32 (1990), 1–225, p. 14.

[228] Article 25, 1899 Hague Convention II.

[229] Article 25, 1907 Hague Regulations. See the comparison between the 1899 and 1907 Hague Regulations, pp. 218–51 in A. Higgins, *The Hague Peace Conferences and other International Conferences concerning the Laws and Usages of War: Texts of Conventions with Commentaries* (Cambridge: Cambridge University Press, 1909), p. 237.

[230] R. Jennings, 'Open towns', BYIL, 22 (1945), 258–64, p. 259; H. Elliott, 'Open cities and (un)defended places', Army Lawy (April 1995), 39–50, p. 43; L. Nurick, 'The distinction between combatant and noncombatant in the law of war', AJIL, 39 (1945), 680–97, p. 690, and A. Rogers, *Law on the Battlefield*, n. 14 supra, fn. 5 on p. 87, but see H. Lauterpacht, 'The problem of the revision of the law of war', BYIL, 29 (1952), 360–82, p. 366, and H. Blix, 'Area bombardment', n. 17 *supra*, p. 41.

[231] R. Jennings, 'Open towns', n. 230 *supra*, p. 260.

[232] *Ibid.*, pp. 260–1. This approach is supported by the War Office with the Assistance of H. Lauterpacht, *Manual of British Military Law Part III: The Law of the War on* Land (London: HMSO, 1958; hereinafter: *British Military Manual*), para. 290.

## Development

The modern approach to undefended or open towns is laid down in Article 59 of AP I, which refers to the prohibition against attacking by any means 'non-defended localities'. Places which may be declared as non-defended localities are 'any inhabited place near or in a zone where armed forces are in contact which is open for occupation by an adverse Party' and must fulfil conditions including the prior evacuation of combatants and the absence of hostile use of fixed military establishments or support of military operations.[233] Attacking such places constitutes a grave breach under Article 85(3)(d) of AP I.

AP I introduces the concept of military objectives,[234] which are also referred to in Article 8(2)(b)(v). However, according to Oeter, non-defended localities under AP I cannot be military objectives, by definition, as 'the adversary has deliberately excluded them from his military activities, so that the intended military advantage could be achieved by mere occupation without combat activity, whereas a bombardment would be evidently unnecessary'.[235] Implicit in this statement is the assumption that locations lying behind the lines of defence cannot be undefended as they are not open to occupation.[236]

To date there have been no prosecutions for attacks upon undefended towns before the ICTY, nor allegations of the breach of this rule either in the Gulf or in Kosovo. One reason may be that the concepts of civilian objects and military objectives have to some extent overtaken the concept of the undefended town. As Elliott comments, '[t]rue sieges are rare in modern warfare'.[237]

## The Rome Statute

The EOC for this offence, in addition those relating to the nature of the conflict, state that the perpetrator must have 'attacked one or more towns, villages, dwellings or buildings' which did not constitute military objectives.[238] In addition the towns, villages, dwellings or buildings must have been 'open for unresisted occupation'.[239] Therefore, the Elements confirm that only a location near the combat zone can constitute an 'open' or 'undefended' location, given that no location behind the lines could be 'open for unresisted occupation' irrespective of its civilian character.

233 Article 59(2), AP I.

234 Article 52, AP I, defined *supra*, pp. 69–71.

235 S. Oeter, 'Methods and means of combat', n. 21 *supra*, para. 458.

236 *Ibid.*, para. 459, and see L. Green, *The Contemporary Law of Armed Conflict* (Manchester: Manchester University Press, 2nd edn, 2000), p. 100, and A. Rogers, *Law on the Battlefield*, n. 14 *supra*, p. 133.

237 H. Elliott, 'Open cities', n. 230 *supra*, p. 48. The author considers the siege of Sarajevo in the Bosnian conflict and concludes that it was not an undefended place, *ibid.*, pp. 48–50.

238 EOC, p. 132.

239 *Ibid.*

This means that locations behind the lines of defence cannot be 'undefended' locations and so could be attacked by air or from the sea without committing this offence.[240] However, the Elements of Article 8(2)(b)(v), unlike the Hague Regulations or AP I, do not prohibit attacks on military objects in 'undefended' towns.[241] This is nonsensical, as attacks against military objects behind the lines are in any case allowed under Article 8(2)(b)(ii) and attacks against military objects which are in places 'open for unresisted occupation' would not appear necessary, as they could be taken without the need for an attack.[242] A footnote to the EOC for this article does, in any case, confirm that '[t]he presence in the locality of persons specially protected under the Geneva Conventions of 1949 or of police forces retained for the sole purpose of maintaining law and order does not by itself render the locality a military objective'.[243]

Finally, given that the EOC do not mention a mental element, the default *mens rea* of Article 30 must apply to this offence. Therefore the perpetrator would have to intend to engage in the attack and be aware of the fact that the location was open for unresisted occupation and that the target was not a military objective.

## Article 8(2)(b)(vi) Killing or wounding a combatant who, having laid down his arms or having no means of defence, has surrendered at discretion

### Origins

Attacks upon wounded and disabled soldiers were prohibited as far back as the American Civil War.[244] More recently Article 23(c) of the 1907 Hague Regulations prohibited killing or wounding combatants who have surrendered or have no means of defence. The term 'surrendered at discretion' was explained by the British *Manual of Military Law* as meaning that the combatant must surrender unconditionally before obtaining the protection of this Article.[245]

Violations of this prohibition were punished in war crimes trials after the Second World War.[246] In the *Peleus* Trial, where the commander of a German submarine ordered the killing of survivors of a sunken vessel, the Judge Advocate stated that it was a 'fundamental usage of war that the killing of unarmed enemies was

[240] Although such an attack would have to be in accordance with Article 8(2)(b)(ii) and (iv).

[241] See Article 25, 1907 Hague Regulations, and Article 59, AP I.

[242] Given that such bombardment would be unnecessary, it would probably fall foul of the proportionality test in 8(2)(b)(iv) in any case.

[243] EOC, fn. 38 on p. 132.

[244] Article 71, Lieber Code.

[245] *British Military Manual*, para. 119.

[246] See cases discussed below, and *Abbaye Ardenne* case, 4 LRTWC 97, *Thiele and Steinert* case, 3 LRTWC 56, *Jaluit Atoll* case, 1 LRTWC 71.

forbidden'.[247] Furthermore, in the *Almelo* Trial, where a British prisoner of war (PoW) and a Dutch civilian who had been hiding were shot, the notes on the case comment that the decision of the military court was based on 'the rule that it is a war crime to kill a captured member of the opposing armed forces'.[248]

### Development

This prohibition was developed by Article 41 of AP I, which stated that '[a] person who is recognized or who, in the circumstances, should be recognized to be *hors de combat* shall not be made the object of attack' and under Article 85(3)(e) of AP I such an attack amounts to a grave breach.[249] The expression *hors de combat* is defined in Article 41(2) as applying to someone who is in the power of an adverse party, has clearly expressed an intention to surrender, or has been rendered unconscious or incapacitated by wounds or sickness and so is incapable of defending himself. The Bothe *et al.* and ICRC commentaries explain that these articles avoid gaps in protection between the time when an individual is rendered *hors de combat* through injury or surrender and when he attains a more secure status such as that of prisoner of war.[250]

An important issue raised by Article 41 of AP I is the nature of 'surrender'. According to McCoubrey and White, 'surrender itself is a positive act and not one which should, or safely could, be inferred from mere inaction or even retreat'.[251] By way of example they refer to the withdrawal of Iraqi troops on the road to Basra during the Iraq–Kuwait Gulf conflict when, despite the Iraqi retreat, the Coalition forces continued to attack the armoured column, causing many casualties.[252] McCoubrey and White argue that the Iraqi withdrawal did not constitute a surrender because the troops were still a 'potent military threat' as a fully armed and unyielding enemy, even if moving temporarily from the battle zone.[253]

The nature of surrender depends upon the type of conflict. In the call for surrender at Goose Green during the Falklands/Malvinas conflict the Argentine forces were instructed to leave the town, forming in military manner, removing their helmets and laying down their weapons.[254] During naval warfare it is customary to signal surrender by hauling down the ship's flag, and possibly by raising a

247 The *Peleus* Trial, 1 LRTWC 1, p. 11.

248 The *Almelo* Trial, 1 LRTWC 35, p. 44.

249 See also Article 20(b)(iv), 1996 ILC Draft Code.

250 Bothe *et al.*, *New Rules for Victims*, pp. 219–21, and Sandoz *et al.*, *Commentary on the Additional Protocols*, p. 481.

251 H. McCoubrey and N. White, *International Law and Armed Conflict* (Aldershot: Dartmouth, 1992), p. 227.

252 *Ibid.*, pp. 227–8.

253 *Ibid.*, p. 228.

254 L. Green, *The Contemporary Law of Armed Conflict*, n. 236 *supra*, p. 94.

white flag and stopping the engines.[255] Shipwrecked persons would automatically come under the protection of this article unless they attempted hostile acts.[256] The ICRC commentary to AP I suggests that in air warfare 'it is generally accepted that a crew wishing to indicate their intention to cease combat should do so by waggling the wings while opening the cockpit (if this is possible)', and this may be supplemented by radio signals.[257] For aircrew parachuting from an aircraft in distress Article 42 of AP I lays down the rule that they are not to be attacked during their descent, although Green suggests that such immunity may cease if the airman 'manoeuvres his parachute so as to land behind his own lines'.[258]

## The Rome Statute

The wording of this article in the Rome Statute is almost identical to Article 23(c) of the Hague Regulations, but the wording of the EOC is drawn from Article 41 of AP I. The Elements state, in addition to the requirements relating to the international status of the conflict, that the perpetrator must have killed or injured one or more persons who must have been *hors de combat* and the perpetrator must have been aware of the factual circumstances establishing that status.[259]

Cottier explains that laying down arms requires that a combatant should not only cease to fight but also demonstrate the intention not to fight any more.[260] Therefore, ceasing to fight and withdrawing, whilst still retaining weapons, would not suffice to bring combatants under the protection of this article, as they could be withdrawing to regroup and to launch a new attack. Cottier defines persons having no longer means of defence as those no longer capable of armed resistance.[261] Therefore the wounded and sick, the shipwrecked and those parachuting from an aircraft in distress (unless manoeuvring back to their own lines) would be considered as having no longer means of defence.

To be brought under the protection of this article the persons *hors de combat* must have 'surrendered at discretion', which is defined by Cottier as meaning that 'the individual concerned is not willing to fight any more and does not resist capture by the enemy'.[262] It is, however, clear that, although a severely wounded or unconscious person would not be capable of positive surrender, such a person

[255] *Ibid.*, p. 175, and Sandoz *et al.*, *Commentary on the Additional Protocols*, p. 487, and see the Trial of *von Ruchteschell*, 9 LRTWC 82, p. 89.

[256] Article 41(2), AP I.

[257] Sandoz *et al.*, *Commentary on the Additional Protocols*, p. 487, but see Spaight on the difficulties of accepting surrender in the air, J. Spaight, *Air Power and War Rights* (London: Longman, 3rd edn, 1947), pp. 126–68.

[258] L. Green, *The Contemporary Law of Armed Conflict*, n. 236 *supra*, p. 152.

[259] EOC, p. 132, and see Cottier *et al.*, 'Article 8', p. 200.

[260] Cottier *et al.*, 'Article 8', p. 200.

[261] *Ibid.*

[262] *Ibid.*

may not be attacked or killed and the willingness to surrender at discretion presumed.[263] In any case, under the EOC it is simply required that the victim should be *hors de combat*, and this would be the case *either* if he had laid down his arms and surrendered *or* if he had no means of defence.[264]

The mental element of this offence is not evident from Article 8(2)(b)(vi), and, as the EOC do not define the *mens rea*, the default mental element of Article 30 of the Rome Statute must apply.[265] Therefore, the perpetrator must have intended or known that in the ordinary course of events his actions would kill or wound the victim and must have been aware of the factual circumstances establishing the victim as *hors de combat*. However, whilst the perpetrator would have to be aware, for example, that the victim had laid down his arms and surrendered, he would not have to understand the legal status of the victim as *hors de combat*, nor the legal consequences of his actions in killing or wounding the victim.

## Article 8(2)(b)(vii) Making improper use of a flag of truce, of the flag or of the military insignia and uniform of the enemy or of the United Nations, as well as of the distinctive emblems of the Geneva Conventions, resulting in death or serious personal injury

### Origins

This article is based primarily on Article 23(f) of the 1907 Hague Regulations, although abuse of the flag of truce, emblems or flags of protection and the enemy's uniform were prohibited as far back as the Lieber Code.[266]

### *Improper use of the flag of truce*

Improper use of the flag of truce is forbidden by Article 23(f) of the Hague Regulations, and Articles 32 to 34 explain the permitted use of the flag of truce on the battlefield. The white flag is used to enter into communication with the opposing belligerent and the bearer has the right to inviolability unless he abuses the position. Whilst the communication may frequently be the negotiation of terms for surrender, this is not the legal meaning of the flag of truce,[267] although the British *Military Manual* comments that 'in practice, the white flag has come to indicate surrender if hoisted by individual soldiers or a small party in the course of an action'.[268]

[263] *Ibid.*, p. 202.

[264] *Ibid.*

[265] See discussion *supra*, pp. 5–8.

[266] Articles 114, 117 and 65, 1863 Lieber Code.

[267] Articles 32–4, 1907 Hague Regulations.

[268] *British Military Manual*, para. 394. This has been supported in similar words in the new British joint services manual, Ministry of Defence (MoD), *The Manual of the Law of Armed Conflict* (Oxford: Oxford University Press, 2004), para. 10.5.1.

The success of the institution of the flag of truce is 'dependent on good faith and lack of abuse'[269] and 'the feigning of an intent to negotiate under a flag of truce or of a surrender' was prohibited as perfidy in Article 37(1)(a) of AP I.[270] Spaight suggests that a white flag raised 'by a retreating force to stay the enemy's hand' may be legally ignored by the adverse party,[271] but it is unclear whether use of a white flag in such a situation would actually amount to the offence of improper use of the flag of truce.

*Improper use of the flag or of military insignia and uniform of the enemy*

Article 23(f) of the Hague Regulations prohibits improper use 'of the national flag or of the military insignia and uniform of the enemy'. Whilst the meaning of 'national flag' is clear, Bothe describes a uniform as 'a means of identification showing that a person is a member of the armed forces of a State or is associated with an international organization' and explains that '[i]t is an established practice that some national insignia or emblem be fixed on the uniform'.[272] It must, however, be noted that these are visual symbols and that this article does not prohibit the ruse of using the enemy's codes or passwords.[273]

A more complex issue is: what is *improper use* of the flags, insignia and uniforms of the enemy? This has long been contentious, and Spaight, writing in 1911, acknowledged the divide between those who believed that use of the enemy's flag, insignia and uniform was illegitimate in all circumstances and those who held that such material could be used provided that the disguise was shed before combat actually commenced.[274] Fleck states that the negotiations for Article 23(f) show that there was no intention by States to legalise any deception during conflict by use of enemy flag, insignia and uniform, asserting that such a ruse 'was regarded as objectionable even prior to the Brussels Conference'.[275] However, he admits of exceptions where the 'acts of deception are not conducive to facilitating acts of combat' such as use of enemy uniforms for training exercises or by prisoners of war to aid escape.[276]

As Rowe indicates, '[t]he unanimous view of writers is that wearing of the uniform of the enemy while *engaging in attacks* is prohibited by international law'[277]

[269] Y. Dinstein, 'Flag of truce', pp. 173–4 in Bernhardt (ed.), *Encyclopaedia Vol. 3*, p. 173.

[270] See *infra*, p. 117.

[271] J. Spaight, *War Rights on Land* (London: Macmillan, 1911), p. 225.

[272] M. Bothe, 'Flags and uniforms in war', pp. 174–5, in Bernhardt (ed.), *Encyclopaedia Vol. 3*, p. 174. See also P. Rowe, 'The use of special forces and the laws of war, wearing the uniform of the enemy or civilian clothes and of spying and assassination', Rev dr milit, 33 (1994), 207–34, pp. 219–20.

[273] Bothe *et al.*, *New Rules for Victims*, p. 214.

[274] J. Spaight, *War Rights on Land*, n. 271 *supra*, pp. 104–6.

[275] D. Fleck, 'Ruses of war and prohibition of perfidy', Rev dr milit, 13 (1974), 269–304, p. 280. This is supported by V. Jobst III, 'Is the wearing of the enemy's uniform a violation of the laws of war?', AJIL, 35 (1941), 435–42, p. 438.

[276] D. Fleck, 'Ruses of war', n. 275 *supra*, p. 282.

[277] P. Rowe, 'The use of special forces', n. 272 *supra*, p. 213.

and this is supported by the British *Manual of Military Law*.[278] Indeed, this rule may be inferred by Article 1(2) of the Hague Regulations, which requires that combatants have a fixed distinctive emblem recognisable at a distance. However, the Second World War case of *Skorzeny*, in which German parachutists were acquitted without a reasoned judgement after having penetrated behind the US lines whist wearing US uniforms under their parachute overalls, has not really assisted in clarifying this area of law further.[279]

The prohibition relating to improper use is restated by Article 39(2) of AP I, which prohibits making use of 'the flags or military emblems, insignia or uniforms of adverse Parties while engaging in attacks or in order to shield, favour, protect or impede military operations'. This clarifies the imprecise wording of Article 23(f) of the Hague Regulations, although Greenwood warns that this article is controversial and should not be regarded as declaratory of customary law.[280] However, it is not contentious to hold that the use during an attack of enemy uniforms or captured military vehicles without first removing enemy insignia would be prohibited, and it seems likely that use of those uniforms during military operations prior to attack would also be 'improper use'.[281] Nevertheless, the weight of evidence suggests that Fleck was correct in contending that the use of such enemy material to assist in training exercises or the escape of a prisoner of war would indeed not constitute 'improper use'.[282]

Article 39(3) of AP I states that this definition of improper use shall not affect existing rules of international law applicable to espionage or 'to the use of flags in the conduct of armed conflict at sea'. With respect to espionage, this suggests that the wearing of the enemy's uniform by a spy behind enemy lines will not constitute a war crime. Whilst this may make little difference to the individual, who may be tried and executed for the act of spying, it has two important consequences. First, the commander who sent the spy will not be responsible for a war crime under the doctrine of command responsibility with regard to the uniform worn by the spy.[283] Second, if the spy returns to his own lines and is caught at a later date during combat and is wearing the uniform of his own forces he must be treated as a prisoner of war and cannot be punished for his previous act of espionage or, it would appear, for the fact that he wore the uniform of the enemy whilst committing such an act.[284]

[278] *British Military Manual*, para. 320. This is supported by MoD, *The Manual of the Law of Armed Conflict*, n. 268 *supra*, para. 5.11.1.

[279] Trial of *Skorzeny and Others*, 9 LRTWC 90, and see P. Rowe, 'The use of special forces', n. 272 *supra*, pp. 215–17, and Sandoz *et al.*, *Commentary on the Additional Protocols*, fn. 26 on p. 467.

[280] C. Greenwood, 'Customary law status of the 1977 Geneva Protocols', pp. 93–114 in A. Delissen and D. Tanja (eds), *Humanitarian Law of Armed Conflict: Challenges Ahead* (Dordrecht: Nijhoff, 1991), p. 105.

[281] See also Bothe *et al.*, *New Rules for Victims*, p. 214.

[282] *Ibid.*, p. 214.

[283] *Ibid.*, p. 215.

[284] See Article 31, 1907 Hague Regulations. For a general discussion of espionage in time of war see J. Kish (ed. D. Turns), *International Law and Espionage* (Dordrecht: Nijhoff, 1995), pp. 123–51.

A more complex issue is the extent to which warships during naval conflicts may use the flag of the enemy. Article 39(3) does not state that the use of such flags is legal, but it leaves the question open.[285] Although there are examples in State practice of warships flying an enemy or neutral flag until just prior to opening fire,[286] there have been no cases of such actions reported in post-Second World War conflicts.[287] Furthermore, such a practice has always been controversial and as early as 1913 was condemned as 'treacherous and barbarous' in the Institute of International Law's *Manual of the Laws of Naval War*.[288]

Finally, with respect to air warfare, the 1923 Hague Draft Rules of Aerial Warfare state in Article 19 that the use of false external marks is forbidden. According to Spaight, the prohibition of false or enemy marks in air warfare has long been customary international law, as demonstrated in the Second World War by accusations and 'indignant denials' of such practice.[289] Furthermore, although Article 39(3) explicitly exempts naval warfare from the provision, it is silent with respect to air warfare, which suggests that air warfare must follow the same rules as land warfare on improper use of enemy emblems.

### *Improper use of the flag or military insignia and uniform of the United Nations*

The basis of this offence can be found in Article 37(d) of AP I, where 'the feigning of protected status by the use of signs, emblems or uniforms of the United Nations' is prohibited, and Article 38(2) which prohibits making unauthorised use 'of the distinctive emblem of the United Nations'.[290] Both commentaries to AP I state with respect to Article 37(d) that the feigning of UN symbols is prohibited as perfidy for only so long as the United Nations are a neutral presence in a conflict.[291] This analysis is supported by Bothe, who comments that 'where the United Nations itself is a party to the conflict, the rules relating to enemy uniforms, insignia, or flags apply'.[292]

[285] M. Bothe, 'Flags and uniforms in war', n. 272 *supra*, p. 174, and G. Politakis, 'Stratagems and the prohibition of perfidy with special reference to the laws of war at sea', Austrian JPIL, 45 (1993), 253–308, p. 270.

[286] For examples of this practice see G. Politakis, 'Stratagems and the prohibition', pp. 272–8 and 287–8.

[287] W. Heintschel von Heinegg, 'The law of armed conflicts at sea', n. 109 *supra*, p. 422.

[288] Article 15(2), Manual of the Laws of Naval War, 9 August 1913, Institute of International Law.

[289] J. Spaight, *Air Power and War Rights*, n. 257 *supra*, pp. 85–6.

[290] Sandoz *et al.*, *Commentary on the Additional Protocols*, p. 459 and fn. 42, comments that the use of the UN flag is governed by a code issued by the Secretary General of the United Nations on 19 December 1947 and amended on 11 November 1952.

[291] Bothe *et al.*, *New Rules for Victims*, p. 206, and Sandoz *et al.*, *Commentary on the Additional Protocols*, p. 439.

[292] M. Bothe, 'Flags and uniforms in war', n. 272 *supra*, p. 174.

### *Improper use of the distinctive emblems of the Geneva Convention*

Improper use of the 'distinctive badges' of the Geneva Conventions was prohibited under Article 23(f) of the 1907 Hague Regulations. The Second World War case of *Hagendorf* recorded the breach of this prohibition by a German soldier who fired a weapon at American soldiers from an ambulance bearing the red cross symbol.[293] He was found guilty and the notes on the case state that '[i]t is hard to conceive of a more flagrant misuse than the firing of a weapon from an ambulance by personnel who were themselves protected by such emblems and by the Conventions'.[294]

The more modern expression 'distinctive emblem' is used in Article 38 of AP I, which prohibits 'use of the distinctive emblem of the red cross, red crescent or red lion and sun', and Article 6 of AP III states that this provision applies equally to the red crystal, the new distinctive emblem recognised under that treaty.[295] Article 8(1) of the Protocol defines 'distinctive emblem' as 'the distinctive emblem of the red cross, red crescent or red lion and sun on a white ground *when used for the protection* of medical units and transports, or medical and religious personnel, equipment or supplies'.[296] Therefore, it is the improper use of the Geneva Convention emblems when used for protective purposes, rather than indicative purposes, that constitutes a war crime.[297]

A definition of improper use of the distinctive emblems of the Geneva Conventions can be arrived at only by examining the 1949 Geneva Conventions and the 1977 Additional Protocol in order to ascertain what amounts to 'proper use' of the protective emblems. Those entitled to wear or display the protective emblems of the Geneva Conventions include medical and religious personnel of armed forces, medical establishments, mobile units, ships and aircraft of armed forces and in certain circumstances civilian medical and religious personnel and civilian medical units and transports.[298]

The medical establishments protected by the red cross, crescent or crystal remain protected at all times, unless 'they are used to commit, outside their humanitarian duties, acts harmful to the enemy'.[299] This suggests that improper use of the

[293] Trial of *Hagendorf*, 13 LRTWC 146.

[294] *Ibid.*, p. 148.

[295] The red lion and sun is no longer in use. AP III entered into force in January 2007 and (as of October 2007) twenty States are parties.

[296] Emphasis added.

[297] Bothe *et al.*, *New Rules for Victims*, p. 103, and Sandoz *et al.*, *Commentary on the Additional Protocols*, pp. 450–1.

[298] See Articles 38–44, Geneva Convention I; Articles 41–5, Geneva Convention II; Articles 18, 20 and 21–2, Geneva Convention IV, and Articles 12–13 and 18, AP I. See generally F. Bugnion, 'The red cross and red crescent emblems', IRRC, 29 (1989), 408–19, A. Bouvier, 'Special aspects of the use of the red cross or red crescent emblem', IRRC, 272, 438–58, and H. Slim, 'Protection of the red cross and red crescent emblems and the repression of misuse', IRRC, 272 (1989), 420–37.

[299] Article 21, Geneva Convention I; Article 34, Geneva Convention II; Article 19, Geneva Convention IV; Article 13, AP I, and see Article 6(1), AP III, which applies provisions of the Geneva Conventions repressing such use equally to the red crystal.

distinctive signs would include using them in such a way as to conduct acts harmful to the enemy, and therefore those personnel and establishments using the protective emblems must indeed be neutral and concerned solely with humanitarian duties.[300] Perfidious use of the red cross, crescent or crystal would also clearly constitute improper use.[301] It must also be noted that this prohibition on misuse of the distinctive emblems of the Geneva Convention applies equally to naval warfare.[302]

## Development

An example of abuse of the flag of truce may be taken from the Iraq–Kuwait Gulf conflict. The US Department of Defense report records an incident where Iraqi soldiers waved a white flag and laid down their weapons but the Saudi Arabian patrol who advanced to accept the surrender were fired upon by other Iraqi forces hidden in buildings on either side of the street.[303] This would clearly be improper use of the flag of truce on the part of the soldiers waving the flag if they knew that their fellow soldiers were intending to open fire. However, during a similar incident in Goose Green, in the Falklands/Malvinas conflict, it would appear that the Argentinian soldiers displaying the white flag did so without authorisation from their commander and the British soldiers who went to investigate were killed by Argentinian troops who were unaware that the white flag had been displayed.[304] This incident would not constitute improper use on the part of the soldiers flying the flag of truce, provided that they had done so in good faith, and instead serves as a warning to those observing the white flag to ensure that the situation is safe before taking action.

Improper use of the flag, military insignia and uniform of the enemy during naval conflicts is dealt with by Article 110 of the San Remo Manual, which states that warships 'are prohibited from launching an attack whilst flying a false flag'. The explanation to the Manual states that '[t]he traditional right regarding the use of false flags is reflected in the present text'.[305] Therefore, whilst the San Remo Manual confirms that launching an attack whilst flying the enemy flag would

[300] See W. Rabus, 'Protection of the wounded, sick and shipwrecked', pp. 293–319, in D. Fleck (ed.), *Handbook of Humanitarian Law*, n. 21 *supra*, para. 640.

[301] Article 85(3)(f), AP I prohibits perfidious use of the distinctive emblems of the Geneva Convention as a grave breach and by virtue of Article 6(1), AP III, this would apply equally to perfidious use of the red crystal.

[302] Note that Article 38, AP I, does not exclude naval warfare, unlike Article 39 on emblems of nationality.

[303] US Department of Defense Report, p. 632.

[304] C. Greenwood, 'Scope of application of humanitarian law', pp. 39–63, in D. Fleck (ed.), *Handbook of Humanitarian Law*, n. 21 *supra*, para. 223. See also MoD, *The Manual of the Law of Armed Conflict*, n. 268 *supra*, fn. 10 of para. 10.5.2.

[305] L. Doswald-Beck (ed.), *San Remo Manual of International Law applicable to Armed Conflict at Sea* (Cambridge: Cambridge University Press, 1995; hereinafter: *San Remo Manual – Explanation)*, p. 185.

constitute 'improper use', it leaves open the question of whether a warship could properly fly an enemy flag during manoeuvres prior to combat.

The San Remo Manual provides a more clear-cut approach to the flying of the UN flag and the emblems of the Geneva Convention. Under Article 110 warships are at all times prohibited from simulating the status of 'vessels protected by the United Nations flag' or 'vessels entitled to be identified by the emblem of the red cross or red crescent'. However, the explanation to the manual restricts the complete prohibition against flying the UN flag to situations where such colours would be protective and states that this would clearly be the case in a conflict where the United Nations was neutral.[306]

## The Rome Statute

The nature of 'improper use', as has already been shown, is dependent in each case upon the current conventional and customary laws which apply to the use of that material. Although Cottier rightly points out that '"[i]mproper use" is not necessarily synonymous to perfidious use', it is generally correct to say that perfidious use of many of the signs or symbols in this article would amount to improper use of that material under customary international law and therefore could be charged as such under this article provided that the criteria of the other elements were fulfilled.[307]

The EOC require, in respect of each of the improper use offences under Article 8(2)(b)(vii), that the conduct has resulted in death or serious personal injury.[308] There is no definition of 'serious personal injury' and no indication of whether this can encompass psychological as well as physical injury. Guidance may be taken from the ICRC commentary to 85(3), which defines 'serious injury to body or health' as injury which will 'affect people in a long-lasting or crucial manner, either as regards their physical integrity or their physical *and mental* health'.[309] This reflects the approach taken by English law, which has held grievous bodily harm, defined as 'really serious harm',[310] to include such injuries as broken bones, internal injuries and serious psychological harm.[311]

The perpetrator must also have been aware that death or serious personal injury could result from his conduct and therefore must have been subjectively reckless in respect of this result.[312] Cottier comments that the death or serious

[306] *Ibid.*

[307] For a discussion of the overlap between Article 8(2)(b)(vii) and Article 8(2)(b)(xi) see *infra*, pp. 117–18.

[308] EOC, pp. 133–4.

[309] Sandoz *et al.*, *Commentary on the Additional Protocols*, p. 995, emphasis added. This approach is taken in Cottier *et al.*, 'Article 8', p. 208.

[310] *DPP v. Smith*, [1961] AC, 290, p. 334.

[311] *Burstow* (1997) AC [1998], 147–67, p. 159.

[312] EOC, pp. 133–4. This requirement is less strict than that which would have been imposed by the default mental element of Article 30, Lee (ed.), *ICC: Elements*, p. 158.

personal injury is not restricted to enemy combatants but includes 'the death of other persons, including civilians, wounded or sick and UN and associated personnel'.[313]

Each of the improper use offences, with the exception of improper use of a flag, insignia or uniform of the United Nations, contains the element '[t]he perpetrator knew *or should have known* of the prohibited nature of such use'.[314] The footnote to this element, in each case, states '[t]his mental element recognizes the interplay between article 30 and article 32. The term "prohibited nature" denotes illegality.'[315] This is an unusual element and appears to give an accused a defence based on lack of knowledge of the law when he could not have known the law. The footnote refers to Article 30, which is the default mental element requiring intent and knowledge on the part of the accused, and Article 32, which provides that a mistake of law may exclude criminal responsibility 'if it negates the mental element required by such a crime'.

Dörmann explains the background to this element as a compromise between those delegates who believed that ignorance of the prohibited use of the signs and symbols should be a complete defence and those who believed that such a defence would encourage States to avoid their responsibility to teach the military the proper use of important signs such as those of the red cross or crescent.[316] The 'knew or should have known' 'standard of negligence' was adopted as a compromise.[317] Therefore the accused would have a defence to an 'improper use' crime if he did not know and was not negligent in such lack of knowledge that the use to which he put the material was illegal.

### *Improper use of the flag of truce*

For the war crime of 'improper use of a flag of truce' the Elements of Crimes, in addition to those discussed above and those regarding the nature of the conflict, state that the perpetrator 'used a flag of truce . . . in order to feign an intention to negotiate when there was no such intention'.[318] This is fairly straightforward, but it must be remembered that it is applied in conjunction with the other elements discussed above. To take Spaight's example, discussed earlier, of using the flag of truce to 'stay the enemy's hand' in order to buy time to retreat, this article would not be breached unless that conduct resulted in death or serious personal injury.[319]

[313] Cottier *et al.*, 'Article 8', p. 208.

[314] EOC, pp. 133–4, emphasis added.

[315] *Ibid.*, fns 39, 40 and 43.

[316] K. Dörmann, 'The first and second sessions of the Preparatory Commission for the International Criminal Court', YIHL, 2 (1999), 283–306, p. 301.

[317] *Ibid.*, p. 302.

[318] EOC, p. 133.

[319] See discussion *supra*, p. 96.

### *Improper use of the flag or military insignia and uniform of the enemy*

The elements which apply specifically to the improper use of enemy material are that the perpetrator must have 'used a flag, insignia or uniform of the hostile party' and made such use 'in a manner prohibited under the international law of armed conflict *while engaged in an attack*'.[320] The elements of this offence have restricted improper use of enemy material to that agreed by all commentators as improper, in land, air and sea warfare,[321] and therefore it appears that this article applies to all types of warfare.

### *Improper use of the flag or military insignia and uniform of the United Nations*

The elements of this improper use offence simply state that the perpetrator must have 'used a flag, insignia or uniform of the United Nations . . . in a manner prohibited under the international law of armed conflict'.[322] This makes it clear that improper use of the insignia and uniform of UN civilian staff is within this prohibition as well as improper use of the military insignia and uniform of UN combat personnel.[323] Furthermore, unlike the other improper use offences, the elements state that the perpetrator 'knew of the prohibited nature of such use' and therefore, for the offence of improper use of UN signs and symbols, ignorance of the law would constitute a defence.[324]

### *Improper use of the distinctive emblems of the Geneva Conventions*

The elements for improper use of the distinctive emblems state that the perpetrator must have used the distinctive emblems of the Geneva Conventions 'for *combatant purposes* in a manner prohibited under the international law of armed conflict'.[325] A footnote to the Elements of this offence states that 'combatant purposes' means 'purposes *directly related to hostilities* and not including medical, religious or similar activities'.[326] Whilst the exact scope of 'directly related to hostilities' is uncertain, the carrying on of activities outside a medical or religious role which militarily assist a combatant party, under the protection of the distinctive emblems, would clearly constitute improper use.

[320] EOC, p. 133, emphasis added.

[321] See P. Rowe, 'The use of special forces', n. 272 *supra*, p. 213 and discussion *supra*, pp. 96–8.

[322] EOC, p. 134.

[323] See Cottier *et al.*, 'Article 8', p. 205.

[324] EOC, p. 134, including fn. 41.

[325] EOC, p. 134, emphasis added. Note that the Elements refer only to the 'distinctive emblems of the Geneva Conventions' and so arguably omit the 'distinctive emblem' added by AP III.

[326] EOC, fn. 42 on p. 134.

## Article 8(2)(b)(viii) The transfer, directly or indirectly, by the Occupying Power of parts of its own civilian population into the territory it occupies, or the deportation or transfer of all or part of the population of the occupied territory within or outside this territory

### Origins

The two alternative offences in this article of the Rome Statute are based on Article 49 of the Fourth Geneva Convention and Article 85(4)(a) of AP I. The offence of deporting or transferring 'all or parts of the population of the occupied territory within or outside this territory' is familiar, as Article 49 of the Fourth Geneva Convention is also the basis of the grave breach of 'unlawful deportation or transfer', dealt with under Article 8(2)(a)(vii) above.[327] The offence of transfer by the Occupying Power 'directly or indirectly . . . of parts of its own civilian population into the territory it occupies' has roots in Article 49 but is prohibited under Article 85(4)(a) of AP I in wording very similar to this offence under the Rome Statute.[328] The following discussion will concentrate on the latter of the alternative offences, commenting only in respect of the former where it differs from the grave breach of 'unlawful deportation or transfer'.

These offences deal with actions by the 'Occupying Power', necessitating an explanation of when territory can be considered to be occupied. Article 42 of the Hague Regulations defines occupied territory as that which is 'actually placed under the authority of the hostile army' and explains that the 'occupation extends only to the territory where such authority has been established and can be exercised'. Article 2 common to the Geneva Conventions of 1949 asserts that an occupation can arise even if it meets with no armed resistance and therefore, as Schindler explains, there is an occupation '[w]henever a State intervenes with its armed forces in another State, be it to alter the régime of that State or to exercise other acts of sovereign power'.[329]

The definition of occupation is elaborated upon by Greenspan, who states that a military occupation occurs when 'organized resistance has been overcome in the area and the troops in possession have established their authority to such an extent that they are in a position to assert that authority within a reasonable time in any part of the occupied area'.[330] The British *Military Manual* further explains that an occupation does not become invalid because of rebellious activities by some of the inhabitants, or even because of occasional successes by resistance fighters, provided that 'the authority of the legitimate government is not effectively re-established and that the Occupant suppresses the rebellion

[327] See *supra*, pp. 53–7.

[328] Pictet (ed.), *Commentary: IV Convention*, pp. 277–83 and Bothe *et al.*, *New Rules*, p. 518.

[329] D. Schindler, 'The different types of armed conflicts according to the Geneva Conventions and Protocols', 163 Rec des Cours (1979) II, 117–63, p. 132.

[330] M. Greenspan, *The Modern Law of Land Warfare* (Berkeley CA: University of California Press, 1959), p. 214, and see J. Spaight, *War Rights on Land*, n. 271 *supra*, pp. 321–7.

at once'.[331] As to the exact commencement and ending of an occupation, Bothe states that it begins 'with the establishment of actual control over the territory' and ends 'when the occupation is in fact terminated by the withdrawal of the Occupying Power or by a determination of the final fate of the territory after the re-establishment of peaceful relations between the parties'.[332]

The commentaries to the Geneva Conventions and AP I do not greatly assist in an understanding of transfer by the Occupying Power of parts of its own civilian population into the territory it occupies.[333] In particular, it is unclear how many people constitute 'part' of the civilian population and it is uncertain whether a transfer is prohibited only if carried out forcefully. Furthermore the necessary link between the perpetrator of the offence and the Occupying Power is not entirely clear. However, it is clear that the prohibition against such transfer by the Occupying Power in Article 49(6) of the Fourth Geneva Convention is absolute, with no derogation permitted;[334] there are no exceptions based on military necessity or the security of the population.

## Development

The offence of transferring parts of the civilian population into the occupied territory has been subjected to scrutiny in recent years because of the policy of Israel (which is party to the 1949 Geneva Conventions but not to AP I) of establishing Jewish settlements in the territories occupied by Israel after the 1967 Six Day War.[335] The view of US State Department Legal Advisor Hansell, in a 1978 letter on this issue, was that the non-forcible as well as forcible transfers of parts of the civilian population into occupied territory breached Article 49(6) of the Fourth Geneva Convention.[336] His argument was based on a comparison between the wording of Article 49(1) of AP I, which specifies 'forcible transfers' in prohibiting transfers of the population out of the occupied territory, and the wording of Article 49(6), which omits the word 'forcible' when prohibiting transfers into occupied territory, raising the presumption that all transfers in this

[331] *British Military Manual*, para. 509. This is supported by MoD, *The Manual of the Law of Armed Conflict*, n. 268 *supra*, para. 11.7.1.

[332] M. Bothe, 'Occupation, belligerent', pp. 64–7 in Bernhardt (ed.), *Encyclopaedia Vol. 4*, pp. 65–6, and see generally H. McCoubrey, 'Civilians in occupied territory', pp. 205–23, in P. Rowe, *The Gulf War*, n. 90 *supra*, pp. 206–8.

[333] Pictet (ed.), *Commentary: IV Convention*, p. 283, and Sandoz *et al.*, *Commentary to the Additional Protocols*, p. 1000.

[334] C. Meindersma, 'Legal issues surrounding population transfers in conflict situations', NILR, 41 (1994), 31–83, p. 52.

[335] Israeli courts have considered this question only in the context of whether Geneva Convention IV was applicable at all and have held that it was not, for example, *Ayub v. Minister of Defence*, Israel Supreme Court sitting as the High Court of Justice, 1978, reproduced in summary in M. Sassòli and A. Bouvier, *How Does Law Protect in War?* (Geneva: ICRC, 1999), Case No. 102, pp. 812–16.

[336] H. Hansell, Letter of the State Department Legal Advisor concerning the legality of Israeli settlements in the occupied territories, 21 April 1978, reprinted in ILM, 17 (1978), 777–9.

context were forbidden.[337] An example of non-forcible methods facilitating transfers, given by Meindersma, is a policy which 'induces or encourages specific population movements by providing financial and other incentives for people to move'.[338]

The subject of 'settlers' has also received scrutiny in recent years by Special Rapporteur Al-Khasawneh for the Commission on Human Rights. In a 1994 progress report, whilst acknowledging that the implantation of settlers into occupied territory was prohibited in order to 'prevent alteration of the composition of a population in an occupied territory in order for it to retain its ethnic identity' and to prevent such transfers from being used 'as a means of asserting title or sovereignty over an occupied territory',[339] he emphasised that transfers remain prohibited irrespective of motive.[340] In his final report he concluded that '[u]nlawful population transfer involves a practice or policy that has the purpose or effect of moving persons into or out of an area, whether within or across an international border, or into or out of an occupied territory, without the free and informed consent of the transferred population or any receiving population'.[341]

With respect to the definition of an 'Occupying Power', the ICJ looked at this issue in the *Case concerning Armed Activities on the Territory of the Congo* (*Democratic Republic of the Congo v. Uganda*).[342] The Court stated that there must be 'sufficient evidence to demonstrate that the said authority was in fact established and exercised by the intervening State in the areas in question' and that in particular the Court must be satisfied that the intervening State had substituted its own authority for that of the territorial State.[343]

However, it is interesting that the ICTY Trial Judgement in *Naletilić and Martinović* held that the law of occupation as it affects individuals as civilians protected under the Fourth Geneva Convention does not require that the occupying power has authority and that '[f]or the purposes of those individuals' rights, a state of occupation exists upon their falling into "the hands of the occupying power"', so preventing the situation of civilians being given less protection in

[337] *Ibid.*

[338] C. Meindersma, 'Legal issues surrounding population transfers', n. 334 *supra*, p. 33.

[339] Mr A. Al-Khasawneh, Special Rapporteur Progress Report, 'The realization of economic, social and cultural rights: the human rights dimensions of population transfer, including the implantation of settlers', Sub-commission on Prevention of Discrimination and Protection of Minorities, UN Doc. E/CN.4/Sub.2/1994/18, 30 June 1994, para. 77.

[340] *Ibid.*, para. 73.

[341] Mr A. Al-Khasawneh, Special Rapporteur, Final Report, 'Freedom of movement: human rights and population transfer', Sub-commission on Prevention of Discrimination and Protection of Minorities, UN Doc. E/CN.4/Sub.2/1997/23, 27 June 1997, para. 66.

[342] *Case concerning Armed Activities on the Territory of the Congo* (*Democratic Republic of the Congo v. Uganda*), 19 December 2005, General List No. 116, available at: <http://www.icj-cij.org/docket/files/116/10455.pdf>.

[343] *Ibid.*, para. 173. This interpretation was supported by the ICC, *Thomas Lubanga Dyilo*, Pre-trial Chamber Decision on the Confirmation of Charges, paras 212–17.

an intermediate period than when the occupation is established.[344] Therefore, if the invading State transferred parts of the civilian population within or outside of the territorial State before an occupation had properly been established, according to this interpretation the offence of transferring civilians would still have been committed.[345] This is a sensible interpretation, for otherwise there would be no recourse for such acts done by the invading forces until they had established themselves as an Occupying Power.

## The Rome Statute

The position of Israel on the issue of transfer of civilians into occupied territory complicated the issue of defining the offence.[346] Indeed, according to Dörmann, this war crime 'gave rise to the most difficult negotiations of all'.[347] The Elements for the first alternative offence, in addition to the requirements relating to the nature of the conflict, state that the perpetrator '(a) Transferred, directly or indirectly, parts of its own population into the territory it occupies.'[348] A footnote to the word 'transferred' states that this term 'needs to be interpreted in accordance with the relevant provisions of international humanitarian law'.[349] Dörmann comments that this 'states the obvious, without giving any further clarification',[350] but, given the expression 'directly or indirectly', it would appear that inducements or facilitation of population transfer, or perhaps even failure to prevent a voluntary transfer, would also be an offence under this section.[351] Suggested examples of such inducements or facilitation given by Cottier include '[c]onfiscation laws, government settlement plans, protection of unlawful settlements and other economic and financial measures such as incentives, subsidies'.[352]

[344] *Naletilić and Martinović*, Trial Judgement, para. 221.

[345] *Ibid.*, para. 222. Note, the Trial Chamber was actually discussing the grave breach of unlawful deportation or transfer, but it is submitted that they should be interpreted similarly.

[346] Schabas states that 'Israel felt itself particularly targeted by the provision', W. Schabas, *An Introduction to the ICC*, n. 7 *supra*, p. 124.

[347] K. Dörmann, 'Preparatory Commission for the International Criminal Court', n. 63 *supra*, p. 481. Israel initially voted against the Rome Statute, primarily because of the inclusion of this offence, but then signed the Statute in December 2000. However, in June 2002 Israel formally announced that it had no intention of ratifying the Rome Statute.

[348] EOC, p. 135.

[349] *Ibid.*, fn. 44.

[350] K. Dörmann, 'Preparatory Commission for the International Criminal Court', n. 63 *supra*, p. 482.

[351] See Cottier *et al.*, 'Article 8', p. 214, and H. von Hebel and D. Robinson, 'Crimes within the jurisdiction of the Court', n. 154 *supra*, p. 113. See also the ICRC working paper submitted to the Preparatory Commission on the Elements of Crimes of Article 8(2)(b), 18 June 1999, available at: <http://www.igc.apc.org/icc>, comments on Article 8(2)(b)(viii).

[352] Cottier *et al.*, 'Article 8', p. 214.

The issue of the number of individuals who must be transferred to commit this offence remains unclear.[353] It is submitted that the number of individuals necessary to constitute part of the population must be sufficient to affect the receiving population in some way, such as creating a settlement of 100 or more people, rather than transferring a few people who may be absorbed into the local population.[354] Another issue is that, whilst the Statute refers to 'parts of its own civilian population', the EOC omit the word 'civilian', raising the question of whether the transferred population must be indeed civilian. However, the Statute is clear in the use of the words 'civilian population' and, whilst the EOC shall be used to assist in the interpretation of the Statute, in the face of a contradiction the Court should apply the wording of the Statute.[355]

On the issue of the necessary link between the perpetrator and the Occupying Power, the Elements are somewhat ambiguous.[356] However, the wording of this offence in the Rome Statute suggests that the transfer must be attributable to the Occupying Power and therefore appears to require government involvement, so that 'individuals who act in a wholly private capacity and whose actions are not attributable to the Occupying Power do not appear to be criminally responsible under article 8 para. 2(b)(viii)'.[357]

The EOC for the second alternative offence read that the perpetrator '[d]eported or transferred all or parts of the population of the occupied territory within or outside this territory'.[358] As previously suggested, this offence should be defined similarly to the grave breach of Article 8(2)(a)(vii), except that the offence requires the transfer or deportation of 'all or parts' of the population of the occupied territory, rather the transfer or deportation of protected persons.[359] For this offence 'parts' of the population should perhaps be read as a reasonably substantial number. However, it is arguable that 'substantial' should be read qualitatively as well as quantitatively, as, if those transferred or deported were the leaders or intellectuals of the population, it would disproportionately affect the population remaining in the occupied territory.[360]

353 Cottier and the ICRC working paper simply state that a 'certain number of individuals' must be transferred, Cottier *et al.*, *ibid.*, and the ICRC working paper on the Elements of Crimes of Article 8(2)(b), n. 351 *supra*, comments on Article 8(2)(b)(viii).

354 This is not to be understood as suggesting an additional mental element for this offence, rather as a method of measuring whether the number of transferred individuals amounts to a 'part' of the population.

355 See Articles 9(1) and 21(1)(a), Rome Statute, and comments by K. Dörmann, 'Preparatory Commission for the International Criminal Court', n. 63 *supra*, p. 482.

356 *Ibid.*

357 *Ibid.* Note that government involvement in this offence could theoretically lead to the prosecution of the Prime Minister or President of a country, given Article 27, Rome Statute, on the irrelevance of official capacity.

358 EOC, p. 135.

359 For a definition of occupied territory see discussion *supra*, pp. 104–5.

360 For discussion of an analogous approach taken with respect to the crime of genocide see C. Byron, 'The crime of genocide', pp. 143–77 in D. McGoldrick, P. Rowe and E. Donnelly (eds), *The Permanent International Criminal Court: Legal and Policy Issues* (Oxford: Hart, 2004), pp. 147–8.

The mental element of this offence is not defined and therefore must be that of intention and knowledge as defined in Article 30 of the Rome Statute.

### Article 8(2)(b)(ix) Intentionally directing attacks against buildings dedicated to religion, education, art, science or charitable purposes, historic monuments, hospitals and places where the sick and wounded are collected, provided they are not military objects

#### Origins

This provision has its roots in Article 27 of the IV Hague Regulations,[361] with the extension of the protection to educational buildings,[362] and is influenced by the provisions for the protection of cultural property in the 1954 Hague Convention and Articles 53 and 85(4)(d) of AP I.[363] Although, in essence, the offence is very similar to Article 52 of AP I, which prohibits attacks against civilian objects, its particular importance is explained by Driver, who states that following a conflict 'refugees will return to their homes and somehow communities will be rebuilt. The preservation of cultural property aids the rebuilding process by facilitating the re-establishment of community identity by linking their past to their present and their future.'[364]

#### Development

The offence of attacking cultural property has been discussed in the ICTY cases of *Blaškić* and *Kordić and Čerkez* in respect of a similar provision in Article 3(d) of the ICTY statute.[365] Both Trial Chambers stated that the 'damage or destruction must have been committed intentionally to institutions which may clearly be identified as dedicated to religion or education and which were not being used for military purposes at the time of the acts',[366] although the *Kordić and Čerkez* Appeal Chamber noted that 'normal educational institutions' would not be protected under this provision.[367]

[361] See also Article 5, 1907 Hague Regulations IX.

[362] This innovation was proposed by New Zealand and Switzerland, M. Arsanjani, 'The Rome Statute', n. 130 *supra*, pp. 33–4.

[363] See generally M. Sersic, 'Protection of cultural property in time of armed conflict', NYIL, 27 (1996), 3–38, pp. 8–27.

[364] M. Driver, 'The protection of cultural property during wartime', RECIEL, 9 (2000), 1–12, p. 1. For a Second World War case of the destruction of monuments in occupied territory under Article 56, 1907 Hague Regulations, see Trial of *Lingenfelder*, 9 LRTWC 67.

[365] *Blaškić*, Trial Judgement, para. 185, and *Kordić and Čerkez*, Trial Judgement, paras 359–62.

[366] *Blaškić*, Trial Judgement, para. 185, and a similar statement is made in *Kordić and Čerkez*, Trial Judgement, para. 361.

[367] *Kordić and Čerkez*, Appeal Judgement, para. 86. Note that in para. 92 the Court commented that 'normal educational' establishments would in any case be protected as civilian objects.

The *Kordić and Čerkez* Trial Judgement emphasised that 'protection of whatever type will be lost if cultural property . . . is used for military purposes' and according to the *Blaškić* Trial Chamber 'the institutions must not have been in the immediate vicinity of military objectives'.[368] This latter statement is questionable and indeed the *Naletilić and Martinović* Trial Chamber rejected the proposition, as did the *Strugar* Trial Judgement, which emphasised that 'it is the use of cultural property and not its location that determines whether and when the cultural property would lose its protection'.[369] Nevertheless, it is clear that in such circumstances cultural objects may be damaged as a result of an attack on a legitimate military objective and the Court in *Strugar* noted that 'the practical result may be that it cannot be established that the acts which caused destruction of or damage to cultural property were "directed against" that cultural property, rather than the military installation or use in its immediate vicinity'.[370]

### The Rome Statute

The EOC for the offence of attacking cultural objects, in addition to the requirements concerning the international nature of the conflict, state that the perpetrator must have directed an attack the object of which 'was one or more buildings dedicated to religion, education, art, science or charitable purposes, historic monuments, hospitals or places where the sick and wounded are collected, which were not military objectives' and furthermore that the perpetrator must have intended such places to be the object of the attack.[371]

The broad category of objects protected by this article of the Rome Statute and reflected by the EOC has been criticised by Gottlieb.[372] His objection to the joint categorisation of cultural property and hospitals, which at first sight appears to favour cultural property with elevated protection, is that hospitals and places where the sick and wounded are collected are protected due to their 'human cargo' or because of the important services they offer and stand to lose that protected status when humans are not within their confines or their services are no longer needed, whilst cultural property 'should be protected regardless of transient factors such as the presence of people within its borders or their need for a particular service'.[373] Gottlieb also makes the valid criticism that protected

[368] *Kordić and Čerkez*, Trial Judgement, para. 362, and *Blaškić*, Trial Judgement, para. 185.

[369] *Naletilić and Martinović*, Trial Judgement, para. 604, and *Strugar*, Trial Judgement, para. 310.

[370] *Strugar*, Trial Judgement, para. 310. It is arguable that cultural objects should be given more weight in the proportionality test than an ordinary civilian object, given that they are considered worthy of specific protection in international humanitarian law.

[371] EOC, p. 135. A footnote to these Elements explains that the presence in the locality of protected persons under the Geneva Conventions or of police forces retained solely to maintain law and order 'does not by itself render the locality a military objective', *ibid.*, fn. 45.

[372] Y. Gottlieb, 'Criminalizing destruction of cultural property: a proposal for defining new crimes under the Rome Statute of the ICC', Penn St Int'l L Rev, 23 (2005), 857–96.

[373] *Ibid.*, pp. 865–6.

buildings 'sometimes contain . . . more significant heritage than the buildings themselves' but that such contents are not protected by this article or EOC.[374]

The EOC also require that the perpetrator directed an attack, which has already been discussed above and defined as combat action by one or more combatants.[375] Neither the Statute nor the Elements impose the requirement of damage or destruction as a result of the attack and therefore an attack which failed because of a weapons malfunction would still constitute an offence under this article.[376] The offence is not committed if the cultural object concerned has become a military objective. However, this in-built defence is more limited than that provided by Article 27 of the Hague Regulations, which removed protection merely on the basis that the property was being used for 'military purposes', because here it is necessary to demonstrate that the object concerned is making an effective contribution to military action and that its destruction would offer a definite military advantage.[377]

Finally the mental element of this offence is an intentional attack upon the cultural object with awareness of the status of the object as religious, educational, etc., and of the fact that it is not a military objective.

## Article 8(2)(b)(x) Subjecting persons who are in the power of an adverse party to physical mutilation or to medical or scientific experiments of any kind which are neither justified by the medical, dental or hospital treatment of the person concerned nor carried out in his or her interest, and which cause death to or seriously endanger the health of such person or persons

### Origins

The background to this offence was the experiments carried out by the Nazis in concentration camps during the Second World War. The Second World War cases *in re Brandt* and the Trial of *Hoess*,[378] among others,[379] looked at these experiments in depth, particularly condemning them for having been carried out upon persons who had not given their consent.[380] Whilst the Judgement *in re Brandt* attempted to lay out 'moral, ethical and legal concepts' which should be satisfied

[374] *Ibid.*, p. 866.

[375] See discussion *supra*, p. 67.

[376] K. Dörmann, 'Preparatory Commission for the International Criminal Court', n. 63 *supra*, pp. 466–7.

[377] See discussion *supra*, pp. 69–71, and comments by M. Arsanjani, 'The Rome Statute', n. 130 *supra*, pp. 33–4.

[378] *In re Brandt and Others*, 14 AD, 296 (also discussed in the 'Notes on the case' of the Trial of *Milch*, 7 LRTWC 27, pp. 49–53), and Trial of *Hoess*, 7 LRTWC 11.

[379] See also Trial of *Milch*, 7 LRTWC 27, and the Trial of *Pohl* (discussed in 'Notes on the case' of the Trial of *Milch*) 7 LRTWC 27, p. 49.

[380] Trial of *Milch*, 7 LRTWC 27, p. 52.

prior to experimentation upon humans,[381] the 1949 Geneva Conventions prohibited such experiments absolutely.[382]

Mutilation and medical or scientific experiments are prohibited under Articles 13 and 32 of the Third and Fourth Geneva Conventions. An important question is whether there is a difference between these types of experiments and the 'biological' experiments prohibited by Article 12(2) of the First and Second Geneva Conventions. It would appear that the terms are interchangeable, given that the grave breach provisions of each Convention refer only to 'biological' experiments, although the expression is used nowhere else in the Third or Fourth Geneva Convention.[383] Additionally, the UN notes on the Trial of *Hoess* make it clear that the 'medical experiments' at Auschwitz were such in name only and in reality were 'devised at finding the most appropriate means with which to lower or destroy the reproductive power of the Jews, Poles, Czechs and other non-German Nations . . . they were preparatory to the carrying out of the crime of genocide'.[384] It would surely be inappropriate to determine whether an experiment was 'biological' or 'medical or scientific' on the basis of the classification given by the defendant.[385]

Mutilations and medical or scientific experiments which endanger the 'physical or mental health and integrity' of persons 'in the power of the adverse Party' and which are 'not indicated by the state of health of the person concerned' have also been prohibited by Article 11 of AP I, which emphasises that even the consent of the individual concerned cannot justify such actions. The Bothe *et al.* commentary states that 'in the power of the adverse Party' is a wide definition which comprises all prisoners held by the adverse party, including those not entitled to PoW status, and all civilians in occupied territory or civilian aliens in the territory of the adverse Party, whether or not interned.[386] The commentary emphasises that not all mutilation or experimentation is prohibited: the amputation of a limb which was necessary to save life would be permissible, as would medical experiments in the situation where new medication, which has not passed all required tests, is administered to a patient in the attempt to save his life when he would otherwise die.[387]

[381] *Ibid.*, pp. 49–53.

[382] As protected persons cannot renounce their rights under the Geneva Conventions, consent could not now legitimate such experiments.

[383] See the ICRC commentary to Article 32, Geneva Convention IV, Pictet (ed.), *Commentary: IV Convention*, p. 224.

[384] Trial of *Hoess*, 7 LRTWC 11, pp. 24–5.

[385] The *Concise Oxford Dictionary* (Oxford: Clarendon Press, 9th edn, 1995), defines 'medical' as 'of or relating to the science of medicine in general' and 'biological' as 'of or relating to biology or living organisms' and therefore it would appear that when conducted upon humans all 'medical' experiments would in any case also be classifiable as 'biological' experiments.

[386] Bothe *et al.*, *New Rules for Victims*, pp. 111–12.

[387] *Ibid.*, p. 114. See M. Gunn and H. McCoubrey, 'Medical ethics and the laws of armed conflict', JACL, 3 (1998), 133–61, p. 148.

## Development

The offence of scientific or medical experiments has not been alleged in recent conflicts but physical mutilation, such as the amputation of arms, hands, feet, breasts, lips and ears occurred upon a large scale during the conflict in Sierra Leone.[388] The Special Court for Sierra Leone has issued a judgement in the case of *Brima, Kamara and Kanu* considering the definition of mutilation under Article 3(a) of the Special Court's Statute (which is identical to Article 4(2)(a) of AP II).[389]

The Court was clearly strongly influenced by the EOC of the ICC and required that the perpetrator 'intentionally subjected the victim to mutilation, in particular by permanently disfiguring the victim, or by permanently disabling or removing an organ or appendage of the victim' and that this conduct 'was neither justified by the medical, dental or hospital treatment of the victim, nor carried out in the victim's interest'.[390] The Trial Chamber did not require that 'the perpetrator's conduct caused death or seriously endangered the physical or mental health of the victim', but this reflected the fact that the conflict in Sierra Leone was non-international and the EOC under Article 8(2)(c)(i)-2 (the war crime of mutilation in a non-international armed conflict) do not require this element either.[391]

The sole ICTY case to comment on mutilation is the *Tadić* case, where the Court identified conduct as 'sexual mutilation' when a prisoner was forced to bite off one of the testicles of another prisoner, although the offences charged did not explicitly include the offence of mutilation.[392]

## The Rome Statute

The EOC describing mutilation states that the perpetrator must have 'subjected one or more persons to mutilation, in particular by permanently disfiguring the person or persons, or by permanently disabling or removing an organ or appendage'.[393] This definition is fairly clear and would cover the situation of 'sexual mutilation' discussed above.[394] The EOC describing forbidden experiments simply states that the perpetrator must have 'subjected one or more

[388] *Brima, Kamara and Kanu*, Trial Judgement, para. 233, and for a general discussion of the Court see R. Cryer, 'A "special court" for Sierra Leone?', ICLQ, 50 (2001), 435–46.

[389] *Brima, Kamara and Kanu*, Trial Judgement, paras 724–5.

[390] *Ibid.*, para. 724.

[391] *Ibid.*, para. 725, in which the Court overturned its Rule 98 decision on this issue. Compare EOC, pp. 136 and 145.

[392] *Tadić*, Trial Judgement, paras 198, 206 and 237. Offences charged included cruel and inhuman treatment, but Tadić was found not guilty with respect to this incident, as, although present, he did not take an active role.

[393] EOC, p. 136.

[394] *Tadić*, Trial Judgement, paras 198, 206 and 237.

persons to a medical or scientific experiment'.[395] The meaning of such experiments and their relation to biological experiments has been discussed earlier.[396]

The other EOC for the offences of mutilation and medical or scientific experiments are very similar. In addition to the requirements relating to the nature of the conflict as international, they both require that the victim must be in the power of an adverse party, an element which should be defined broadly.[397] Furthermore the conduct or experiment must have 'caused death or seriously endangered the physical or mental health' or additionally, in the case of experiments, the 'integrity' of the persons concerned.[398] It must be noted that this element does not require the victim's health to have *actually* been seriously affected, rather it must have been seriously 'endangered'.[399] Zimmermann interprets this as meaning that 'the act or omission causes an objective danger in the concrete case which . . . could have easily turned into a violation of the health of the victim'.[400]

Finally, it must also be shown that the 'conduct was neither justified by the medical, dental or hospital treatment of the person or persons concerned nor carried out in such person's or persons' interest'.[401] A footnote to this element explains that consent is not a defence to this crime.[402] It further attempts to show when such actions may take place legally by explaining that:

> [t]he crime prohibits any medical procedure which is not indicated by the state of health of the person concerned and which is not consistent with generally accepted medical standards which would be applied under similar medical circumstances to persons who are nationals of the party conducting the procedure and who are in no way deprived of liberty.[403]

This footnote is taken directly from Article 11(1) of AP I, and the ICRC commentary explains that the tempering of generally accepted medical standards with 'an element related to local medical conditions' demonstrates acknowledgement that medical treatment may be unavoidably inadequate in times of armed conflict.[404]

[395] EOC, p. 136. Dörmann suggests that the World Medical Association's guidelines may assist in an interpretation of this Element. The most recent guidelines are entitled 'Ethical principles for medical research involving human subjects', available at: <http://www.wma.net/e/policy/b3.htm>, K. Dörmann, *Elements of War Crimes*, n. 207 *supra*, pp. 236–9.

[396] See *supra*, p. 112.

[397] EOC, p. 136, and Cottier *et al.*, 'Article 8', p. 216.

[398] EOC, p. 136.

[399] Cottier *et al.*, 'Article 8', p. 217.

[400] *Ibid.*

[401] EOC, p. 136.

[402] *Ibid.*, fn. 46.

[403] *Ibid.*

[404] Sandoz *et al.*, *Commentary on the Additional Protocols*, p. 155, and see M. Gunn and H. McCoubrey, 'Medical ethics', n. 387 *supra*, pp. 139–40. Dörmann suggests that the World Medical Association's 'Regulations in time of armed conflict', available at: <http://www.wma.net/e/policy/a20.htm>, may assist in an interpretation of this Element, K. Dörmann, *Elements of War Crimes*, n. 207 *supra*, pp. 232–3.

The Elements do not specify the *mens rea* of this offence and therefore the perpetrator must, according to the default mental element laid down in Article 30, intend to mutilate or perform medical or scientific experiments on the persons concerned and know that the conduct was not justified by their medical treatment and that it was not in their interest. This would mean that an operation, with the consent of the person in the power of an adverse party, to remove a kidney in order to transplant it into the body of a seriously ill relative would, on the face of it, contravene the article. The removal of the organ would amount to mutilation and it would not be justified by the medical condition of the donor, nor would it be in his physical interest, although it could be argued that it was in his emotional interest.[405]

## Article 8(2)(b)(xi) Killing or wounding treacherously individuals belonging to the hostile nation or army

### Origins

Perfidy or treachery has long been prohibited in warfare – indeed, the Lieber Code proclaimed that 'the common law of war allows even capital punishment for clandestine or treacherous attempts to injure an enemy'.[406] More recently Article 23(b) of the Hague Regulations stated that it is forbidden '[t]o kill or wound treacherously individuals belonging to the hostile nation or army' and this is the basis of the offence in the Rome Statute. However, given that Article 24 of the Hague Regulations confirmed the permissibility of ruses of war, the difficulty arose of differentiating between forbidden treachery and permissible ruses.

An example of treacherous killing is the Second World War assassination of SS General Heydrich, who was killed by two Czech nationals in civilian clothing parachuted from a British plane. Kelly states that '[t]he treachery lay . . . in the fact that the attackers hid their intent under the cloak of civilian innocence'.[407] The difference between treacherous killing and ruses was raised by Spaight, who argued that the Second World War air fighting practice of simulating a fall out of control in order to induce attacking aircraft to draw off was a legitimate ruse of war even if the airman intended to resume combat immediately after recovering from the nosedive.[408]

### Development

The prohibition against treacherous killing or wounding was significantly developed by Article 37 of AP I, which defined perfidy as: killing, injuring or

[405] See J. Paust, 'The Preparatory Committee's "definition of crimes": war crimes', Crim LF, 8 (1997), 431–44, pp. 434–5.

[406] Article 101, Lieber Code.

[407] J. Kelly, 'Assassination in wartime', Milit LR, 30 (1965), 101–11, p. 104.

[408] J. Spaight, *Air Power and War Rights*, n. 257 *supra*, pp. 170–2.

capturing an adversary through '[a]cts inviting the confidence of an adversary to lead him to believe that he is entitled to, or is obliged to accord, protection under the rules of international law applicable in armed conflict, with intent to betray that confidence'.[409] The Bothe *et al.* commentary explains that the objectives of this article were 'to reaffirm the prohibitions of Hague Regulations, Art. 23(b), as unambiguously as possible, to define perfidy using objective and easily understandable criteria . . . and to distinguish perfidy from permissible ruses by defining ruses and providing illustrative examples'.[410]

Examples of perfidy given by Article 37 of AP I include 'the feigning of incapacitation by wounds or sickness' and 'the feigning of civilian, noncombatant status'.[411] Article 37 also provides a definition of ruses of war, describing them as 'acts which are intended to mislead an adversary or to induce him to act recklessly but which infringe no rule of international law applicable in armed conflict and which are not perfidious because they do not invite the confidence of an adversary with respect to protection under that law'.[412] However, as the ICRC commentary emphasises, '[a] ruse can never legitimize an act which is not lawful'.[413]

Applying the AP I definition to the assassination of Heydrich and the example of the aeroplane pilot feigning distress, discussed above, the former would clearly constitute perfidy, as the killers invited the confidence of the adversary as to their protected 'civilian' status by wearing civilian clothes, which they used to get close enough to kill him. However, in the latter example, the pilot's actions would have been intended to enable him to escape, not to kill, injure or capture his adversary, and therefore would not amount to perfidy under this article.[414] An example of perfidy or treacherous killing, or at least an attempt to commit the offence, is described in the US report on the Gulf War, where 'an Iraqi officer approached Coalition forces with his hands in the air, indicating his intention to surrender. When near his would-be captors, he drew a concealed pistol from his boot, fired, and was killed during the combat that followed.'[415]

[409] See Article 2, AP I, for a definition of 'rules of international law applicable in armed conflict' and see Sandoz *et al.*, *Commentary on the Additional Protocols*, p. 435.

[410] Bothe *et al.*, *New Rules for Victims*, p. 203, and see p. 204, *ibid.*, which suggests that treacherous killing is broader than perfidy.

[411] This is subject to the provisions of Article 44, AP I.

[412] See generally Sandoz *et al.*, *Commentary on the Additional Protocols*, p. 443, and K. Ipsen, 'War, ruses', pp. 330–1, in Bernhardt (ed.), *Encyclopaedia Vol. 4*.

[413] Sandoz *et al.*, *Commentary on the Additional Protocols*, p. 441.

[414] For further comments on perfidy in air warfare see J. Gómez, 'The law of air warfare', IRRC, 323 (1998), 347–63, p. 356, and regarding perfidy in sea warfare see Article 111, 1994 San Remo Manual, and *San Remo Manual: Explanation*, p. 185.

[415] It is unclear from the report whether anyone was killed or wounded by this man, see US Department of Defense Report, p. 632.

## The Rome Statute

An important question when dealing with this offence under the Rome Statute is whether treacherous wounding or killing is equivalent to perfidy as defined in Article 37 of AP I. Cottier argues, when discussing this offence under the Rome Statute, that 'the terms perfidy and treachery can be understood as synonyms'.[416] This approach is supported by the EOC, which, in very similar language to that of Article 37, state that the perpetrator 'invited the confidence or belief of one or more persons that they were entitled to, or were obliged to accord, protection under the rules of international law applicable in armed conflict',[417] and that the perpetrator intended to betray that confidence or belief and in killing or injuring persons of the adverse party 'made use of that confidence or belief'.[418]

There is an overlap between this offence and the offence under Article 8(2)(b)(vii) of the Rome Statute of 'improper use of a flag of truce, of the flag or of the military insignia and uniform of the enemy or of the United Nations, as well as of the distinctive emblems of the Geneva Conventions, resulting in death or serious personal injury'.[419] However, whilst the two offences have much in common, they are not identical. For example, an offence under both articles would be committed by the use of the flag of truce with intent to shoot soldiers of the adverse party when they approached and thus wound or kill one of them. This would amount to both improper use of the flag of truce, by feigning an intention to negotiate when there was no such intention, and treacherous killing, as the perpetrator was inviting the adverse party to believe that they were obliged to accord him protection, an obligation he was intending to betray.

On the other hand, improper use of the uniform of the hostile party by attacking the enemy whilst wearing their uniform would amount only to an offence under Article 8(2)(b)(vii) and would not constitute treachery, as the confidence obtained from the uniforms would not be in respect of the rules of international law applicable in armed conflict.[420] Finally, an example of treacherous killing, which would not amount to an improper use crime, would be the use of civilian clothing in order to attack soldiers of the adverse party, as it would be inviting and betraying the belief that the adverse party was obliged to accord protection to the individual as a civilian under the laws of armed conflict[421] but would not contravene Article 8(2)(b)(vii), as this does not prohibit improper use of civilian clothing.

It must be emphasised that the offence of treacherous wounding or killing is committed only if the perpetrator made use of the confidence or belief in the entitlement or obligation of protection under the laws of armed conflict in

[416] Cottier *et al.*, 'Article 8', p. 219.
[417] EOC, p. 137.
[418] *Ibid.*
[419] See discussion *supra*, pp. 95–103.
[420] K. Ipsen, 'Perfidy', pp. 130–3, in Bernhardt (ed.), *Encyclopaedia Vol. 4*.
[421] This is subject to the proviso in Article 44(3), AP I.

killing or injuring members of the adverse party. Therefore the use of civilian clothing by a POW in order to escape from the enemy would not be prohibited by the article, nor would feigning death in order to save one's life or to prevent capture.[422] The mental element required is that the perpetrator intended to betray the confidence or belief in the entitlement or obligation of protection under the laws of armed conflict, knowing that he was making use of that confidence or belief which he had created in killing or injuring persons from the adverse party. There is no requirement that the persons who are killed or injured as a result of this offence must be combatants, and they could equally be innocent enemy civilians.

## Article 8(2)(b)(xii) Declaring that no quarter will be given

### Origins

The denial of quarter was condemned by Grotius as early as 1646, and with some exceptions the practice was prohibited by the Lieber Code in 1863.[423] However, it was not until 1899 that the denial of quarter was absolutely prohibited by what is now Article 23(d) of the IV Hague Regulations of 1907. Despite this provision the 'commando order', issued by Hitler and circulated by his officers during the Second World War, clearly breached this prohibition by ordering that 'all members of Allied "commando" units . . . whether armed or not, were to be "slaughtered to the last man" even if they attempted to surrender'.[424] In several war crimes trials following the Second World War German officers were found guilty of ordering that no quarter should be given, both on land, in the cases of *Wickman* and *Meyer*, and at sea, in the case of *Moehle*.[425]

### Development

The prohibition against declaring that no quarter shall be given was reaffirmed in more modern wording in 1977 by Article 40 of AP I, which states that '[i]t is prohibited to order that there shall be no survivors, to threaten an adversary therewith, or to conduct hostilities on this basis'.[426] The British *Manual of Military Law* emphasises that the old rule that quarter could be denied to an enemy under siege who refused to surrender is now obsolete.[427]

[422] Cottier, *et al.*, 'Article 8', p. 224.

[423] H. Grotius, *On the Rights of War and Peace: An Abridged Translation, by William Whewell* (Cambridge: Cambridge University Press, 1853), pp. 375–7, and Articles 60–3, Lieber Code.

[424] 22 Trial of German Major War Criminals (London: HMSO, 1950; hereinafter: *IMT Judgement*), p. 450. See also Trial of *Falkenhorst*, 11 LRTWC 18, especially pp. 27–9.

[425] Trial of *Wickman*, 15 LRTWC 133, Trial of *Meyer*, 4 LRTWC 97, and Trial of *Moehle*, 9 LRTWC 75.

[426] Note that this extends the prohibition against denial of quarter to the threat of such denial as a method of combat, Bothe *et al.*, *New Rules for Victims*, p. 216.

[427] *British Military Manual*, para. 118.

### The Rome Statute

The EOC of this offence incorporate the approach of Article 40 of AP I. In addition to the elements in respect of the nature of the conflict, it must be shown that '[t]he perpetrator declared or ordered that there shall be no survivors' and that such declaration or order 'was given in order to threaten an adversary or to conduct hostilities on the basis that there shall be no survivors'.[428] An additional element requires that the perpetrator 'was in a position of effective command or control over the subordinate forces to which the declaration or order was directed'.[429]

The *actus reus* of this offence is the declaration or order that there shall be no survivors. It is not necessary to show that the order was in fact carried out. Therefore a declaration that 'adversaries proffering surrender be killed or left to a foreseeable death' would amount to this offence,[430] and Kittichaisaree suggests that making surrender impossible by ordering a particular method or means of warfare should amount to a denial of quarter if the accused possesses the mental element of this offence.[431] This mental element is the intention to 'conduct hostilities on the basis that there shall be no survivors' or 'to threaten an adversary'. The alternative *mens rea* ensures that a superior who uses the declaration that no quarter shall be given in order to strike fear into an adversary, perhaps to make him surrender immediately or to withdraw, without the intention that the order be carried out, will still commit this offence.

Finally, the Elements state that the order or declaration that there shall be no survivors must be given by a superior to subordinate forces. A declaration that there should be no quarter given by a soldier to others of his rank and above would not, therefore, breach this prohibition.[432] The expression 'effective command and control' encompasses both those superiors with official, *de jure*, command and those with *de facto* command over troops,[433] such as an officer who assumes command of a unit which has been cut off from its *de jure* superior.

## Article 8(2)(b)(xiii) Destroying or seizing the enemy's property unless such destruction or seizure be imperatively demanded by the necessities of war

### Origins

This offence is based upon Article 23(g) of the Regulations attached to the 1907 Hague Convention IV and bears similarities to the grave breach of

[428] EOC, p. 137.

[419] *Ibid.*

[430] Cottier *et al.*, 'Article 8', p. 226.

[431] K. Kittichaisaree, *International Criminal Law* (Oxford: Oxford University Press, 2001), p. 174.

[432] Although he could be liable for inducing the offence under Article 25(3)(b), Rome Statute, provided that the offence occurred.

[433] See W. Fenrick, 'Article 28, responsibility of commanders and other superiors', pp. 515–22 in O.Triffterer, *Commentary on the Rome Statute*, p. 518.

extensive destruction and appropriation of property not justified by military necessity.[434] Whilst Article 23(g) is situated in Section II, Chapter I, of the Hague Regulations dealing with hostilities and means of injuring the enemy, sieges and bombardments, this does not necessarily restrict the application of the offence to the battlefield.[435] Indeed, Articles 46, 53, 55 and 56 of the 1907 Hague Regulations IV, which lay down limits for belligerent dealings with property, are situated in Section III of the Convention, dealing with military authority in occupied territories.

Second World War war crimes trials in respect of seizure or destruction of property under the 1907 Hague Regulations emphasise that a belligerent does not through occupation 'acquire the right to dispose of property in that territory, except according to the strict rules laid down in the Regulations'.[436] Indeed, the *Flick* Trial noted that this offence may be committed, even though the original seizure was within the rules set down in the 1907 Hague Regulations, if the 'subsequent detention from the rightful owners was wrongful'.[437] Finally, the notes on the case of *Szabados* comment that the exception of imperative military necessity can only 'exist in the course of active military operations'.[438]

### Development

The crime of destroying or seizing the enemy's property unless such destruction or seizure be imperatively demanded by the necessities of war has been developed by the rules on the protection of property in the Geneva Conventions of 1949. Therefore, when deciding whether military necessity admits of seizure or destruction, any particular protection of property set out in the Geneva Conventions must also be considered.[439]

The Iran–Kuwait Gulf conflict raised two potential issues. First, 'the abolition of the Kuwaiti dinar and its replacement by the Iraqi dinar at an artificial exchange rate of 1:1', when the pre-war rate had been 12:1, as McCoubrey observed, had the effect of devastating personal and public savings and amounted to 'a seizure of private and public assets without compensation upon a huge scale'.[440] Second, there was the environmental damage caused by Iraq. In respect of this, Liebler concluded that the expression 'property' indicates that

[434] Discussed *supra*, pp. 44–9, and therefore identical aspects of the offence under this article will not be discussed in detail.

[435] This is supported by Trial of *Szabados*, 9 LRTWC 59.

[436] *Krupp* Trial, 10 LRTWC 69, p. 134, and see comments in *In re Weizsaecker and Others* (*Ministries* Trial), 16 AD (1949), 344, pp. 360–1. See generally W. Downey, 'Captured enemy property: booty of war and seized enemy property', AJIL, 44 (1950), 488–504.

[437] *Flick* Trial, 9 LRTWC 1, p. 23.

[438] Trial of *Szabados*, 9 LRTWC 59.

[439] Discussion, pp. 44–5.

[440] H. McCoubrey, 'Civilians in occupied territory', n. 332 *supra*, pp. 214–15.

the object seized or destroyed must be the subject of ownership in order to be protected, and that 'objects such as the climate, the atmosphere, the sea and marine life, which are not capable of being the objects of such a "proprietary relationship" ' could not be characterized as 'property'.[441] Lijnzaad and Tanja concurred with this conclusion, but considered that this offence may be helpful for environmental damage to real or personal property.[442]

## The Rome Statute

An important question is the scope of this offence under the Rome Statute and whether it is broader than the grave breach of extensive destruction and appropriation of property prohibited under Article 8(2)(a)(iv) of the Rome Statute.[443] It has already been suggested that this offence should not be restricted to means and methods of warfare, and this is supported by Zimmermann, who comments that, as Article 8(2)(b)(ii) and (iv) already deals with means and methods of warfare, such a restriction of this offence would render it largely superfluous.[444] He therefore argues that this offence should apply only to destruction or seizure of property located in occupied territories.[445] However, it is submitted that in light of the history of the article it should apply to both situations and that, in the case of an overlap, the prosecutor should charge the more appropriate offence in the circumstances. Furthermore, unlike Article 8(2)(a)(vi), this offence is not restricted to the property of 'protected persons' but applies to 'the enemy's property', which should be read as including all property of the belligerent State and all the property of its nationals or those acting on behalf of the belligerent State.[446]

Another question which arises is whether there is a difference between the word 'appropriation' used in the grave breach provision in respect of property and the expression 'seizing' used in this provision. The ICRC working paper on Article 8(2)(b) comments that 'the terms "seizure" and "appropriation" seem to have different meanings' but did not discover a specific meaning for the word 'seizure' in international law.[447] A dictionary definition of 'appropriation' is to 'take possession of, especially without authority', whereas the dictionary

[441] A. Leibler, 'Deliberate wartime environmental damage', n. 179 *supra*, pp. 105–6.

[442] L. Lijnzaad and G. Tanja, 'Protection of the environment in times of armed conflict: the Iraq–Kuwait war', NILR, 40 (1993), 169–99, p. 176, and A. Leibler, 'Deliberate wartime environmental damage', n. 179 *supra*, p. 106.

[443] This was suggested by the ICRC working paper on the Elements of Crimes of Article 8(2)(b), n. 351 *supra*, comments on Article 8(2)(b)(xiii).

[444] Cottier *et al.*, 'Article 8', p. 228.

[445] *Ibid.*, p. 229.

[446] *Ibid.*, p. 230.

[447] ICRC working paper on the Elements of Crimes of Article 8(2)(b), n. 351 *supra*, comments on Article 8(2)(b)(xiii).

definition of 'seize' is 'to take hold of forcibly or suddenly', or to be 'put in possession of'.[448] It therefore seems that for all practical purposes these words must have the same meaning under international law, as, by definition, all destruction or taking of property by a belligerent during conflict or in occupied territory would be carried out by force, coercion or compulsion. Kittichaisaree suggests that seizure 'encompasses any kind of depriving a person of the property legally belonging to him; it may be temporary or permanent in nature' and this definition, if expanded to include taking property belonging to legal personalities or to the State, would be an appropriate description of the expression 'seizure'.[449]

The EOC of this offence follow the wording of this article in the Rome Statute closely and require that the perpetrator 'destroyed or seized certain property' and that the property 'was property of a hostile party'.[450] Furthermore, the property must have been 'protected from that destruction or seizure under the international law of armed conflict' and the perpetrator was 'aware of the factual circumstances that established the status of the property'.[451] The final element, apart from those in respect of the nature of the conflict, requires that the 'destruction or seizure was not justified by military necessity'.[452]

Therefore the *mens rea* of this offence, taking into account the wording of the Elements and the default mental element of Article 30 of the Rome Statute, is that the perpetrator must have intended to destroy or seize property and must have been aware that such property belonged to a hostile party and was aware of the factual circumstances which established the protected status of the property. The *actus reus* of this offence is the destruction or seizure of protected property not justified by military necessity.

Military necessity has been discussed in respect of Article 8(2)(a)(iv).[453] It is interesting, however, that the Elements do not repeat the phrase 'imperative' military necessity. Zimmermann suggests that the expression 'imperatively demanded by the necessities of war' in this article means that 'there are no other means to secure military safety'.[454] Therefore, although the Elements do not use the expression 'imperative', the wording of the Rome Statute demands that for this offence a high level of necessity, such as that suggested by Zimmermann, is applied by the Court.

[448] *Concise Oxford Dictionary*, n. 385 *supra*, although in English law 'appropriation' has the specific legal meaning of 'any assumption by a person of the rights of an owner', s. 3, Theft Act 1968. See discussion *infra*, pp. 128–9.

[449] K. Kittichaisaree, *International Criminal Law*, n. 431 *supra*, p. 174.

[450] EOC, pp. 137–8.

[451] *Ibid.*

[452] *Ibid.*

[453] See discussion *supra*, pp. 45–6.

[454] Cottier *et al.*, 'Article 8', p. 232.

## Article 8(2)(b)(xiv) Declaring abolished, suspended or inadmissible in a court of law the rights and actions of the nationals of the hostile party

### Origins

This offence is based upon the first paragraph of Article 23(h) of the 1907 Hague Regulations. However, even at the time of its adoption the offence caused some confusion. Higgins suggested in his commentary on the Hague Conventions that this article constitutes a 'reversal of a rule of the English and American Common Law that contracts entered into by British subjects and subjects of the belligerent states, before the outbreak of war, become extinguished or suspended according to their nature'.[455] This view of Article 23(h) as purely affecting contracts between the civilians of opposing belligerents was questioned by Professor Oppenheim in a letter to the Foreign Office in 1911. The reply from the Foreign Office reasoned that, owing to its placing in the section dealing with hostilities in the Hague Regulations, the effect of Article 23(h) was restricted to the armies in the field and it was intended to prevent a commander from attempting to 'terrorize the inhabitants of the theatre of war by depriving them of existing opportunities of obtaining relief to which they are entitled in respect of private claims'.[456]

However, this reply is not without ambiguities, as it is unclear whether the prohibition extends to criminal law actions in addition to civil actions. In this respect Spaight commented that the *Times* reports of the work of the Hague Conference showed that the German delegate proposed 'that the inviolability which the existing Convention secures for private property should be extended to contracts, and that the exigencies of military occupation should not furnish sufficient reason for annulling these'.[457] He concluded that the article protects the civil law actions of inhabitants of occupied territories.[458] This approach was supported by a 1915 English Court of Appeal case, *Porter v. Freudenberg*, in which Lord Reading stated that Article 23(h) was 'to be read, in our judgement, as forbidding any declaration by the military commander of a belligerent force in the occupation of the enemy's territory which will prevent the inhabitants of that territory from using their courts of law in order to assert or protect their civil rights'.[459]

[455] A. Higgins, *The Hague Peace Conferences*, n. 229 *supra*, p. 265.

[456] L. Oppenheim, 'Letter to the Foreign Office', 28 February 1911, and F. Campbell, 'Letter from Foreign Office to L. Oppenheim', 27 March 1911, reprinted in 'International Law Pamphlets', Lodon School of Economics Library, E(I) 651–60, 665.

[457] J. Spaight, *War Rights on Land*, n. 271 *supra*, p. 141, footnoted as *Times*, 4 July 1907.

[458] *Ibid.*, p. 141.

[459] *Porter v. Freudenberg*, All ER Reprint [1914–15], 918, p. 929.

## Development

The treatment of inhabitants of occupied territories during the Second World War gave rise to a discussion of Article 23(h) in post-war tribunals. The Netherlands Special Court of Cassation in the Trial of *Zuehlke* held that Article 23(h) of the Hague Regulations 'was meant only to protect rights at civil law' and therefore did not apply in respect of a charge of detaining civilians on account of their race or religion contrary to the Netherlands constitution.[460] However, a US military tribunal in the Trial of *Altstötter* held that the introduction and enforcement of discriminatory laws against Poles and Jews, the purpose of which was their extermination, was a violation of Article 23(h),[461] which suggests that criminal rights and actions are also protected by this article.

This approach is supported by Freeman, who argues that:

> outrageous devices such as refusal of counsel and prohibition of any plea other than guilty in abrogation of essential rights guaranteed by the local law; the exclusion of entire groups of the population from legal recourse; and the application of retroactivity of the criminal law could also be viewed as a violation of Article 23(h) of the regulations.[462]

However, there have been no recent deliberations in respect of this article and the contents of this prohibition remain unclear.

## The Rome Statute

The ICRC working paper for the Preparatory Committee stated that the object of this offence was 'to prohibit belligerents from depriving enemy subjects by legislation or otherwise of the means of enforcing their legal rights through resort to courts'.[463] However, the EOC of this article do not greatly clarify the definition given in Article 8(2)(b)(xvi) and state that the perpetrator must have 'effected the abolition, suspension or termination of admissibility in a court of law of certain rights or actions', that this abolition, suspension or termination must have been directed at, and intended to be directed at, 'the nationals of a hostile party'.[464]

The question of whether these rights and actions can include criminal law rights in addition to civil rights and actions is left unclear. Cottier argues that it is unlikely that the delegates at the diplomatic conference at Rome intended to restrict the offence to civil contracts and claims, arguing that '[n]othing in the wording of the article necessarily restricts it to civil claims', and that it is possible that the

460 Trial of *Zuehlke*, 14 LRTWC 139, p. 145.

461 Trial of *Altstötter*, 6 LRTWC 1, pp. 62–3.

462 A. Freeman, 'War crimes by enemy nationals administering justice in occupied territory', AJIL, 41 (1947), 579–610, p. 600.

463 ICRC working paper on the Elements of Crimes of Article 8(2)(b), n. 351 *supra*, comments on Article 8(2)(b)(xiv).

464 EOC, p. 138. Use of the word 'effected' requires a result, Lee (ed.), *ICC: Elements*, pp. 173–4.

Second World War 'abolition of most or all rights of Poles and Jews or other groups in occupied territories or in Germany had influenced the support for this provision and its inclusion in the ICC Statute'.[465]

Therefore, whilst there is still some doubt, it would appear that the mental element of this offence is an intention to suspend or remove certain rights or actions in a court of law, either civil or criminal, by nationals of the hostile party and that the *actus reus* of the offence is the suspension or removal of those rights.[466] The weight of authority suggests that the offence applies in occupied territory, but it may also apply to aliens in the territory of one of the belligerents. Cottier comments that the wording 'the rights and actions' suggests 'that the denial must be a general one . . . [but] the abolition, suspension and inadmissibility of the rights and actions of solely one particular group within the entirety of adversary nationals, for instance and ethnic group, should also qualify'.[467]

## Article 8(2)(b)(xv) Compelling the nationals of the hostile party to take part in the operations of war directed against their own country, even if they were in the belligerent's service before the commencement of the war

### Origins

This article is based on the second paragraph of Article 23(h) of the IV Hague Regulations of 1907 and is very similar to the grave breach of 'compelling a prisoner of war or other protected person to serve in the forces of a hostile power' prohibited under Article 8(2)(a)(v) of the Rome Statute.[468] However, this offence appears to be broader, as the prohibition extends to all 'operations of war' against a national's own country. The expression 'operations of war' has been described as 'unsatisfactorily vague' by Higgins,[469] but Spaight suggested that it would include such acts as 'building fortifications, making munitions, repairing arms, or giving information as to the enemy's position and numbers'.[470]

### Development

Whilst the post-Second World War war crimes trials were quick to condemn forced conscription, they were slower to deal with the issue of employing prisoners of war or the civilians of occupied territory in operations of war.[471] Indeed, as the

[465] Cottier *et al.*, 'Article 8', p. 234.

[466] For a discussion of the rights of a defendant in a criminal trial see *supra*, pp. 51–2.

[467] Cottier *et al.*, 'Article 8', p. 235.

[468] *Supra*, pp. 49–50.

[469] A. Higgins, *The Hague Peace Conferences*, n. 229 *supra*, p. 268.

[470] J. Spaight, *War Rights on Land*, n. 271 *supra*, p. 152.

[471] Trial of *Wagner*, 3 LRTWC 23, *In re Weizsaecker and Others*, 16 AD (1949), 344, p. 357, and see discussion *supra*, pp. 49–50.

notes on the Trial of *Von Leeb and Others* comment, 'prosecuting staffs have preferred to charge accused with exposing prisoners of war to danger rather than with employing them in work directly connected with operations of war, when the facts of cases could have given reasonable prospects of a conviction on either'.[472] However, the Trial *of Krauch* condemned using prisoners of war for work with a direct relation to war operations and held that the employment of prisoners of war in coal mines was contrary to the laws of war.[473]

## The Rome Statute

The EOC of this offence are similar to those for the grave crime of compelling a protected person to serve in the forces of a hostile power under Article 8(2)(a)(v).[474] They require that the perpetrator 'coerced one or more persons by act or threat to take part in military operations against that person's own country or forces' and that '[s]uch person or persons were nationals of a hostile power'.[475] Given that no specific *mens rea* is laid down, the default mental element of Article 30 applies and the perpetrator would have to have intended to coerce the persons to take part in the military operations against their own forces and to have been aware that they were nationals of a hostile power.

The concept of coercion by act or threat has already been discussed in respect of Article 8(2)(a)(v), as has the expression 'military operations'.[476] However, it is interesting that the EOC use the expression 'military operations' rather than 'operations of war'.[477] Although Higgins suggests that the latter is wider in scope,[478] the Preparatory Commission cannot be taken to have intended to narrow the scope of this prohibition and therefore either the two expressions must be read as identical in meaning or the wording of the Rome Statute must prevail.[479]

It is left to the Court to decide in the circumstances of the case whether employing hostile nationals upon a particular type of work is prohibited by this offence. Cottier suggests that the expression 'operations of war' is wider than direct participation in hostilities and includes 'other implication in war-related work'.[480] Guidance may be taken from the EOC proposed by Costa Rica, Hungary and Switzerland, which included the Element '[t]he compelled acts were not permissible as prisoner of war or civilian labour, as defined under international humanitarian

[472] Trial of *Von Leeb and Others*, 12 LRTWC 1, p. 101.

[473] Trial of *Krauch*, 10 LRTWC 1, p. 54, although it is not entirely clear to what extent the dangers of working in a coal mine and the conditions faced by the PoWs contributed to this decision.

[474] Discussed *supra*, p. 50.

[475] EOC, p. 138.

[476] Discussed *supra*, p. 50.

[477] See Lee, *ICC: Elements*, p. 175.

[478] A. Higgins, *The Hague Peace Conferences*, n. 229 *supra*, p. 269.

[479] See Article 21(1)(a), Rome Statute.

[480] Cottier *et al.*, 'Article 8', p. 236.

law'.[481] This suggests that work specifically allowed under international humanitarian law would not breach the prohibition but any other work must be scrutinised as potentially involving 'operations of war'.[482]

## Article 8(2)(b)(xvi) Pillaging a town or place, even when taken by assault

### Origins

Pillage has been forbidden since the 1863 Lieber Code,[483] but this article of the Rome Statute is based upon the prohibition of pillage in the second sentence of Article 23(h) of the IV Hague Regulations. After the Second World War the Nuremberg Charter included the similar offence of 'plunder of public or private property', an offence also charged under Council Control Law (CCL) No. 10 in the *Krupp* Trial among others.[484] However, neither pillage nor plunder was adequately defined under international law, and the words have often been used synonymously.[485] Steinkamm commented that in the traditional sense pillage implied 'an element of violence' but that '[t]he notion of appropriation or obtaining against the owner's will . . . with the intention of unjustified gain, is inherent in the idea of pillage so that it is also perceived as a form of theft through exploitation of the circumstances and fortunes of war'.[486]

### Development

The prohibition of pillage was repeated by Article 33 of the Fourth Geneva Convention, and the commentary states that this prohibition 'concerns not only pillage through individual acts without the consent of the military authorities, but also organized pillage . . . it leaves no loophole'.[487] Furthermore, the commentary contends, this prohibition 'is applicable to the territory of a Party to the conflict as well as to occupied territories. It guarantees all types of property, whether they belong to private persons or to communities or the State.'[488]

481 Proposal submitted by Costa Rica, Hungary and Switzerland on certain provisions of Article 8(2)(b) of the Rome Statute of the International Criminal Court, submitted to the Preparatory Commission for the International Criminal Court Working Group on Elements of Crimes, 26 July–13 August 1999, available at: <http://www.igc.apc.org/icc>.

482 See Articles 50 and 51 of 1949 Geneva Conventions III and IV on permitted labour.

483 Article 44, Lieber Code.

484 *Krupp* Trial, 10 LRTWC 69, p. 138, and see Trial of *Baus*, 9 LRTWC 68, and Trial of *Bommer*, 9 LRTWC 62.

485 A. Steinkamm, 'Pillage', pp. 139–40, in Bernhardt, *Encyclopaedia Vol. 4*, p. 139, and G. Schwarzenberger, *International Law as applied by International Courts and Tribunals*, Vol. II, *The Law of Armed Conflict* (London: Stevens, 1968), p. 250.

486 *Ibid.*

487 Pictet (ed.), *Commentary: IV Convention*, p. 226.

488 *Ibid.*, pp. 226–7, and see *Naletilić and Martinović*, Trial Judgement, para. 615.

The crime of pillage has been examined by the ICTY in respect of the offence of 'plunder of public or private property' under Article 3(e) of the ICTY Statute.[489] The *Čelebici* Judgement held that action taken by an Occupying Power to levy contributions and make requisitions in accordance with international humanitarian law does not amount to pillage.[490] However, it supported the commentary to the 1949 Geneva Conventions by emphasising that both 'looting committed by individual soldiers for their private gain' and 'the organized seizure of property undertaken within the framework of a systematic economic exploitation of occupied territory' are prohibited under this offence.[491]

The Special Court for Sierra Leone in the *Fofana and Kondewa* case considered the definition of pillage under count 5 of the indictment, which was entitled 'Looting and burning'.[492] The court held that pillage was intentional unlawful appropriation of property without the consent of the owner and found that '[d]estruction of property by burning . . . does not, by itself, necessarily involve any unlawful appropriation' and so 'while both looting and burning deprive the owner of their property, the two actions are distinct since the latter crime may be committed without appropriation *per se*'.[493]

No decisions upon whether the expressions 'pillage' and 'plunder' were synonymous were made by the *Čelebici* Trial Chamber, which viewed it as unnecessary in this case, although the Judgement referred to the fact that 'pillage in the traditional sense implied an element of violence'.[494] The *Kordić and Čerkez* Appeal Chamber acknowledged that plunder included acts traditionally described as 'pillage' but did not attempt to draw any distinction between them.[495]

## The Rome Statute

Zimmermann acknowledges that there is no official definition of the word 'pillage' and suggests that it should be understood as 'the unauthorised appropriation or

[489] See also comments on looting by Iraqi soldiers in US Department of Defense Report at p. 620.

[490] *Čelebici*, Trial Judgement, paras 587–91, followed in *Blaškić*, Trial Judgement, para. 184, *Kordić and Čerkez*, Trial Judgement, paras 351–3, and the *Kordić and Čerkez* Appeal Judgement, para. 53. See also *Jelisić*, Trial Judgement, para. 48, which defined plunder as 'the fraudulent appropriation of public or private funds belonging to the enemy'.

[491] *Čelebici*, Trial Judgement, para. 590.

[492] *Fofana and Kondewa*, Trial Judgement, paras 165–6.

[493] *Ibid.* Note that because of the wide definition of appropriation in English criminal law set out in the case of *R. v. Morris, Anderton and Burnside*, [1984] AC, 320 (that appropriation involves the assumption of any of the rights of the owner), and *R. v. Gomez*, [1993] AC 442 (appropriation may exist notwithstanding consent), burning another person's property would amount to an appropriation. Nevertheless, it is not necessarily apposite for such a wide interpretation of appropriation to be imported into international law.

[494] *Čelebici*, Trial Judgement, para. 591.

[495] *Kordić and Čerkez*, Appeal Judgement, para. 79, approving of the definition of plunder in the *Kordić and Čerkez* Trial Judgement, para. 352, which in turn used the definition given in the *Čelebici* Trial Judgement, para. 591.

obtaining by force of property in order to confer possession of it on oneself or on a third party'.[496] This definition includes the concept of taking property by force which is referred to by the tribunal in the *Čelebici* Judgement.[497] However, the EOC do not include this concept, requiring only, in addition to the Elements in respect of the nature of the conflict, that the perpetrator 'appropriated certain property' 'without the consent of the owner' and 'intended to deprive the owner of the property and to appropriate it for private or personal use'.[498]

A footnote to this last element states that 'appropriations justified by military necessity cannot constitute the crime of pillaging'.[499] This is in line with the decision of the *Čelebici* Judgement discussed above.[500] The ICTY Judgement in *Hadžihasanović and Kubura* also provide for the exception of necessity to this offence.[501] The Trial Chamber sets out conditions for this defence, including that the acts of plunder were the only means to avoid 'a real and imminent threat of severe and irreparable harm to life' which was not voluntarily brought about by the perpetrator him or herself and were not disproportionate.[502]

In practical terms this definition does not alter the nature of the offence. For example, in a conflict situation it is difficult to imagine pillage taking place in the presence of the owner without the use of force or at the least coercion. The Elements do not expand upon the type of property which may be the subject of pillage and it is therefore submitted that, in light of the history of this offence, Zimmermann is correct in stating that 'the prohibition extends to all types of property, whether they belong to private persons or to communities or the State'.[503]

Finally, the mental element of the offence is defined as the intention to deprive the owner of the property and 'to appropriate it for private or personal use'. This clearly prohibits the situation where a soldier takes possession of an article of value, such as jewellery, for personal enrichment. However, this wording should not exclude the situation of mass organised pillage upon the orders of commanding officers where the individual soldier does not gain personally, referred to in the *Čelebici* Judgement as 'the organized seizure of property undertaken within the framework of a systematic economic exploitation of occupied territory'.[504] The concept of 'private use' should be read as including such a situation, or the EOC would have unacceptably restricted this provision.

[496] Cottier *et al.*, 'Article 8', p. 238.

[497] *Supra*, p. 128.

[498] EOC, pp. 138–9.

[499] EOC, fn. 47 on p. 139.

[500] See *Čelebici*, Trial Judgement, paras 587–91, referred to at n. 490 *supra*.

[501] *Hadžihasanović and Kubura*, Trial Judgement, para. 53.

[502] *Ibid.* Note that Article 55, Geneva Convention IV, allows the requisition of materials for occupying forces in wider situations provided that the requirements of the civilian population have been taken into account and provided fair value is paid for requisitioned goods.

[503] Cottier *et al.*, 'Article 8', p. 238.

[504] *Čelebici*, Trial Judgement, para. 590.

## Article 8(2)(b)(xvii) Employing poison or poisoned weapons

### Origins

The use of poisoned weapons has been condemned since the time of Grotius and was prohibited by the Lieber Code.[505] This offence in the Rome Statute is taken from Article 23(a) of the 1907 Hague Regulations, which state that it is especially forbidden to 'employ poison or poisoned weapons' but does not define poison. In the absence of a legal definition of poison, the dictionary definition of poison as 'a substance that when introduced into or absorbed by a living organism causes death or injury, especially one that kills by rapid action even in a small quantity' should be taken as a guide.[506]

### Development

There are no recorded post-Second World War trials in respect of the use of poison or poisoned weapons,[507] nor have any ICTY or International Criminal Tribunal on Rwanda (ICTR) indictments charged this offence.

### The Rome Statute

The EOC relating to the use of poison and poisoned weapons do not define 'poison'. In addition to the requirements relating to the nature of the conflict, they state that the perpetrator must employ 'a substance or a weapon that releases a substance as a result of its employment'.[508] Then, rather than defining poison, the Elements establish a 'specific threshold with regard to the effects of the substance'[509] and require that 'it causes death or serious damage to health in the ordinary course of events, through its toxic properties'.[510] No specific mental element is provided in the EOC and so, applying the default mental element of Article 30, the perpetrator must intentionally use a specific substance or weapon and know that in the ordinary cause of events the substance or weapon would cause death or serious injury to health through its toxic properties.

[505] Article 70, Lieber Code, and see H. Grotius, *On the Rights of War and Peace*, n. 423 *supra*, pp. 327–8.

[506] *Concise Oxford Dictionary*, n. 385 *supra*. A similar definition is suggested by A. Thomas and A. Thomas, *Legal Limits on the Use of Chemical and Biological Weapons* (Dallas TX: Southern Methodist University Press, 1970), p. 50.

[507] W. Fenrick, 'New developments in the law concerning the use of conventional weapons in armed conflict', Can. YBIL, 19 (1981), 229–56, p. 237.

[508] EOC, p. 139.

[509] K. Dörmann, 'Preparatory Commission for the International Criminal Court', n. 63 *supra*, p. 476.

[510] EOC, p. 139.

## Article 8(2)(b)(xviii) Employing asphyxiating, poisonous or other gases, and all analogous liquids, materials or devices

### Origins

The 1899 Hague Declaration II prohibited the 'use of projectiles the sole object of which is the diffusion of asphyxiating or deleterious gases' in war between States Parties. However, this did not prevent the use of gas in the First World War, when 90,000 men were killed by chlorine, mustard and other chemical agents and another million were blinded, disfigured or injured,[511] although technically it could be argued that the Germans had opened cylinders rather than used projectiles.[512]

The prohibition was reaffirmed in broader terms by the 1925 Geneva Protocol, which forbade the 'use in war of asphyxiating, poisonous or other gases and of all analogous liquids materials or devices', a definition which forms the basis of this article of the Rome Statute.[513] The impact of the Protocol was restricted to a prohibition of first use of such weapons owing to a series of reservations.[514] However, in terms of the actual prohibition, Baxter and Buergenthal comment that the Geneva Protocol 'could hardly have been expressed in more sweeping and all-embracing language'.[515] In view of this it can be said with certainty that the Protocol does not merely prohibit the use of toxic substances which are gaseous at room temperature but also prohibits atomised toxic liquids.[516] Falk comments that '[t]he operative clause of the Protocol, in effect, restates a preexisting prohibition on poison gas that clearly pertained to chemical weaponry'.[517]

McDougal and Feliciano observe that the Geneva Protocol's 'prohibition is cast in language of such inclusive compass as to permit future interpreters mechanically to subsume thereunder even nonlethal chemical agents, which produce merely temporary if distressing effects entailing no enduring damage to the human

[511] Organisation for the Prohibition of Chemical Weapons, Fact Sheet 1, 'The Chemical Weapons Convention and the OPCW: how they came about', available at: <http://www.opcw.org>, and see M. Eshbaugh, 'The Chemical Weapons Convention: with every step forward, we take two steps back', Ariz J Int'l & Comp L, 18 (2001), 209–44, pp. 212–13, who gives slightly different figures.

[512] M. Eshbaugh, *ibid.*, p. 216.

[513] The 1925 Geneva Protocol also extended this prohibition 'to the use of bacteriological methods of warfare' but as this is not included in the Rome Statute it will not be discussed here.

[514] M. Bothe, 'Chemical warfare', pp. 83–5 in Bernhardt (ed.), *Encyclopaedia Vol. 3*, p. 85.

[515] R. Baxter and T. Buergenthal, 'Legal aspects of the Geneva Protocol of 1925', AJIL, 64 (1970), 853–79, p. 856.

[516] See the OPCW website, discussion of 'Chemical warfare agents', available at: <http://www.opcw.org>.

[517] R. Falk, 'Inhibiting reliance on biological weaponry: the role and relevance of international law', Am UJ Int'l L & Pol'y, 1 (1986), 17–34, p. 21, and see K. Fitzgerald, 'The Chemical Weapons Convention: inadequate protection from chemical warfare', Suffolk Transnat'l LR, 20 (1997), 425–48, p. 430, and M. Bothe, 'War crimes', n. 198 *supra*, p. 407.

organism'.[518] This raises the contentious issue of whether the Geneva Protocol prohibits the use of non-lethal riot gases or herbicides,[519] the United States being the main proponent of the view that such non-lethal substances are excluded from its ambit.[520]

## Development

The United States used both CS gas and defoliants in Vietnam, prior to ratification of the 1925 Geneva Protocol.[521] Partially in response to this the General Assembly adopted a resolution which recognised that the Geneva Protocol prohibited 'all biological and chemical methods of warfare' and declared that the use in international armed conflicts of '[a]ny chemical agents of warfare – chemical substances, whether gaseous, liquid or solid – which might be employed because of their direct toxic effects on man, animals or plants' were prohibited.[522] Although upon ratification of the Geneva Protocol the United States maintained its position that non-lethal gases or defoliants were not prohibited, an Executive Order prescribed new limited circumstances in which such substances would be used.[523]

The Geneva Protocol was briefly analysed by the ICJ in the *Nuclear Weapons* Advisory Opinion in the context of whether it could be found to prohibit the use of nuclear weapons. Whilst the Court found that '[c]hemical and bacteriological weapons were then prohibited by the 1925 Geneva Protocol',[524] it explained that

[518] M. McDougal and F. Feliciano, *The International Law of War: Transnational Coercion and World Public Order* (New Haven CT: New Haven Press, 1994), p. 636.

[519] This is controversial, as the French text used the words 'ou similaires', a more restrictive expression than 'or other gases', used in the English text, I. Detter, *The Law of War* (Cambridge: Cambridge University Press, 2nd edn, 2000), p. 256, and R. Baxter and T. Buergenthal, 'Legal aspects of the Geneva Protocol of 1925', n. 515 *supra*, pp. 856–7.

[520] International Affairs Department of the British Council of Churches, Friends' Peace and International Relations Committee and the UN Association, 'Geneva Protocol: CS gas' (London: Headley, 1970, held in BLPES, Special Pamphlets Collection, HU B49), US position, para. 4, other UN member positions, para. 11. See also UK support of the US view, statement of S. Stewart, Secretary of State, Foreign and Commonwealth Office, Official Report, Fifth Series, Hansard, Vol. 795 (1969–70), written answers, 2 February 1970, cols 17–18.

[521] See H. Levie, 'Weapons of war', pp. 153–60, in P. Trooboff (ed.), *Law and Responsibility in Warfare: The Vietnam Experience* (Chapel Hill NC: University of North Carolina Press, 1975).

[522] General Assembly Resolution (GA Res.) 2603 A (XXIV), 16 December 1969, opposed only by the United States, Australia and Portugal.

[523] Statement by the President on the Geneva Protocol, 22 January 1975, ILM, 14 (1975), p. 299 and United States, 'Executive order on the renunciation of certain uses in war of chemical herbicides and riot control agents', 8 April 1975, *ibid.*, p. 794. See comments by F. Kalshoven, 'Arms, armaments and international law', 191 Rec des Cours (1985) II, 183–341, pp. 268–70, and D. Fidler, 'The international legal implications of "non-lethal" weapons', Mich J Int'l L, 21 (1999), 51–100, pp. 72–4.

[524] *Legality of the Threat or Use of Nuclear Weapons*, Advisory Opinion, ICJ Rep (1996), 226, para. 76.

the term 'analogous materials or devices' in the Protocol has been understood in the practice of States as 'covering weapons whose prime, or even exclusive, effect is to poison or asphyxiate' and therefore it is clear that the Protocol does not prohibit nuclear weapons.[525]

A recent allegation of use of chemical weapons, contrary to the Geneva Protocol, was the use of mustard and nerve gas in the 1980–88 Iran–Iraq war.[526] This use was condemned as contrary to international law by a Security Council resolution but no legal action was taken.[527]

## The Rome Statute

The EOC for this offence, in addition to those relating to the nature of the conflict, require that the perpetrator 'employed a gas or other analogous substance or device' and that the 'gas, substance or device was such that it causes death or serious damage to health in the ordinary course of events, through its asphyxiating or toxic properties'.[528] Therefore the Preparatory Commission defined this weapon by reference to its effects, a similar approach to that taken with poisoned weapons.[529] Dörmann comments that as a result of this method 'the use of riot control agents in most circumstances would not be covered'.[530]

A footnote to the EOC states that '[n]othing in this element shall be interpreted as limiting or prejudicing in any way existing or developing rules of international law with respect to the development, production, stockpiling and use of chemical weapons'.[531] Although it seems clear that most chemical weapons would be prohibited by this article of the Rome Statute, this proviso ensures that the exclusion of riot control agents and defoliants from the jurisdiction of the ICC does not necessarily reflect the situation under customary international law.

Therefore the *actus reus* of this offence is the employment of a gas or other analogous substance or device. Although the *mens rea* is not explicit in the Elements, applying the default mental element of Article 30, it must be shown that the perpetrator intentionally employed the weapon with the knowledge that it would ordinarily cause death or serious damage to health through its asphyxiating or toxic properties.

[525] *Ibid.*, paras 55–6.

[526] H. McCoubrey, 'The regulation of biological and chemical weapons', pp. 123–39 in H. Fox and M. Meyer (eds), *Armed Conflict and the New Law*, n. 211 *supra*, p. 132, and T. McCormack, 'International law and the use of chemical weapons in the Gulf War', Calif West ILJ, 21 (1990–91), 2–30, pp. 20–1.

[527] Security Council Resolution (SC Res.) 582, 24 February 1986, and 598, 20 July 1987.

[528] EOC, p. 139.

[529] See comments *supra*, p. 130.

[530] K. Dörmann, 'Preparatory Commission for the International Criminal Court', n. 63 *supra*, p. 477.

[531] EOC, fn. 48 on p. 139.

## Article 8(2)(b)(xix) Employing bullets which expand or flatten easily in the human body, such as bullets with a hard envelope which does not entirely cover the core or is pierced with incisions

### Origins

Expanding bullets were first prohibited by the 1899 Hague Declaration III in words identical to this article of the Rome Statute. They are often referred to as 'dum-dum' bullets, having been originally manufactured at the Dum Dum arsenal near Calcutta, where they were created for big game hunting before being adapted for military use by the British army.[532]

### Development

Whilst there have been no recent cases in which the use of expanding bullets has been alleged, more modern bullets with a tumbling effect in the body have been compared to expanding bullets. McCoubrey and White conclude that *prima facie* such bullets fall beyond the scope of the 1899 Declaration but emphasise that the proscription against expanding bullets is not limited to bullets *manufactured* in contravention of the Declaration and that 'the "conversion" of a standard bullet to the same effect would be equally unlawful'.[533] However, there is a move towards the extension of the prohibition against expanding bullets, and the German Military Manual also prohibits projectiles 'of a nature to burst or deform while penetrating the human body, to tumble early in the human body, or to cause shock waves leading to extensive tissue damage or even lethal shock'.[534]

### The Rome Statute

The EOC for this offence, in addition to the elements related to the nature of the conflict, require that the perpetrator 'employed certain bullets' and that '[t]he bullets were such that their use violates the international law of armed conflict because they expand or flatten easily in the human body'.[535] Furthermore the accused must have been aware that 'the nature of the bullets was such that their employment would uselessly aggravate suffering or the wounding effect'.[536]

[532] H. McCoubrey and N. White, *International Law and Armed Conflict*, n. 251 *supra*, p. 252.

[533] *Ibid.*

[534] Translation of this part of the German Military Manual in Fleck, *Handbook of Humanitarian Law*, n. 21 *supra*, p. 122, and see H. Meyrowitz, 'The principle of superfluous injury or unnecessary suffering', IRRC, 299 (1994), 98–122, p. 118.

[535] EOC, p. 140. Dörmann comments that the phrase 'their use violates the international law of armed conflict' was inserted as a reminder 'that expanding bullets are not prohibited absolutely, but may be lawfully used in certain domestic law enforcement operations', K. Dörmann, *Elements of War Crimes*, n. 207 *supra*, p. 292.

[536] *Ibid.*, and see Lee (ed.), *ICC: Elements*, p. 182.

The second element may allow the defence that the accused was not aware that expanding bullets violate the laws of armed conflict, given that Article 32 allows a mistake of law to exclude criminal responsibility 'if it negates the mental element required by such a crime'.[537] However, the *mens rea* of this offence is unclear and it is arguable that the second element simply contains an objective requirement that the bullets breached the laws of armed conflict, rather than a requirement that the accused was aware of the fact.[538] This can be supported by the wording of the third element, which, unlike the second element, specifies that the perpetrator must have been 'aware' that the nature of the bullets was such that 'their employment would uselessly aggravate suffering or the wounding effect'.[539]

Therefore, although there is some doubt in the matter,[540] this offence appears to require that the perpetrator employed bullets which objectively breached the law of armed conflicts because of their expanding or flattening effect in the human body. Additionally, it must be shown that the perpetrator was aware that the bullets were such that 'their employment would uselessly aggravate suffering or the wounding effect'. This third element may be difficult to establish, requiring proof of an assessment by the defendant at the time of the employment of the bullets. How will the ICC deal with a defendant who claims that he did not know, or care, about the effect of the bullets when he employed them?

## Article 8(2)(b)(xx) Employing weapons, projectiles and material and methods of warfare which are of such a nature to cause superfluous injury or unnecessary suffering or which are inherently indiscriminate, in violation of the international law of armed conflict, provided that such weapons, projectiles and material and methods of warfare are the subject of a comprehensive prohibition and are included in an annex to this statute, by an amendment in accordance with the relevant provisions set forth in Articles 121 and 123

### Origins

The basis for the prohibition referred to in this article of the Rome Statute was laid down in the 1868 St Petersburg Declaration, which stated that the only legitimate object of warfare was to weaken the military forces of the enemy, for which

[537] Article 32(2).

[538] Garraway suggests that this provision would allow the argument that the bullets were used in a domestic law enforcement capacity and so did not breach the laws of armed even if an international armed conflict was under way, C. Garraway in Lee (ed.), *ICC: Elements*, p. 181.

[539] For a discussion of how this definition was agreed see C. Garraway, *ibid.*, p. 182.

[540] The default *mens rea* of Article 30 requires that unless 'otherwise provided' the material elements must be committed 'with intent and knowledge'. Therefore, knowledge would be required in relation to the second Element, unless it can be argued that the 'awareness' required in the third Element shows that the mental element is 'otherwise provided', so Article 30 does not apply.

it was sufficient to disable the greatest possible number of men. The Declaration further pronounced that 'this object would be exceeded by the employment of arms which uselessly aggravate the sufferings of disabled men, or render their death inevitable' and that such employment would be 'contrary to the laws of humanity'.

## Development

The concept of the prohibition of certain types of weapons on the basis of their effects was developed by Article 22 and 23(e) of the regulations attached to the 1907 Hague Convention IV. These articles state that '[t]he right of belligerents to adopt means of injuring the enemy is not unlimited' and that it is forbidden 'to employ arms, projectiles, or material calculated to cause unnecessary suffering'.[541] This prohibition was developed by Article 35(2) of AP I, which states that '[i]t is prohibited to employ weapons, projectiles and material and methods of warfare of a nature to cause superfluous injury or unnecessary suffering'.[542] Additionally, AP I also prohibited indiscriminate attacks in Article 50(4), defining them in part as 'those which employ a method or means of combat which cannot be directed at a specific military objective' or 'those which employ a method or means of combat the effects of which cannot be limited as required by this protocol'.

### *Weapons, projectiles and material and methods of warfare*

The phrase used in the Hague Regulations, 'arms, projectiles, or material', became 'weapons, projectiles and material or methods of warfare' in AP I, and indeed in this article of the Rome Statute. Whilst the words 'weapons', 'projectiles' and 'material' are fairly self-explanatory, the expression 'methods of warfare' has been the subject of more discussion. Hays Parks explained that '*means* of warfare traditionally has been understood to refer to the effect of weapons in their use against combatants, while *method* of warfare refers to the way weapons are used in a broader sense'.[543] He suggested that in Article 35(2) of AP I the word 'means' would have been more appropriate than 'methods'.[544]

### *Of a nature to cause superfluous injury or unnecessary suffering*

The expression 'of a nature to cause' used in AP I is wider than the phrase 'calculated to cause' used in the Hague Regulations, as the former includes weapons

[541] The expression 'unnecessary suffering' was initially translated from the French *propres à causer des maux superflus* as 'superfluous injury' in Article 23(e), 1899 Hague Convention.

[542] A similar expression is also used in the Preamble of the 1980 Conventional Weapons Convention and a reference to the prohibition is made in Article 3(3) of the 1996 Amended Protocol II.

[543] W. Hays Parks, 'Memorandum of law: *travaux préparatoires* and legal analysis of blinding laser weapons protocol', Army Lawy (1997), 33–41, Department of the Army Pamphlet 27-50-295, pp. 34–5, emphasis added, and see Sandoz *et al.*, *Commentary on the Additional Protocols*, p. 621.

[544] W. Hays Parks, 'Memorandum of law', n. 543 *supra*, p. 35, but see H. Meyrowitz, 'The principle of superfluous injury', n. 534 *supra*, p. 103.

which were not designed to cause superfluous injury or unnecessary suffering and yet have such an outcome as an inevitable side effect of their use.[545] The expression 'superfluous injury or unnecessary suffering' is more complex.[546] The ICRC commentary to AP I states that this double expression is an appropriate translation of the French *maux superflus* because the French term covers 'simultaneously the sense of moral and physical suffering'.[547]

Article 35(2) of AP I, according to the ICRC commentary, requires that the 'nature of the injury or the intensity of suffering' is weighed against the 'military necessity', in order to decide whether there is a case of superfluous injury or unnecessary suffering.[548] However, as the commentary acknowledges, this concept has a 'relative and imprecise character'.[549] Cassese suggests that the construction of this prohibition in military manuals reveals three factors that this balancing test should take into account: whether the effect of the weapons is disproportionate to their aim; whether the use of weapons with such an effect is not absolutely necessary when measured against the military advantage to be gained from their use and when the weapons are analogous to other weapons which have already been prohibited.[550]

Robblee suggests that factors 'such as medical effects, the degree of disability inflicted, the risk of death, and the strain on medical resources' resulting from the use of a particular weapon are factors which may weigh against a particular weapon in this balancing act, as indeed might 'public opinion, the laws of humanity, and treachery'.[551] This list demonstrates an issue identified by Meyrowitz, that 'those factors which define the unnecessary or superfluous character of suffering or injury . . . may be either quantitative or qualitative in nature'.[552]

[545] F. Kalshoven, 'The Conference of Government Experts on the Use of Certain Conventional Weapons, Lucerne, 24 September–18 October 1974', NYIL, 6 (1975), 77–102, p. 90.

[546] See comments by S. Oeter, 'Methods and means of combat', n. 21 *supra*, para. 402.

[547] Sandoz *et al.*, *Commentary on the Additional Protocols*, p. 407.

[548] *Ibid.*, p. 408. Hays Parks suggests a similar balancing test, W. Hays Parks, 'Memorandum of law: sniper use of open-tip ammunition', Army Lawy (1991), 86–9, Department of the Army Pamphlet, 27-50-218, p. 87.

[549] Sandoz *et al.*, *Commentary on the Additional Protocols*, p. 410.

[550] A. Cassese, 'Weapons causing unnecessary suffering: are they prohibited?', RDI, 58 (1975), 12–42, pp. 26–30, note that this comment was written prior to the conclusion of AP I and was therefore an analysis of Article 23(e) of the 1907 Hague Convention IV.

[551] P. Robblee, 'The legitimacy of modern conventional weaponry', Milit LR, 71 (1976), 95–148, pp. 96–7.

[552] H. Meyrowitz, 'The principle of superfluous injury', n. 534 *supra*, p. 111. See generally R. Coupland and P. Herby, 'Review of the legality of weapons: a new approach, the SIrUS Project', 835 IRRC, 835 (1999), 583–92; J. sur Vevey, 'ICRC expert meeting on legal reviews of weapons and the SIrUS Project', 842 IRRC (2001), 539–42, and R. Coupland, 'The SIrUS Project: towards a determination of which weapons cause "superfluous injury or unnecessary suffering"', pp. 99–118 in H. Durham and T. McCormack (eds), *The Changing Face of Conflict*, n. 184 *supra*.

#### *Inherently indiscriminate*

Indiscriminate attacks are prohibited by Article 50(4) of AP I, which defined them in part as 'those which employ a method or means of combat which cannot be directed at a specific military objective' or 'those which employ a method or means of combat the effects of which cannot be limited as required by this protocol'. Therefore the definition of 'indiscriminate' includes both the method by which a particular weapon is used in an attack and the use of a type of weapon which is by nature indiscriminate, such as the use of a contagious disease as a weapon.[553]

### The Rome Statute

No EOC have as yet been drafted for this offence because no 'weapons, projectiles or material or methods of warfare' are at present included in an annex to the Statute.[554] Prohibited weapons may be added to this annex as an amendment to the Rome Statute under Articles 121 and 123 at the Review Conference to be held in 2009. However, in the opinion of Cassese, an amendment to this article is so unlikely to be agreed upon that in all probability the Court will never have jurisdiction over such offences.[555]

Mathews and McCormack comment that this article 'introduces an unprecedented nexus between the prohibition on "superfluous injury or unnecessary suffering" and the conclusion of multilateral negotiations for a comprehensive ban on a weapons type'.[556] For example, whilst the 1980 Weapons Convention refers to this prohibition in its preamble, 'the Conference ended with no finding that the restrictions and prohibitions contained in the weapons convention were imposed because of any agreed belief or finding that those weapons were in fact excessively injurious or had indiscriminate effects or that its rules were statements of customary international law'.[557]

The requirement that the weapon must be subject to a comprehensive prohibition prior to being included in the annex to the Statute would appear to rule out the possibility of nuclear weapons being prohibited under this article for the

[553] See generally F. Kalshoven, 'Arms, armaments and international law', n. 523 *supra*, pp. 236–7, the same author, 'The Conference of Government Experts', n. 545 *supra*, pp. 90–2, and M. Schmitt, 'Direct participation in hostilities', n. 39 *supra*, p. 55.

[554] See comment in the EOC, p. 140.

[555] A. Cassese, 'The statute of the International Criminal Court: some preliminary reflections', EJIL, 10 (1999), 144–71, p. 152.

[556] R. Mathews and T. McCormack, 'The relationship between international humanitarian law and arms control', pp. 65–98 in H. Durham and T. McCormack (eds), *The Changing Face of Conflict*, n. 184 *supra*, p. 88.

[557] J. Roach, 'Certain Conventional Weapons Convention: arms control or humanitarian law?', Milit LR, 105 (1984), 3–72, p. 35, and see W. Fenrick, 'New developments in the law', n. 507 *supra*, p. 240.

foreseeable future.[558] However, Cottier suggests that the concept of a 'comprehensive prohibition' may include a prohibition under customary international law in addition to a prohibition under conventional law.[559] The obvious candidates for prohibition include: chemical weapons,[560] to the extent they are not already prohibited by Article 8(2)(b)(xviii); biological weapons,[561] in particular contagious diseases, and land mines.[562]

## Article 8(2)(b)(xxi) Committing outrages upon personal dignity, in particular humiliating and degrading treatment

### Origins

The wording of this article is identical to that of Article 3(1)(c), common to the four Geneva Conventions of 1949. Whilst Common Article 3 applies by its terms solely to non-international armed conflicts, according to the ICJ in the *Nicaragua* case, 'these rules also constitute a minimum yardstick . . . which are also to apply to international conflicts'.[563] Indeed, AP I repeats this prohibition in Article 75(2)(b), and in Article 85(4)(d) condemns as a grave breach 'practices of apartheid and other inhuman and degrading practices involving outrages upon personal dignity, based on racial discrimination'. The commentary to Article 75(2)(b) states that this offence 'refers to acts which, without directly causing harm to the integrity and physical and mental well-being of persons, are aimed at humiliating and ridiculing them, or even forcing them to perform degrading acts'.[564]

[558] See R. Mathews and T. McCormack, 'The relationship between international humanitarian law and arms control', n. 556 *supra*, pp. 88–9.

[559] Cottier *et al.*, 'Article 8', p. 243. Although, given the advisory opinion in the *Legality of the Threat or Use of Nuclear Weapons*, it would be difficult to state definitively that nuclear weapons were subject to a comprehensive prohibition under customary international law, ICJ Rep (1996), 226, Decision para. E. See also the 'understanding' of several States to AP I, including the United Kingdom, France, Canada and Spain, that AP I does not restrict the use of nuclear weapons, and the similar 'understanding' made by France in relation to Article 8 of the Rome Statute, available at: <http://www.icrc.org>.

[560] 1993 Chemical Weapons Convention. See generally M. Eshbaugh, 'The Chemical Weapons Convention', n. 511 *supra*.

[561] 1972 Biological Weapons Convention. See H. Dagen, 'Bioterrorism: perfectly legal', Catholic ULR, 49 (2000), 535–73, and B. Appleyard, 'When the wind blows', 14 October 2001, *The Sunday Times Magazine*, 67–75.

[562] 1996 Amended Protocol II and 1997 Ottawa Land Mine Convention. See M. Lacey, 'Passage of Amended Protocol II', Army Lawy (2000), 7–15, Department of the Army Pamphlet 27-50-328, and A. Petrarca, 'An impetus of human wreckage? The 1996 amended Land Mine Protocol', Calif West ILJ, 27 (1996), 205–39.

[563] *Case concerning Military and Paramilitary Activities in and against Nicaragua* (*Merits*) Nicaragua v. US, ICJ Rep (1986) 14, para. 218.

[564] Sandoz *et al.*, *Commentary on the Additional Protocols*, p. 873.

Second World War jurisprudence reveals three cases which today might be considered to breach this prohibition.[565] The *Maelzer* Trial concerned the parade of British and American prisoners of war through the streets of Rome, where, according to the prosecution witness, the population threw stones and sticks at the prisoners.[566] The accused was found guilty of exposing prisoners of war to acts of violence, insults and public curiosity.[567] In the Trial of *Chuichi and Others* the accused were found guilty of ill treatment of Indian Sikh prisoners of war.[568] The physical ill treatment was aggravated by the fact that the PoWs had their hair and beards cut off and one was forced to smoke a cigarette, when this was forbidden by their religion.[569] Finally, the Trial of *Schmid* concerned the ill treatment of an unknown dead US serviceman.[570] The accused, a German medical officer, removed the head from the body of the serviceman, boiled it, removed the skin and flesh and then bleached the skull, which he kept on his desk for several months.[571] Despite his claim that he had not acted out of hatred and had kept the skull only for instructional purposes, he was found guilty of the offence.[572]

### Development

This crime has been examined in some depth by the ICTY.[573] In *Furundžija* the Trial Chamber found that the rapes and sexual assaults upon the victim, in front of soldiers who were watching and laughing, caused 'severe physical and mental pain, along with public humiliation' and amounted to 'outrages upon her personal dignity and sexual integrity'.[574] In the *Aleksovski* case the Trial Chamber defined outrages upon personal dignity as a particularly deplorable species of inhuman treatment which occasioned 'more serious suffering than most prohibited acts falling within the *genus*'.[575] They defined the mental element of the crime as the intention to humiliate or ridicule the victim,[576] but the *Aleksovski* Appeal Judgement explained that the offence did not necessarily require 'a *specific intent* on the part of a perpetrator to humiliate, ridicule or degrade the victims'.[577]

[565] Identified by the ICRC in the ICRC working paper on the Elements of Crimes of Article 8(2)(b), n. 351 *supra*, comments on Article 8(2)(b)(xxi).

[566] Trial of *Maelzer*, 11 LRTWC 53.

[567] *Ibid.*, p. 55.

[568] Trial of *Tanaka Chuichi and Others*, 11 LRTWC 62.

[569] *Ibid.*

[570] Trial of *Schmid*, 14 LRTWC 151.

[571] *Ibid.*, p. 151.

[572] *Ibid.*, and see the examples on p. 152.

[573] See also the ICTR Judgement in *Musema*, Trial Judgement, para. 285.

[574] *Furundžija*, Trial Judgement, para. 272.

[575] *Aleksovski*, Trial Judgement, para. 54.

[576] *Ibid.*, para. 56. The Trial Chamber specifically ruled out recklessness from the mental element, *ibid.*

[577] *Aleksovski*, Appeal Judgement, para. 27, original emphasis. However, this was not the subject of the appeal and so this statement was effectively *obiter dicta*.

With respect to the *actus reus* of the crime the *Aleksovski* Trial Chamber held that the act 'must cause serious humiliation or degradation to the victim', which it interpreted as entailing 'real and lasting suffering to the individual arising from the humiliation or ridicule'.[578] Although this necessitated a subjective element to this offence, as sensitive persons would be more prone to perceive their treatment as humiliating, they added an objective element that 'the humiliation to the victim must be so intense that the reasonable person would be outraged'.[579]

The Trial Chamber in the *Kunarać* case re-examined the offence of outrages upon personal dignity and criticised part of the *Aleksovski* Judgement. It found both the Trial and the Appeal Judgements ambiguous on the issue of the mental element of this offence.[580] The *Kunarać* Judgement stated that the perpetrator must, in addition to intending the relevant act or omission, be aware of its objective character and therefore know that his act or omission could cause 'serious humiliation, degradation or affront to human dignity'.[581] The Trial Chamber also commented that a perpetrator who has met the objective threshold of the offence is unlikely to be unaware of the nature of his acts.[582]

With respect to the *actus reus*, the *Kunarać* Trial Chamber concurred with the definition of an outrage upon personal dignity as an act causing 'serious humiliation or degradation to the victim'.[583] However, it did not agree that humiliation or degradation which was real and serious also needed to be lasting and stated that a minimum temporal requirement of the effects of an outrage was not an element of the offence.[584] The *Kunarać* Judgement summarised the *actus reus* of the offence as 'any act or omission which would be generally considered to cause serious humiliation, degradation or otherwise be a serious attack on human dignity', and this was approved on appeal.[585]

This approach to both the *mens rea* and the *actus reus* of outrages upon personal dignity was followed in the case of *Kvočka*.[586] However, the *Kvočka* Judgement approved the part of the *Aleksovski* Trial Chamber Judgement which took subjective criteria into account, including the victim's temperament or sensitivity, in addition to applying a 'reasonable person' standard, when deciding

[578] *Aleksovski*, Trial Judgement, para. 56.

[579] *Ibid.*

[580] *Kunarać*, Trial Chamber, para. 508.

[581] *Ibid.*, para. 512. This has been criticised by Erikkson on the basis that a body cavity search under any circumstances would appear to constitute a violation of humanitarian law on a strict application of this test, but such a search could be 'legitimately based on corroborated information of smuggled contraband', S. Erikkson, 'Humiliating and degrading treatment under international humanitarian law: criminal accountability, State responsibility and cultural considerations', AFLR, 55 (2004), 269–311, p. 285.

[582] *Kunarać*, Trial Chamber, para. 513, approved on appeal, *Kunarać*, Appeal Judgement, paras 165–6.

[583] *Kunarać*, Trial Judgement, para. 501.

[584] *Ibid.*

[585] *Ibid.*, para. 507, and *Kunarać*, Appeal Judgement, para. 163.

[586] *Kvočka, et al.*, Trial Judgement, para. 168.

whether the act was an outrage upon personal dignity.[587] Finally, the *Kvočka* Trial Chamber held that the conditions of confinement in Omarska camp amounted to an outrage upon personal dignity as '[t]he detainees were forced to perform subservient acts demonstrating Serb superiority, forced to relieve bodily functions in their clothing, and they endured the constant fear of being subjected to physical, mental, or sexual violence in the camp'.[588]

### The Rome Statute

The EOC for this offence, in addition to the elements in respect of the nature of the conflict, require that the perpetrator 'humiliated, degraded or otherwise violated the dignity of one or more persons'.[589] This text clarifies the fact that humiliating and degrading treatment are merely examples of outrages upon personal dignity and that an outrage upon personal dignity could be committed by some other violation of dignity.[590] Although the Elements do not elaborate upon the nature of this other violation of dignity, it is submitted that it could be found in some form of inhuman treatment.[591] The Elements also include the objective requirement that '[t]he severity of the humiliation, degradation or other violation was of such degree as to be generally recognized as an outrage upon personal dignity'.[592] Erikkson's comment that '[h]umiliation is a piercing arrow that wounds the heart and, in the worst of cases, kills healthy esteem' is useful in describing the type of humiliation covered by this element and the seriousness of the offence.[593]

A footnote to the first element explains that '[f]or this crime, "persons" can include dead persons', and that the victim 'need not personally be aware of the existence of the humiliation or degradation or other violation',[594] which shows that the offence may equally be committed against sleeping, unconscious or dead victims. The footnote also explains that '[t]his element takes into account relevant aspects of the cultural background to the victim', so retaining a subjective aspect to the offence, whereby a cultural or religious specific humiliation, degradation or violation of dignity could constitute an outrage upon personal dignity, even if the same action perpetrated against a person from a different background would not amount to this offence. In such a situation the objective element could be satisfied by showing that the violation was severe enough to be generally recognised as an outrage upon personal dignity when perpetrated against persons of that particular cultural or religious background.

[587] *Ibid.*, para. 167.

[588] *Ibid.*, para. 173.

[589] EOC, p. 140.

[590] Lee (ed.), *ICC: Elements*, p. 184, but Kittichaisaree takes a more restrictive view, K. Kittichaisaree, *International Criminal Law*, n. 431 *supra*, p. 181.

[591] See Cottier *et al.*, 'Article 8', p. 246, and discussion *supra*, pp. 29, 36–8 and 40.

[592] EOC, p. 140.

[593] S. Erikkson, 'Humiliating and degrading treatment', n. 581 *supra*, p. 288.

[594] EOC, fn. 49 on p. 140.

Therefore the Rome Statute and the EOC define the crime of outrages upon personal dignity in much the same way as the jurisprudence of the ICTY.[595] In respect of the *actus reus* of the offence, both subjective and objective elements are present. The EOC do not refer to the requirement for the harm to be lasting, suggested by the *Aleksovski* Trial Chamber,[596] and so it would seem that this would not need to be proved in a case before the ICC. The standard of *mens rea* is not explicit in the EOC and so the default mental element of Article 30 of intent and knowledge applies.[597] Therefore, it would seem that the perpetrator must intend to commit the act concerned in the knowledge that it will humiliate, degrade or violate the dignity of the victim.[598]

The treatment of prisoners at Abu Ghraib has already been discussed as an example of the grave breach of torture.[599] However, whilst the ICC did not in fact have jurisdiction in that case, it is clear that forcibly arranging detainees into various sexually explicit positions for photographing, forcing male detainees to masturbate whilst being photographed and videotaped and parading male detainees outside cells naked and with women's underwear over their heads would have amounted to the offence of outrages upon personal dignity under the Rome Statute.[600]

## Article 8(2)(b)(xxii) Committing rape, sexual slavery, enforced prostitution, forced pregnancy, as defined in Article 7, paragraph 2 (f), enforced sterilisation, or any other form of sexual violence also constituting a grave breach of the Geneva Conventions

### Origins

Rape and sexual assault have been described as 'one of the oldest and most horrible aspects of war',[601] though the Rome Statute is not the first instrument

[595] Most of the ICTY jurisprudence for this offence concerns sexual violence, but see comments of B. Moshan, 'Women, war, and words: the gender component in the permanent International Criminal Court's definition of crimes against humanity', Fordham Int'l LJ, 22 (1998), 154–84, p. 180, and J. Campanaro, 'Women, war and international law: the historical treatment of gender-based war crimes', Geo LJ, 89 (2001), 2557–92, p. 2589.

[596] See *supra*, p. 141.

[597] See *supra*, pp. 5–8.

[598] This is the mental element suggested in the *Kunarać* Trial Chamber Judgement, para. 512.

[599] See *supra*, pp. 39–40.

[600] These abuses are detailed in Article 15-6, Investigation of the 800th Military Police Brigade, Findings of Fact following Part I of Investigation, March 2004, para. 6, available at: <http://news.findlaw.com/usatoday/docs/iraq/tagubarpt.html> and Report of the International Committee of the Red Cross (ICRC) on the Treatment by Coalition Forces of Prisoners of War and other Protected Persons by the Geneva Conventions in Iraq during Arrest, Internment and Interrogation, February 2004, para. 25, available at: <http://www.globalsecurity.org/military/library/report/2004/icrc_report_iraq_Feb2004.pdf>.

[601] P. Davis, 'The politics of prosecuting rape as a war crime', Int Law, 34 (2000), 1223–48, p. 1223.

to prohibit this abhorrent crime, and rape has long been considered an offence against the laws of war. In 1646 Grotius opined that, in respect of the 'violation of women', the act 'ought to be no more unpunished in peace than in war: and this latter rule is the Law of Nations, not of all, but of the best'.[602] In 1863 the Lieber Code prohibited sexual violence against women in two articles, Article 37, which stated that offences against 'the persons of the inhabitants, especially those of women: and the sacredness of domestic relations' should be rigorously punished, and Article 44, which proclaimed that rape was punishable by the death penalty.[603]

Whilst the 1899 and 1907 Hague Regulations did not expressly prohibit sexual offences, such an offence could be read into Article 46, which stated, somewhat obliquely, that '[f]amily honor and rights . . . must be respected'.[604] Nevertheless, rape and sexual violence occurred during the First World War and were committed on a massive scale during the Second World War.[605] Crimes of sexual violence were not among those charged in the Leipzig Trials after the First World War, and the Nuremberg Charter following the Second World War did not even list rape either as a war crime or as a crime against humanity.[606] Furthermore, although evidence of sexual violence was given during the Nuremberg Trial, the Judgement of the Tribunal did not even mention the word 'rape'.[607]

Crimes of sexual violence were prosecuted after the Second World War in the International Military Tribunal for the Far East (IMTFE), particularly in respect of the 'rape of Nanking'. On this atrocity the Judgement stated that even 'girls of tender years and old women were raped in large numbers' and found that 'approximately 20,000 cases of rape occurred in the city during the first month

[602] H. Grotius, *On the Rights of War and Peace*, n. 423 *supra*, p. 330.

[603] Lieber Code.

[604] See comments of M. Lippman, 'Humanitarian law: war on women', Mich SU-Detroit Col L JIL, 9 (2000), 33–119, p. 38.

[605] On the First World War see M. Lippman, *ibid.*, pp. 35–7. and the inclusion of 'rape' and 'enforced prostitution' on the list of charges suggested by the Commission on the Responsibility of the Authors of the War and on Enforcement of Penalties, Report Presented to the Preliminary Peace Conference, 29 March 1919, reprinted in AJIL, 14 (1920), 95–126, p. 114. On the Second World War see C. Niarchos, 'Women, war, and rape: challenges facing the International Tribunal for the former Yugoslavia', HRQ, 17 (1995), 649–90, pp. 663–6, and T. Meron, 'Shakespeare's *Henry the Fifth* and the law of war', AJIL, 86 (1992), 1–45, p. 30. See also S. Ryan, 'From the furies of Nanking to the Eumenides of the International Criminal Court: the evolution of sexual assaults as international crimes', Pace ILR, 11 (1999), 447–86, pp. 454–9; T. Meron, 'Rape as a crime under international humanitarian law', AJIL, 87 (1993), 424–8, pp. 425–6, and S. Chesterman, 'Never again . . . and again: law, order, and the gender of war crimes in Bosnia and beyond', Yale J Int'l L, 22 (1997), 299–343, pp. 329–31.

[606] Article 6(b) and 6(c), Nuremberg Charter. However, Article II(1)(c), CCL No. 10, listed rape as a crime against humanity.

[607] C. Niarchos, 'Women, war, and rape', n. 605 *supra*, p. 665, and J. Campanaro, 'Women, war and international law', n. 595 *supra*, pp. 2560–2.

of occupation'.[608] Although the Tokyo Charter did not specifically include the offence of rape, nevertheless the findings of the IMTFE implicitly recognised rape as a war crime.[609]

Another well known military trial in the Far East after the Second World War which implicitly accepted that rape was a breach of humanitarian law was the Trial of *Yamashita*.[610] The Judgement stated that 'where murder and rape and vicious, revengeful actions are widespread offences, and there is no effective attempt by a commander to discover and control the criminal acts, such a commander may be held responsible, even criminally liable, for the lawless acts of his troops'.[611] A further Second World War military trial in the East Indies considered a charge of forced prostitution in the Trial of *Awochi*.[612] The defendant, a Japanese hotel keeper, was charged with the war crime of enforced prostitution of Dutch women in his club. The Court found the defendant guilty on the basis that he confined the women to part of the club's premises and threatened them with the Japanese military police when they wished to leave, threats which were 'rightly considered as being synonymous with ill-treatment, loss of liberty or worse'.[613]

The 1949 Geneva Conventions contain prohibitions against crimes of sexual violence against women. However, they do not develop the elements of these offences, and indeed the provision of Article 14 in the Third Geneva Convention states in euphemistic language that prisoners of war are entitled to 'respect for their persons and their honour' and that '[w]omen shall be treated with all the regard due to their sex', and it is left to the commentary, under the heading of 'honour and modesty', to spell out that '[t]he main intention is to defend women prisoners against rape, forced prostitution and any form of indecent assault'.[614] Article 27 on sexual violence in the Fourth Geneva Convention is more explicit, but the prohibition of 'rape, enforced prostitution or any form of indecent assault' is still framed in terms of an attack on women's honour.

Classifying sexual violence as a crime against modesty and honour is both an inadequate description of the suffering caused by the offence and 'on the scale of wartime violence, rape as a mere injury to honor or reputation appears less worthy of prosecution than injury to the person'.[615] The 1977 Additional Protocols also contain prohibitions against rape, forced prostitution and indecent assault, expressions which are not further elaborated either in the Protocols or

[608] B. Röling and C. Rüter (eds), 1 *The Tokyo Judgment: The International Military Tribunal for the Far East, 29 April 1946–12 November 1948* (Amsterdam: UPA University Press, 1977–78), p. 389.

[609] M. Cherif Bassiouni, *Crimes against Humanity in International Criminal Law* (The Hague: Kluwer, 2nd edn, 1999), p. 348, and see also M. Lippman, 'Humanitarian law: war on women', n. 604 *supra*, pp. 60–1, and J. Campanaro, 'Women, war and international law', n. 595 *supra*, pp. 2563–5.

[610] Trial of *Yamashita*, 4 LRTWC 1.

[611] *Ibid.*, p. 35.

[612] Trial of *Awochi*, 13 LRTWC 122.

[613] *Ibid.*, p. 124.

[614] Pictet (ed.), *Commentary: III Convention*, p. 147.

[615] C. Niarchos, 'Women, war, and rape', n. 605 *supra*, p. 674.

in the commentaries.[616] Whilst under the Protocols references to honour have been dropped in favour of 'outrages upon personal dignity', it is arguable that this is still not a satisfactory description of sexual offences.[617]

## Development

Events in the former Yugoslavia and Rwanda have been the catalyst for in-depth legal examination of sexual violence as a breach of humanitarian law and the elements of the various sexual offences before the ICTY and ICTR. The Final Report of the Yugoslavia Commission of Experts described rape as a 'crime of violence of a sexual nature against the person' and emphasised that 'acts of sexual assault against women, men and children are prohibited by international humanitarian law through normative provisions prohibiting violence against the physical integrity and dignity of the person'.[618] Thus rape was recognised as a crime of violence and the Commission of Experts also acknowledged that crimes of sexual violence could be perpetrated against both sexes.[619] This approach of treating rape as a crime of violence was later confirmed by the ICTR in the *Akayesu* Judgement, which emphasised that 'rape is a form of aggression'.[620]

### *Rape*

Rape has various definitions in different national laws, and prior to the establishment of the ICTY and ICTR there was no authoritative definition of rape in international law.[621] The first judgement of an international tribunal to define the elements of the crime of rape, albeit as a crime against humanity, was the ICTR Trial Chamber Judgement in the case of *Akayesu*.[622] The accused was the *bourgmestre* (mayor) in the commune of Taba, in Rwanda, where, *inter alia*, he was found to have ordered, instigated and aided and abetted sexual violence, including rape, against Tutsi women.[623]

The Tribunal found that 'the central elements of the crime of rape cannot be captured in a mechanical description of objects and body parts' and therefore

[616] See Articles 75(2)(b) and 76(1), AP I, and 4(2)(e), AP II.

[617] See comments by K. Askin, 'Sexual violence in decisions and indictments of the Yugoslav and Rwandan tribunals: current status', AJIL, 93 (1999), 97–123, p. 101.

[618] Final Report of the Commission of Experts established pursuant to SC Res. 780 (1992), UN Doc. S/1994/674, 27 May 1994, para. 103.

[619] This approach has academic support, see J. Falvey, 'Criminal sexual conduct as a violation of international humanitarian law', St John's JLC, 12 (1997), 385–410, pp. 389–90.

[620] *Akayesu*, Trial Judgement, para. 687.

[621] The ILC's 1996 Draft Code prohibits rape in Article 20(d) but does not define it. For a general discussion of rape before the ICTY and ICTR see B. Stephens, 'Humanitarian law and gender violence: an end to centuries of neglect?', H of LPS, 3 (1999), 87–109, and K. Askin, 'Prosecuting wartime rape and other gender-related crimes under international law: extraordinary advances, enduring obstacles', Berkeley J Int'l L, 21 (2003), 288–349.

[622] *Akayesu*, Trial Judgement, para. 688.

[623] *Ibid.*, paras 692–7.

defined rape broadly as 'a physical invasion of a sexual nature, committed on a person under circumstances which are coercive'.[624] This definition included coercive circumstances as opposed to lack of consent as an element of the offence, the latter being consigned to the Rules of Procedure and Evidence (RPE) as an evidential rule.[625] The Judgement explained that coercive circumstances may be constituted by '[t]hreats, intimidation, extortion and other forms of duress which prey on fear or desperation', that they 'need not be evidenced by a show of physical force' and that 'coercion may be inherent in certain circumstances, such as armed conflict'.[626] This definition of rape was followed by the ICTY in the *Čelebici* case, which stated that it was wide enough to include forced oral sex.[627]

In *Furundžija* a Bosnian Croat commander was found guilty of torture and aiding and abetting rape and serious sexual violence upon a Bosnian Muslim woman in his custody.[628] Although the Trial Chamber considered the *Akayesu* definition, it derived a more detailed definition of rape by examining national laws on this offence.[629] The Judgement set out the elements of rape as '(i) the sexual penetration, however slight: (a) of the vagina or anus of the victim by the penis of the perpetrator or any other object used by the perpetrator; or (b) of the mouth of the victim by the penis of the perpetrator; (ii) by coercion or force or threat of force against the victim or a third person'.[630]

Therefore the *Furundžija* Trial Chamber defined rape more precisely than *Akayesu*,[631] but still used the concept of coercion, rather than consent, as part of the definition of rape, consent being dealt with under the RPE.[632] However, in the *Kunarać* case, where three accused were found liable for crimes including enslaving Bosnian Muslim women and subjecting them to rape and sexual

[624] *Ibid.*, paras 687–8, and see *Musema*, Trial Judgement, paras 226–9.

[625] Rule 96, ICTR RPE, '(ii) Consent shall not be allowed as a defence if the victim: (a) Has been subjected to or threatened with or has had reason to fear violence, duress, detention or psychological oppression; or (b) Reasonably believed that if the victim did not submit, another might be so subjected, threatened or put in fear; (iii) Before evidence of the victim's consent is admitted, the accused shall satisfy the Trial Chamber in camera that the evidence is relevant and credible', available at: <http://69.94.11.53/ENGLISH/rules/101106/rop101106.pdf>. Rule 96 in the ICTY RPE contains the same provision on consent, available at: <http://www.un.org/icty/legaldoc-e/basic/rpe/IT032Rev38e.pdf>. Rule 96 has remained unchanged despite several amendments to the ICTY and ICTR RPE.

[626] *Akayesu*, Trial Judgement, para. 688.

[627] *Čelebici*, Trial Judgement, paras 479 and 1065–6, and on the issue of forced oral sex also see *Furundžija*, Trial Judgement, para. 183.

[628] *Furundžija*, Trial Judgement, paras 269 and 275.

[629] *Ibid.*, paras 176–84.

[630] *Ibid.*, para. 185.

[631] See *Muhimana*, Trial Judgement, paras 549–51, where the Court attempted to reconcile the approaches of *Akayesu* and *Furundžija/Kunarać*.

[632] *Furundžija*, Trial Judgement, para. 185. See comments by C. Coan in 'Rethinking the spoils of war: prosecuting rape as a war crime in the International Criminal Tribunal for the former Yugoslavia', NCJIL & Com Reg, 26 (2000), 183–237, p. 217.

violence for prolonged periods,[633] the Judgement replaced the expression 'by coercion or force or threat of force', used in *Furundžija*, with the expression 'where such sexual penetration occurs without the consent of the victim'.[634] The Trial Chamber also defined the mental element of rape as 'the intention to effect this sexual penetration, and the knowledge that it occurs without the consent of the victim'.[635] This definition of the *actus reus* and *mens rea* of rape was followed by the Trial Chamber in *Kvočka*.[636]

On the issue of consent to sexual intercourse, the *Kunarać* Trial Chamber explained further that it must be 'given voluntarily, as a result of the victim's free will, assessed in the context of the surrounding circumstances'.[637] However, it acknowledged that in practice lack of consent may be evidenced by the presence of various factors such as 'force, threats of force, or taking advantage of a person who is unable to resist'.[638] This statement was clarified by the *Kunarać* Appeal Chamber, which emphasised that whilst force or threat of force may provide clear evidence of non-consent, 'force is not an element *per se* of rape'.[639]

Nevertheless, in practical terms the difference between the focus on coercion in *Furundžija* and the focus on consent in *Kunarać* did not greatly affect the outcome, given the limited circumstances in which the issue of consent could be raised under Rule 96 of the RPE.[640] The *Furundžija* Judgement stated that in the Court's opinion 'any form of captivity vitiates consent',[641] and the Appeal Chamber in *Kunarać* asserted that the circumstances which prevail in most cases charged as war crimes or crimes against humanity will be almost 'universally coercive' and so true consent will not be possible.[642] The ICTR Trial Chamber in *Muhimana* in response to these decisions stated that 'coercion is an element

[633] *Kunarać*, Trial Judgement, paras 883, 886 and 888. For a commentary on this case see C. Maravilla, 'Rape as a war crime: the implications of the International Criminal Tribunal for the former Yugoslavia's decision in Prosecutor v. Kunarać, Kovać, and Vuković on international humanitarian law', Fla J Int'l L, 13 (2001), 321–41.

[634] *Kunarać*, Trial Judgement, para. 460, approved on appeal, *Kunarać*, Appeal Judgement, para. 128. This approach was also supported by J. Falvey, 'Criminal sexual conduct', n. 619 *supra*, p. 391.

[635] *Kunarać*, Trial Judgement, para. 460.

[636] *Kvočka et al.*, Trial Judgement, paras 176–7 and 179.

[637] *Kunarać*, Trial Judgement, para. 460.

[638] *Ibid.*, para. 458. Compare with the requirement of forcible resistance by the victim in the US court-martial of a serviceman accused of rape in Vietnam, *United States v. Steele*, 30 March 1971, 43 CMR 845.

[639] *Kunarać*, Appeal Judgement, para. 129.

[640] See Rule 96, n. 625 *supra*.

[641] *Furundžija*, Trial Judgement, para. 271, followed by *Kvočka et al.*, Trial Judgement, para. 178. This approach was also taken by G. McDougall, Special Rapporteur, Final Report, 'Contemporary forms of slavery: systematic rape, sexual slavery and slavery-like practices during armed conflict', Sub-commission on Prevention of Discrimination and Protection of Minorities, UN Doc. E/CN.4/Sub.2/1998/13, 22 June 1998 (hereinafter: G. McDougall, Contemporary forms of slavery, Final Report), para. 25.

[642] *Kunarać*, Appeal Judgement, para. 130.

that may obviate the relevance of consent as an evidentiary factor in the crime of rape'.[643]

The issue of consent to rape in detention was examined by the Trial Chamber in the case of *Kvočka*.[644] Here a witness complained of forced sexual intercourse by Radić, a guard shift leader in the Omarska camp.[645] Although the witness admitted in cross-examination that Radić had helped her by bringing her food and water and moving her husband to another detention building, the Trial Chamber found that this did not discredit the witness.[646] The evidence suggested that Radić 'regularly attempted to bribe or coerce victims to "agree" to sexual intercourse in exchange for favors' and the Trial Chamber recalled with approval previous holdings by the ICTY that 'a status of detention will normally vitiate consent in such circumstances'.[647]

### *Sexual violence*

The definition of sexual violence has also been considered in cases before the ICTY and ICTR. The Judgement in *Akayesu* defined sexual violence as 'any act of a sexual nature which is committed on a person under circumstances which are coercive' and explained that '[s]exual violence is not limited to physical invasion of the human body and may include acts which do not involve penetration or even physical contact'.[648] The Trial Chamber gave as an example of this an incident in which Akayesu 'ordered the Interahamwe to undress a student and force her to do gymnastics naked in the public courtyard of the bureau communal, in front of a crowd'.[649]

The definition of sexual violence given by *Akayesu* was followed by the ICTY in the *Čelebici* and *Kvočka* cases.[650] However, the Trial Chamber in *Furundžija* defined sexual violence as 'all serious abuses of a sexual nature inflicted upon the physical and moral integrity of a person by means of coercion, threat of force or intimidation in a way that is degrading and humiliating for the victim's dignity'.[651] This is a narrower definition of sexual assault than the one given in *Akayesu*, requiring, in addition to a serious sexual act in coercive circumstances, that the abuse is carried out in a way degrading and humiliating for the victim's dignity. An alternative and broader definition of sexual violence was given by the Special Rapporteur for the Human Rights Commission on Contemporary Forms

[643] *Muhimana*, Trial Judgement, para. 546.

[644] *Kvočka et al.*, Trial Judgement, paras 554–5.

[645] The exact status of Radić was a contested issue but on the facts the Trial Chamber found that he was a guard shift leader at the camp, *ibid.*, para. 517.

[646] *Ibid.*, para. 555.

[647] *Ibid.*

[648] *Akayesu*, Trial Judgement, para. 688.

[649] *Ibid.*

[650] *Čelebici*, Trial Judgement, para. 479, and *Kvočka et al.*, Trial Judgement, para. 180.

[651] *Furundžija*, Trial Judgement, para. 186.

of Slavery, Gay McDougall, as 'any violence, physical or psychological, carried out through sexual means or by targeting sexuality'.[652] Indeed, the Trial Chamber in *Kvočka* suggested in a footnote that the crime of sexual violence was broad enough to include 'sexual mutilation, forced marriage, and forced abortion'.[653]

### *Sexual slavery*[654]

The issue of sexual slavery in armed conflict has been considered in detail by McDougall, who defined slavery as 'the status or condition of a person over whom any or all of the powers attaching to the right of ownership are exercised, including sexual access through rape or other forms of sexual violence'.[655] Therefore, 'sexual' was an adjective to describe a form of slavery and McDougall gave as particularly severe examples of sexual slavery the 'comfort stations'[656] maintained by the Japanese during the Second World War and the 'rape camps'[657] from the former Yugoslavia.[658]

In an update of her final report McDougall explained that '[c]ritical elements in the definition of slavery are limitations on autonomy and on the power to decide matters relating to one's sexual activity and bodily integrity',[659] but that slavery differs from imprisonment or arbitrary detention in that these limitations on autonomy can be 'solely psychological or situational, with no physical restraints'.[660] In particular, McDougall argued that, 'while slavery requires the treatment of a person as chattel, the fact that a person was not bought, sold or traded does not in any way defeat a claim of slavery'[661] and that '[t]he mere ability to extricate

[652] G. McDougall, Contemporary forms of slavery, Final Report, para. 21.

[653] *Kvočka et al.*, Trial Judgement, para. 180, fn. 343.

[654] See discussion of enslavement *infra*, pp. 212–18.

[655] G. McDougall, Contemporary forms of slavery, Final Report, para. 27.

[656] See T. Okada, 'The "comfort women" case: judgement of April 27, 1998, Shimonoseki Branch, Yamaguchi Prefectural Court, Japan', Pac Rim LPJ, 8 (1999), 63–108, and E. Totsuka, 'Commentary on a victory for "comfort women": Japan's judicial recognition of military sexual slavery', Pac Rim LPJ, 8 (1999), 47–61. See also the summary of findings of the Women's International War Crimes Tribunal, in *The Prosecutors and the Peoples of the Asia–Pacific Region v. Emperor Hirohito et al. and the Government of Japan*, 12 December 2000, and the discussion of this in C. Chinkin, 'Women's International Tribunal on Japanese military sexual slavery', AJIL, 95 (2001), 335–41.

[657] See *Kunarać*, although sexual slavery was dealt with as rape and as enslavement as a crime against humanity, see discussion *supra*, para. 3.89.1 and *infra*, pp. 147–8 and 214–15.

[658] G. McDougall, Contemporary forms of slavery, Final Report, para. 30.

[659] G. McDougall, Special Rapporteur, Update to Final Report, 'Contemporary forms of slavery: systematic rape, sexual slavery and slavery-like practices during armed conflict', Sub-commission on Prevention of Discrimination and Protection of Minorities, UN Doc. E/CN.4/Sub.2/2000/21, 6 June 2000 (hereinafter: G. McDougall, Contemporary forms of slavery, update to Final Report), para. 8.

[660] *Ibid.*, para. 50.

[661] G. McDougall, Contemporary forms of slavery, Final Report, para. 28.

oneself at substantial risk of personal harm from a condition of slavery should not be interpreted as nullifying a claim of slavery'.[662]

Two examples of sexual slavery in modern conflicts given by McDougall are, first, the practice of the Ugandan Lord's Resistance Army of abducting children, including girls as young as twelve, to give to commanders as 'wives'.[663] McDougall stated that '[t]he repeated rape and sexual abuse of women and girls under the guise of "marriage" constitutes slavery, as the victims do not have the freedom to leave, to refuse the sham "marriage" or to decide whether and on what terms to engage in sexual activity'.[664] Second, young virgin girls in Sierra Leone were ordered to report each night for sexual abuse by rebel fighters, who abducted some of the girls when they retreated.[665] Again McDougall described this as sexual slavery, as 'the victims did not have the freedom to leave or to refuse to comply with the orders, and as repeated sexual access to the victims was gained through the use and threat of force, the control of the physical environment and abduction'.[666]

## The Rome Statute

### *Rape*

In addition to the Elements in respect of the nature of the conflict, the Elements of the crime of rape require that '[t]he Perpetrator invaded the body of a person by conduct resulting in penetration, however slight, of any part of the body of the victim or of the perpetrator with a sexual organ, or of the anal or genital opening of the victim with any object or any other part of the body'.[667] A footnote to the expression 'invaded' states that this concept is intended to be broad enough to be gender-neutral.[668] Therefore, this element clarifies the fact that the crime of rape may be perpetrated by either sex upon a victim of either sex and additionally reflects the nature of the offence as 'an assault upon the integrity of a person'.[669] It appears to reflect a compromise between the somewhat vague language used in *Akayesu* and the more specific wording of this offence in *Furundžija*.

[662] *Ibid.*

[663] G. McDougall, Contemporary forms of slavery, update to Final Report, para. 13.

[664] *Ibid.*, para 13.

[665] *Ibid.*, para. 17.

[666] *Ibid.*, para. 17.

[667] EOC, p. 141.

[668] *Ibid.*, fn. 50.

[669] C. Hall, 'The first five sessions of the UN Preparatory Commission for the International Criminal Court', AJIL, 94 (2000), 773–89, p. 778, and see K. Boon, 'Rape and forced pregnancy under the ICC Statute: human dignity, autonomy, and consent', Colum Hum Rts L Rev, 32 (2001), 625–75, pp. 630–1.

The second Element of rape states that:

> [t]he invasion was committed by force, or by threat of force or coercion, such as that caused by fear of violence, duress, detention, psychological oppression or abuse of power, against such person or another person, or by taking advantage of a coercive environment, or the invasion was committed against a person incapable of giving genuine consent.[670]

A footnote to the word 'consent' states that '[i]t is understood that a person may be incapable of giving genuine consent if affected by natural, induced or age-related incapacity'.[671]

Once more this seems to be a compromise between different approaches taken by judgements of the ICTY and ICTR, with the 'coercion' approach of *Akayesu*, *Čelebici* and *Furundžija* prevailing over the 'consent' approach of *Kunarać*.[672] The Women's Caucus for Gender Justice, an NGO group at the Preparatory Commission, expressed approval of the inclusion of the word 'coercion' as opposed to 'force' on the basis that it deals with a less direct, although equally menacing, situation.[673] They suggest that 'abuse of authority and threats to deny or promises to provide the means of survival' should be viewed as constituting coercive circumstances, rendering any apparent consent immaterial.[674]

### *Sexual slavery*

The EOC of sexual slavery require that the perpetrator 'exercised any or all of the powers attaching to the right of ownership over one or more persons, such as by purchasing, selling, lending or bartering such a person or persons, or by imposing on them a similar deprivation of liberty'.[675] This element reflects

[670] EOC, p. 141. Hansen-Young objects to any use of the word 'consent' as opposed to 'coercion', T. Hansen-Young, 'Defining rape: a means to achieve justice in the Special Court for Sierra Leone', Chi J Int'l L, 6 (2005), 479–94, especially pp. 489–92.

[671] EOC, p. 141, fn. 51. See *Brima, Kamara and Kanu*, Trial Judgement, para. 694, which comments that '[c]hildren below the age of 14 cannot give valid consent', although this was based on Sierra Leonean national law on the age of consent.

[672] However, as with the ICTY/R, consent is dealt with in the RPE, where Rule 70 states that '[i]n cases of sexual violence, the Court shall be guided by and, where appropriate, apply the following principles: (a) Consent cannot be inferred by reason of any words or conduct of a victim where force, threat of force, coercion or taking advantage of a coercive environment undermined the victim's ability to give voluntary and genuine consent; (b) Consent cannot be inferred by reason of any words or conduct of a victim where the victim is incapable of giving genuine consent; (c) Consent cannot be inferred by reason of the silence of, or lack of resistance by, a victim to the alleged sexual violence', Rules of Procedure and Evidence, Assembly of States Parties to the Rome Statute of the ICC, Official Records, First Session, ICC-ASP/1/3, 3–10 September 2002, 10–107, p. 44.

[673] Women's Caucus for Gender Justice, 'Priority concerns relating to the elements annex', submitted to the 16–26 Preparatory Committee for the International Criminal Court, available at: <http://www.iccwomen.org/icc/>.

[674] *Ibid.*

[675] EOC, p. 141. A similar deprivation of liberty would include those not physically locked up but in fear of their lives and with nowhere else to go, Lee (ed.), *ICC: Elements*, pp. 191–2.

exactly that of enslavement as a crime against humanity, demonstrating that the ICC has taken the same position as McDougall in seeing 'sexual' as an adjective to the offence of slavery.[676] The second element in respect of the 'sexual' nature of this offence requires that '[t]he perpetrator caused such person or persons to engage in one or more acts of a sexual nature'.[677] This is very broad expression and would include any conceivable sexual exploitation of a person enslaved during an armed conflict.

### *Enforced prostitution*

The Elements of enforced prostitution were difficult to agree upon, given that many delegates were of the opinion that 'in situations of armed conflict, most factual scenarios that could be described as forced prostitution would also amount to sexual slavery and could more appropriately and more easily be characterized and prosecuted as slavery'.[678] However, they require that:

> [t]he perpetrator caused one or more persons to engage in one or more acts of a sexual nature by force, or by threat of force or coercion, such as that caused by fear of violence, duress, detention, psychological oppression or abuse of power, against such person or persons or another person, or by taking advantage of a coercive environment or such person's or persons' incapacity to give genuine consent.[679]

Furthermore the perpetrator 'or another person obtained or expected to obtain pecuniary or other advantage in exchange for or in connection with the acts of a sexual nature'.[680] Given this definition, it is still difficult to imagine a situation in which forced prostitution, other than as a 'one-off', would not amount to sexual slavery,[681] although the requirement of pecuniary or other advantage arising from the acts of a sexual nature has the implication that not all crimes of sexual slavery will amount to forced prostitution. For example, the situation of the Dutch women in the case of *Awochi*,[682] although charged at the time as forced prostitution, would also appear to constitute sexual slavery. The women had deprivation of liberty imposed upon them, given that they were kept in a particular place without freedom of movement, and they were also forced to engage in acts of a sexual nature.

### *Forced pregnancy*

This offence was included as a result of the practice during the conflict in the former Yugoslavia of raping women and then detaining them until it was too

[676] See discussion *infra*, pp. 214–17.

[677] EOC, p. 141.

[678] G. McDougall, Contemporary forms of slavery, Final Report, para. 33, and see K. Dörmann, 'Preparatory Commission for the International Criminal Court', n. 63 *supra*, p. 480.

[679] EOC, p. 142.

[680] *Ibid.*

[681] But see K. Askin, 'Crimes within the jurisdiction of the International Criminal Court', Crim LF, 10 (1999), 33–59, pp. 44–5, and N. Demleitner, 'Forced prostitution: naming an international offence', Fordham Int'l LJ, 18 (1994), 163–97, pp. 193–4.

[682] Discussed *supra*, p. 145.

late for them to obtain an abortion, thus forcing them to bear a child of a different ethnicity.[683] However, it proved difficult to frame at the Rome Conference, owing to fears by delegates that it could be construed as giving all women the right to an abortion.[684]

Article 7(2)(f), to which Article 8(2)(b)(xxii) refers, defines 'forced pregnancy' as 'the unlawful confinement of a woman forcibly made pregnant, with the intent of affecting the ethnic composition of any population or carrying out other grave violations of international law' and explicitly states that '[t]his definition shall not in any way be interpreted as affecting national laws relating to pregnancy'. It must be noted, however, that sexual intercourse is not a necessary ingredient of this offence and indeed that 'forced pregnancy is broader than rape in that it applies to any situation or technology by which a woman is made pregnant against her will'.[685]

The Elements merely repeat this definition and therefore the mental element of this offence would include knowledge that the woman was forcibly made pregnant and that she was being confined,[686] coupled with the intention to affect the ethnic composition of a population, or to commit another grave violation of international law.[687] Boon suggests that an intention to commit another crime within the Rome Statute, such as persecution, torture or inhuman treatment, would fulfil the mental element of this offence by amounting to an intention to commit another grave violation of international law.[688]

### *Enforced sterilisation*

The Elements of this offence require that the perpetrator 'deprived one or more persons of biological reproductive capacity' and that this conduct 'was neither justified by the medical or hospital treatment of the person or persons concerned nor carried out with their genuine consent'.[689] Footnotes to these EOC explain that birth control measures which have a non-permanent effect are not included in the offence and that 'genuine consent' does not include consent obtained through deception.[690]

Therefore, any method of permanent sterilisation which was not justified by medical or hospital treatment would amount to this offence, provided that the

[683] Yugoslavia Commission of Experts' Report, n. 618 *supra*, para. 248.

[684] H. von Hebel and D. Robinson, 'Crimes within the jurisdiction of the court', n. 154 *supra*, p. 100.

[685] K. Boon, 'Rape and forced pregnancy under the ICC Statute', n. 669 *supra*, p. 661.

[686] Lack of knowledge that the confinement was unlawful should not constitute a defence for an accused on the basis that ignorance of the law is no defence, but see Articles 32(1) and 33 of the Rome Statute.

[687] EOC, p. 142. Therefore the Elements raise the *mens rea* requirement for this crime above the *actus reus*, and further ensure that depriving a woman forcibly made pregnant of an abortion because national law did not allow abortions would not amount to this offence.

[688] K. Boon, 'Rape and forced pregnancy under the ICC Statute', n. 669 *supra*, p. 665.

[689] EOC, p. 142.

[690] *Ibid.*, fns 54 and 55.

perpetrator intended to sterilise the victim and knew that it was not justified and that he did not have the genuine consent of the person affected. It is difficult to imagine a conflict situation in which genuine consent could truly be obtained in respect of permanent sterilisation which was not justified by medical or hospital treatment. An example of justified treatment which might result in permanent sterilisation could include emergency treatment for testicular or ovarian cancer.

### *Sexual violence*

The Elements of sexual violence were difficult to frame, as Article 8(2)(b)(xxii) uses the expression 'or any other form of sexual violence also constituting a grave breach of the Geneva Conventions'. This gave rise to two different interpretations at the Preparatory Commission, an affirmation that gender crimes could already be prosecuted as grave breaches or an additional requirement that gender offences must also fulfil all the requirements of one of the grave breaches of the Geneva Conventions.[691] The compromise is reflected in the Elements, with this comment being restricted to the sexual violence offence and requiring that '[t]he conduct was of a gravity comparable to that of a grave breach of the Geneva Conventions' and the perpetrator must have been 'aware of the factual circumstances that established the gravity of the conduct'.[692]

It is submitted that when measuring the gravity of the conduct in order to decide whether it is comparable to a grave breach, the cultural circumstances of the incident must be taken into account. For example, the forced nudity of a Muslim woman from a traditional society would probably be much more severe in its effects upon the victim than the forced nudity of a woman from a Western country who was used to sunbathing topless on the beach.[693]

The element which defines sexual violence states that the perpetrator 'committed an act of a sexual nature against one or more persons or caused such person or persons to engage in an act of a sexual nature'. The phrase 'act of a sexual nature' is a broad expression which would cover such things as 'sexual contact or conduct, sexual mutilation, forced or coerced performance of sexual acts or sexual entertainment, forced or coerced nudity'.[694] The act of a sexual nature must be 'by force, or by threat of force or coercion, such as that caused by fear of violence, duress, detention, psychological oppression or abuse of power, against such person or persons or another person, or by taking advantage of a coercive environment or such person's or persons' incapacity to give genuine consent'.[695]

[691] K. Dörmann, 'Preparatory Commission for the International Criminal Court', n. 63 *supra*, pp. 480–1.

[692] EOC, p. 143, and see Lee (ed.), *ICC: Elements*, p. 198.

[693] This is not to suggest that in either circumstance such conduct would not be comparable in gravity to a grave breach.

[694] Women's Caucus for Gender Justice, 'Priority concerns relating to the elements annex', n. 673 *supra*.

[695] EOC, p. 143.

This expression is essentially the one used in the EOC for rape and enforced prostitution.[696]

### Article 8(2)(b)(xxiii) Utilising the presence of a civilian or other protected person to render certain points, areas or military forces immune from military operations

#### Origins

The 1949 Geneva Conventions prohibited the presence of civilians or prisoners of war from being used to 'render certain points or areas immune from military operations'.[697] These provisions arose from a few instances of the use of 'human shields' during the Second World War to protect areas of strategic importance and to accompany military convoys, although the practice had in fact been employed by the British forces during the Boer War.[698] The commentary to the Geneva Conventions defines 'military operations' as 'any acts of warfare committed by the enemy's land, air or sea forces, whether it is a matter of bombing or bombardments of any kind or of attacks by units near at hand'.[699]

The prohibition of the use of human shields was extended by Article 51(7) of AP I to forbid such use of the 'movement' as well as the 'presence' of civilians and forms the basis of this provision of the Rome Statute. The concept of movement in this article of AP I covers both the situation in which a belligerent takes advantage of the 'voluntary' movement of people, such as fleeing refugees, as well as the situation where a belligerent forces civilians into an area to impede the movement of the adversary's troops.[700]

#### Development

The crime of using human shields has attracted much attention in recent years, most notably because of the use of this tactic in the Iraq–Kuwait Gulf War and in the Balkan conflict.[701] The use of Western and Kuwaiti civilian hostages and prisoners of war by Iraq in an attempt to render certain military objectives

[696] See discussion *supra*, pp. 152–3.

[697] Article 28, Geneva Convention IV, and Article 23, Geneva Convention III, respectively.

[698] Pictet (ed.), *Commentary: IV Convention*, p. 208, and Lord Wright, 'The killing of hostages as a war crime', BYIL, 25 (1948), 296–310, p. 301.

[699] Pictet (ed.), *Commentary: IV Convention*, p. 209. See definition of 'military operations' in S. Oeter, 'Methods and means of combat', n. 21 *supra*, para. 441(2).

[700] Sandoz *et al.*, *Commentary on the Additional Protocols*, p. 627, and Bothe *et al.*, *New Rules for Victims*, p. 316.

[701] Turns also comments that Hizbollah made use of the presence of the United Nations and civilians as shields when launching attacks against Israel in the Lebanon, D. Turns, 'Some reflections on the conflict in southern Lebanon: the "Qana incident" and international humanitarian law', JCSL, 5 (2000), 177–209, pp. 203–4.

immune from attack led to worldwide condemnation as a breach of the Geneva Conventions.[702]

With respect to the Balkan conflict, the ICTY indictment of *Karadžić and Mladić* accuses them of the grave breach of inhuman treatment for using UN peacekeepers as human shields, a charge confirmed by the Rule 61 decision.[703] The peacekeepers were held against their will at potential NATO air targets, including ammunition bunkers, and a communications centre 'in order to render these locations immune from further NATO airstrikes'.[704] Inhumane and cruel treatment was also charged in the case of Blaškić, a Bosnian Croat, who was found to have used Bosnian Muslim civilians as human shields to protect his headquarters.[705] However, as a result of the characterisation of this conduct as inhuman or cruel treatment in both of the above cases, the elements of the offence of detaining an individual as a human shield *per se* were not elaborated, although the *Blaškić* Appeal Chamber commented that '[u]sing protected detainees as human shields constitutes a violation of the provisions of the Geneva Conventions regardless of whether those human shields were actually attacked or harmed' and that the 'prohibition is designed to protect detainees from being exposed to the risk of harm, and not only to the harm itself'.[706]

### The Rome Statute

The EOC for this offence, in addition to those concerning the nature of the conflict, first require that the perpetrator 'moved or otherwise took advantage of the location of one or more civilians or other persons protected under the international law of armed conflict' in order to fulfil the *actus reus* of the offence.[707] Importantly, the wording of this element, which reflects that of the Rome Statute, confirms that other protected persons, such as prisoners of war, are protected by the article in addition to civilians. This element also demonstrates that, as with Article 51(7) of AP I, rendering areas immune from military operations through the movement of such individuals as well as their presence is prohibited.

The second element lays down the *mens rea* of the offence by requiring that the perpetrator 'intended to shield a military objective from attack or shield, favour

[702] Note that Iraq is not a party to AP I, but this still constituted a breach of Articles 28 and 23, Geneva Conventions IV and III, respectively. See A. DeSaussure, 'The role of the law of armed conflict during the Persian Gulf War', n. 88 *supra*, pp. 52–4; R. Bailey, 'Why do States violate the law of war? A comparison of Iraqi violations in two Gulf wars', Sy J Int L, 27 (2000), 103–29, p. 125, and US Department of Defence Report, pp. 624–6.

[703] First indictment of *Karadžić and Mladić*, 24 July 1995, counts 15 and 16, and *Karadžić and Mladić*, Rule 61 Review, para. 20.

[704] First indictment of *Karadžić and Mladić*, 24 July 1995, para. 47.

[705] *Blaškić*, Trial Judgement, paras 716 and 743. On appeal *Blaškić* was found to have omitted to prevent the use of civilians in this way, *Blaškić*, Appeal Judgement, para. 670.

[706] *Blaškić*, Appeal Judgement, para. 654.

[707] EOC, p. 143.

or impede military operations'.[708] This is phrased somewhat differently from the article in the Rome Statute, which prohibits the perpetrator from using the presence or movement of individuals 'to render certain points, areas or military forces immune from military operations'. *Prima facie* it appears unlikely that human shields would be used to render objectives without military value immune to attack. However, it is possible that a belligerent could hold civilians or prisoners of war in a building of debatable military value, such as a television and radio station, claiming that it was not a military objective and should not be attacked in any event, yet clearly utilising their presence to render the point immune from military operations. Nevertheless, such a situation would probably constitute an intention to 'shield, favour or impede military operations' and thereby still fulfil the *mens rea* of the offence. The wording of this element also demonstrates that the offence may be committed when an individual uses a human shield with the intention of rendering an area immune from military operations; it is not necessary to show the plan was successful and that the area was not attacked.

Upon ratification of the ICC, France entered an interpretative declaration to this article of the Rome Statute, stating that the use of human shields contrary to the article 'does not preclude France from directing attacks against objectives considered as military objectives under international humanitarian law'.[709] Whilst this is a valid statement, an attack against a military objective with a large human shield would risk breaching Article 8(2)(b)(iv) of the Statute prohibiting excessive incidental loss of life or injury to civilians.[710]

## Article 8(2)(b)(xxiv) Intentionally directing attacks against buildings, material, medical units and transport, and personnel using the distinctive emblems of the Geneva Conventions in conformity with international law

### Origins

The distinctive emblems of the Geneva Conventions are defined by Article 8(1) of AP I as 'the red cross, red crescent or red lion and sun', although the red lion and sun has since fallen out of use. A further distinctive emblem, the red crystal, was added by Additional Protocol III to the Geneva Conventions in 2005.[711] The Geneva Conventions and Protocols do not contain an article prohibiting attacks upon personnel, transport or buildings using the distinctive emblems *per se*, though attacks upon such persons and objects entitled to use the distinctive emblems

[708] *Ibid.*

[709] France's interpretative declaration, para. 4, available from the ICRC website: <http://www.icrc.org>.

[710] See Article 51(8), AP I.

[711] Additional Protocol III came into force on 14 January 2007.

are in any case prohibited.[712] The Conventions and Protocols also set out provisions for the proper use of the emblems as a protective device under international law.[713]

## Development

There have been no recent prosecutions or legal debate on the issue of attacking objects or persons using the emblems of the Geneva Conventions.[714]

## The Rome Statute

The EOC of this offence, in addition to those in relation to the nature of the conflict, require that the perpetrator 'attacked one or more persons, buildings, medical units or transports or other objects using, in conformity with international law, a distinctive emblem or other method of identification indicating protection under the Geneva Conventions'.[715] This element is broad enough to include an attack on an object using the red crystal, although AP III was agreed after the adoption of the Rome Statute. Additionally, it must be shown that the perpetrator 'intended such persons, buildings, units or transports or other objects so using such identification to be the object of the attack'.[716]

The wording of this offence in the Rome Statute commences with the phrase 'intentionally directing attacks', the same expression as that used in the offences defined by Article 8(2)(b)(i)–(iii) and (ix). However, the EOC for this crime, unlike those referred to, state that '[t]he perpetrator attacked . . .', rather than '[t]he perpetrator directed an attack'. Nevertheless, it seems unlikely that this slight alteration in wording was intended to alter the sense of this crime, and in line with the other offences it is submitted that this is referring to combat action by one or more combatants.[717]

The *actus reus* of the offence is fulfilled only if the persons or objects attacked are using the distinctive emblems of the Geneva Conventions in conformity with international law. Therefore the emblems must be used in conformity with the regulations set out in the Geneva Conventions and their Additional Protocols.[718] The Elements also prohibit an attack on a person or object

[712] See Articles 19, 24–6, 33 and 36, Geneva Convention I; Articles 22, 24–5, 27, 36–7 and 39, Geneva Convention II; Articles 18 and 20–2, Geneva Convention IV, and Articles 18(3–4) and 23–4, AP I.

[713] See Articles 38–44, Geneva Convention I; Articles 41–5, Geneva Convention II; Articles 18, 20 and 21–2, Geneva Convention IV, and Articles 12–13 and 18, AP I, and see discussion *supra*, p. 99.

[714] But see reference to an Israeli attack on an ambulance in the Lebanon during Operation Grapes of Wrath in D. Turns, 'Some reflections on the conflict in southern Lebanon', n. 701 *supra*, pp. 202–3.

[715] EOC, pp. 143–4.

[716] *Ibid.*, p. 144.

[717] See *supra*, p. 67.

[718] *Ibid.*

using any 'other method of identification indicating protection under the Geneva Conventions'. This ensures that an attack upon an Israeli military hospital displaying the red shield of David would contravene the provision.[719] Additionally, this would encompass an attack upon a hospital ship or medical helicopter transmitting an agreed distinctive signal.[720]

Finally, the *mens rea* of the offence is clear from the second element. The perpetrator must intend the persons or objects displaying the emblem to be the object of the attack. This suggests that the accused must either see the emblem, or see or hear a distinctive signal (or other method of identification) used to show that the persons or objects are protected under the Geneva Conventions. There is no suggestion that the perpetrator must attempt a legal analysis of whether such emblem or identification is being used in conformity with international law, or indeed be aware of the fact that such an emblem demonstrates protection under international law. This appears to be an objective part of the *actus reus* and is in accordance with the general principle that knowledge of the law is not a relevant factor when assessing liability for an alleged offence.[721]

## Article 8(2)(b)(xxv) Intentionally using starvation of civilians as a method of warfare by depriving them of objects indispensable to their survival, including wilfully impeding relief supplies as provided for under the Geneva Conventions

### Origins

Starvation has been used as a method of warfare throughout history,[722] and even the Lieber Code admitted that '[i]t is lawful to starve the hostile belligerent, armed or unarmed, so that it leads to the speedier subjection of the enemy'.[723] Nevertheless, although the 1907 Hague Regulations did not outlaw starvation as a method of warfare directly, such actions were indirectly limited by the prohibition against destroying or seizing the enemy's property unless imperatively demanded by the necessities of war.[724] Furthermore, '[d]eliberate starvation

[719] Israel uses the Red Shield of David in place of the red cross or crescent as its distinctive emblem, see reservation entered to Geneva Conventions I, II and IV, available from the ICRC website: <http://www.icrc.org/>. The new emblem, the red crystal, established by APIII, was intended to address this problem but to date (as of October 2007) Israel has not ratified the treaty.

[720] See Article 18(4) and (5). This phrasing is important to prevent a loophole where the person targeting an aircraft or ship is not close enough to see whether or not the distinctive emblem is displayed.

[721] Although ignorance of the law is a limited defence under Articles 32 and 33 of the Rome Statute.

[722] E. Rosenblad, *International Humanitarian Law of Armed Conflict: Some Aspects of the Principle of Distinction and Related Problems* (Geneva: Henri Dunant Institute, 1979), pp. 103–4.

[723] Article 17, Lieber Code, but see C. Allen, 'Civilian starvation and relief during armed conflict: the modern humanitarian law', Georgia J Int Comp L, 19 (1989), 1–85, pp. 33–5.

[724] Article 23(h), 1907 Hague Regulations, C. Allen, *ibid.*, pp. 35–6, and discussion, *supra*, pp. 119–22.

of civilians' was listed as a war crime after the First World War by the Commission on the Responsibility of the Authors of the War and on Enforcement of Penalties.[725]

Starvation of civilians in the context of siege warfare was considered in post-Second World War tribunals. In particular, the US Military Tribunal reviewed the orders of Field Marshal von Leeb, who authorised his artillery to fire upon Russian civilians attempting to leave the besieged city of Leningrad. However, the tribunal held that this act was not unlawful, as 'the cutting off of every source of sustenance from without is deemed legitimate', and that 'if the commander of a besieged place expels the noncombatants, in order to lessen the number of those who consume his stock of provisions, it is lawful, though an extreme measure, to drive them back so as to hasten the surrender'.[726] Additionally, during both the First World War and the Second World War naval blockades were used by several States and excluded all shipping from the declared areas, including those transporting foodstuffs, leading to hardship and even starvation among civilians.[727]

In the light of these experiences the Geneva Conventions of 1949 laid down provisions to ensure an adequate food supply for prisoners of war and civilians in occupied areas.[728] However, they failed to prohibit starvation of civilians as a method of combat or to deal adequately with the situation of sieges or blockades. The Fourth Convention merely requires that the Parties 'endeavour' to agree to allow certain vulnerable persons to leave besieged areas.[729] During a blockade the Parties are required to allow free passage of 'essential foodstuffs, clothing and tonics intended for children under fifteen, expectant mothers and maternity cases' only provided that certain conditions are met.[730]

[725] Commission on the Responsibility of the Authors of the War and on Enforcement of Penalties, Report presented to the Preliminary Peace Conference, 29 March 1919, reprinted in AJIL, 14 (1920), 95–126, p. 114.

[726] Trial of *von Leeb and Others*, 12 LRTWC 1, p. 84. See comments of E. Rosenblad, *International Humanitarian Law of Armed Conflict*, n. 722 *supra*, p. 109, and Y. Dinstein, 'Siege warfare and the starvation of civilians', pp. 145–52, in A. Delissen and D. Tanja, *Humanitarian Law Challenges*, n. 280 *supra*, pp. 146–7.

[727] Adler comments on the British blockade of Germany in the First World War, G. Adler, 'Targets in war: legal considerations', Hous LR, 8 (1970), 1–46, p. 38. Levie comments on the US blockade of Japan in the Second World War in 'Means and methods of combat at sea', pp. 227–37 in M. Schmitt and L. Green (eds), *Levie on the Law of War*, 70 US Naval War College International Law Studies (Newport, RI: Naval War College, 1998), p. 229. The International Military Tribunal (IMT) at Nuremberg found the commander-in-chief of the German navy, Dönitz, not guilty on the charge of unrestricted submarine warfare on the basis that British merchant ships were armed and the British and US navies acted similarly, *IMT Judgement*, pp. 507–10.

[728] See Articles 20 and 26, Geneva Convention III, and Articles 55 and 59, Geneva Convention IV.

[729] Article 17, Geneva Convention IV.

[730] Article 23, Geneva Convention IV. See comments by Y. Dinstein, 'Siege warfare and the starvation of civilians', n. 726 *supra*, p. 148, and E. Rosenblad, *International Humanitarian Law of Armed Conflict*, n. 722 *supra*, pp. 113–14.

Starvation of civilians as a method of warfare was finally prohibited unambiguously by Article 54 of AP I,[731] the basis of this article of the Rome Statute.[732] Article 54 states that '[s]tarvation of civilians as a method of warfare is prohibited', and that:

> [i]t is prohibited to attack, destroy, remove or render useless objects indispensable to the survival of the civilian population, such as foodstuffs, agricultural areas for the production of foodstuffs, crops, livestock, drinking water installations and supplies and irrigation works, for the specific purpose of denying them for their sustenance value to the civilian population or to the adverse Party, whatever the motive, whether in order to starve out civilians, to cause them to move away, or for any other motive.

Furthermore, Article 70 of AP I states that if the civilian population in a non-occupied territory (which would include a besieged city) does not have an adequate food supply, 'relief actions which are humanitarian and impartial in character and conducted without any adverse distinction shall be undertaken, subject to the agreement of the Parties concerned in such relief actions'.[733] Detter comments that these articles 'prohibit siege in the old meaning and function of the term'.[734]

The ICRC commentary to AP I states that to use starvation as a method of warfare would be to use it as 'a weapon to annihilate or weaken the population', provoking starvation deliberately, 'causing the population to suffer hunger, particularly by depriving it of its sources of food or supplies'.[735] Oeter argues that the list of objects indispensable to the survival of the civilian population in Article 54(2) of AP I is illustrative only, and that in harsh climates other items such as clothing or basic shelter would be included, hence deprivation of such items as a method of warfare would amount to this offence.[736] However, Allen comments that in view of the fact that the items illustrated are all consumables it is unlikely that other objects are protected under this provision.[737]

[731] This advance may have been influenced by starvation in the Biafran and Vietnam conflicts, G. Mudge, 'Starvation as a means of warfare', Int Law, 4 (1969–70), 228–68, and R. Falk, 'Methods and means of warfare', pp. 37–53 in P. Trooboff (ed.), *Law and Responsibility in Warfare*, n. 521 *supra*, pp. 45–6.

[732] See J. Paust, 'The human rights to food, medicine and medical supplies, and freedom from arbitrary and inhumane detention and controls in Sri Lanka', Vand J Transnat'l L, 31 (1998), 617–42, p. 628.

[733] See C. Allen, 'Civilian starvation and relief during armed conflict', n. 723 *supra*, pp. 71–2.

[734] I. Detter, *The Law of War*, n. 519 *supra*, p. 298.

[735] Sandoz *et al.*, *Commentary on the Additional Protocols*, p. 653.

[736] S. Oeter, 'Methods and means of combat', n. 21 *supra*, para. 463(4), G. Aldrich, 'New life for the laws of war', n. 36 *supra*, p. 779, and see Y. Dinstein, *The Conduct of Hostilities under the International Law of Armed Conflict* (Cambridge: Cambridge University Press, 2004), p. 132.

[737] C. Allen, 'Civilian starvation and relief during armed conflict', n. 723 *supra*, p. 64, and C. Shotwell, 'Food and the use of force: the role of humanitarian principles in the Persian Gulf crisis and beyond', Rev dr milit, 30 (1991), 345–85, p. 366, but see Bothe *et al.*, *New Rules for Victims*, p. 340.

It must be noted that AP I does not prohibit the destruction of objects indispensable to the survival of the civilian population as an incidental side effect of military action, but only where the perpetrator intended to deny their sustenance value to the civilian population. Therefore 'a belligerent might reasonably attack an irrigation canal used as a defensive position, a water tower used as an observation post, or an orchard used as cover for the enemy'.[738] However, if the intention of the perpetrator is to deny the sustenance value to the civilian population, the motive behind such action, whether to kill the civilians or force them to move, is irrelevant. Finally, despite the fact that Article 49(3) states that this section of AP I (including Article 54) does not alter humanitarian law applicable to war at sea, nevertheless the article also states that this section is binding upon naval and air operations where they affect the civilian population on land. Therefore, it is evident that a naval blockade may not starve civilians on land as a method of warfare and must in any case comply with Article 70 by allowing relief operations in favour of civilians.[739]

## Development

Starvation of civilians and impeding relief supplies for civilians by armed forces and groups have been all too common in recent conflicts.[740] In particular, aid convoys and relief supplies were attacked both in Somalia and in the former Yugoslavia.[741] However, the elements of this offence have not as yet received detailed examination before the ICTY, although the *Milošević* indictment charged obstruction of aid to the enclaves of Bihać, Goražde, Srebrenica and Žepa as the crime against humanity of persecution.[742]

Nevertheless, the content of this provision in relation to naval blockades has been examined in the San Remo Manual, which states that a blockade would be unlawful under Article 54 if 'it has the sole purpose of starving the civilian population or denying it other objects essential for its survival'.[743] Furthermore, the Manual states that '[i]f the civilian population of the blockaded territory is inadequately provided with food and other objects essential for its survival,

[738] C. Allen, 'Civilian starvation and relief during armed conflict', n. 723 *supra*, p. 66, and see G. Aldrich, 'New life for the laws of war', n. 36 *supra*, p. 779, and M. Bothe, 'War crimes', n. 198 *supra*, p. 402. However, such action would have to conform to the law relating to proportionality, see discussion *supra*, pp. 81–9.

[739] C. Shotwell, 'Food and the use of force', n. 737 *supra*, p. 365, but see arguments to the contrary in Y. Dinstein, *The Conduct of Hostilities*, n. 736 *supra*, pp. 137–40.

[740] See 'Report of the Secretary General to the Security Council on the protection of civilians in armed conflict', 8 September 1999, UN Doc. S/1999/957, para. 19, and D. Buckingham, 'A recipe for change: towards an integrated approach to food under international law', Pace ILR, 6 (1994), 285–321, pp. 299–300.

[741] SC Res. 794, 3 December 1992, para. 5, and SC Res. 787 of 1992, para. 7, condemned these actions.

[742] *Milosević*, Bosnia Indictment, para. 35(k).

[743] Article 102, 1994 San Remo Manual, and *San Remo Manual: Explanation*, p. 179.

the blockading party must provide for free passage of such foodstuffs and other essential supplies'.[744]

## The Rome Statute

The EOC for this offence, in addition to those in respect of the nature of the conflict, require that the perpetrator 'deprived civilians of objects indispensable to their survival' and 'intended to starve civilians as a method of warfare'.[745] Therefore, intention to starve civilians is necessary in order to fulfil the mental element of this offence; it is not sufficient that the perpetrator is reckless as to the starvation, or that the starvation is an unintended effect of his military strategy.[746]

According to Dörmann the delegates at the Preparatory Commission, when composing the EOC, were agreed that starvation 'was meant to cover not only the more restrictive meaning of starving as killing by hunger or depriving of nourishment, but also the more general meaning of deprivation or insufficient supply of some essential commodity, or something necessary to live'.[747] Therefore deprivation of 'medicine or in certain circumstances blankets, could be covered by this crime, if, in the latter case, such blankets were indispensable for survival owing to the very low temperature in a region'.[748] This is a sensible approach, in line with the spirit of Article 54 of AP I, the basis of this provision in the Rome Statute. Cottier's suggestion that the use of such starvation 'with an aim to gain a military advantage' would amount to its use as a 'method of warfare' is a good explanation of this phrase.[749]

The *actus reus* of this offence is fulfilled by depriving civilians of objects indispensable to their survival.[750] This is a wide expression and the list given in Article 54(2) should be taken as a guide, in addition to medicine, clothing, blankets and shelter, where climatic conditions make the latter necessary. Although this article in the Rome Statute refers to the wilful impeding of relief supplies, this is not referred to in the Elements, presumably because it is only an example of depriving civilians of objects indispensable to their survival. However, if impeding relief supplies for the civilian population, provided for by Articles 55 and 59 of the Fourth Geneva Convention and Article 70 of AP I, amounts to deprivation of

[744] Article 103, 1994 San Remo Manual. This essentially implements Article 70 of AP I in relation to relief supplies.

[745] EOC, p. 144.

[746] See comments by C. Rottensteiner, 'The denial of humanitarian assistance as a crime under international law', IRRC, 835 (1999), 555–82, p. 569.

[747] K. Dörmann, 'Preparatory Commission for the International Criminal Court', n. 63 *supra*, p. 475. This approach is supported in Cottier *et al.*, 'Article 8', p. 256.

[748] K. Dörmann, 'Preparatory Commission for the International Criminal Court', n. 63 *supra*, p. 475, and see Lee (ed.), *ICC: Elements*, p. 204.

[749] Cottier *et al.*, 'Article 8', p. 259.

[750] See comments by J. Paust, 'The Preparatory Committee's "definition of crimes": war crimes', n. 405 *supra*, p. 443.

objects indispensable to civilian survival, then it could constitute the *actus reus* of the offence.[751] Finally, it must be noted that the Elements do not require that as a result of the perpetrator's actions one or more civilians died from starvation.[752]

Therefore the *mens rea* of this offence requires that the perpetrator intended to starve civilians, an expression encompassing starvation by lack of nourishment or by an insufficient supply of another commodity essential for life, in order to gain a military advantage. The *actus reus* is fulfilled if the perpetrator deprives civilians of objects indispensable to their survival, and such a deprivation could be caused by the intentional impeding of relief supplies, but it need not be shown that the actions or omissions actually resulted in any civilians dying of starvation. This offence could be committed by land forces, by a naval blockade or by air strikes which would affect civilians on land in the manner proscribed.

## Article 8(2)(b)(xxvi) Conscripting or enlisting children under the age of fifteen years into the national armed forces or using them to participate actively in hostilities

### Origins

Children are often employed in armed conflicts, as they make obedient and cheap soldiers, yet those who survive such employment 'are often physically injured and psychologically scarred, having lost years of schooling and socialization'.[753] The use of children in armed conflicts has not decreased in recent years, with an estimated 250,000 soldiers currently under eighteen years old, and, furthermore, technological advances such as 'automatic weapons and lightweight arms have increased the desirability and utility of child soldiers'.[754] However, although the 1949 Geneva Conventions provide extra protection for children under fifteen, they are silent as to the employment of children in warfare.[755]

The prohibition upon the use of soldiers under fifteen years old which forms the basis for this provision of the Rome Statute is contained in both Article 77(2) of AP I and, in very similar wording, in Article 38 of the 1989 Convention

[751] See Cottier *et al.*, 'Article 8', p. 258.

[752] K. Dörmann, 'Preparatory Commission for the International Criminal Court', n. 63 *supra*, p. 476.

[753] 'Children and armed conflict: Report of the Secretary General', 19 July 2000, UN Doc. A/55/163-S/2000/712, para. 38.

[754] Estimate in Report of the Special Representative of the Secretary General for Children and Armed Conflict, 17 August 2006, UN Doc. A/61/275, para. 11, and see A. Abbott, 'Child soldiers: the use of children as instruments of war', Suffolk Transnat'l LR, 23 (2000), 499–573, pp. 510–1 and p. 516, on why some children enlist voluntarily.

[755] G. van Bueren, 'The international legal protection of children in armed conflicts', ICLQ, 43 (1994), 809–26, and C. Hamilton and T. Abu El-Haj, 'Armed conflict: the protection of children under international law', International Journal of Children's Rights, 5 (1997), 1–46.

on the Rights of the Child.[756] Article 77 of AP I has been censured as a weak provision in that it requires the parties to a conflict only to 'take *all feasible measures* in order that children who have not attained the age of fifteen years do not take a *direct part* in hostilities'.[757] Therefore it does not institute a completely unambiguous prohibition of the use of child soldiers and fails to prohibit the indirect participation of children in hostilities.[758]

## Development

The use of child soldiers has been prohibited by three international instruments: the 1990 African Charter on the Rights and Welfare of the Child, which prohibits the use of children under eighteen from taking 'a direct part in hostilities';[759] the 1999 ILO Convention No. 182 on Child Labour, which prohibits forced or compulsory recruitment of children under eighteen for 'use in armed conflict'[760] and the 2000 Optional Protocol to the Convention on the Rights of the Child, which extends the original prohibition from children under fifteen to those under eighteen.[761] Additionally, the Statute of the Special Court for Sierra Leone in Article 4(c) gave the Court jurisdiction over '[a]bduction and forced recruitment of children under the age of fifteen years into armed forces or groups for the purpose of using them to participate actively in hostilities'. In respect of the phrase 'using them to participate actively in hostilities' the Secretary General commented that this element of the offence amounts to the 'transformation of the child into, and its use as, among other degrading uses, a "child combatant"'.[762]

The phrase 'to participate actively in hostilities' used by this provision in the Rome Statute has been indirectly analysed by the ICTR.[763] The Trial Chamber in *Akayesu* found that the expression 'active part in the hostilities' in Common Article 3 and 'direct part in the hostilities' in Article 4 of AP II were so similar that they may be treated as synonymous.[764] The Trial Chamber Judgement in

[756] See M. Dutli, 'Captured child combatants', IRRC, 278 (1990), 421–34, pp. 425–6, and I. Cohn and G. Goodwin-Gill, *Child Soldiers: the Role of Children in Armed Conflict* (Oxford: Clarendon Press, 1994), pp. 68–70, and J. Kuper, *International Law concerning Child Civilians in Armed Conflict* (Oxford: Clarendon Press, 1997), pp. 102–3.

[757] Emphasis added.

[758] See H. Mann, 'International law and the child soldier', ICLQ, 36 (1987), 32–57, pp. 44–5, and A. Delissen, 'Legal protection of child-combatants after the protocols: reaffirmation, development or a step backwards?', pp. 153–64 in A. Delissen and D. Tanja, *Humanitarian Law Challenges*, n. 280 *supra*, p. 154.

[759] Articles 2 and 22.

[760] Articles 2 and 3(a).

[761] Articles 1 and 2, adopted by GA Res. 54/263 on 25 May 2000, entered into force on 12 February 2002 and has 119 States parties (as of October 2007).

[762] Report of the Secretary General, UN Doc. S/2000/915, p. 4.

[763] The ICTR considered these expressions in order to decide whether the individuals concerned were protected under Common Article 3 and AP II.

[764] *Akayesu*, Trial Judgement, para. 629.

*Rutaganda* defined 'direct part in hostilities' as 'acts of war which by their nature or purpose are likely to cause actual harm to the personnel and equipment of the enemy armed forces'.[765] This suggests that the prohibition against using children to participate actively in hostilities in Article 72 of AP I allows their use in circumstances that would not lose their civilian immunity from attack, such as 'the gathering or transmission of military information, the transportation of arms and munitions or the provision of supplies'.[766]

### The Rome Statute

The EOC for this offence, in addition to the Elements in relation to the nature of the conflict, require that the perpetrator 'conscripted or enlisted one or more persons into the national armed forces or used one or more persons to participate actively in hostilities'.[767] The persons, so conscripted, enlisted or used must have been under the age of fifteen years and it must be shown that the perpetrator 'knew or should have known that such person or persons were under the age of fifteen years'.[768]

The expression 'conscripted or enlisted' covers the administrative act of putting the name of a person on the armed forces list and therefore applies to both voluntary as well as forced enrolment into the armed forces.[769] The Pre-trial Chamber of the ICC in the case of *Lubanga Dyilo* explained that 'conscripting' was forcible recruitment and 'enlisting' voluntary recruitment and therefore emphasised that as both were prohibited by this article 'the child's consent is not a valid defence'.[770]

The word 'national' was inserted before 'armed forces' to deal with the concerns of certain Arab states that wished to exclude from this provision young Palestinians joining the *intifadah*.[771] However, Cottier suggests that the basis for the interpretation of 'national armed forces' should be that provided by Article 43(1) of AP I, 'all organized armed forces, groups and units which are under a command responsible to that Party for the conduct of its subordinates'.[772] This

[765] *Rutaganda*, Trial Judgement, para. 100, referring to Sandoz *et al.*, *Commentary on the Additional Protocols*, in respect of Article 13(3) at p. 1453 (identical to commentary on Article 51(3) at p. 619). See discussion *supra*, pp. 64–7 and 174–6.

[766] M. Happold, *Child Soldiers in International Law* (Manchester: Manchester University Press, 2005), p. 64.

[767] EOC, p. 144.

[768] *Ibid.*

[769] H. von Hebel and D. Robinson, 'Crimes within the jurisdiction of the court', n. 154 *supra*, p. 118, and Cottier *et al.*, 'Article 8', p. 260. See also *Fofana and Kondewa*, Trial Judgement, para. 192.

[770] *Thomas Lubanga Dyilo*, Pre-trial Chamber Decision on the Confirmation of Charges, paras 246–7.

[771] Cottier *et al.*, 'Article 8', p. 261.

[772] *Ibid.*

is supported by the decision of the Pre-trial Chamber in *Lubanga Dyilo*, which, after some analysis, stated that the term 'the national armed forces' is not limited to the armed forces of a State.[773]

The expression 'used such one or more persons to *participate actively* in hostilities'[774] was explained in a footnote to the text submitted to the Rome Conference by the Preparatory Committee, and, although the footnote did not survive the drafting process, its contents appear to reflect the general understanding of this phrase.[775] The footnote states that the words were 'adopted in order to cover both direct participation in combat and also active participation in military activities linked to combat such as scouting, spying, sabotage and the use of children as decoys, couriers or at military checkpoints'.[776]

This approach has been supported by the Pre-trial Chamber in *Lubanga Dyilo*, which stated that the use of children to guard military objectives or as bodyguards for military commanders would breach the article.[777] The Special Court of Sierra Leone Trial Chamber in the case of *Brima, Kamara and Kanu*, having quoted the footnote to the preparatory text,[778] stated that '[a]ny labour or support that gives effect to, or helps maintain, operations in a conflict constitutes active participation' and gave examples of 'carrying loads for the fighting faction, finding and/or acquiring food, ammunition or equipment, acting as decoys, carrying messages, making trails or finding routes, manning checkpoints or acting as human shields' as actions that would amount to active participation.[779] Therefore, despite the jurisprudence of the *ad hoc* tribunals above,[780] under this offence in the Rome Statute the phrase 'participate actively in hostilities' should be read more widely than the phrase 'direct participation in hostilities'. This is an appropriate distinction, as whilst the former phrase removes immunity from attack from civilians and so should be interpreted narrowly, the latter is intended to protect

[773] *Thomas Lubanga Dyilo*, Pre-trial Chamber Decision on the Confirmation of Charges, para. 285, and see analysis in paras 272–84. See a criticism of this interpretation of the phrase 'national armed forces' in M. Happold, 'Current developments, International Criminal Court: IV *Prosecutor v. Thomas Lubanga*, Decision of Pre-trial Chamber 1 of the International Criminal Court, 29 January 2007', ICLQ, 56 (2007), 713–24, pp. 721–2. See also Happold's comment that even if the recruitment of children into armed groups is not prohibited by this article, their use to participate in hostilities by armed groups is prohibited, M. Happold, *Child Soldiers in International Law*, n. 766 *supra*, p. 135.

[774] Emphasis added.

[775] Report of the Preparatory Committee on the Establishment of an ICC, 14 April 1998, UN Doc. A/Conf.183.2/Add.1, p. 21, fn. 12. K. Dörmann, *Elements of War Crimes*, n. 207 *supra*, p. 376.

[776] Report of the Preparatory Committee on the Establishment of an ICC, n. 775, *supra*.

[777] *Thomas Lubanga Dyilo*, Pre-trial Chamber Decision on the Confirmation of Charges, para. 263. This has also been criticised, M. Happold, 'Current developments: International Criminal Court', n. 773 *supra*, pp. 720–1.

[778] *Brima, Kamara and Kanu*, Trial Judgement, para. 736.

[779] *Ibid.*, para. 737.

[780] Discussed *supra*, pp. 166–7.

children from involvement in armed conflicts and so should be interpreted more broadly.[781]

The *mens rea* of this offence, in addition to intending to conscript, enlist or use the persons concerned, requires that the perpetrator 'knew or should have known' that the individuals were under fifteen years of age.[782] Therefore the accused would have a defence to this crime if he did not know and was not negligent in his lack of knowledge that the persons concerned were under fifteen. Fenrick, albeit with respect to Article 28(a)(i) of the Rome Statute on command responsibility, suggests that an accused 'should have known' where 'he or she fails to obtain or wantonly disregards information of a general nature within his or her reasonable access'.[783] Therefore, where an accused, who was recruiting, did not enquire into the age of a child despite an appearance close to the protected minimum age, he would have sufficient *mens rea* under the 'should have known' standard.[784]

To conclude, the *actus reus* of this offence would be committed if the perpetrator enrolled, voluntarily or otherwise, a child under fifteen years into the organised armed forces or into groups under the command of a Party to the conflict. Alternatively, the *actus reus* would be fulfilled if the perpetrator used such a child to participate in combat, either directly or indirectly, in a combat support function. The mental element of this crime requires that the perpetrator either knew, or was criminally negligent in his lack of knowledge, that the child concerned was under fifteen.[785] Finally, the Pre-trial Chamber considered the crime of enlisting and conscripting to be 'an offence of a continuing nature . . . [that] continues to be committed as long as the children remain in the [national] armed groups or forces and consequently ceases to be committed when these children leave the groups or reach age fifteen'.[786]

[781] However, the phrase 'active part in hostilities' is also used in the *chapeau* of Article 8(2)(c), discussed *infra*, pp. 174–6, where it is used to remove immunity from civilians and so should be interpreted in exactly the same way as 'direct participation in hostilities'.

[782] See criticism of this age limit in D. Momtaz, 'War crimes in non-international armed conflicts under the Statute of the International Criminal Court', YIHL, 2 (1999), 177–92, p. 184.

[783] W. Fenrick, 'Article 28', n. 433 *supra*, p. 519.

[784] Cottier *et al.*, 'Article 8', p. 262.

[785] The age limit of under fifteen for this offence implies that individuals between fifteen and seventeen can legitimately take part in a conflict, although under Article 26, Rome Statute, the ICC has jurisdiction only over individuals of eighteen or older.

[786] *Thomas Lubanga Dyilo*, Pre-trial Chamber Decision on the Confirmation of Charges, para. 248.

# 4

# War crimes (III): non-international armed conflicts

## Background to non-international armed conflicts

The extent of jurisdiction over war crimes committed in non-international armed conflicts in the Statute of the International Criminal Court (ICC) was a controversial issue at the Diplomatic Conference in Rome.[1] International humanitarian law relating to internal conflicts is less well developed than that relating to international armed conflicts, although in 1949 Common Article 3 of the Geneva Conventions established basic rules with respect to those persons not taking part in the hostilities, and this was developed in 1977 by Additional Protocol II (AP II).[2] From this limited start there has been an enormous expansion of the law applicable in non-international armed conflicts in recent years,[3] in particular as a result of the jurisprudence of the International Criminal Tribunal for the former Yugoslavia (ICTY) and International Criminal Tribunal for Rwanda (ICTR).[4]

[1] M. Cottier, W. Fenrick, P. Viseur Sellers and A. Zimmermann, 'Article 8, war crimes', pp. 173–288 in O. Triffterer (ed.), *Commentary on the Rome Statute of the International Criminal Court* (Baden-Baden: Nomos, 1999; hereinafter: Cottier *et al.*, 'Article 8'), p. 262.

[2] L. Moir, 'The historical development of the application of humanitarian law in non-international armed conflicts to 1949', ICLQ, 47 (1998), 337–61; D. Forsythe, 'Legal management of internal war: the 1977 Protocol on non-international armed conflicts', AJIL, 72 (1978), 272–95; C. Lysaght, 'The scope of Protocol II and its relation to Common Article 3 of the Geneva Conventions of 1949 and other human rights instruments', AULR, 33 (1983), 9–27, and D. Plattner, 'The penal repression of violations of international humanitarian law applicable in non-international armed conflicts', IRRC, 278 (1990) 409–20.

[3] Aldrich compares the expansion of law in this area to the 'big bang', G. Aldrich, 'The laws of war on land', AJIL, 94 (2000), 42–63, p. 61.

[4] See generally: D. Turns, 'War crimes without war? The applicability of international humanitarian law to atrocities in non-international armed conflicts', RADIC, 7 (1995), 804–30; R. Müllerson, 'International humanitarian law in internal conflicts', JACL, 2 (1997), 109–33; L. Lopez, 'Uncivil wars: the challenge of applying international humanitarian law to internal armed conflicts', NYUR, 69 (1994), 916–62; I. Corey, 'The fine line between policy and custom: Prosecutor v. Tadić and the customary international law of internal armed conflict', Milit LR, 166 (2000), 145–57, pp. 152–5, and 'Declaration on the rules of international humanitarian law governing the conduct of hostilities in non-international armed conflicts' (Council of the International Institute of Humanitarian Law, San Remo, 7 April 1990).

These developments have both affirmed that the principle of individual criminal responsibility applies to breaches of international humanitarian law in non-international armed conflicts by both State and non-State actors and have expanded the substantive rules of international humanitarian law applicable to such conflicts.[5] Therefore, Article 8 of the Rome Statute is not limited to Common Article 3, but in paragraph 2(e) also contains provisions on other violations of the laws of war applicable in non-international armed conflicts, drawn from both AP II and customary international law. Most of these articles will not be discussed in depth here, as they 'exactly mirror provisions already contained in article 8 para. 2(b) dealing with international armed conflict'.[6] Indeed, their substantive elements are almost identical, demonstrating the view of the delegates that 'there is no difference in substance between the elements of war crimes in an international armed conflict and those in a non-international armed conflict'.[7] Therefore only those articles not already discussed, or raising special issues because of their application to non-international armed conflicts, will be examined below.

## The threshold for the application of Article 8(2)(c) and (e)

When dealing with internal hostilities it is necessary to set out the level of violence which will amount to an armed conflict and so trigger jurisdiction.[8] Paragraphs 2(d) and 2(f) of Article 8 set out the preconditions necessary for the application of paragraph 2(c), containing Common Article 3, and paragraph 2(e), containing other provisions applicable in non-international armed conflicts. Both paragraphs contain an identical first sentence, taken from Article 1(2) of AP II,

[5] *Tadić*, Interlocutory Appeal Decision, paras 96–127 on the extension of the substantive law applicable to non-international armed conflicts, and *ibid.*, paras 128–34 on individual criminal responsibility in non-international armed conflicts. *Norman*, Appeal Decision on Preliminary Motion based on Lack of Jurisdiction (Child Recruitment), para. 22, on the fact that non-State parties are bound by humanitarian law; this is followed by *Fofana and Kondewa*, Trial Judgement, para. 95. See also T. Graditzky, 'Individual criminal responsibility for violations of international humanitarian law committed in non-international armed conflicts', IRRC, 322 (1998), 29–56; T. Meron, 'International criminalization of internal atrocities', AJIL, 89 (1995), 554–77, and C. Meindersma, 'Violations of Common Article 3 of the Geneva Conventions as violations of the laws or customs of war under Article 3 of the Statute of the International Criminal Tribunal for the former Yugoslavia', NILR, 42 (1995), 375–97.

[6] Cottier *et al.*, 'Article 8', p. 263.

[7] K. Dörmann, 'Preparatory Commission for the International Criminal Court: the elements of war crimes, Part II: Other serious violations of the laws and customs applicable in international and non-international armed conflicts', IRRC, 842 (2001), 461–87, p. 483.

[8] See P. Kooijmans, 'In the shadowland between civil war and civil strife: some reflections on the standard-setting process', pp. 225–47 in A. Delissen and G. Tanja (eds), *Humanitarian Law of Armed Conflict: Challenges Ahead* (Dordrecht: Nijhoff, 1991), and T. Meron, 'Towards a humanitarian declaration on internal strife', AJIL, 78 (1984), 859–68.

stating that the provisions apply 'to armed conflicts not of an international character' and not to 'situations of internal disturbances and tensions, such as riots, isolated and sporadic acts of violence or other acts of a similar nature'. This is the sole guidance with respect to the threshold for the application of Article 8(2)(c).

Common Article 3 of the Geneva Conventions itself contains no reference as to a threshold for its applicability, which could assist in explaining when Article 8(2)(c) applies. Although it is difficult to differentiate between the internal disturbances excluded by Article 8(2)(d) and a non-international armed conflict, the ICTR in the *Akayesu* case stated that 'an armed conflict is distinguished from internal disturbances by the level of intensity of the conflict and the degree of the organization of the parties to the conflict'.[9] The ICTY Trial Chamber in the *Limaj, Bala and Musliu* case expanded upon the meaning of 'degree of organization of the parties', stating that 'Chambers of the Tribunal have taken into account factors including the existence of headquarters, designated zones of operation, and the ability to procure, transport, and distribute arms'.[10]

Other criteria suggested by the commentary to the Geneva Conventions in order to assist an assessment of whether the level of violence has risen to that of an armed conflict include that 'the legal Government is obliged to have recourse to the regular military forces against insurgents organized as military' and that 'the dispute has been admitted to the agenda of the Security Council or the General Assembly of the United Nations as being a threat to international peace, a breach of the peace, or an act of aggression'.[11] It is submitted that the ICC should consider these criteria in addition to the extent of organisation of non-governmental groups and the intensity of the conflict, to support the decision on whether the threshold for the applicability of Article 8(2)(c) has been reached in a particular case.

With respect to Article 8(2)(e), paragraph 8(2)(f) adds the further explanation that the section applies 'to armed conflicts that take place in the territory of a State when there is protracted armed conflict between governmental authorities and organized armed groups or between such groups'.[12] Although this definition

[9] *Akayesu*, Trial Judgement, para. 625. See also G. Draper, 'The Geneva Conventions of 1949', 114 Rec des Cours (1965) I, 59–165, p. 89; M. Greenspan, *The Modern Law of Land Warfare* (Berkeley CA: University of California Press, 1959), pp. 624–5; J. Pictet (ed.), *The Geneva Conventions of 12 August 1949: Commentary: IV Geneva Convention* (Geneva: ICRC, 1952–60; hereinafter: Pictet (ed.), *Commentary: I/II/III/IV Convention*) p. 35; F. Ni Aolain, 'The relationship between situations of emergency and low-intensity armed conflict', Israel Yrbk Hum Rts, 28 (1998), 97–106, pp. 102–5; W. Solf, 'The status of combatants in non-international armed conflicts under domestic law and transnational practice', AULR, 33 (1983), 53–65, p. 64, and C. Meindersma, 'Applicability of humanitarian law in international and internal armed conflict', Hague Yrbk Int'l L, 7 (1994), 113–40, p. 124.

[10] *Limaj, Bala and Musliu*, Trial Judgement, para. 90.

[11] Pictet (ed.), *Commentary: IV Geneva Convention*, p. 35.

[12] See comments on this by T. Graditzky, 'War crime issues before the Rome diplomatic conference on the establishment of an international criminal court', UC Davis J Int'l L & Pol'y, 5 (1999), 199–217, pp. 209–10.

bears some similarities to Article 1(1) of AP II, nevertheless it is a broader threshold based upon the definition given by the ICTY Appeal Chamber in *Tadić*.[13]

Zimmermann comments that the expression 'protracted' in Article 8(2)(e) does not have the same meaning as 'sustained' in Article 1(1) of AP II, as the word 'protracted' does not require that the military actions are continuous, merely that they take place over a prolonged period of time.[14] In addition, Zimmerman comments that the expression 'governmental authorities', used in this paragraph, is broad enough to include 'units of national guards, the police forces, border police or other armed authorities of a similar nature' as well as the regular armed forces of a State.[15] It seems clear that the fighting does not necessarily have to take place between rebels and government forces in order to amount to a non-international armed conflict. Such a conflict can arise in the context of two opposed non-governmental parties.

The Appeal Chamber in *Tadić* also discussed the temporal and geographical limits of non-international armed conflicts. It stated that:

> [i]nternational humanitarian law applies from the initiation of such armed conflicts and extends beyond the cessation of hostilities until a general conclusion of peace is reached; or, in the case of internal conflicts, a peaceful settlement is achieved. Until that moment, international humanitarian law continues to apply in the whole territory . . . under the control of a party, whether or not actual combat takes place there.[16]

This approach, applicable irrespective of the type of conflict, has been consistently followed by other Judgements of the ICTY and ICTR and it is submitted that it should be applied by the ICC.[17]

## Article 8(2)(c)

### The *chapeau* to Article 8(2)(c) Serious violations of Common Article 3

The *chapeau* to Article 8(2)(c) limits the jurisdiction of the ICC in respect to violations of Common Article 3 in two ways. First, only 'serious' violations of

[13] *Tadić*, Interlocutory Appeal Decision, para. 70. This has been consistently followed by subsequent judgements of the ICTY and ICTR and has also been followed by the SCSL in *Fofana and Kondewa*, Trial Judgement, para. 124. See C. Kreß, 'War crimes committed in non-international armed conflict and the emerging system of international criminal justice', pp. 103–77 in D. Fleck (ed.), *Humanitarian Protection in Non-international Armed Conflicts* (San Remo: International Institute of Humanitarian Law, 2001), pp. 117–21.

[14] Cottier *et al.*, 'Article 8', p. 285. Zimmermann also comments that, given that this definition does not apply to 8(2)(c), there is no minimum duration of the conflict for the application of Common Article 3, *ibid.*, p. 270.

[15] *Ibid.*, p. 286.

[16] *Tadić*, Interlocutory Appeal Decision, para. 70.

[17] See *Furundžija*, Trial Judgement, para. 59; *Blaškić*, Trial Judgement, para. 63, and *Akayesu*, Trial Judgement, para. 635.

this article will come within its jurisdiction.[18] The *Tadić* Interlocutory Appeal decision defined the expression 'serious' in a similar context as an action constituting 'a breach of a rule protecting important values, and the breach must involve grave consequences for the victim'.[19] Although it is difficult to imagine a breach of one of the paragraphs of 8(2)(c) as anything other than serious,[20] this expression can be understood as reflecting the statement in Article 5 that the 'jurisdiction of the Court shall be limited to the most serious crimes of concern to the international community as a whole'.[21]

Second, the *chapeau* defines those persons against whom the offences defined in paragraphs (i) to (iv) of 8(2)(c) may be committed. This definition is taken from Common Article 3 and protects 'persons taking *no active part in the hostilities*, including members of armed forces who have laid down their arms and those placed *hors de combat* by sickness, wounds, detention or any other cause'.[22] According to the Trial Chamber in *Tadić* '[t]his protection embraces, at the least, all of those protected persons covered by the grave breaches regime applicable to conflicts of an international character: civilians, prisoners of war, wounded and sick members of the armed forces in the field and wounded sick and shipwrecked members of the armed forces at sea'.[23] The Trial Chamber of the Special Court for Sierra Leone (SCSL) added in the case of *Fofana and Kondewa* that the 'armed law enforcement agencies of a State are generally mandated only to protect and maintain the internal order of a State' and so 'as a general presumption and in the execution of their typical law enforcement duties, such forces are considered to be civilians for the purposes of international humanitarian law'.[24]

The expression 'active part in the hostilities' in Common Article 3 is similar to 'direct part in hostilities' in Article 53(1) of AP I, discussed earlier.[25] The phrase 'active part in the hostilities' was analysed by the Trial Chamber in *Akayesu*, which stated that the two phrases were so similar that they should be treated as synonymous.[26] Indeed, McDonald comments that '[b]oth the terms "direct" and "active" participation in hostilities occur in Geneva law, although it can

[18] See discussion *supra*, pp. 16–17.

[19] *Tadić*, Interlocutory Appeal Decision, para. 93(iii).

[20] See J. Pejic, 'The International Criminal Court Statute: an appraisal of the Rome package', Int Law, 34 (2000), 65–84, p. 71.

[21] See also Article 17(d) on admissibility and Cottier *et al.*, 'Article 8', p. 270.

[22] Common Article 3(1), 1949 Geneva Conventions, emphasis added.

[23] *Tadić*, Trial Judgement, para. 615. (This part of the Judgement was not challenged on appeal.)

[24] *Fofana and Kondewa*, Trial Judgement, para. 136; but in para. 137, *ibid.*, the Trial Chamber explains that if a civilian police force in time of armed conflict was incorporated into the armed forces, then the police officers would be classified as combatants.

[25] See discussion *supra*, pp. 64–7.

[26] *Akayesu*, Trial Judgement, para. 629. Note that the Trial Chamber was comparing the wording in Common Article 3 with the wording in Article 4 of AP II, but Article 4 uses the same language as Article 51(3) in AP I.

be questioned whether there is any substantive difference between them. Many commentators use these terms interchangeably.'[27]

Nevertheless, some problems unique to the targeting of civilians taking an 'active part in the hostilities' in non-international armed conflicts were discussed by the Expert meeting in Geneva.[28] Some experts commented that in a non-international armed conflict all the rebels were essentially civilians participating in the conflict and that 'state armed forces could not prevail in an armed conflict in which everyone belonging to the opposing party was protected and where the state was only allowed to respond to attacks against its armed forces, without ever taking military initiatives of its own'.[29] This is essentially an argument for a 'membership approach' to the phrase 'active part in the hostilities' and that it should be lawful to attack those civilians who are fighting members of rebel forces at any time.[30]

However, some experts argued that the lack of clarity of the notion of active or direct participation in hostilities constituted a gap in international humanitarian law which 'had to be bridged by reference to human rights law'.[31] They therefore argued that this phrase 'could not be interpreted to allow the use of lethal force beyond the restrictive standards of human rights law' and stated that 'any approach that would allow direct attacks against civilians outside a situation of actual or imminent fighting opened the door to summary or arbitrary executions'.[32]

Perhaps the solution may be found in the arguments of the experts who suggested that civilian membership of the group was insufficient to allow attack at all times and that it is also necessary to show the existence of military necessity.[33] An attack by rebels would necessitate an armed response, which would be lawful under both human rights law and humanitarian law. However, human rights law also accepts that lethal force may be used when capture or arrest is too risky and 'the risk posed by attempting to capture a group of thousands of

[27] A. McDonald, 'The challenges to international humanitarian law and the principles of distinction and protection from the increased participation of civilians in hostilities', in Spotlight on Issues of Contemporary Concern in International Humanitarian Law and International Criminal Law, p. 16, available at: <http://www.wihl.nl>. See discussion of this phrase *supra*, pp. 166–7, with respect to the prohibition against using child soldiers, and see the broader reading of this given by the EOC, Assembly of States Parties to the Rome Statute of the ICC, Official Records, First Session, ICC-ASP/1/3, 3–10 September 2002 (hereinafter: EOC), pp. 108–55, discussed *supra*, p. 168.

[28] Third Expert Meeting on the Notion of Direct Participation in Hostilities, Summary Report, Geneva, 23–25 October (hereinafter: ICRC Expert Meeting), pp. 42–58, available at: <http://www.icrc.org/web/eng/siteeng0.nsf/htmlall/participation-hostilities-ihl-311205>.

[29] *Ibid.*, p. 44.

[30] See discussion *supra*, pp. 66–7.

[31] ICRC Expert Meeting, p. 51. On the interaction between human rights and humanitarian law see C. Byron, 'A blurring of the boundaries: the application of international humanitarian law by human rights bodies', Va JIL, 47 (2007), 839–96; W. Abresch, 'A human rights law of internal armed conflict: the European Court of Human Rights in Chechnya', EJIL, 16 (2005), 741–67, and N. Lubell, 'Challenges in applying human rights law to armed conflict', IRRC, 860 (2005), 737–54.

[32] ICRC Expert Meeting, pp. 51–2.

[33] *Ibid.*, p. 45.

heavily armed insurgents holed up in a village' may justify an armed attack,[34] whereas in other situations 'off-duty' rebels may be captured without great risk.[35]

### Elements of Crimes common to Article 8(2)(c)(i)–(iv)

There are four elements common to the offences laid out in the Elements of Crimes (EOC) for Article 8(2)(c). It must be shown that the conduct 'took place in the context of and was associated with an armed conflict not of an international character' and that the perpetrator 'was aware of factual circumstances that established the existence of an armed conflict'.[36] Therefore, the offence must occur during an armed conflict, there must be a nexus between the conflict and the offence and the perpetrator must be aware that he is acting within the circumstances which objectively amount to an armed conflict.[37] These elements are also common to the offences listed under 8(2)(e).[38]

The other elements common to Article 8(2)(c) require that the 'person or persons were either *hors de combat*, or were civilians, medical personnel or religious personnel taking no active part in the hostilities' and that the perpetrator was aware 'of the factual circumstances that established this status'.[39] Although the definition of protected persons in the EOC differs somewhat from the *chapeau*, Dörmann comments that this was done in order to avoid ambiguities and that '[i]t was the understanding of the drafters in informal consultations that the term *hors de combat* should not be narrowly interpreted'.[40] In requiring awareness of the status of the victim, the Elements do not demand a legal evaluation upon the part of the perpetrator, but merely an awareness of the factual situation which objectively demonstrates the legal status of the victim.[41]

### Article 8(2)(c)(i) Violence to life and person, in particular murder of all kinds, mutilation, cruel treatment and torture

The EOC for these offences reflect almost exactly those of wilful killing, mutilation, inhuman treatment and torture in Article 8(2)(a)(i) (b)(x)-1 (a)(ii)-2 and

[34] See comments of W. Abresch, 'A human rights law of internal armed conflict', n. 31 *supra*, p. 753.

[35] See provisions on the right to life; Article 2, European Convention for the Protection of Human Rights and Fundamental Freedoms; Article 6, International Covenant of Civil and Political Rights, and Article 4, American Convention on Human Rights.

[36] EOC, pp. 144–8.

[37] See discussion *supra*, pp. 14–16.

[38] EOC, pp. 148–55.

[39] *Ibid.*, pp. 144–8.

[40] K. Dörmann, 'The first and second sessions of the Preparatory Commission for the International Criminal Court', YIHL, 2 (1999), 283–306, p. 299.

[41] Note also that the common EOC do not include a discriminatory intent, one of the grounds of the appeal of the *Aleksovski* defence, rejected by the Appeal Chamber, *Aleksovski*, Appeal Judgement, para. 17.

(a)(ii)-1 respectively.[42] This approach follows that taken by the ICTY, which has held that there is no substantive difference between wilful killing and murder or inhuman treatment and cruel treatment or torture in international or non-international armed conflicts.[43] The only difference in the EOC is that the elements of mutilation, unlike those in Article 8(2)(b)(x) do not require the victim to have been in the power of an adverse party, nor do they require that the conduct 'caused death or seriously endangered the physical or mental health of such persons'.[44]

The EOC do not deal with the issue of whether violence to life and person other than the specific acts listed could also constitute an offence under this paragraph. On a plain reading of the Statute, the expression 'in particular' suggests that 'murder . . . mutilation, cruel treatment and torture' are simply examples of violence to life and person. Therefore, it is arguable that the Prosecutor of the ICC could charge another form of violence to life and person, not expressly mentioned in Article 8(2)(c)(i), provided that it was of the same general nature as the acts specified.[45]

Nevertheless, the ICTY Trial Chamber in the case of *Vasiljević* dealt with the issue of whether 'violence to life and person' *per se* amounted to a crime within the jurisdiction of the tribunal.[46] The tribunal held that whilst 'both "life" and the "person" are protected in various ways by international humanitarian law', the principle of *nullum crimen sine lege* means that 'under no circumstances may the court create new criminal offences after the act charged against an accused . . . by giving a definition to a crime which had none'.[47] The Trial Chamber announced that '[i]n the absence of any clear indication in the practice of states as to what the definition of the offence of "violence to life and person" . . . may be under customary law' it was not satisfied that 'such an offence giving rise to individual criminal responsibility exists under that law'.[48]

[42] Compare EOC, pp. 125, 136 and 126, respectively. See comments of K. Dörmann, 'Preparatory Commission for the International Criminal Court: the elements of war crimes', IRRC, 839 (2000), 771–95, p. 792.

[43] This approach was taken in *Čelebici*, Trial Judgement, paras 422 and 437–9 in respect of wilful killing and murder; paras 551–2 in respect of inhuman and cruel treatment and para. 443 in respect of torture. It was followed by *Kordić and Čerkez*, Trial Judgement, paras 233 and 265 in respect of wilful killing and murder and inhumane and cruel treatment. *Furundžija*, Trial Judgement, para. 160, followed *Čelebici* in respect of the consistent definition of torture.

[44] EOC, p. 136, discussed *supra*, p. 114. See also *Brima, Kamara and Kanu*, Trial Judgement, paras 724–5.

[45] Following the *ejusdem generis* rule of statutory interpretation. This interpretation of 'violence to life and person' under Common Article 3 has also been taken by A. Cassese, 'Black letter lawyering *v.* constructive interpretation: the *Vasiljević* case', J Int'l Crim Just 2 (2004) 265–74, p. 272. Note that, under Article 21(1)(a), Rome Statute, the Statute itself has priority over the EOC as applicable law for the ICC.

[46] *Vasiljević*, Trial Judgement, paras 193–204.

[47] *Ibid.*, paras 195–6. Note that the principle of *nullum crimen* is enshrined in the Rome Statute in Article 22.

[48] *Vasiljević*, Trial Judgement, para. 203. See criticism of this finding in A. Cassese, 'Black letter lawyering', n. 45 *supra*, pp. 271–3.

This approach was followed by the SCSL Trial Chamber in the case of *Fofana and Kondewa* when it stated that 'the category of "violence to life and person" does not exist as an independent offence in customary international law'.[49] Therefore, it seems unlikely that the Prosecutor of the ICC will charge 'violence to life and person' *per se* or indeed another new category of such violence not covered by the Elements unless he or she can adduce evidence that such an act has been defined under international law and accepted as giving rise to individual criminal responsibility.

## Article 8(2)(c)(iv) The passing of sentences and the carrying out of executions without previous judgement pronounced by a regularly constituted court, affording all judicial guarantees which are generally recognised as indispensable

### Origins

The commentary to the Geneva Conventions states that '[a]ll civilized nations surround the administration of justice with safeguards aimed at eliminating the possibility of judicial errors. The Convention has rightly proclaimed that it is essential to do this even in time of war.'[50] The offence is similar in origin to the grave breach of depriving a protected person of the right to a fair and regular trial, requiring, in addition, that the victim has been executed or sentenced.[51]

### Development

A similar offence was included in 1977 in Article 6 of AP II, stating that '[n]o sentence shall be passed and no penalty shall be executed on a person found guilty of an offence except pursuant to a conviction pronounced by a court offering the essential guarantees of independence and impartiality'.[52] The article proceeded to list examples of these essential guarantees, which may act as a guideline as to which guarantees are indispensable under Common Article 3.[53] They include the right to be informed of the charges and to prepare a defence, the principle of non-retroactivity of criminal offences, the presumption of innocence, the right to silence and a prohibition against trials *in absentia*.

In the US Supreme Court decision of *Hamdan v. Rumsfeld* Justice Stevens opined that the content of the indispensable judicial guarantees could be found in Article 75 of AP I, which he implied was accepted as 'an articulation of

[49] *Fofana and Kondewa*, Trial Judgement, para. 145.

[50] Pictet (ed.), *Commentary: IV Geneva Convention*, p. 39.

[51] See discussion *supra*, p. 51.

[52] Article 6(2), AP II.

[53] Zimmermann supports this proposition, see Cottier *et al.*, 'Article 8', p. 275.

safeguards to which all persons in the hands of an enemy are entitled'.[54] In addition to the guarantees provided in Article 6 of AP II, Article 75 includes the right of the accused to examine witnesses against him or herself and to call and examine witnesses on his or her behalf. It is arguable that additional guidance on this may be drawn from Article 14 of the International Covenant of Civil and Political Rights (ICCPR), which also includes the right of a person accused of a criminal offence to be tried without undue delay and the right to an interpreter if he cannot understand or speak the language used in court.[55]

## The Rome Statute

The EOC for this offence, in addition to those relating to the nature of the conflict and status of the victim under Common Article 3, require that the perpetrator 'passed sentence or executed one or more persons' and that:

> [t]here was no previous judgement pronounced by a court, or the court that rendered judgement was not 'regularly constituted', that is, it did not afford the essential guarantees of independence and impartiality, or the court that rendered judgement did not afford all other judicial guarantees generally recognized as indispensable under international law.[56]

Finally the Elements require that the perpetrator 'was aware of the absence of a previous judgement or of the denial of relevant guarantees and the fact that they are essential or indispensable to a fair trial'.[57] The expression 'sentence' is not defined and may feasibly range from a fine to imprisonment or corporal punishment. However, as the jurisdiction of the ICC is limited to serious breaches of Common Article 3, it is unlikely that a fine would be considered serious enough unless it was very high with serious consequences for the victim.[58] Sentencing or execution would amount to an offence under this paragraph, according to the EOC, if there were no previous court judgement. Therefore, if a commander ordered the execution or imprisonment of detainees alleged to have assisted the opposing party in a non-international armed conflict, without holding a trial, the offence would be committed.

The offence may also be committed where the sentencing or execution follows a court judgement in two instances. First, where the court was not 'regularly constituted'. This is defined by the Elements as a court which 'did not afford the

[54] *Hamdan v. Rumsfeld*, 548 US (2006), No. 05-184, 29 June 2006, Opinion of Justice Stevens, section VI-D-iv, with Justices Souter, Ginsburg and Breyer concurring, available at: <http://www.supremecourtus.gov/opinions/05pdf/05–184.pdf>.

[55] Article 14(3)(c) and (f), ICCPR. It is not suggested that the full panoply of fair trial rights must be respected under this provision and therefore care should be taken when taking human rights provisions as guidance.

[56] EOC, p. 147.

[57] *Ibid.*, and see K. Dörmann, 'The first and second sessions of the Preparatory Commission', n. 40 *supra*, p. 299.

[58] See discussion *supra*, pp. 173–4.

essential guarantees of independence and impartiality'.[59] Guidance on this may be taken from the General Comment of the Human Rights Committee on the right to a fair trial under Article 14 of the ICCPR.[60] The Human Rights Committee (HRC) commented on issues affecting the independence and impartiality of judges, such as their qualifications for office, the manner in which they are appointed, the duration of an appointment and the conditions governing the cessation of their functions and the 'actual independence of the judiciary from the executive branch and the legislative'.[61]

However, it must be taken into consideration that the HRC comment was aimed at States, whereas this offence applies during non-international armed conflicts. Clearly, the high level of independence and impartiality required of State-appointed judges in peacetime cannot apply to a non-State group during a conflict. Therefore, provided that the party carrying out prosecutions establishes judges who are as independent as possible in the circumstances, without attempting to assert undue influence over them, and that the judges, in good faith, 'decide without personal influence and objectively, only according to their best knowledge and conscience',[62] the court should be considered to be 'regularly constituted'.

Second, sentencing or execution following a judgement from a court not 'affording all other judicial guarantees generally recognized as indispensable under international law' would breach this provision. A footnote to this element comments that the ICC should consider whether 'in the light of all relevant circumstances, the cumulative effect of factors with respect to guarantees deprived the person or persons of a fair trial'.[63] Therefore the deprivation of one particular judicial guarantee may not amount to an offence under this provision, provided that as a whole in the circumstances the trial could be considered fair.

Kreß comments that this restrictive definition of indispensable judicial guarantees 'is crucial in order not to exceed the justifiable level of international criminalization'.[64] It is submitted that this is a practical approach, taking into account the application of this offence to rebels and States in non-international armed conflicts. Provided that the *indispensable* judicial guarantees are respected and that this results in a trial that is fair, considered as a whole, in the circumstances, then the *actus reus* is not made out.

The mental element of this offence requires either that the perpetrator was aware of the lack of a previous judgement or that he was aware 'of the denial

[59] EOC, p. 147.

[60] HRC General Comment 13, Article 14, ICCPR, UN Doc. HRI/GEN/1/Rev.1 at 14 (1994), available at: <http://www1.umn.edu/humanrts/gencomm/hrcom13.htm>.

[61] *Ibid.*

[62] ICRC working paper submitted to the Preparatory Commission on the Elements of Crimes of Article 8(2)(c), 28 May 1999, available at: <http://www.igc.apc.org/icc>, comments on Article 8(2)(c)(iv) at 2(b)(2).

[63] EOC, fn. 59 on p. 147.

[64] C. Kreß, 'War crimes committed in non-international armed conflict', n. 13 *supra*, p. 137.

of relevant guarantees and the fact that they are essential or indispensable to a fair trial'.[65] This is quite a high standard of *mens rea*, demanding proof of an understanding of fair trial standards on the part of the perpetrator. It seems likely that this may provide a loophole for defendants unless there is a severe lack of due process prior to sentencing or execution.[66]

## Article 8(2)(e)

### Article 8(2)(e)(ii) Intentionally directing attacks against buildings, material, medical units and transport, and personnel using the distinctive emblems of the Geneva Conventions in conformity with international law

This offence reflects exactly, in wording and Elements, the equivalent offence relating to international armed conflicts under Article 8(2)(b)(xxiv).[67] However, it merits attention here because the rules for the use of the emblems in conformity with international law are laid down primarily in the four Geneva Conventions and AP I, which do not apply in non-international armed conflicts.[68] Therefore the question of which law regulates the use of the distinctive emblems in non-international armed conflicts must be resolved before a prosecution under this provision may take place.

Common Article 3 does not address the use of the distinctive emblems of the red cross or crescent, but Article 12 of AP II states that under the direction of the competent authority the distinctive emblems 'shall be displayed by medical and religious personnel and medical units, and on medical transports' and concludes that it shall 'be respected in all circumstances . . . [and] shall not be used improperly'. According to Slim this article has codified customary international law and is therefore binding upon all States.[69] Therefore the ICC could rely on Article 12 of AP II when dealing with a defendant charged under this provision.

However, as Bouvier comments, this article does not explicitly define protected medical personnel.[70] Relying upon the official records of the Diplomatic

[65] EOC, p. 147.

[66] See C. Byron and D. Turns, 'The Preparatory Commission for the International Criminal Court', ICLQ, 50 (2001), 420–35, p. 428.

[67] Discussed *supra*, pp. 158–60, and see K. Dörmann, *Elements of War Crimes under the Rome Statute of the International Criminal Court: Sources and Commentary* (Cambridge: Cambridge University Press and ICRC, 2002), p. 447.

[68] Article 2(3), AP III, states that 'The conditions for use of and respect for the third Protocol emblem are identical to those for the distinctive emblems established by the Geneva Conventions and, where applicable, the 1977 Additional Protocols'.

[69] H. Slim, 'Protection of the red cross and red crescent emblems and the repression of misuse', IRRC, 272 (1989), 420–37, p. 427.

[70] A. Bouvier, 'Special aspects of the use of the red cross or red crescent emblem', IRRC, 272 (1989), 438–58, p. 454.

Conference on Humanitarian Law, he concludes that in addition to military medical services, local relief organisations, such as the national Red Cross or another voluntary aid society carrying on activities under the supervision of a party to the conflict, may also use the distinctive emblems in non-international armed conflicts.[71] However, when dealing with an attack upon a civilian using the distinctive emblem, a charge could alternatively be brought under Article 8(2)(e)(i) of attacking an individual civilian not taking a direct part in hostilities.

### Article 8(2)(e)(vii) Conscripting or enlisting children under the age of fifteen years into armed forces or groups or using them to participate actively in hostilities

This offence is identical to that in Article 8(2)(b)(xxvi), the equivalent article applicable in international armed conflicts, in all respects except for the expression 'armed forces or groups' which has been used in this article rather than 'national armed forces', used in the former article.[72] Additionally, whilst the expression 'conscripting' is used in both articles, it is clear that it is not restricted to the actions of States. The Special Court for Sierra Leone in the case of *Brima, Kamara and Kanu* commented that the expression 'conscripting' would also encompass 'acts of coercion, such as abductions, and forced recruitment' by a non-State armed group.[73]

With respect to the expression 'armed forces or groups', the Trial Chamber in *Brima et al.* stated that such 'armed forces or groups must be under responsible command, which entails a degree of organization which should be such as to enable the armed groups to plan and carry out concerted military operations and to impose discipline within the armed group'.[74] A similar definition is given by the Trial Chamber in *Fofana and Kondewa*, which also makes the point that 'such a group may be either State or non-State controlled'.[75] This makes it clear that this article is intended to prohibit the use of children in non-international armed conflicts by both State and non-State parties. Furthermore, with respect to non-State parties, it is intended to criminalise the use of children in hostilities by organised rebel groups, rather than all possible misuse of children by individuals.

[71] *Ibid.*, p. 455. In respect to supervision by a party to the conflict see Y. Sandoz, C. Swinarski and B. Zimmermann (eds), *Commentary on the Additional Protocols of 8 June 1977 to the Geneva Conventions of 12 August 1949* (Geneva: ICRC and Nijhoff, 1987; hereinafter: Sandoz *et al.*, *Commentary on the Additional Protocols*), p. 1441, and A. Bouvier, 'Special aspects of the use of the red cross', n. 70 *supra*, p. 456.

[72] Article 8(2)(b)(xxvi) is discussed *supra*, pp. 165–9.

[73] *Brima, Kamara and Kanu*, Trial Judgement, para. 734.

[74] *Ibid.*, para. 738.

[75] *Fofana and Kondewa*, Trial Judgement, para. 194.

## Article 8(2)(e)(viii) Ordering the displacement of the civilian population for reasons related to the conflict, unless the security of the civilians involved or imperative military reasons so demand

### Origins

This prohibition is taken from Article 17 of AP II and is not directly reflected by the international armed conflict offences of the Rome Statute, although it bears similarities to Article 8(2)(b)(viii). The Bothe *et al.* commentary to AP II states that this article was intended to prevent counter-insurgency operations of 'drying up the sea in which guerrilla fish swim', where civilians are relocated to secure centres in order to deprive rebel groups of support, and to prevent 'displacements of ethnic groups in order to facilitate the domination of the area involved by another more favoured group'.[76]

It is clear that displacements for reasons not related to the conflict, such as natural disasters, are not prohibited by this article. However, AP II also allows exceptions when displacement linked with the conflict may take place. First, such displacement may be allowed if it is in the interests of the security of civilians, and the ICRC commentary states in this regard that 'a displacement designed to prevent the population from being exposed to grave danger cannot be expressly prohibited'.[77] Second, imperative military reasons may provide an exception to this prohibition, but the commentary warns that '[m]ilitary necessity as a ground for derogation from a rule always requires the most meticulous assessment of the circumstances' and that 'the adjective "imperative" reduces to a minimum cases in which displacement may be ordered'.[78] However, as Bothe *et al.* note, 'there is nothing in Art. 17 which precludes voluntary movement of civilians'.[79]

### Development

Events in the Bosnian conflict demonstrate how the provisions of Article 17, relating to the security of civilians, could be exploited. It is possible to argue that Bosnian Muslims were displaced from certain areas for their own safety, the armed forces being unable to guarantee protection from local militia or other civilians.[80] Rogers also argues that, in circumstances where regular armed forces oppose guerrillas in close combat in built-up areas, such displacement could genuinely be in the interests of civilians, avoiding severe casualties among local inhabitants.[81]

[76] M. Bothe, K. Partsch and W. Solf, *New Rules for Victims of Armed Conflicts* (The Hague: Nijhoff, 1982; hereinafter: Bothe *et al.*, *New Rules for Victims*), p. 691.

[77] Sandoz *et al.*, *Commentary on the Additional Protocols*, p. 1472.

[78] *Ibid.*, pp. 1472–3.

[79] M. Bothe *et al.*, *New Rules for Victims*, p. 692.

[80] See M. Roch, 'Forced displacement in the former Yugoslavia: a crime under international law?', Dick J Int'l L, 14 (1995), 1–29, p. 16.

[81] A. Rogers, 'Zero-casualty warfare', IRRC, 837 (2000), 165–81, pp. 167–8.

He suggests that the Russian provision of safe corridors for the civilian population to escape the fighting in Grozny in the Chechen conflict was an example of the most humanitarian course of action in such circumstances.[82]

Defendants charged with this offence may also exploit the fact that only the 'ordering' of civilian displacement is criminalised.[83] Therefore, as Roch and Carey suggest, the 'voluntary' displacement of civilians because of human rights abuses committed against them by the armed forces could not amount to this offence, although other offences would almost certainly be committed in such a situation.[84]

## The Rome Statute

In addition to the EOC related to the nature of the conflict, the elements of this crime require that the perpetrator 'ordered a displacement of a civilian population', that the order 'was not justified by the security of the civilians involved or by military necessity' and finally that the perpetrator 'was in a position to effect such displacement by giving such order'.[85] The expression 'ordered' restricts this offence to a situation where an order to displace civilians has been given and would not include circumstances where the civilian population felt compelled to flee because of the dangers of the conflict or ethnic violence or moved on a genuinely voluntary basis.[86]

There must be a displacement of 'a civilian population'.[87] The word 'displacement' is used in AP II to describe movements of civilians within their territory, with an extra paragraph forbidding the movement of civilians outside of their territory.[88] However, it cannot be argued that simply displacing the civilians over an international frontier would circumvent this offence in the Rome Statute and therefore 'displacement' must be understood in a wide sense as referring to any movement of civilians away from their place of residence either within or outside their State.[89] A dictionary definition of 'population' is 'the inhabitants of a place, country, etc., referred to collectively' or 'any specified group within this (*the Irish population of Liverpool*)'.[90] Therefore the expression 'civilian population' in the EOC suggests that the perpetrator must order, at least, the

[82] *Ibid.*, p. 168.

[83] This includes other criminal participation in the offence, such as aiding and abetting the giving of such an order.

[84] M. Roch, 'Forced displacement in the former Yugoslavia', n. 80 *supra*, pp. 16–17, and C. Carey, 'Internal displacement: is prevention through accountability possible? A Kosovo case study', Am ULR, 49 (1999), 243–88, pp. 287–8.

[85] EOC, p. 153.

[86] See comments of A. Zimmermann in Cottier *et al.*, 'Article 8', p. 281.

[87] According to the Rome Statute this must be 'for reasons related to the conflict'.

[88] Article 17(2), AP II.

[89] Cottier *et al.*, 'Article 8', p. 281.

[90] *Concise Oxford Dictionary* (Oxford: Clarendon Press, 9th edn, 1995).

displacement of a significant number of a specified civilian group within a village, town or region in order to commit this offence.[91]

The exceptions to the rule against displacing civilians are repeated in the EOC, with the difference that the Elements refer only to 'military necessity' and not to 'imperative military reasons', as is stated in the Rome Statute. This cannot be taken as enlarging the scope of this exception, as in the case of divergence between the EOC and the definitions in the Rome Statute the latter prevails.[92] Finally, the EOC require that the perpetrator 'was in a position to effect such displacement by giving such order'.[93] Dörmann comments that this formulation refers to both *de jure* and *de facto* authority, thus encompassing the individual who 'has effective control of a situation by sheer force'.[94] Although the mental element of this offence is not defined in the EOC, under Article 30 it would appear to be an intention to order the displacement of a civilian population in the knowledge that it was not justified by imperative military necessity or the security of the civilians.

## Article 8(2)(e)(ix) Killing or wounding treacherously a combatant adversary

The wording of this offence is similar to that of 8(2)(b)(xi) relating to international armed conflicts, except that the term 'combatant adversaries' is used, rather than 'individuals belonging to the hostile nation or army'. This reflects the fact that in non-international armed conflicts both parties to the conflict normally have the same nationality. However, the expression 'combatant adversary' is more restrictive than the equivalent for international armed conflicts, as it criminalises only the treacherous killing or wounding of those adversaries participating in the fighting and not the civilians of the adverse party.[95]

## Article 8(2)(e)(xii) Destroying or seizing the property of an adversary unless such destruction or seizure be imperatively demanded by the necessities of the conflict

This offence is similar to that under Article 8(2)(b)(xiii), applicable in international armed conflicts. The differences again reflect the difference in nature of the conflict, with the phrases 'the property of an adversary' and 'the conflict' being used in this subsection of the Rome Statute rather than 'enemy's

[91] See comments of K. Dörmann, 'Preparatory Commission for the International Criminal Court', n. 7 *supra*, pp. 484–5.

[92] See discussion *supra*, p. 8.

[93] EOC, p. 153.

[94] K. Dörmann, 'Preparatory Commission for the International Criminal Court', n. 7 *supra*, p. 485.

[95] See discussion *supra*, pp. 117–18.

property' and 'war'. Similarly, the EOC refer to the property of 'an adversary' rather than the property of 'a hostile party' and state that the destruction or seizure must not be 'required' by military necessity, rather than 'justified'.[96]

Although both articles appear identical, except with respect to the nature of the conflict, the items which may be lawfully seized or destroyed during a non-international armed conflict cannot automatically be considered the same as those in an international armed conflict and must be decided with reference to AP II and customary international law.[97] Kreß comments upon the confusion regarding the exact ambit of this article, stating that it appears to introduce the war crime of attacking civilian objects, not included in the list in Article 8(2)(e), 'through the back door of Article 8(2)(e)(xii), as the term "adversary" used in this provision certainly extends to civilians'.[98]

Under AP II, objects particularly protected against destruction include dams, dykes and nuclear electricity-generating stations,[99] historic monuments, works of art or places of worship,[100] medical facilities,[101] foodstuffs, agricultural areas, livestock and drinking water installations.[102] It is therefore suggested that the destruction and, in certain cases, seizure of such property on a sufficiently serious scale should, if not imperatively demanded by the necessities of the conflict, amount to an offence under this article.

## Article 8(3)

This article states that the offences set out in paragraphs 8(2)(c) and (e) shall not 'affect the responsibility of a Government to maintain or re-establish law and order in the State or to defend the unity and territorial integrity of the State, by all legitimate means' and it is based on Article 3(1) of AP II. It was included in the Statute to assuage the fears of some States that the provisions on internal conflict might be used to justify interference in their domestic affairs.[103]

However, it is clear that an individual wishing to rely on this section would first have to show that he was acting on behalf of the government of a State and not an opposition movement.[104] Second, it would have to be shown that the

[96] EOC, comparison between pp. 155 and 137–8.

[97] See comments of ICRC, ICRC working paper submitted to the Preparatory Commission on the Elements of Crimes of Article 8(2)(e), 29 June 1999, available at: <http://www.igc.apc.org/icc>, comments on Article 8(2)(e)(xii).

[98] C. Kreß, 'War crimes committed in non-international armed conflict', n. 13 *supra*, p. 139.

[99] Article 15, AP II.

[100] Article 16, AP II.

[101] Article 11, AP II.

[102] Article 14, AP II.

[103] D. Robinson and H. von Hebel, 'War crimes in internal conflicts: Article 8 of the ICC Statute', YIHL, 2 (1999), 193–209, p. 205.

[104] Cottier *et al.*, 'Article 8', p. 287.

actions were taken for the purposes enunciated and not for the 'pursuance of illegitimate goals'.[105] Finally, Article 8(3) is only satisfied if the means used are legitimate and therefore this article cannot negate responsibility for war crimes committed in a non-international armed conflict.[106]

[105] *Ibid.*, emphasis removed.

[106] *Ibid.*, pp. 287–8 and D. Robinson and H. von Hebel, 'War crimes in internal conflicts', n. 103 *supra*, p. 205. See J. Pejic, 'The International Criminal Court Statute', n. 20 *supra*, p. 72.

# 5

# Crimes against humanity

## Background to crimes against humanity

The origins of crimes against humanity are less clear than those of war crimes, but the concept was first invoked in the early nineteenth century in order to condemn brutal treatment by a State of its own citizens.[1] The concept of crimes against humanity was also referred to in the preambular paragraphs of the 1868 St Petersburg Declaration and the 1907 Hague Convention, which alluded to limits imposed by the 'laws of humanity' during armed conflicts, but the notion remained undefined.[2]

The First World War led to the concept of crimes against humanity being invoked again, first in a 1915 declaration condemning the Turkish massacre of Armenians and then by the 1919 Commission on the Responsibility of the Authors of the War, which recommended a tribunal to try those individuals suspected of acting 'in breach of the laws and customs of war and the laws of humanity'.[3] The Commission listed over thirty suggested charges, including murder, torture, rape and deportation of civilians, but did not differentiate in that list between war crimes and crimes against humanity.[4] Ultimately the peace treaties with the

[1] Final Report of the Commission of Experts Established Pursuant to Security Council Resolution 935 (1994), UN Doc. S/1994/1405, 9 December 1994, para. 132, and L. Sunga, *Individual Responsibility in International Law for Serious Human Rights Violations* (Dordrecht: Nijhoff, 1992), p. 41.

[2] 1868 St Petersberg Declaration and the Preamble to the 1907 Hague Convention IV, and see M. Boot, R. Dixon and C. Hall, 'Article 7, crimes against humanity', pp. 117–72 in O. Triffterer (ed.), *Commentary on the Rome Statute of the International Criminal Court: Observers' Notes, Article by Article* (Baden-Baden: Nomos, 1999; hereinafter: Boot *et al.*, 'Article 7'), p. 121.

[3] Declaration of Great Britain, France and Russia, 24 May 1915, cited in E. Schwelb, 'Crimes against humanity', BYIL, 23 (1946), 178–226, p. 181, and Commission on the Responsibility of the Authors of the War and on Enforcement of Penalties: Report presented to the Preliminary Peace Conference, 29 March 1919, reprinted in AJIL, 14 (1920), 95–126, p. 122.

[4] Commission on the Responsibility of the Authors of the War and on Enforcement of Penalties, *ibid.*, pp. 114–15.

defeated Powers did not in any case contain any reference to the 'laws of humanity'.[5]

The atrocities committed in the Second World War acted as the catalyst for the fuller development of this new and previously undefined crime.[6] The 1945 London Agreement promulgated the Nuremberg Charter, with jurisdiction, *inter alia*, over crimes against humanity.[7] The Charter defined these crimes for the first time in international law as:

> murder, extermination, enslavement, deportation, and other inhumane acts committed against any civilian population, before or during the war, or persecutions on political, racial or religious grounds in execution of or in connection with any crime within the jurisdiction of the Tribunal, whether or not in violation of the domestic law of the country where perpetrated.[8]

Similar definitions were included in the Tokyo Charter and Control Council Law (CCL) No. 10.[9]

Crimes against humanity have been described as 'an attack on all humanity';[10] indeed Orentlicher comments that the prosecution of such crimes is so important that 'it justifies an exception to the bedrock principle of international law respect for national sovereignty'.[11] Nevertheless, this category of crimes has never been authoritatively defined by an international Convention,[12] and suffers from a multiplicity of conflicting definitions.[13] The inclusion of crimes against humanity in the Rome Statute, supported by the Elements of Crimes (EOC),

[5] See Articles 227–9, 1919 Treaty of Versailles, reprinted in AJIL, 13 (Supp. 1919), 151–385, and comments by L. Sadat Wexler, 'The interpretation of the Nuremberg Principles by the French Court of Cassation: from Touvier to Barbie and back again', Colum J Transnat'l Law, 32 (1994), 289–380, pp. 298–300. See also the 1920 Treaty of Sèvres, reprinted in AJIL, 15 (Supp. 1921), 179–295, which was eventually replaced by the 1923 Treaty of Lausanne, reprinted in AJIL, 18 (Supp. 1925), 1–53.

[6] W. Fenrick, 'Should crimes against humanity replace war crimes?', Colum J Transnat'l Law, 37 (1999), 767–85, pp. 772–4, and see A. Cassese, 'Crimes against humanity', pp. 353–78 in A. Cassese, P. Gaeta and J. Jones (eds), *The Rome Statute of the International Criminal Court: A Commentary*, Vol. I (Oxford: Oxford University Press, 2002), p. 354.

[7] See M. Bassiouni, *Crimes against Humanity in International Criminal Law* (Dordrecht: Nijhoff, 1992), pp. 5–6 and 17.

[8] Article 6(c), Nuremberg Charter.

[9] Article 5(c), Tokyo Charter, and Article II(c), CCL No. 10.

[10] D. Matas, 'Prosecution in Canada for crimes against humanity', NYL Sch J Int'l & Comp L, 11 (1990), 347–55, p. 350.

[11] D. Orentlicher, 'Settling accounts: the duty to prosecute human rights violations of a prior regime', Yale LJ, 100 (1991), 2537–615, p. 2593, and see M. Frulli, 'Are crimes against humanity more serious than war crimes?', EJIL, 12 (2001), 329–50.

[12] M. Bassiouni, '"Crimes against humanity": the need for a specialized convention', Colum J Transnat'l Law, 31 (1994), 457–94.

[13] L. Sadat, *The International Criminal Court and the Transformation of International Law: Justice for the New Millennium* (New York: Transnational, 2002), p. 148, and compare Article 5, ICTY Statute, Article 3, ICTR Statute, and Article 18, ILC Draft Code.

provides an invaluable opportunity to clarify these offences and provide a proper framework for their prosecution.

## Article 7(1) *chapeau*

### Nexus with armed conflict?

The definition of crimes against humanity in the Nuremberg Charter applied only 'in execution of or in connection with' war crimes or crimes against peace.[14] Nevertheless, two of the defendants at Nuremberg were held liable solely on charges of crimes against humanity which had only a tenuous link with war crimes or crimes against peace.[15] This limitation was not repeated in CCL No. 10, although the discrepancy led to conflicting decisions over whether tribunals conducted pursuant to this ordinance were indeed bound by a conflict nexus.[16]

The Nuremberg Principles as formulated by the International Law Commission (ILC) did not include a conflict nexus, a position maintained in the ILC's Draft Code of Offences against the Peace and Security of Mankind.[17] This approach was also reflected in the Genocide Convention, which defined genocide, a specific type of crime against humanity,[18] as a crime under international law whether committed in time of peace or war,[19] and in the Convention on the Non-applicability of Statutory Limitations to War Crimes and Crimes against

[14] Article 6(c), Nuremberg Charter. See E. Schwelb, 'Crimes against humanity', n. 3 *supra*, p. 188, and B. Van Schaack, 'The definition of crimes against humanity: resolving the incoherence', Colum J Transnat'l Law, 37 (1999), 787–850, p. 801.

[15] Judgement of Streicher and Von Schirach, 22 Trial of German Major War Criminals (London: HMSO, 1950; hereinafter *IMT Judgement*), pp. 502 and 514; comments by B. Van Schaack, 'The definition of crimes against humanity', n. 14 *supra*, para. 576.

[16] Contrast the *Flick* Trial, 9 LRTWC 1, pp. 25–6 and 44–8, with *In re Ohlendorf*, 15 AD (1948), 656, p. 664, and see M. Lippman, 'Crimes against humanity', BC Third World LJ, 17 (1997), 171–273, pp. 219–20; P. Hwang, 'Defining crimes against humanity in the Rome Statute of the International Criminal Court', Fordham Int'l LJ, 22 (1998), 457–504, pp. 451–60, and S. Ratner and J. Abrams, *Accountability for Human Rights Atrocities in International Law: Beyond the Nuremberg Legacy* (Oxford: Oxford University Press, 2nd edn, 2001), pp. 51–2.

[17] See D. Johnson, 'The Draft Code of Offences against the Peace and Security of Mankind', ICLQ, 4 (1955), 445–68, pp. 449–50 and 465–8; Article 2(11), 1954 ILC Draft Code; Article 21, 1991 ILC Draft Code, and Article 18, 1996 ILC Draft Code.

[18] B. Whitaker, 'Revised and updated report on the question of the prevention and punishment of the crime of genocide', UN Sub-commission on Prevention of Discrimination and Protection of Minorities, 2 July 1985 (UN Doc. E/CN.4/Sub.2/1985/6), p. 11; ECOSOC, 'Report of the *Ad Hoc* Committee on Genocide', 24 May 1948, UN Doc. E/794, p. 7, and 1996 ILC Draft Code Commentary, para. 2 on Article 17, and see the *Justice* Trial, 6 LRTWC 1, pp. 32 and 48, and *Kayishema and Ruzindana*, Trial Judgement, para. 89.

[19] Article 1, Genocide Convention.

Humanity, which specifically allowed that crimes against humanity could be 'committed in time of war or in time of peace'.[20]

Therefore the reinstatement of a conflict nexus for crimes against humanity by the International Criminal Tribunal for the former Yugoslavia (ICTY) Statute in 1993 appeared to be a retrograde step.[21] However, the Appeal Chamber in *Tadić* emphasised that the nexus was reintroduced solely for the purposes of the ICTY, '[s]ince customary international law no longer requires any nexus between crimes against humanity and armed conflict'.[22] This approach was confirmed in *Nikolić*, where the Trial Chamber stated that since the Judgement at Nuremberg the concept of crimes against humanity 'has taken on a certain autonomy as there is no longer any need to determine a link with a crime against the peace or a war crime'.[23]

Although this issue caused vigorous debate in the Preparatory Committee, the majority of delegates shared the view of the US delegate, who declared that there was 'no sound reason in theory or precedent' to require a conflict nexus.[24] Therefore the International Criminal Court (ICC) will have jurisdiction over crimes against humanity whether committed in time of peace or conflict and this is confirmed by the introduction to these crimes in the EOC, which states that there need not be a military attack.[25]

## Widespread or systematic

The requirement that crimes against humanity must be widespread or systematic was not present in the Nuremberg or Tokyo Charters, nor was it a requirement of CCL No. 10.[26] However, those tribunals were established to deal with offences committed during or in connection with the Second World War, and so necessarily related to situations where both widespread and systematic atrocities had taken place.[27]

[20] Article 1(b), 1968 Convention on the Non-applicability of Statutory Limitations to War Crimes and Crimes against Humanity.

[21] Article 5, ICTY Statute, but see Article 3, ICTR Statute, and Article 2, Special Court for Sierra Leone (SCSL) Statute.

[22] *Tadić*, Interlocutory Appeal Decision, para. 78, but see *ibid.*, para. 141, in which the tribunal was more tentative with respect to the necessity of a conflict nexus.

[23] *Nikolić* Rule 61 Review, para. 26.

[24] H. von Hebel and D. Robinson, 'Crimes within the jurisdiction of the court', pp. 79–126 in R. Lee (ed.), *The International Criminal Court: The Making of the Rome Statute: Issues, Negotiations, Results* (The Hague: Kluwer, 1999), pp. 92–3, and C. Hall, 'The first two sessions of the UN Preparatory Committee on the Establishment of an International Criminal Court', AJIL, 91 (1997), 177–87, p. 180.

[25] Elements of Crimes, Assembly of States Parties to the Rome Statute of the ICC, Official Records, First Session, ICC-ASP/1/3, 3–10 September 2002 (hereinafter: EOC), p. 116.

[26] Article 6(c), Nuremberg Charter; Article 5(c), Tokyo Charter and Article II(c), CCL No. 10.

[27] See *In re Albrecht* (No. 2), 16 AD (1949), 396, p. 398.

The 1996 ILC Draft Code of Crimes' definition of crimes against humanity states that such crimes must have been committed 'in a systematic manner or on a large scale'.[28] The commentary to the Draft Code defines 'large scale' as meaning that the acts are directed against a multiplicity of victims 'as a result of the cumulative effect of a series of inhumane acts or the singular effect of an inhumane act of extraordinary magnitude' and states that 'systematic' means pursuant to a preconceived plan or policy, excluding random acts.[29]

The expression 'widespread or systematic' is part of the definition of crimes against humanity in both the Statute of the International Criminal Tribunal on Rwanda (ICTR) and the Statute of the Special Court for Sierra Leone.[30] Conversely, the ICTY Statute omits any mention of this element, but both the report of the Yugoslavia Commission of Experts and the report of the Secretary General on the establishment of the ICTY confirm that the attacks must be carried out in a widespread or systematic manner.[31]

In *Akayesu* the ICTR Trial Chamber stated that 'widespread may be defined as massive, frequent, large scale action, carried out collectively with considerable seriousness and directed against a multiplicity of victims' and defined 'systematic' as 'thoroughly organised and following a regular pattern on the basis of a common policy involving substantial public or private resources'.[32] The Trial Chamber in *Rutaganda* concurred with this definition and noted that 'customary international law requires that the attack be either of a widespread *or* systematic nature and need not be both', thus confirming a disjunctive approach to this element.[33]

In the ICTY the Trial Chamber in *Blaškić* explained that the widespread characteristic 'refers to the scale of the acts perpetrated and to the number of victims' and, relying upon the ILC Draft Code, stated that a single inhumane act 'of extraordinary magnitude' could satisfy the 'widespread' requirement.[34] With respect to the systematic nature of crimes against humanity, the Trial Chamber in *Jelisić* suggested that the 'repeated, unchanging and continuous nature of the violence committed' would be a factor demonstrating this.[35]

[28] Article 18, 1996 ILC Draft Code.

[29] 1996 ILC Draft Code Commentary, para. 4, on Article 18.

[30] Article 3, ICTR Statute, and Article 2, SCSL Statute.

[31] Final Report of the Commission of Experts established pursuant to Security Council Resolution 780 (1992), UN Doc. S/1994/674, 27 May 1994 (hereinafter: Yugoslavia Commission of Experts' Report), para. 84, and Report of the Secretary General pursuant to Paragraph 2 of Security Council Resolution 808 (1993), UN Doc. S/25704, para. 48.

[32] *Akayesu*, Trial Judgement, para. 580, but K. Ambos and S. Wirth criticise the reference to substantial resources in 'The current law of crimes against humanity: an analysis of UNTAET Regulation 15/2000', Crim LF, 13 (2002), 1–90, pp. 18–19.

[33] *Rutaganda*, Trial Judgement, paras 68–70, original emphasis. See also the ICTY in *Kunarać*, Appeal Judgement, para. 97 and *Stakić*, Appeal Judgement, para. 246.

[34] *Blaškić*, Trial Judgement, para. 206, and see *Kordić and Čerkez*, Trial Judgement, para. 179.

[35] *Jelisić*, Trial Judgement, para. 53.

The *Kunarać* Trial Judgement held that the expression 'systematic' 'signifies the organised nature of the acts of violence and the improbability of their random occurrence' and that '[p]atterns of crimes – that is the non-accidental repetition of similar criminal conduct on a regular basis – are a common expression of such systematic occurrence'.[36] This was approved by the Appeal Chamber, which also emphasised that 'neither the attack nor the acts of the accused needs to be supported by any form of "policy" or "plan"' and that whilst such a policy may be useful evidentially in establishing that the attack was indeed directed against a civilian population and was widespread or systematic 'it is not a legal element of the crime'.[37]

Therefore the ICTY, the ICTR and the ILC appear to take a similar approach to the definition of the phrase 'widespread or systematic', which is also used in a disjunctive manner in Article 7(1) of the Rome Statute. On the whole, the cases treat 'widespread' as interchangeable with 'large scale' and some cases interpret it as referring to the number of victims affected, rather than simply to the extent of the geographical area in which victims are situated.[38] If the ICC adopted this interpretation it could treat a single attack, such as the terrorist attack on the World Trade Center on 11 September 2001, as coming within the definition of widespread.[39] The cases do not suggest a minimum number of victims to constitute a widespread attack, but it is submitted that for the ICC to take jurisdiction they would have to be in the high hundreds or thousands.[40]

A dictionary definition of 'systematic' is 'methodical; done or conceived according to a plan or system'.[41] This is similar to the concept of systematic as

[36] *Kunarać*, Trial Judgement, para. 429, approved in *Kunarać*, Appeal Judgement, para. 94, and followed by *Blaškić*, Appeal Judgement, para. 101, and *Kordić and Čerkez*, Appeal Judgement, para. 94.

[37] *Kunarać*, Appeal Judgement, para. 98, followed by *Blaškić*, Appeal Judgement, paras 100 and 120. The ICTR has taken the same approach in *Semanza*, Appeal Judgement, para. 269, and *Gacumbitsi*, Appeal Judgement, para. 84, in which the Appeal Chamber stated that neither a plan or policy nor tolerance by the State was a legal element of a crime against humanity.

[38] Although a dictionary definition of 'widespread' is 'widely distributed', *Concise Oxford Dictionary* (Oxford: Clarendon Press, 9th edn, 1995).

[39] See R. Lee, 'An assessment of the ICC Statute', Fordham Int'l LJ, 25 (2001), 750–66, p. 756, and S. Chesterman, 'An altogether different order: defining the elements of crimes against humanity', Duke J Comp & Int'l L, 10 (2000), 307–43, p. 316. See also discussions of 11 September on websites: 'Terrorism and the Laws of War', at <http://www.crimesofwar.org/expert/attack-intro.html> and 'Terrorist Attacks on the World Trade Centre and the Pentagon' at <http://www.asil.org/insights/insigh77.htm>.

[40] Based on the *Akayesu* requirement of large-scale serious action, Trial Judgement, para. 580, and the *Blaškić* comment that a single act would have to be of 'extraordinary magnitude', Trial Judgement, para. 206. See also the threshold for seriousness of crimes against humanity in para. 1 of the Introduction to Crimes against Humanity, EOC, p. 116, and Article 17(1)(d) of the Rome Statute, and see P. Akhavan, 'Contributions of the International Criminal Tribunals for the Former Yugoslavia and Rwanda to development of definitions of crimes against humanity and genocide', ASIL Proceedings, 94 (2000), 279–84, p. 280.

[41] *Concise Oxford Dictionary*, n. 38 *supra*.

entailing crimes which are thoroughly organised and following a regular pattern of similar criminal conduct, which arises from the ICTY and ICTR jurisprudence. Von Hebel and Robinson comment that at the ICC Preparatory Commission the expression 'systematic' was considered to be a stringent requirement which involved 'highly organized and orchestrated execution . . . in accordance with a developed plan'.[42]

## Part of the attack, with knowledge of the attack

The *Kunarać* Trial Chamber defined 'attack' as a 'course of conduct involving the commission of acts of violence' and further noted that this expression held a different meaning in the context of a crime against humanity than in the laws of war.[43] The Appeal Chamber further explained that an attack in this context 'is not limited to the use of armed force; it encompasses any mistreatment of the civilian population'.[44] This approach was also taken by the ICTR Trial Chamber in *Akayesu*, which stated that an 'attack' may be 'non-violent in nature, like imposing a system of apartheid . . . or exerting pressure on the population to act in a particular manner . . . if orchestrated on a massive scale or in a systematic manner'.[45] The Special Court for Sierra Leone has defined attack in this context as meaning a 'campaign, operation or course of conduct' in the *Fofana and Kondewa* Trial Judgement.[46]

The Rome Statute defines 'attack directed against any civilian population' in Article 7(2)(a) as 'a course of conduct involving the multiple commission of acts referred to in paragraph 1 against any civilian population' and, in contrast with the *ad hoc* tribunals approach, requires that this is 'pursuant to or in furtherance of a State or organizational policy to commit such attack'.[47] This wording is repeated in the introduction to crimes against humanity in the EOC, which also emphasises that the acts 'need not constitute a military attack'.[48] Askin comments that the expression 'multiple' in Article 7(2)(a) 'implies that more than one attack, or at least a prolonged attack, is necessary'.[49] However, Hwang alludes to the

[42] H. von Hebel and D. Robinson, 'Crimes within the jurisdiction of the court', n. 24 *supra*, p. 97, fn. 52.

[43] *Kunarać*, Trial Judgement, paras 415–16.

[44] *Kunarać*, Appeal Judgement, para. 86, followed by *Limaj, Bala and Musliu*, Trial Judgement, para. 182.

[45] *Akayesu*, Trial Judgement, para. 581, followed by *Rutaganda*, Trial Judgement, para. 70. However, see comments of Luban that the word 'attack' 'suggests something dynamic, something moving and ongoing' rather than 'the erection of a stable system of group subordination or oppression', D. Luban, 'A theory of crimes against humanity', Yale J Int'l L, 29 (2004), 85–166.

[46] *Fofana and Kondewa*, Trial Judgement, para. 111.

[47] The concept of a state or organisational policy will be discussed *infra*, pp. 202–6.

[48] EOC, Introduction to Crimes against Humanity, para. 3, p. 116.

[49] K. Askin, 'Crimes within the jurisdiction of the International Criminal Court', Crim LF, 10 (1999), 33–59, p. 40.

literal interpretation of 'multiple' taken by an Indian delegate at the Preparatory Commission, that 'anything more than one could be multiple'.[50]

Therefore the requirement for an 'attack' to consist of a multiple commission of acts listed in Article 7 will not normally amount to an onerous burden on the prosecution. It is arguable that this definition would exclude from crimes against humanity a single act which has serious consequences for many civilians, such as the detonation of a 'dirty bomb' in the middle of a city.[51] However, while an incident such as the attack on the World Trade Center could result from one course of conduct, nevertheless that attack would result in many of the acts or crimes referred to in Article 7, such as several murders, and thus arguably satisfy the 'multiple' requirement.[52]

The *mens rea*, and additional objective elements of crimes against humanity, are summed up in the condition that the perpetrator's crime must form 'part' of the widespread or systematic attack against a civilian population, and that he must have had 'knowledge of the attack'. These requirements have been discussed in the Judgements of the ICTY and ICTR as, although their Statutes exclude the phrase 'with knowledge of the attack', their case law has effectively inserted this requirement into their definitions of crimes against humanity.[53]

On an objective basis, it is necessary to prove only that the perpetrator's crime was 'by its nature or consequences' part of the attack.[54] Therefore there is no need to prove the commission of more than one offence by the accused, as it is the overall attack, rather than his part in it, which must have been widespread or systematic.[55] This approach was affirmed by the *Kunarać* Appeal Chamber, which stated that, provided that the acts of the accused are a part of the attack, 'all other conditions being met, a single or relatively limited number of acts on his or her part would qualify as a crime against humanity, unless those acts may be said to be isolated or random'.[56]

Furthermore, although there has to be a nexus between the acts of the accused and the attack, the Trial Chamber in *Krnojelac* stated that '[a] crime committed several months after, or several kilometres away from, the main attack against the civilian population could still, if sufficiently connected, be part of that

[50] P. Hwang, 'Defining crimes against humanity', n. 16 *supra*, p. 502.

[51] A conventional explosive device that spreads nuclear contamination.

[52] See K. Ambos and S. Wirth, 'The current law of crimes against humanity', n. 32 *supra*, p. 17, and S. Chesterman, 'An altogether different order', n. 39 *supra*, p. 316.

[53] Article 5, ICTY Statute (the Statute also omits the words 'as part of', but these have been inserted by case law), Article 3, ICTR Statute.

[54] *Kunarać*, Trial Judgement, para. 418.

[55] *Mrkšić*, Rule 61 Review, para. 30; *Kunarać*, Trial Judgement, para. 431; *Kunarać*, Appeal Judgement, para. 96; *Blaškić*, Appeal Judgement, para. 101; *Kordić and Čerkez*, Appeal Judgement, para. 94, and *Deronjić*, Appeal Judgement, para. 109.

[56] *Kunarać*, Appeal Judgement, para. 96, followed by *Blaškić*, Appeal Judgement, para. 101; *Kordić and Čerkez*, Appeal Judgement, para. 94 and *Deronjić*, Appeal Judgement, para. 109.

attack'.[57] The *Semanza* Trial Judgement added that '[t]he victim(s) of the enumerated act need not necessarily share geographic or other defining features with the civilian population that forms the primary target of the underlying attack' but held that 'such characteristics may be used to demonstrate that the enumerated act forms part of the attack'.[58]

With respect to the mental element of crimes against humanity, the ICTY and ICTR cases all require that, in addition to the *mens rea* for the crime committed, the accused knew of the widespread or systematic attack,[59] was aware that it was directed against a civilian population[60] and knew that his acts formed a part of that attack.[61] However, proof that the perpetrator had knowledge of all the details of the attack is not required.[62] Moreover, the case law shows that knowledge of the overall attack can be inferred and that wilful blindness will not be a defence.[63]

The issue of whether personal motives of the defendant are relevant to a crime against humanity and whether a crime can truly be said to be part of the overall attack if it is carried out for purely personal reasons was discussed by the ICTY in *Tadić*. The Appeal Chamber, relying upon a series of German national Second World War cases[64] and the general irrelevance of motive in criminal law,[65] reversed the decision of the Trial Chamber on this issue.[66] The Appeal Judgement held that, provided the perpetrator's offence was committed in the context of widespread or systematic crimes directed against a civilian

[57] *Krnojelac*, Trial Judgement, para. 55, and *Kunarać*, Appeal Judgement, para. 100. Note that both *Kunarać*, *ibid.*, and *Blagojević and Jokić*, Trial Judgement, para. 547, warn that the attack must not be an isolated act. For suggested indicia of the nexus between the accused's acts and the attack see Boot *et al.*, 'Article 7', pp. 125–6.

[58] *Semanza*, Trial Judgement, para. 330.

[59] *Tadić*, Trial Judgement, para. 656; *Tadić*, Appeal Judgement, para. 248; *Jelisić*, Trial Judgement, para. 56; *Blaškić*, Trial Judgement, para. 247; *Kupreškić*, Trial Judgement, para. 556; *Kordić and Čerkez*, Trial Judgement, para. 185; *Kayishema and Ruzindana*, Trial Judgement, paras 133–4; *Bagilishema*, Trial Judgement, para. 94, and see *R. v. Finta*, Supreme Court, Canada, 104 ILR, 285, p. 362.

[60] *Tadić*, Appeal Judgement, paras 248 and 271; *Kupreškić*, Trial Judgement, para. 557; *Kordić and Čerkez*, Trial Judgement, para. 185; *Krnojelac*, Trial Judgement, para. 59, and *Kayishema and Ruzindana*, Trial Judgement, para. 134.

[61] *Kunarać*, Appeal Judgement, para. 99; *Blaškić*, Appeal Judgement, para. 124, and *Kordić and Čerkez*, Appeal Judgement, para. 99.

[62] *Kunarać*, Trial Judgement, para. 434; *Krnojelac*, Trial Judgement, para. 59, and *Kunarać*, Appeal Judgement, para. 102.

[63] *R. v. Finta*, Supreme Court, Canada, 104 ILR, 285, p. 363; *Tadić*, Trial Judgement, para. 657, and *Kayishema and Ruzindana*, Trial Judgement, para. 134. The latter was supported in *Blaškić*, Trial Judgement, para. 249; *Kupreškić*, Trial Judgement, para. 557; *Kordić and Čerkez*, Trial Judgement, para. 185, and *Blagojević and Jokić*, Appeal Judgement, para. 102.

[64] *Tadić*, Appeal Judgement, paras 257–62 and fns 318–25.

[65] *Ibid.*, paras 268–9, and see *Bagilishema*, Trial Judgement, para. 95.

[66] *Tadić*, Appeal Judgement, paras 255 and 270, reversing *Tadić*, Trial Judgement, paras 656–9.

population, and that the accused knew that his acts 'fitted into such a pattern', a crime against humanity could be committed for purely personal reasons.[67]

Subsequent ICTY Judgements have followed the *Tadić* Appeal Judgement and shed more light upon this approach to personal motives. The Trial Chamber in *Blaškić* stated that '[t]he accused need not have sought all the elements of the context in which his acts were perpetrated; it suffices that . . . he knowingly took the risk of participating in the implementation of that context'.[68] This interpretation was adopted by the *Kunarać* and *Krnojelac* cases, and it is submitted that this interpretation is to be preferred to that of the *Blaškić* Appeal Chamber, which emphasised that the accused should *know*, rather than merely take the risk, that his act formed part of the widespread attack.[69]

It is also submitted that the ICC should follow the *Tadić* approach to personal motives as expanded by the *Blaškić* Trial Chamber.[70] The EOC do not require proof of motive in respect of crimes against humanity,[71] so the question becomes whether the defendant's crime is 'part' of the overall attack, irrespective of his motives. For example, in the *Kunarać* case, the Trial Chamber stated that the accused, who raped and enslaved Muslim women, knew about the attack against the Muslim population and 'committed the offences charged by directly taking advantage of the situation created'.[72] Therefore, an argument that the defendants acted from purely sexual motives, rather than intending their acts to be part of the overall attack, would have been unsuccessful.[73]

## Directed against any civilian population

From the Nuremberg Charter onwards the majority of definitions of crimes against humanity have included the provision that the attack must be committed or directed 'against any civilian population'.[74] However, although CCL No. 10 included this

[67] *Tadić*, Appeal Judgement, para. 255, but see the Dissenting Opinion of Judge Shahabuddeen, *ibid.*, para. 35, and, in support of the Dissenting Opinion, M. Sassòli and L. Olson, 'The judgment of the ICTY Appeals Chamber on the merits in the Tadić case', IRRC, 839 (2000), 733–69, pp. 757–8. Nevertheless the *Tadić* Appeal Judgement was followed by *Kunarać*, Appeal Judgement, para. 103; *Blaškić*, Appeal Judgement, para. 124, and *Kordić and Čerkez*, Appeal Judgement, para. 99. See also the comments on the distinction between motive and intent in *Krnojelac*, Appeal Judgement, para. 102.

[68] *Blaškić*, Trial Judgement, para. 251, and see *Marques, Da Costa et al.*, Trial Judgement, Dili District Court, Special Panel for Serious Crimes, para. 641.

[69] *Kunarać*, Trial Judgement, para. 434; *Krnojelac*, Trial Judgement, para. 59, and *Kunarać*, Appeal Judgement, para. 102. See also *Blaškić*, Appeal Judgement, para. 44.

[70] *Tadić*, Appeal Judgement, para. 255, and *Blaškić*, Trial Judgement, para. 251. See K. Ambos and S. Wirth, 'The current law of crimes against humanity', n. 32 *supra*, pp. 37–40.

[71] See common Elements to crimes against humanity, EOC, 7(1)(a), paras 2–3, p. 116.

[72] *Kunarać*, Trial Judgement, para. 592.

[73] *Kunarać*, Appeal Judgement, para. 137; this argument was unsuccessfully put forward as a defence to the charge of torture.

[74] But see Article 5(c), Tokyo Charter, as amended on 26 April 1946, and K. Askin, 'Crimes within the jurisdiction of the International Criminal Court', n. 49 *supra*, p. 40, and an exception in Article 18, 1996 ILC Draft Code.

provision, charges of crimes against humanity were upheld in two cases relating to the treatment of captured members of the Allied armed forces.[75] This flexible approach to the expression 'civilians' was also shown in the trial of *Barbie*, a case under French national legislation, where the Court of Cassation stated that '[n]either the driving force which motivated the victims, nor their possible membership of the Resistance' could exclude the possibility that Barbie committed crimes against humanity.[76]

When considering the cases before the ICTY and ICTR and how the ICC should interpret these terms it is necessary to keep two issues separate which were not necessarily separated in earlier cases. The first issue is the meaning of a 'civilian population' against which the widespread or systematic attack must take place. The second issue is whether, in order to form part of the wider attack, the acts of the accused need to be against individual civilians, and if so, the definition of 'a civilian' for the purposes of crimes against humanity.

With respect to an understanding of the phrase 'civilian population', the *Kunarać* Appeal Judgement states that 'the use of the word "population" does not mean that the entire population of the geographical entity in which the attack is taking place must have been subjected to that attack', but that '[i]t is sufficient to show that enough individuals were targeted in the course of the attack, or they were targeted in such a way as . . . [to show] the attack was in fact directed against a civilian "population" '.[77] ICTY jurisprudence has also considered the relevance of the expression 'any civilian population' and held that the word 'any' makes it clear that there is no necessity to link civilians to one side of a conflict (if one exists) and that crimes against humanity can be committed against persons of the same nationality.[78] *Tadić* and *Kunarać* suggest that the expression 'population' was included to prevent isolated or random acts from being characterised as a crime against humanity.[79] This interpretation, however, was necessary in order to 'read in' a widespread or systematic requirement into the ICTY Statute.[80]

Both the ICTY and ICTR Judgements stress that, while the civilian population must be the primary object of the attack,[81] the presence of some non-civilians does not change the character of the population provided that it is 'predominantly

[75] *In re Rohde and Others*, 13 AD (1948), 294, p. 295, and Trial of *Altstötter and Others*, 6 LRTWC 1, p. 81.

[76] *Fédération Nationale des Déportés et Internés Résistants et Patriotes and Others v. Barbie*, 78 ILR, 136, p. 140, and see p. 137.

[77] *Kunarać*, Appeal Judgement, para. 90 (approving of *Tadić*, Trial Judgement, para. 644, and *Kunarać*, Trial Judgement, para. 424) and followed by *Stakić*, Appeal Judgement, para. 247.

[78] *Tadić*, Trial Judgement, para. 635, and *Kunarać*, Trial Judgement, para. 423.

[79] *Ibid.*, paras 644 and 422 respectively, and see *Kunarać*, Appeal Judgement, para. 90.

[80] See P. Hwang, 'Defining crimes against humanity', n. 16 *supra*, pp. 482–4.

[81] *Kunarać*, Trial Judgement, para. 421, and *Kunarać*, Appeal Judgement, para. 91.

civilian in nature'.[82] Indeed, the *Blaškić* Appeal Chamber comments that 'the presence within a population of members of resistance groups, or former combatants who have laid down their arms, does not alter its civilian characteristic' and suggests that when determining 'whether the presence of soldiers within a civilian population deprives the population of its civilian character, the number of soldiers, as well as whether they are on leave, must be examined'.[83]

On the issue of whether the defendant's act, in the context of the attack against the civilian population, must have been directed against 'a civilian', the Trial Chamber in *Kunarać* required that 'as a minimum the perpetrator must have known or considered the possibility that the victim of his crime was a civilian'.[84] This requirement is debatable, as it is the overall attack which must be directed against a civilian population and it has to be shown only that the defendant's crime formed part of that attack. For example, the murder of a soldier, who was trying to protect some civilian political opponents of the government from a mob taking part in a widespread attack aimed at such opponents, could arguably constitute murder as a crime against humanity if carried out to remove an obstacle to further crimes against that civilian population.[85] Nevertheless, this is not the approach taken by the ICC and so the question of what is 'a civilian' remains important, especially when considering a situation in which a defendant is accused of killing prisoners of war or imprisoned resistance fighters.

The ICTY Judgements, in their analysis of 'a civilian', reflect the fact that the ICTY Statute links crimes against humanity with armed conflict and primarily contrasts civilians with members of the armed forces or combatants.[86] Therefore, their definition of 'civilian' relies on an analysis of this word in the Geneva Conventions and Additional Protocols.[87] Nevertheless, initially, the ICTY Judgements followed *Barbie* in their inclusion of resistance fighters in the definition of 'a civilian'.[88] The Trial Chamber in *Blaškić* went even further and

[82] *Tadić*, Trial Judgement, para. 638, and see *Kupreškić*, Trial Judgement, para. 549; *Blaškić*, Trial Judgement, para. 214; *Kordić and Čerkez*, Trial Judgement, para. 180; *Kunarać*, Trial Judgement, para. 425; *Krnojelac*, Trial Judgement, para. 56, and ICTR Judgements: *Kayishema and Ruzindana*, Trial Judgement, para. 128; *Bagilishema*, Trial Judgement, para. 79, and *Semanza*, Trial Judgement, para. 330.

[83] *Blaškić*, Appeal Judgement, paras 113 and 115.

[84] *Kunarać*, Trial Judgement, para. 435.

[85] This could be supported by the *Kunarać* Appeal Judgement, para. 103, comment that 'It is the attack, not the acts of the accused, which must be directed against the target population', albeit that it was said in the context of irrelevance of personal motive. However, if the attack was truly against a civilian population, the vast majority of victims would be civilian.

[86] See S. Chesterman, 'An altogether different order', n. 39 *supra*, pp. 322–5.

[87] *Tadić*, Trial Judgement, para. 639; *Blaškić*, Trial Judgement, para. 209, and *Kunarać*, Trial Judgement, para. 425. The Yugoslavia Commission of Experts' Report, n. 31 *supra*, paras 77–8, also took this approach.

[88] *Mrkšić*, Rule 61 Review, para. 29; *Tadić*, Trial Judgement, para. 643; *Kordić and Čerkez*, Trial Judgement, para. 180; *Kupreškić*, Trial Judgement, para. 549, and *Krnojelac*, Trial Judgement, para. 56. Cassese suggests that the ICC should follow this approach, A. Cassese, 'Crimes against humanity', n. 6 *supra*, p. 375.

stated that crimes against humanity could be committed against 'those who were members of a resistance movement and former combatants – regardless of whether they wore uniform or not – but who were no longer taking part in hostilities when the crimes were perpetrated because they had either left the army or were no longer bearing arms or, ultimately, had been placed *hors de combat*, in particular, due to their wounds or their being detained'.[89]

This Trial Judgement seemed to suggest that 'a civilian' was a very broad expression and that an individual could be prosecuted, for example, for the crime against humanity of murder if he killed a prisoner of war or a captured resistance fighter. The *Blaškić* Appeal Chamber also required that the victim of an individual crime against humanity should be civilian but reassessed the interpretation of 'a civilian' and stated that 'the specific situation of the victim at the time the crimes are committed may not be determinative of his civilian or non-civilian status' and emphasised that '[i]f he is indeed a member of an armed organization, the fact that he is not armed or in combat at the time of the commission of crimes does not accord him civilian status'.[90]

Nevertheless, it is questionable whether the ICTY definition of 'a civilian' is an appropriate precedent for the ICC, given that the definition of crimes against humanity in the Rome Statute, unlike the Statute of the ICTY, does not require a link with an armed conflict. Only the ICTR in the case of *Kayishema and Ruzindana* specifically considered the definition of 'a civilian' during peacetime.[91] The Trial Chamber stated that the term civilian must be read widely and includes 'all persons except those who have the duty to maintain public order and have the legitimate means to exercise force'.[92] This negative test could be workable as a method of providing the ICC with the same definition of 'a civilian' in peacetime as in wartime in order to maintain consistency in an offence which can be committed irrespective of the existence of a conflict.[93] This would have the effect of classifying the police force and the armed forces as non-civilian, at least when using the force to maintain public order or during a conflict, but would not exclude from the definition of 'civilian' those resistance fighters who would

[89] *Blaškić*, Trial Judgement, para. 214, followed by *Kordić and Čerkez* Trial Judgement, para. 180. The same approach was taken in *Akayesu*, Trial Judgement, para. 582, and *Bagilshema*, Trial Judgement, para. 79.

[90] *Blaškić*, Appeal Judgement, para. 114. Post-*Blaškić* ICTY cases show confusion about the different definitions of 'civilian population' and 'a civilian', see *Blagojević and Jokić*, Trial Judgement, para. 544, and *Limaj, Bala and Musliu*, Trial Judgement, para. 186, but the distinction is drawn clearly in *Stakić*, Appeal Judgement, para. 144.

[91] *Kayishema and Ruzindana*, Trial Judgement, para. 127. Note that those ICTR Judgements which have discussed the definition of 'a civilian' as a separate issue from a 'civilian population' have followed the *Blaškić* Trial Chamber Judgement (rather than the *Blaškić* Appeal Judgement), see *Bagilishema*, Trial Judgement, para. 79; *Kajelijeli*, Trial Judgement, para. 874; *Bisengimana*, Trial Judgement, para. 49, and *Muvunyi*, Trial Judgement, para. 513.

[92] *Kayishema and Ruzindana*, Trial Judgement, para. 127.

[93] But see K. Ambos and S. Wirth, 'The current law of crimes against humanity', n. 32 *supra*, pp. 24–6.

not be considered legitimate combatants with prisoner of war (PoW) status under the Geneva Conventions or Additional Protocols.[94]

The approach that the ICC will take to the expression 'civilian population' is unclear and not addressed in the EOC. Robinson states that the Preparatory Commission felt that this complex and still evolving notion was better left to resolution in case law, but agreed that it was a 'flexible test'.[95] The ICTY approach of holding that the presence of some non-civilians does not change the character of the population if it is predominantly civilian is a sensible interpretation.

The approach the ICC should take to the expression 'any population' is more complex. Certainly, the word 'any' should be read in line with the ICTY jurisprudence as confirming that the victims of crimes against humanity can hold the same nationality, or be on the same side in a conflict, as the perpetrators.[96] However, the expression 'population', if read solely as a requirement that the acts must be more than isolated and random, would appear to be otiose in the ICC Statute in light of the 'widespread or systematic' requirement.[97] Mettraux suggests that a 'population' must 'form a self-contained group of individuals, either geographically or as a result of other common features' and therefore excludes from this '[a] group of individuals randomly or fortuitously assembled – such as a crowd at a football game'.[98]

Nevertheless, the ICC must be careful not to allow the interpretation of 'population' to reintroduce the requirement that all crimes against humanity must be based on discrimination. First, it is debatable whether discrimination was, in fact, needed for all crimes against humanity in the Nuremberg Charter.[99] Second, whilst the ICTR definition of crimes against humanity expressly included a discrimination requirement, the ICTY definition did not, and indeed the *Tadić* Appeal Chamber held that discrimination is only a condition for the specific crime of persecution.[100] Third, Robinson confirms that '[t]he negotiations in Rome

[94] See definition of civilians discussed *supra*, pp. 61–2, but see L. Sadat, *The International Criminal Court and the Transformation of International Law*, n. 13 *supra*, p. 153.

[95] R. Lee (ed.), *The International Criminal Court: Elements of Crimes and Rules of Procedure and Evidence* (New York: Transnational, 2001; hereinafter: Lee (ed.), *ICC: Elements*), p. 78, and see H. von Hebel and D. Robinson, 'Crimes within the jurisdiction of the court', n. 24 *supra*, p. 97, fn. 54.

[96] *Tadić*, Trial Judgement, para. 635, and *Kunarać*, Trial Judgement, para. 423.

[97] See K. Ambos and S. Wirth, 'The current law of crimes against humanity', n. 32 *supra*, pp. 21–2.

[98] G. Mettraux, 'Crimes against humanity in the jurisprudence of the International Criminal Tribunals for the Former Yugoslavia and for Rwanda', Harv ILJ, 43 (2002), 237–316, p. 255, and see *R. v. Finta*, Supreme Court, Canada, 104 ILR, 285, pp. 358–9, which required an 'identifiable group of people'.

[99] Compare the Trial of *Altstötter and Others*, 6 LRTWC 1, p. 40 with *Attorney General v. Enigster*, 18 ILR, 540, p. 541, and see D. Robinson, 'Defining "crimes against humanity" at the Rome Conference', AJIL, 93 (1999), 43–57, p. 46, fn. 17.

[100] *Tadić*, Appeal Judgement, para. 305, followed by *Kordić and Čerkez*, Trial Judgement, para. 186. Indeed, the Appeal Chamber in *Akayesu* noted that the requirement that crimes against humanity must be based upon discrimination was a purely jurisdictional requirement of the ICTR and did not reflect customary international law on this issue, *Akayesu*, Appeal Judgement, paras 464–6.

produced agreement that a discriminatory motive is not an element required for all crimes against humanity'.[101]

Therefore the approach taken by Chesterman of using the word 'population' loosely has merit.[102] He suggests that the expression confirms that, as in humanitarian law, the civilian population comprises all those who are civilians and that 'the presence of individuals who do not come within the definition of "civilians" does not deprive a population of its civilian character'.[103] This reflects the findings of the ICTY that the attack need only be directed against a population which is *predominantly* civilian in nature.[104] However, an interpretation of 'population' as requiring merely a loose objective link between the civilians attacked, rather than as discriminatory *mens rea* on the part of any individual perpetrator, could have the benefit of making the 'widespread or systematic' element easier to prove.[105] For example, if the attack was only against civilians of a particular religion, it would have to be shown that the attack was widespread or systematic only in the context of *that* civilian population, not in the context of the civilian population as a whole.[106]

### Pursuant to or in furtherance of a State or organisational policy to commit such attack

The explicit requirement of a State or organisational policy underlying the overall attack was not included in the Nuremberg Charter, the Tokyo Charter, CCL No. 10, or the ICTY or ICTR statutes.[107] Indeed, whether or not an underlying policy is a necessary part of crimes against humanity has been strongly contested.[108] The Nuremberg Judgement is of limited assistance because, whilst it describes the Nazi policy of terror and persecution, it is unclear whether this was raised

[101] D. Robinson, 'Defining "crimes against humanity"', n. 99 *supra*, p. 46, and see H. von Hebel and D. Robinson, 'Crimes within the jurisdiction of the court', n. 24 *supra*, pp. 93–4.

[102] S. Chesterman, 'An altogether different order', n. 39 *supra*, pp. 325–6.

[103] *Ibid.*, and Article 50, API.

[104] *Tadić*, Trial Judgement, para. 638, and see *Kupreškić*, Trial Judgement, para. 549; *Blaškić*, Trial Judgement, para. 214; *Kordić and Čerkez*, Trial Judgement, para. 180; *Kunarać*, Trial Judgement, para. 425; *Krnojelac*, Trial Judgement, para. 56, and ICTR Judgements: *Kayishema and Ruzindana*, Trial Judgement, para. 128; *Bagilishema*, Trial Judgement, para. 79, and *Semanza*, Trial Judgement, para. 330.

[105] G. Mettraux, 'Crimes against humanity in the jurisprudence of the International Criminal Tribunals', n. 98 *supra*, pp. 255–6.

[106] *Ibid.*, p. 256. If this interpretation were applied, the civilians in the World Trade Center would have to be considered as part of the civilian population of Manhattan in order to be victims of crimes against humanity.

[107] Article 6(c), Nuremberg Charter; Article 5(c), Tokyo Charter; Article II(c), CCL No. 10; Article 5, ICTY Statute, and Article 3, ICTR Statute.

[108] Contrast the approach of D. Robinson, 'Defining "crimes against humanity"', n. 99 *supra*, pp. 48–51, with that of G. Mettraux, 'Crimes against humanity in the jurisprudence of the International Criminal Tribunals', n. 98 *supra*, pp. 270–82.

as the factual circumstance in which the crimes took place or whether it was a necessary element of crimes against humanity.[109]

Nevertheless, some Second World War tribunals referred to State involvement in crimes against humanity as an element of the offence, including the Trial of *Altstötter*, which stated that crimes against humanity must have been 'conducted by or with the approval of government'.[110] More recent cases taking this approach include the French judgements in the cases of *Barbie* and *Touvier*, which both held that an essential element of crimes against humanity was that 'the acts charged were performed in a systematic manner in the name of a State practising by those means a policy of ideological supremacy'.[111]

A similar requirement was included in the 1996 ILC Draft Code of Crimes, which stated that crimes against humanity must have been 'instigated or directed by a Government or by any organization or group'.[112] The commentary to the Draft Code explains that such instigation or direction 'gives the act its great dimension' and excludes inhumane acts of an individual 'acting on his own initiative pursuant to his own criminal plan in the absence of any encouragement or direction from either a Government or a group or organization'.[113] Ambos and Wirth suggest that the link with 'an authority or power' has been necessary to transform a criminal act into an act of international concern since the abandonment of the war nexus which previously internationalised such acts.[114]

Certain ICTY and ICTR Judgements have quoted the ILC definition and explanation of the policy element of crimes against humanity with approval.[115] However, most Judgements do not accept that a policy element is really a requirement of crimes against humanity, as opposed to merely providing evidence that

[109] *IMT Judgement*, p. 468, although it is possible that this issue of policy was raised in connection with planning an aggressive war, rather than in connection with crimes against humanity, p. 79.

[110] Trial of *Altstötter and Others*, 6 LRTWC 1, p. 40, and see *In re Ahlbrecht (No. 2)*, 16 ILR, 396, p. 397, and *In re Ohlendorf and Others*, 15 AD (1948), 656, p. 664.

[111] *Barbie*, 100 ILR, 330, p. 336, and *Touvier*, 100 ILR, 337, p. 352. See also *Public Prosecutor v. Menten*, 75 ILR, 331, p. 363, and *R. v. Finta*, Supreme Court, Canada, 104 ILR, 285, p. 359. For a critical discussion of the French cases see: L. Sadat, 'Prosecutions for crimes against humanity in French municipal law: international implications', ASIL Proceedings, 91 (1997), 270–4, pp. 271–2; L. Sadat Wexler, 'The interpretation of the Nuremberg Principles by the French Court of Cassation', n. 5 *supra*, pp. 341–4 and 353–5; M. Tigar, S. Casey, I. Giordani and S. Mardemootoo, 'Paul Touvier and the crime against humanity', Texas Int'l LJ, 30 (1995), 285–310; J. Viout, 'The Klaus Barbie trial and crimes against humanity', Hof LPS, 3 (1999), 155–66, and N. Doman, 'Aftermath of Nuremberg: the trial of Klaus Barbie', U Col LR, 60 (1989), 449–69.

[112] Article 18, 1996 ILC Draft Code.

[113] 1996 ILC Draft Code Commentary, para. 5 to Article 18, and see D. Johnson, 'The Draft Code of Offences', n. 17 *supra*, p. 465.

[114] K. Ambos and S. Wirth, 'The current law of crimes against humanity', n. 32 *supra*, p. 12.

[115] *Tadić*, Trial Judgement, para. 655; *Blaškić*, Trial Judgement, para. 205, and *Kayishema and Ruzindana*, Trial Judgement, para. 125.

a crime is 'systematic'.[116] Nevertheless, those Judgements which include a policy component accept that this requirement is not limited to a State policy,[117] and indeed the *Tadić* Trial Chamber accepts that this requirement could be satisfied by an entity exercising *de facto* control over a particular territory or even by a terrorist group.[118]

The policy requirement is inserted into the definition of crimes against humanity in the Rome Statute through the expression 'attack directed against any civilian population', which is defined in Article 7(2)(a) as 'a course of conduct . . . pursuant to or in furtherance of a State or organizational policy to commit such attack'. This expression is expanded upon by the introduction to crimes against humanity in the EOC, which state that a 'policy to commit such attack' 'requires that the State or organization actively promote or encourage such attack against a civilian population'.[119] A footnote to this paragraph explains that the attack would be implemented by the State or organisational action and that '[s]uch a policy may, in exceptional circumstances, be implemented by a deliberate failure to take action, which is consciously aimed at encouraging such attack', although '[t]he existence of such a policy cannot be inferred solely from the absence of governmental or organizational action'.[120]

The complexity of this definition, when the supplementing and somewhat contradictory introduction and footnotes in the EOC are taken into account, demonstrates the controversial nature of the provision.[121] Furthermore, it raises several questions. First, although the concept of a State policy is relatively clear, what is an organisational policy and does the exclusion of the 'group' policy, referred to by the ILC, curtail the breadth of this definition? A comparison between the dictionary definitions of 'group' and 'organisation' suggest that the latter must have a more orderly structure.[122] An organisational policy would clearly include the policy of 'an entity holding *de facto* authority over a territory', referred to

[116] *Kunarać*, Appeal Judgement, para. 98, followed by *Blaškić*, Appeal Judgement, paras 100 and 120. The ICTR has taken the same approach in *Akayesu*, Trial Judgement, para. 580; *Semanza*, Appeal Judgement, para. 269, and *Gacumbitsi*, Appeal Judgement, para. 84, in which the Appeal Chamber stated that neither a plan or policy nor tolerance by the State was a legal element of a crime against humanity. The Yugoslavia Commission of Experts' Report, n. 31 *supra*, para. 84, also treated this as part of the 'systematic' requirement.

[117] *Nikolić*, Rule 61 Review, para. 26, and *Kupreškić*, Trial Judgement, paras 551–2, although in para. 555 the Trial Chamber is more tentative. *Blaškić*, Trial Judgement, para. 205; *Kayishema and Ruzindana*, Trial Judgement, paras 125–6, and *Bagilishema*, Trial Judgement, para. 78, are more definite.

[118] *Tadić*, Trial Judgement, para. 654.

[119] EOC, Introduction to Crimes against Humanity, p. 116, para. 3.

[120] EOC, fn. 6 on p. 116.

[121] H. von Hebel and D. Robinson, 'Crimes within the jurisdiction of the court', n. 24 *supra*, p. 96; C. Hall, 'The first five sessions of the UN Preparatory Commission for the International Criminal Court', AJIL, 94 (2000), 773–89, p. 780, and Lee (ed.), *ICC: Elements*, pp. 75–6.

[122] *Concise Oxford Dictionary*, n. 38 *supra*, and see P. Hwang, 'Defining crimes against humanity', n. 16 *supra*, p. 504.

in *Kupreškić*,[123] but could a terrorist 'group' also amount to an organisation?[124] It is submitted that a well established and organised terrorist group could in certain circumstances amount to an 'organisation' and therefore could form the policy behind an attack against a civilian population.[125]

A second question is: what amounts to 'active promotion or encouragement' of the policy? Robinson explains that at the Preparatory Commission this expression was understood as encompassing the direction or instigation of policy referred to in the ILC Draft Code, in addition to 'passive, deliberate encouragement'.[126] Furthermore, the explanatory footnote in the Elements confirms that included within an active promotion or encouragement of a policy is 'deliberate failure to take action', provided it is 'consciously aimed at encouraging such attack'.[127] Although a policy cannot be inferred solely from the absence of action, such an inference would clearly be appropriate if the State or organisation knew of the crimes and had the ability to prevent or punish them but failed to do so.[128] Nevertheless, the restriction of this category of offences to those actively encouraging an attack against civilians, as opposed to simply tolerating or condoning it, has been strongly criticised by Cassese and Politi.[129]

Third, how formal is the policy required to be, and does this policy requirement effectively amount to imposing a mandatory 'systematic' requirement? Von Hebel and Robinson comment that the delegates at the Preparatory Commission understood the policy element as a 'flexible test' and emphasised that the policy need not be formal,[130] an approach taken by the ICTY in *Kupreškić*.[131] Moreover, Robinson stresses that the policy test does not require the high degree of organisation or orchestration required by the term 'systematic'.[132]

[123] *Kupreškić*, Trial Judgement, para. 552.

[124] *Tadić*, Trial Judgement, para. 654, refers to a 'terrorist group or organization'.

[125] See comments of S. Ratner and J. Abrams, *Accountability for Human Rights Atrocities*, p. 69, F. Lattanzi, 'Crimes against humanity in the jurisprudence of the International Criminal Tribunals for the Former Yugoslavia and Rwanda', pp. 473–504, in H. Fischer, C. Kreß and S. Lüder (eds), *International and National Prosecution of Crimes under International Law: Current Developments* (Berlin: Berlin Verlag, 2001), p. 485, and G. Robertson, *Crimes against Humanity: The Struggle for Global Justice* (New York: New Press, 2000), pp. 335–6, who specifically mentions Bin Laden, but K. Ambos and S. Wirth disagree, 'The current law of crimes against humanity', n. 32 *supra*, p. 27.

[126] Lee (ed.), *ICC: Elements*, p. 77.

[127] EOC, p. 116.

[128] Lee (ed.), *ICC: Elements*, p. 76, and see P. Hwang, 'Defining crimes against humanity', n. 16 *supra*, p. 503, and Women's Caucus for Gender Justice, 'Recommendations and Commentary for the Elements of Crimes and Rules of Procedure and Evidence', submitted to the Preparatory Commission for the ICC, 12–30 June 2000, on the *chapeau* to crimes against humanity.

[129] A. Cassese, 'Crimes against humanity', pp. 353–78, and M. Politi, 'Elements of crimes', pp. 443–73 in A. Cassese *et al.*, *ICC Commentary*, n. 6 *supra*, pp. 375–6 and 465–6 respectively.

[130] H. von Hebel and D. Robinson, 'Crimes within the jurisdiction of the court', n. 24 *supra*, p. 97 and fn. 51.

[131] *Kupreškić*, Trial Judgement, para. 551, and see *Akayesu*, Trial Judgement, para. 580.

[132] D. Robinson, 'Defining "crimes against humanity"', n. 99 *supra*, pp. 50–1.

He describes the definition of attack in Article 7 of the Rome Statute as resulting in 'a high-threshold but disjunctive test (widespread or systematic) coupled with a low-threshold but conjunctive test (multiple and policy)'.[133] It should also be noted that the policy required is merely 'to commit such an attack' and not to impose a particular political ideology, to discriminate or to commit specific acts.[134]

Finally, it is unclear whether the mental element 'with knowledge of the attack' necessarily requires knowledge of the policy to which the attack is pursuant. It is clear, however, that neither knowledge of all the details of the policy nor participation in the formulation of the policy is a necessary element of crimes against humanity.[135] It is submitted that, while the policy element must be proved materially, the perpetrator need be aware of only the basic factual outline of the widespread or systematic attack against a civilian population. Otherwise a loophole would be created in which defendants could escape liability by claiming that they did not know that there was a State or organisational policy to commit the attack.[136]

## Article 7(1) offences

### Elements of Crimes common to Article 7(1) offences

The elements common to crimes against humanity require that the conduct of the perpetrator 'was committed as part of a widespread or systematic attack directed against a civilian population' and that the perpetrator 'knew that the conduct was part of or intended the conduct to be part of' such an attack.[137] These elements basically repeat the provisions of the *chapeau* discussed above. However, the expression 'intended the conduct to be part' of the attack was included in order to deal with a perpetrator committing his offence in an emerging crime against humanity.[138] This issue is clarified in the introduction to crimes against humanity in the EOC, which states that '[i]n the case of an emerging widespread or systematic attack against a civilian population, the intent clause of the last element indicates that this mental element is satisfied if the perpetrator intended to further such an attack'.[139]

[133] D. Robinson, in Lee (ed.), *ICC: Elements*, p. 63.

[134] P. Hwang, 'Defining crimes against humanity', n. 16 *supra*, p. 504.

[135] See discussion of knowledge of details of the attack, *supra*, pp. 195–7, and H. von Hebel and D. Robinson, 'Crimes within the jurisdiction of the court', n. 24 *supra*, p. 97 and fn. 51.

[136] See M. McAuliffe deGuzman, 'The road from Rome: the developing law of crimes against humanity', HRQ, 22 (2000), 335–403, pp. 380–1, and J. Pejic, 'The International Criminal Court Statute: an appraisal of the Rome package', Int Law, 34 (2000), 65–84, p. 74.

[137] EOC, pp. 116–24.

[138] Lee (ed.), *ICC: Elements*, p. 73.

[139] EOC, Introduction to Crimes against Humanity, p. 116, para. 2.

## Article 7(1)(a) Murder

The crime of murder has been discussed in the context of war crimes. The *actus reus* was defined as being a substantial cause of the death of the victim and the mental element was defined as intention to kill or cause serious injury, reckless as to the probability of death.[140] This definition has also been used by the ICTR in respect of murder as a crime against humanity.[141] Confusion was caused by the French term *assassinat*, used in the ICTR Statute for murder as a crime against humanity, as opposed to *meurtre*, which was used for murder contrary to Common Article 3, causing the judgements to differ in substance over whether the intention to kill or cause really serious harm, reckless as to the probability of death, must be premeditated or not.[142]

However, the ICTY Judgements have confirmed that the basic elements of murder, whether as a war crime or crime against humanity, remain the same.[143] The identical EOC for murder as a crime against humanity, wilful killing in an international armed conflict and murder in an internal conflict suggest that the basic *actus reus* and mental element of the crime of murder should be interpreted similarly in all three cases before the ICC.[144] Whilst the Elements do not entirely clarify the *mens rea* for this offence they clearly do not require premeditation for this offence.

## Article 7(1)(b) Extermination

### Origins

Extermination has been listed in all instruments concerning crimes against humanity since the Second World War.[145] Nevertheless, the post-Second World War tribunals did not assist in defining this offence.[146] However, Schwelb in his

[140] *Supra*, para. 2.10, but see *Marques, Da Costa et al.*, Trial Judgement, Dili District Court, Special Panel for Serious Crimes, paras 643–9.

[141] *Akayesu*, Trial Judgement, para. 589; *Rutaganda*, Trial Judgement, para. 80, and *Musema*, Trial Judgement, para. 215.

[142] *Kayishema and Ruzindana*, Trial Judgement, paras 139–40; *Bagilishema*, Trial Judgement, paras 83–4; *Semanza*, Trial Judgement, para. 339; *Ntagerura, Bagambiki and Imanishimwe*, Trial Judgement, para. 700, and *Muhimana*, Trial Judgement, para. 569, hold that premeditation is necessary for a conviction of murder as a crime against humanity. *Akayesu*, Trial Judgement, paras 588–90; *Rutaganda*, Trial Judgement, para. 81, and *Musema*, Trial Judgement, paras 214–15, hold that premeditation is unnecessary.

[143] *Kordić and Čerkez*, Trial Judgement, para. 236; *Krnojelac*, Trial Judgement, para. 323; *Kvoca et al.*, Trial Judgement, para. 132; *Milosević*, Prosecution's Second Pre-trial Brief, para. 1054; *Brđanin*, Trial Judgement, para. 380, and *Blagojević and Jokić*, Trial Judgement, para. 556.

[144] EOC, compare the Element for murder in pp. 116, 125 and 144.

[145] Boot *et al.*, 'Article 7', p. 131. See Article 6(c), Nuremberg Charter; Article 5(c), Tokyo Charter; Article II(c), CCL No. 10; Article 5, ICTY Statute; Article 3, ICTR Statute; Article 18, 1996 ILC Draft Code, and Article 2, SCSL Statute.

[146] See the analysis of post-Second World War trials in *Krstić*, Trial Judgement, para. 492, fn. 1132.

analysis of Article 6(c) of the Nuremberg Charter commented that the inclusion of 'extermination' within the Charter was intended to ensure that 'steps which are too remote from an individual act of homicide to constitute complicity in that act may be punishable as complicity in the crime of extermination'.[147] Another interpretation of this offence in the commentary to the Fourth Geneva Convention describes extermination as a denial of the right of whole groups of human beings to exist and states that 'it is a collective crime consisting of a number of individual murders'.[148]

## Development

The ILC commentary to the 1996 Draft Code also depicts extermination as 'a crime which by its very nature is directed against a group of individuals' and states that it involves 'an element of mass destruction which is not required for murder'.[149] However, unlike the commentary to the Geneva Convention above, the ILC distinguishes extermination from genocide by explaining that '[e]xtermination covers situations in which a group of individuals who do not share any common characteristics are killed' and that '[i]t also applies to situations in which some members of a group are killed while others are spared'.[150]

The definition of the crime of extermination has been developed by both ICTY and ICTR Trial and Appeal Chambers but their definitions have not always been consistent. In respect of the *actus reus* of the offence, the majority of the decisions, including the three Appeal Judgements on this issue, have held that the crime of extermination 'is the act of killing on a large scale' and 'requires proof that the accused participated in a widespread or systematic killing or in systematically subjecting a widespread number of people to conditions of living that would inevitably lead to death'.[151]

Whilst it is clear that an event of extermination must involve 'killing on a large scale', it is not clear that the Appeal Judgements necessarily had to hold that the defendant him or herself must have participated in the killing of a large number of people rather than concluding that killing a small number of people in the context of a mass killing event would suffice. In fact, the latter approach was taken by an earlier ICTR Trial Judgement in *Kayishema and Ruzindana* which defined the *actus reus* to include the killing of *at least one person* by action or omission through the participation in a mass killing of others or the creation of conditions which lead to the mass killing of others.[152] Interestingly, the

[147] E. Schwelb, 'Crimes against humanity', n. 3 *supra*, p. 192.

[148] J. Pictet (ed.), *The Geneva Conventions of 12 August 1949: Commentary: IV Geneva Convention* (Geneva: International Committee of the Red Cross, 1952–60), p. 223.

[149] 1996 ILC Draft Code Commentary, para. 8, to Article 18.

[150] *Ibid.* This was essentially the definition used in *Akayesu*, Trial Judgement, para. 591.

[151] *Ntakirutimana and Ntakirutimana*, Appeal Judgement, paras 516 and 522; followed by *Gacumbitsi*, Appeal Judgement, para. 86, and *Stakić*, Appeal Judgement, paras 259–60.

[152] *Kayishema and Ruzindana*, Trial Judgement, paras 144 and 147.

understanding of genocide by some of the ICTY and ICTR cases and the EOC of the ICC suggest that an individual with the specific intent of genocide could be charged with the offence despite killing only one or two people in the context of an ongoing genocide.[153] It is strange, therefore, that the ICTY and ICTR appear to have created a stricter *actus reus* for the crime against humanity of extermination and so it is arguable that the *Kayishema* Trial Judgement is to be preferred.

The meaning of 'mass' killing has also been the cause of discussion. The *Kayishema* Trial Chamber defined 'mass' as 'large scale' and stated that it 'does not command a numerical imperative' but should be defined on a case-by-case basis.[154] This interpretation has been followed by other ICTR and ICTY Trial Chambers.[155] The *Nahimana, Barayagwiza and Ngeze* Trial Judgement also added to this approach by stating that the 'distinction between extermination and murder is a conceptual one that relates to the victims of the crime and the manner in which they were targeted'.[156] This, perhaps, is related to the fact that some judgements suggest that the crime of extermination must take place against a group.

The *Krstić* Trial Judgement held that there must be evidence that 'a particular population was targeted'.[157] The Trial Chamber in *Stakić* expanded upon this, stating that the victims should be 'defined by political affiliation, physical attributes or simply the fact that they happened to be in a certain geographical area' and also accepted that they could be defined in the negative 'as not belonging to, not being affiliated with or loyal to the perpetrator or the group to which the perpetrator belongs'.[158] However, both the *Brđanin* and *Martić* Trial Judgements accept that 'the element of massiveness of the crime allows for the possibility to establish the evidence of the *actus reus* of extermination on an accumulation of separate and unrelated incidents, meaning on an aggregated basis' and therefore make no mention of a 'group' requirement.[159] This area has not yet been clarified by an appeal judgement.

Another element required by the *Akayesu* Trial Chamber was that the prosecution must demonstrate that the accused participated in the killing of named or described persons.[160] The *Krstić* Trial Chamber also stated that the prosecution

[153] *Akayesu*, Trial Judgement, para. 521; *Ntagerura, Bagambiki and Imanishimwe*, Trial Judgement, para. 664; *Semanza*, Trial Judgement, para. 319, and *Stakić*, Trial Judgement, paras 505 and 513, and see EOC, p. 113.

[154] *Kayishema and Ruzindana*, Trial Judgement, para. 145.

[155] *Bagilishema*, Trial Judgement, para. 87; *Kajelijeli*, Trial Judgement, para. 891; *Kamuhanda*, Trial Judgement, para. 692; *Stakić*, Trial Judgement, para. 640, and *Blagojević and Jokić*, Trial Judgement, para. 573.

[156] *Nahimana, Barayagwiza and Ngeze*, Trial Judgement, para. 1061.

[157] *Krstić*, Trial Judgement, para. 503.

[158] *Stakić*, Trial Judgement, para. 639, and see *Kajelijeli*, Trial Judgement, para. 893, which refers to 'a group, such as a neighbourhood'.

[159] *Brđanin*, Trial Judgement, para. 391, and *Martić*, Trial Judgement, para. 63.

[160] *Akayesu*, Trial Judgement, para. 592.

must identify the victims.[161] However, the *Ntakirutimana* Appeal Chamber, which was followed by the *Stakić* Appeal Chamber, held that '[i]t is not an element of the crime of extermination that a precise identification of "certain named or described" persons be established' but it is 'sufficient that the Prosecution satisfy the Trial Chamber that mass killings occurred'.[162] This decision properly allows the prosecution to charge an accused with extermination despite the fact, for example, that the vast majority of victims in a mass grave are not identified.

Finally, with respect to the mental element of this offence, whilst some judgements have found that killing by recklessness and even gross negligence suffices,[163] the majority of decisions, including the ICTY Appeal Chamber in *Stakić* and the ICTR Appeal Chamber in *Ntakirutimana* and *Gacumbitsi*, have held that only intention to participate in the killing will suffice.[164] The Trial Chamber in *Vasiljevic* also held that the defendant 'must have known of the vast scheme of collective murder and been willing to take part therein';[165] however, the *Stakić* Appeal Judgement stated that this was not an element of the crime of extermination and that the mental element of this offence was simply 'that the accused intended, by his acts or omissions, either killing on a large scale, or the subjection of a widespread number of people, or the systematic subjection of a number of people, to conditions of living that would lead to their deaths'.[166]

### The Rome Statute

An elaboration of the crime of extermination is included in Article 7(2)(b) of the Rome Statute, which states that this offence 'includes the intentional infliction of conditions of life, *inter alia* the deprivation of access to food and medicine, calculated to bring about the destruction of part of a population'. This is incorporated into the Elements, which require that the perpetrator 'killed one or more persons, including by inflicting conditions of life calculated to bring about the destruction of part of a population'.[167] Footnotes to the Elements emphasise that the killing can be committed indirectly, including by deprivation of food or

[161] *Krstić*, Trial Chamber, para. 499.

[162] *Ntakirutimana and Ntakirutimana*, Appeal Judgement, para. 521, and *Stakić*, Appeal Judgement, fn. 552.

[163] *Kayishema and Ruzindana*, Trial Judgement, paras 144 and 146; *Bagilishema*, Trial Judgement, para. 89, and *Bisengimana*, Trial Judgement, para. 71.

[164] *Stakić*, Appeal Judgement, para. 260; *Ntakirutimana and Ntakirutimana*, Appeal Judgement, para. 522, and *Gacumbitsi*, Appeal Judgement, para. 86.

[165] *Vasiljević*, Trial Judgement, para. 228.

[166] *Stakić*, Appeal Judgement, para. 259, following *Ntakirutimana and Ntakirutimana*, Appeal Judgement, para. 522.

[167] EOC, p. 117. According to *Vasiljević*, Trial Judgement, fn. 586, this element was directly inspired by the definition of extermination given in the *Kayishema and Ruzindana* Trial Judgement, para. 147.

medicine.[168] However, according to the Rome Statute and the first element, if 'conditions of life' are imposed they must be 'calculated to bring about the destruction of a part of the population'.[169] This expression was interpreted by the *Krstić* Trial Chamber as meaning that a numerically significant part of a specific population must have been targeted.[170]

The second element describes the surrounding circumstances of the perpetrator's killing and requires that the 'conduct constituted, or took place as part of, a mass killing of members of a civilian population'.[171] Mass killing suggests large-scale murder,[172] and this element makes it clear that, if the perpetrator's actions of themselves amount to a mass killing, there is no need to prove further killing on the part of others. Alternatively, the perpetrator would still be liable if his or her conduct was part of a mass killing and a footnote explains that the term 'as part of' would include 'the initial conduct in a mass killing'.[173]

The expressions 'part of a population' and 'a civilian population' remain undefined. It is submitted that if these expressions are interpreted too strictly they would raise the threshold of this offence to an unacceptably high level.[174] Neither the ILC Draft Code, nor the ICTR in *Kayishema and Ruzindana*, required that those individuals targeted for extermination should share specific characteristics.[175] The word 'population' should be interpreted as loosely as possible and include not only 'political, social, linguistic groups and groups based on their sexual orientation', but groups existing only in the mind of the perpetrator, such as 'all persons believed to be traitors to the State or "subversives"'.[176] Furthermore, the expression 'part of a population' should not be interpreted as entailing a higher numerical significance than is necessarily inherent in the expression 'mass killing'.

Finally, the *mens rea* of the crime of extermination is not defined in the Elements, and so, applying the default mental element in Article 30, the perpetrator must intend to kill at least one person either directly or indirectly. Furthermore the perpetrator must have been aware of the factual circumstances which made his act a mass killing, for example that his denial of food supplies to a particular area would result in many deaths from starvation, or be aware of the surrounding mass killings of which his actions formed part.

[168] EOC, fns 8 and 9 on p. 117.

[169] Article 7(2)(b), Rome Statute, and EOC, p. 117.

[170] *Krstić*, Trial Judgement, paras 502–3.

[171] EOC, p. 117.

[172] Boot *et al.*, 'Article 7', p. 132.

[173] EOC, p. 117, fn. 10, and see Lee (ed.), *ICC: Elements*, p. 83.

[174] See G. Mettraux, 'Crimes against humanity in the jurisprudence of the International Criminal Tribunals', n. 98 *supra*, pp. 285–6.

[175] See discussion *supra*, p. 208, and comments by W. Rückert and G. Witschel, 'Genocide and crimes against humanity in the Elements of Crimes', pp. 59–93 in H. Fischer, C. Kreß and S. Lüder (eds), *International and National Prosecution of Crimes under International Law*, n. 125 *supra*, p. 75.

[176] Boot *et al.*, 'Article 7', p. 132.

## Article 7(1)(c) Enslavement

### Origins

Slavery has existed since ancient times and the African slave trade was an established institution by the sixteenth century.[177] Nevertheless, between 1815 and 1957 approximately 300 international agreements attempted to suppress this abhorrent practice.[178] The exact point at which enslavement became prohibited under customary international law is difficult to judge,[179] but the 1926 Slavery Convention, which bound States Parties to prevent and suppress slavery and the slave trade, was a significant development. This convention also produced an enduring definition of slavery as 'the status or condition of a person over whom any or all of the powers attaching to the right of ownership are exercised'.[180]

Despite the international agreements prohibiting slavery, slave labour was used in the First World War, and the Second World War saw slave labour in atrocious conditions on a massive scale.[181] The definition of crimes against humanity in the Nuremberg Charter included both enslavement and deportation to slave labour,[182] but the Nuremberg Judgement neither defined these concepts nor drew 'a systematic distinction' between them.[183] Nevertheless, two CCL No. 10 cases explained slavery in more depth. In the case of *Pohl* the US military tribunal explained that slavery may exist even though the slaves are treated humanely, that 'the admitted fact of slavery – compulsory uncompensated labour – would still remain'.[184] In the *Milch* case the tribunal questioned whether anyone believed 'that the vast hordes of Slavic Jews who laboured in Germany's war industries were accorded the rights of contracting parties' before holding that '[t]hey were slaves, nothing less – kidnapped, regimented, herded under armed guards, and worked until they died from disease, hunger, exhaustion'.[185]

[177] R. Redman, 'The League of Nations and the right to be free from enslavement: the first human right to be recognized as customary international law', Chi-Kent LR, 70 (1994), 759–800, p. 765.

[178] D. Weissbrodt and Anti-slavery International, 'Contemporary forms of slavery: updated review of the implementation and follow-up to the conventions on slavery', Commission on Human Rights, Sub-commission on the Promotion and Protection of Human Rights, UN Doc. E/CN.4/Sub.2/2000/3, 26 May 2000, para. 3. See also M. Bassiouni, 'Enslavement as an international crime', NYUJ Int L & Pol, 23 (1991), 445–517, pp. 459–517, and H. Fisher, 'The suppression of slavery in international law', ILQ, 3 (1950), 28–51, pp. 43–51.

[179] G. Robertson, *Crimes against Humanity*, n. 125 *supra*, p. 209.

[180] Article 1, 1926 Slavery Convention, and see comments in D. Weissbrodt and Anti-slavery International, 'Contemporary forms of slavery', n. 178 *supra*, para. 16.

[181] M. Bassiouni, *Crimes against Humanity in International Criminal Law*, n. 7 *supra*, p. 296; D. Christopher, '*Jus cogens*, reparation agreements, and Holocaust slave labor litigation', L & Pol Int Bus, 31 (2000), 1227–53, p. 1228, and J. Roy, 'Strengthening human rights protection: why the Holocaust slave labor claims should be litigated', Scholar: St Mary's LR Min Issues, 1 (1999), 153–205, pp. 169–76.

[182] Article 6(c), Nuremberg Charter.

[183] *Kunarać*, Trial Judgement, para. 523, and see *IMT Judgement*, pp. 460–3.

[184] *In re Pohl and Others*, 14 AD (1947), 290, pp. 291–2.

[185] Trial of *Milch*, 7 LRTWC 27, pp. 38–9.

The cases discussed above dealt with concepts of forced labour and slavery without really defining the difference between the two, although forced labour has been described as a practice 'similar to, but distinct from slavery'.[186] Forced labour was condemned in an International Labour Organisation (ILO) Convention prior to the Second World War and defined as 'all work or service which is exacted from any person under the menace of any penalty and for which the said person has not offered himself voluntarily'.[187] However, various forms of work, including compulsory military service and work exacted as a consequence of conviction in a court of law, were exempted from this definition.[188] The Third Geneva Convention also allows the compulsory labour of prisoners of war, but places limitations upon the type and conditions of work, which should be performed in similar conditions to the nationals of the detaining power.[189] Further, under the Fourth Geneva Convention, the occupying power may compel work from persons in occupied territory only for very limited purposes and must pay a fair wage.[190]

Additional Protocol (AP) II deals with the issues of forced labour and slavery in non-international armed conflicts. Article 5 provides that those persons whose liberty has been restricted shall 'if made to work, have the benefit of working conditions and safeguards similar to those enjoyed by the local civilian population'.[191] Nevertheless, such persons also have the protection of Article 4, which expressly forbids 'slavery and the slave trade in all their forms'.[192] This implies that enforced labour during armed conflicts, if used strictly in accordance with the Geneva Conventions and Protocols, does not amount to slavery. However, the 1956 Supplementary Slavery Convention prohibited slavery-like practices which impose a servile status, such as debt bondage, serfdom, compulsory marriage or transfer of women and the delivery of children for the exploitation of their labour, which suggests that in certain circumstances forced labour would be prohibited as a slavery-like practice.[193]

Alongside the treaties defining and outlawing slavery were instruments dealing with the associated problem of trafficking. Both the 1926 Slavery Convention and AP II outlawed the 'slave trade' in addition to slavery, but from 1904 to 1933 there was a series of conventions primarily aimed at prohibiting

[186] D. Weissbrodt and Anti-slavery International, 'Contemporary forms of slavery', n. 178 *supra*, para. 30.

[187] Article 2(1), 1930 ILO Convention No. 29, and see Article 1, 1957 ILO Convention No. 105.

[188] Article 2(2), 1930 ILO Convention No. 29.

[189] Articles 49–57 and 62, Geneva Convention III.

[190] Article 51, Geneva Convention IV.

[191] Article 5(1)(e), AP II.

[192] Article 4(2)(f), AP II.

[193] Article 1, 1956 Supplementary Convention on the Abolition of Slavery, the Slave Trade, and Institutions and Practices similar to Slavery.

the trafficking of women.[194] These were consolidated by the 1949 Convention for the Suppression of the Traffic in Persons and of the Exploitation of the Prostitution of Others, although this treaty has been criticised as focusing only upon the issue of trafficking for the purposes of prostitution.[195] Nevertheless, it is important to note that the 1949 Convention does not require an international border crossing as an element of trafficking, nor does it allow consent as a defence to trafficking.[196]

## Development

An explanation of enslavement as a crime against humanity is contained in the commentary to the ILC's Draft Code of Crimes. The ILC defines enslavement broadly as 'establishing or maintaining over persons a status of slavery, servitude or forced labour contrary to well-established and widely recognized standards of international law'.[197] An extensive definition of enslavement is also favoured by Rassam, who comments that bonded labour is essentially slavery, as 'the debt is rarely, if ever, paid off due to high interest rates charged by the "lender" ' and because such servitude can be passed on from one generation to the next within the same family.[198] She also suggests that forced labour often amounts to slavery '[d]ue to the common element of coercive "ownership" of the labor and/or the body of a human being and the inability of many of these victims to seek any judicial or administrative recourse'.[199]

The ICTY in the *Kunarać* case considered enslavement in some depth. The Trial Chamber defined the *actus reus* of enslavement as 'the exercise of any or all of the powers attaching to the right of ownership over a person' and the *mens rea* as 'the intentional exercise of such powers'.[200] This broad definition of enslavement was supported by the *Kunarać* Appeal Chamber, which accepted that the

[194] R. Coomaraswamy, Special Rapporteur, 'Report on trafficking in women, women's migration and violence against women in accordance with Commission on Human Rights Resolution 1997/44', Commission on Human Rights, UN Doc. E/CN.4/2000/68, 29 February 2000, paras 18–19, and S. Toepfer and B. Wells, 'The worldwide market for sex: a review of international and regional legal prohibitions regarding trafficking in women', Mich J Gender & L, 2 (1994), 83–128, pp. 97–8.

[195] Article 1, 1949 Convention for the Suppression of the Traffic in Persons and of the Exploitation of the Prostitution of Others (approved by GA Res. 317 (IV), 2 December 1949, but not opened for signature until 21 March 1950), and see R. Coomaraswamy, 'Report on trafficking in women', n. 194 *supra*, para. 22.

[196] S. Inglis, 'Expanding international and national protections against trafficking for forced labor using a human rights framework', Buff Hum Rts LR, 7 (2001), 55–104, pp. 63–4 and 67.

[197] 1996 ILC Draft Code Commentary, para. 10, commenting on Article 18.

[198] A. Rassam, 'Contemporary forms of slavery and the evolution of the prohibition of slavery and the slave trade under customary international law', Va JIL, 39 (1999), 303–52, pp. 326–9, and M. Bassiouni, ' "Crimes against humanity": the need for a specialized convention', n. 12 *supra*, pp. 457–8.

[199] A. Rassam, 'Contemporary forms of slavery', n. 198 *supra*, p. 329.

[200] *Kunarać*, Trial Judgement, para. 540.

traditional concept of slavery, 'often referred to as "chattel slavery", has evolved to encompass various contemporary forms of slavery' where the victim 'is not subject to the exercise of the more extreme rights of ownership . . . but in all cases . . . there is some destruction of the juridical personality'.[201]

The Trial Chamber in *Kunarać* stated that indicia of enslavement included 'control of someone's movement, control of physical environment, psychological control, measures taken to prevent or deter escape, force, threat of force or coercion, duration, assertion of exclusivity, subjection to cruel treatment and abuse, control of sexuality and forced labour'.[202] The Appeal Chamber approved these factors but emphasised that 'it is not possible exhaustively to enumerate all of the contemporary forms of slavery which are comprehended in the expansion of the original idea'.[203] Additionally, the Trial Chamber held that '"[a]quisition" or "disposal" of someone for monetary or other compensation, is *not* a requirement for enslavement'[204] and that the duration of the exercise of powers attaching to ownership is a factor to be considered when deciding if enslavement has taken place, but not an overriding one.[205]

The *Kunarać* Trial Chamber stated that in a case of enslavement the victim's consent is either absent or negated through 'the threat or use of force or other forms of coercion; the fear of violence, deception or false promises; the abuse of power; the victim's position of vulnerability; detention or captivity, psychological oppression or socio-economic conditions'.[206] However, the Appeal Chamber clarified the fact that lack of consent is not an element of enslavement, but is relevant only as evidence to show that the accused has exercised powers attaching to the right of ownership.[207]

The specific issue of whether forced labour amounts to slavery was discussed in the Trial Chamber Judgement of *Krnojelac*. The Judgement suggested that an important issue is whether the labour is involuntary, a factual question to be determined on a case-by-case basis, and that it is important to establish whether the persons in question 'had no real choice as to whether they would work'.[208] It is submitted that the consent of a person to enslavement through forced labour should not operate as a defence if a refusal by that person would either not have been successful in preventing the labour or would have caused them serious detriment. The *Krnojelac* Judgement also reviewed the provisions relating to labour in AP

[201] *Kunarać*, Appeal Judgement, para. 117.

[202] *Kunarać*, Trial Judgement, para. 543.

[203] *Kunarać*, Appeal Judgement, para. 119.

[204] See also G. McDougall, Special Rapporteur, 'Contemporary forms of slavery: systematic rape, sexual slavery and slavery-like practices during armed conflict', update to Final Report, Commission on Human Rights, Sub-commission on the Promotion and Protection of Human Rights, UN Doc. E/CN.4/Sub.2/2000/21, 6 June 2000, para. 8.

[205] *Kunarać*, Trial Judgement, para. 542, emphasis added, and see *Kunarać* Appeal Judgement, para. 121.

[206] *Kunarać*, Trial Judgement, para. 542.

[207] *Kunarać*, Appeal Judgement, para. 120.

[208] *Krnojelac*, Trial Judgement, para. 359.

II and held that the violation of the Protocol's guarantees would allow the performance of labour to be treated as an indication of enslavement.[209] The Tribunal further held that where payment is not specified in the Geneva Conventions and Protocols, such as in AP II, the court should 'determine on a case by case basis whether labour performed should have been compensated in some way'.[210]

Although neither the ILC nor the ICTY has defined trafficking, alongside enslavement it is a major contemporary problem.[211] The Protocol to Prevent, Suppress and Punish Trafficking in Persons, especially Women and Children provides a modern definition of trafficking.[212] Article 3 defines trafficking as:

> the recruitment, transportation, transfer, harbouring or receipt of persons, by means of the threat or use of force or other forms of coercion, of abduction, of fraud, of deception, of the abuse of power or of a position of vulnerability or of the giving or receiving of payments or benefits to achieve the consent of a person having control over another person, for the purpose of exploitation. Exploitation shall include, at a minimum, the exploitation of the prostitution of others or the other forms of sexual exploitation, forced labour or services, slavery or practices similar to slavery, servitude or the removal of organs.

The article further states that consent is irrelevant if coercion or other methods mentioned have been used. This definition is important, as it demonstrates that lack of consent is not an element of trafficking and so refocuses the legal inquiry 'away from the victim and on to the actions of the trafficker/exploiter reflecting a recognition that deception or coercion nullifies any meaningful, fully informed consent'.[213] The issue of pressure which renders consent irrelevant is discussed in the *travaux préparatoires* to the Protocol, which clarify that the reference to

[209] *Ibid.*, para. 360.

[210] *Ibid.*

[211] L. Malone, 'Economic hardship as coercion under the Protocol on International Trafficking in Persons by Organized Crime Elements', Fordham Int'l LJ, 25 (2001), 54–94, pp. 54–5; S. Tiefenbrun, 'Sex sells but drugs don't talk: trafficking of women sex workers', Thomas Jefferson LR, 23 (2001), 199–226, p. 199; K. Hyland, 'The impact of the Protocol to Prevent, Suppress and Punish Trafficking in Persons, especially Women and Children', HR Brief, 8 (2001), 30–2, p. 30, and A. Cole, 'Reconceptualising female trafficking: the inhuman trade in women', Cardozo JL & Gender, 12 (2006), 789–820. See also Article 6, 1979 Convention on the Elimination of all Forms of Discrimination against Women, and Article 35, 1989 Convention on the Rights of the Child. On the prevalence of women and child victims see International Organisation of Migration *Quarterly Bulletin*, 'Trafficking in migrants', Vol. 23, April 2001, available at: <http://www.iom.int>.

[212] In force 2003, 115 States parties (as of October 2007), and supplements the 2000 United Nations Convention against Transnational Organised Crime. See K. Hyland, 'The impact of the Protocol to Prevent, Suppress and Punish Trafficking', n. 211 *supra*, p. 31, and see Global Alliance against Trafficking in Women (GAATW), 'Human Rights Standards for the Treatment of Trafficked Persons' (1999), pp. 2–4, available at: <http://www.inet.co.th/org/gaatw>, and T. Obokata, 'Trafficking of human beings as a crime against humanity: some implications for the international legal system', ICLQ, 54 (2005), 445–57.

[213] S. Inglis, 'Expanding international and national protections against trafficking for forced labor', n. 196 *supra*, p. 67.

abuse of a position of vulnerability 'is understood to refer to any situation in which the person involved has no real and acceptable alternative but to submit to the abuse involved'.[214] Further, Article 3(c) and (d) protects children under eighteen by establishing an irrebuttable presumption that children cannot consent to trafficking for the purpose of exploitation, irrespective of coercion or deception.[215]

### The Rome Statute

The definition of enslavement for the purposes of crimes against humanity is given in Article 7(2)(c) as 'the exercise of any or all of the powers attaching to the right of ownership over a person and includes the exercise of such power in the course of trafficking in persons, in particular women and children'. This definition is amplified in the Elements, which require that the perpetrator 'exercised any or all of the powers attaching to the right of ownership over one or more persons, such as by purchasing, selling, lending or bartering such a person or persons, or by imposing on them a similar deprivation of liberty'.[216] A footnote confirms that this conduct could include trafficking in persons.[217]

This definition was drawn from the war crime of sexual slavery and is similar to the definition of slavery given by the ICTY in *Kunarać*.[218] The examples of the exercise of powers of ownership given in the EOC were controversial and, despite the commercial character of the terms 'purchasing, selling, lending or bartering', Robinson states that the Preparatory Commission did not intend the expression 'imposing on them a similar deprivation of liberty' to be understood as implying that 'some sort of commercial or pecuniary exchange was required'.[219] This expansive interpretation of enslavement is confirmed by a footnote which states that 'such deprivation of liberty may, in some circumstances, include exacting forced labour or otherwise reducing a person to a servile status as defined in the Supplementary Convention on the Abolition of Slavery, the Slave Trade, and Institutions and Practices similar to Slavery of 1956'.[220]

The significance of the victim's consent is not mentioned in the EOC. It is submitted that a person cannot consent to enslavement and that, in line with the *Kunarać* Appeal Judgement, consent is relevant only as evidence that the perpetrator did indeed exercise powers of ownership over the victim.[221] Other evidence of such powers include the indicia suggested by the ICTY in *Kunarać*

[214] *Travaux préparatoires* of the Negotiations for the Protocol to Prevent, Suppress and Punish Trafficking in Persons, especially Women and Children, UN Doc. A/55/383/Add.1, p. 12.

[215] See also Article 2, 1994 Inter-American Convention on International Traffic in Minors.

[216] EOC, p. 117.

[217] *Ibid.*, fn. 11.

[218] Lee (ed.), *ICC: Elements*, p. 85, and *Kunarać*, Trial Judgement, para. 540.

[219] Lee (ed.), *ICC: Elements*, p. 85.

[220] EOC, fn. 11 on p. 117, and see Boot *et al.*, 'Article 7', p. 134.

[221] *Kunarać*, Appeal Judgement, para. 120.

and could also include the use of force, coercion and abuse of a position of vulnerability as defined in the Trafficking Protocol.[222] Further, when deciding whether powers of ownership have been exercised in the course of trafficking, the ICC could draw upon Article 3 of the Trafficking Protocol and define trafficking as 'the recruitment, transportation, transfer, harbouring or receipt of persons'.[223] The gender or age of the trafficked person does not need to be proved as a part of the offence.

The *mens rea* of this offence is not defined in the EOC and so the default mental element of Article 30, intention to exercise any or all of the powers attaching to the right of ownership and knowledge of the surrounding circumstances, would have to be shown. Knowledge of surrounding circumstances would be particularly relevant in the case of a person accused of enslavement through trafficking, to demonstrate that the accused was aware he was not dealing with voluntary migrants.

## Article 7(1)(d) Deportation or forcible transfer of population

### Origins

The background to deportation and forcible transfer is discussed in the context of the grave breach of unlawful deportation or transfer.[224] In this respect the Trial Chamber in *Krnojelac* commented that the content of the underlying offence 'does not differ whether perpetrated as a war crime or as a crime against humanity'.[225]

### Development

The commentary to the ILC Draft Code on the crime of 'arbitrary deportation or forcible transfer' states that, whilst 'deportation implies expulsion from the national territory', the 'forcible transfer of population could occur wholly within the frontiers of one and the same State'.[226] This approach has been adopted by most of the ICTY Judgements,[227] which were also greatly influenced by the definition of deportation or forcible transfer in Article 7(2)(d) of the Rome Statute.[228]

The *Krstić* and *Krnojelac* Trial Chambers emphasised that only forcible or involuntary displacements of populations breach this provision and used a

[222] *Kunarać*, Trial Judgement, para. 543, and Article 3, 2000 Protocol to Prevent, Suppress and Punish Trafficking in Persons, especially Women and Children.

[223] Article 3, *ibid.*

[224] Discussed *supra*, pp. 53–4.

[225] *Krnojelac*, Trial Judgement, para. 473, and see *Stakić*, Appeal Judgement, para. 289.

[226] Article 18(g), 1996 ILC Draft Code.

[227] *Krstić*, Trial Judgement, para. 521; *Krnojelac*, Trial Judgement, para. 474; *Stakić*, Appeal Judgement, paras 278 and 317, and *Simić, Tadić and Zarić*, Trial Judgement, para. 123.

[228] See particularly *Blaškić*, Trial Judgement, para. 234, and *Krnojelac*, Trial Judgement, para. 474.

definition of 'forcibly' drawn from the EOC.[229] The *Krstić* Trial Chamber, whilst acknowledging that departures motivated by discrimination may not amount to forceful transfer, stated that the Bosnian Muslims who fled after the fall of Srebrenica 'were not exercising a genuine choice to go, but reacted reflexively to a certainty that their survival depended on their flight'.[230] The Judgement stated, however, that displacement necessary for 'the security of the population or imperative military reasons' could legitimate a forced transfer.[231] Additional legitimate reasons for displacement contemplated by the ILC commentary included those essential for 'public health or well being, in a manner consistent with international law'.[232] Nevertheless, the *Stakić* Appeal Chamber emphasised that displacement for humanitarian reasons 'is not justifiable where the humanitarian crisis that caused the displacement is itself the result of the accused's own unlawful activity'.[233]

With respect to the *mens rea* of forcible transfer or deportation, earlier Trial Chamber Judgements suggested that the perpetrator must intend that the victim is removed and found that this must include the aim that the victims do not return.[234] The *Stakić* Appeal Judgement, however, after reconsidering the basis of this offence in Article 49 of the Fourth Geneva Convention, concluded that 'deportation does not require an intent that the deportees should not return' and appeared to imply that the same principle applied to forcible transfer.[235] Finally, with respect to the intended destination of the victim, for the crime of deportation the *Stakić* Appeal Chamber stated that there must be displacement across a State or *de facto* border.[236] With respect to victims of forcible transfer the *Simić, Tadić and Zarić* Trial Chamber stated that the intended destination does not need to be a distant part of the territory provided that it is sufficiently distant that the victim is prevented from effectively exercising the right to stay in his or her home and community.[237]

## The Rome Statute

The Rome Statute defines 'deportation or forcible transfer of population' in Article 7(2)(d) as 'forced displacement of the persons concerned by expulsion or other

[229] *Krstić*, Trial Judgement, paras 521 and 529; *Krnojelac*, Trial Judgement, para. 475; *Stakić*, Trial Judgement, para. 682; *Stakić*, Appeal Judgement, para. 281, and *Simić, Tadić and Zarić*, Trial Judgement, para. 125. See discussion of EOC, *infra*, p. 220.

[230] *Krstić*, Trial Judgement, paras 528–30.

[231] *Ibid.*, para. 524.

[232] 1996 ILC Draft Code Commentary, para. 13, commenting on Article 18.

[233] *Stakić*, Appeal Judgement, para. 287.

[234] *Naletilić and Martinović*, Trial Judgement, para. 520 and fn. 1362; *Stakić*, Trial Judgement, para. 687, and *Simić, Tadić and Zarić*, Trial Judgement, paras 133–4.

[235] *Stakić*, Appeal Judgement, para. 307.

[236] *Ibid.*, para. 302, but see the partially dissenting Judgement of Judge Shahabudden in this case, especially para. 72.

[237] *Simić, Tadić and Zarić*, Trial Judgement, para. 130.

coercive acts from the area in which they are lawfully present, without grounds permitted under international law'. This definition is amplified by the EOC which state that the perpetrator 'deported or forcibly transferred, without grounds permitted under international law, one or more persons to another State or location, by expulsion or other coercive acts', that the persons 'were lawfully present' in that area and that the perpetrator 'was aware of the factual circumstances that established the lawfulness of such presence'.[238]

This offence is very similar to the grave breach of unlawful deportation or transfer under Article 8(2)(a)(vii) of the Statute, but under that provision the offence could be committed upon the transfer of one protected person.[239] However, Article 7(1)(d) prohibits the 'deportation or forcible transfer of *population*'.[240] Therefore, although the Elements allow that a perpetrator may incur responsibility for the transfer of 'one or more' persons, it would appear that this must take place in the context of the transfer of a 'population'. However, this expression should not be interpreted as requiring that the entire population of a particular area is transferred, but it necessarily requires that a significant number of people are deported or transferred.[241]

A footnote to the Elements states that 'deported or forcibly transferred' is interchangeable with 'forcibly displaced', thus indicating that both deportation and transfer of the population must be done 'forcibly'.[242] However, another footnote defines 'forcibly' in a broad manner, similar to the definition of 'force' in the EOC of rape, as 'not restricted to physical force, but may include threat of force or coercion, such as that caused by fear of violence, duress, detention, psychological oppression or abuse of power against such person or persons or another person, or by taking advantage of a coercive environment'.[243]

The forced displacement must be without grounds permitted under international law. Therefore, forced movement of populations as a result of genuine emergencies, such as threats to the public arising from serious infectious diseases or natural disasters, either in peacetime or during a conflict, would not amount to this offence. Additionally, during a conflict a displacement could also be rendered lawful if carried out under Article 49 of Geneva Convention IV, or Article 17 of AP II, as absolutely necessary owing to the security of the population or imperative military reasons.[244] 'Expulsion or coercive acts' are not defined, but Hall suggests that these 'must include the full range of coercive pressures on people to flee their homes, including death threats, destruction of their homes, and other acts of persecution, such as depriving members of a group of

[238] EOC, p. 118.
[239] Discussed *supra*, p. 57.
[240] Emphasis added.
[241] See discussion of 'population' *supra*, pp. 198 and 211.
[242] EOC, fn. 13 on p. 118.
[243] EOC, fn. 12 on p. 118, and see discussion *supra*, p. 152.
[244] See *Krstić*, Trial Judgement, para. 524.

employment, denying them access to schools and forcing them to wear a symbol of their religious identity'.[245]

The EOC also require that the persons transferred were 'lawfully present' in the area.[246] The inclusion of lawful presence has caused debate as to whether this standard should be judged according to national or international law. The EOC left the question open, to be decided by case law, but it is submitted that Kittichaisaree is correct in asserting that in such circumstances 'national law must also be measured against the yardstick of international law' or a State could avoid breaching the provision simply by passing draconian laws.[247]

The *mens rea* of this offence, applying Article 30, is that the perpetrator intended to forcibly displace one or more persons, in the knowledge that a population was being forcibly displaced. The Elements state explicitly that the perpetrator does not have to perform a legal evaluation of the lawfulness of the presence of the person or persons in the area from which he or she displaces them, but should merely be aware of the factual circumstances establishing this.[248] The EOC do not clarify whether the perpetrator must have performed a legal evaluation in respect of whether the grounds for forcible displacement were permitted under international law, but it is submitted that, again, awareness of the factual circumstances should suffice.[249]

## Article 7(1)(e) Imprisonment or other severe deprivation of physical liberty in violation of fundamental rules of international law

### Origins

The offence of imprisonment as a crime against humanity is similar to unlawful confinement as a grave breach, and indeed this was the approach of the Trial Chamber in the case of *Kordić and Čerkez*.[250]

### Development

The ILC prohibited arbitrary imprisonment in the Draft Code, which was defined by the commentary as deprivation of liberty 'without due process of law'.[251]

[245] Boot *et al.*, 'Article 7', p. 162.

[246] See J. Nicolai, 'Operation Murambatsvina: a crime against humanity under the Rome Statute?', Am U Int LR, 21 (2005–06), 813–44, pp. 837–8.

[247] K. Kittichaisaree, *International Criminal Law* (Oxford: Oxford University Press, 2001), p. 109, and see Lee (ed.), *ICC: Elements*, p. 87, and Boot *et al.*, 'Article 7', p. 161.

[248] EOC, p. 118, and W. Rückert and G. Witschel, 'Genocide and crimes against humanity', n. 175 *supra*, p. 78.

[249] See Articles 32 and 33, Rome Statute.

[250] *Kordić and Čerkez*, Trial Judgement, paras 298 and 301, and *Milosević*, Prosecution's Second Pre-trial Brief, para. 1057. See discussion *supra*, para. 2.40.2.

[251] Article 18(h), 1996, ILC Draft Code and Commentary.

This definition was adopted by the ICTY in the cases of *Kordić and Čerkez* and *Krnojelac* for the offence of imprisonment as a crime against humanity under the ICTY Statute.[252] Nevertheless, the Judgement of *Kordić and Čerkez* only really examined imprisonment as a crime against humanity in the context of an armed conflict and therefore held that such imprisonment was unlawful when civilians were detained contrary to or without the procedural safeguards of the fourth Geneva Convention.[253]

The ILC commentary, however, made reference to human rights instruments and stated that 'concentration camps or detention camps or other forms of long-term detention' could amount to the crime of arbitrary imprisonment.[254] The Trial Chamber in *Krnojelac* also reviewed human rights instruments, but found that they did not 'adopt a common approach to the issue of when a deprivation of liberty is or becomes arbitrary'.[255] Taking an interpretation which could be applied in peacetime or conflict, the *Krnojelac* Judgement held that the deprivation of an individual's liberty will be unlawful if 'no legal basis can be called upon to justify the initial deprivation of liberty' and that the legal basis for deprivation of liberty 'must apply throughout the period of imprisonment' or an 'initially lawful deprivation of liberty may become unlawful at that time and be regarded as arbitrary imprisonment'.[256] The Judgement also stated that the legal basis to justify deprivation of liberty must not be contrary to international law.[257]

### The Rome Statute

This offence is not defined in Article 7(2) of the Rome Statute, but the EOC state that the perpetrator must have 'imprisoned one or more persons or otherwise severely deprived one or more persons of physical liberty'.[258] The gravity of the conduct must have been such that it was 'in violation of fundamental rules of international law' and the perpetrator was aware of the factual circumstances establishing the gravity of the conduct.[259] The expression 'deprivation of physical liberty' is wider than imprisonment and would include such examples as house arrest, restriction to a particular village or similar restrictions.[260] Hall

[252] Article 5(e), 1993, ICTY Statute, and *Kordić and Čerkez*, Trial Judgement, para. 302; *Krnojelac*, Trial Judgement, para. 113, and *Kordić and Čerkez*, Appeal Judgement, para. 116.

[253] Articles 42–3, Geneva Convention IV, *Kordić and Čerkez*, Trial Judgement, para. 303.

[254] 1996, ILC Draft Code, Commentary, referring to Article 9, 1948, UDHR, and Article 9, 1966, ICCPR.

[255] *Krnojelac*, Trial Judgement, para. 113.

[256] *Ibid.*, para. 114, followed by *Ntagerura, Bagambiki, and Imanishimwe*, Trial Judgement, para. 702, and *Krajišnik*, Trial Judgement, paras 752–3.

[257] *Ibid.* The analysis was influenced by the report of the Working Group on Arbitrary Detention, 'Question of the Human Rights of all Persons subjected to any Form of Detention or Imprisonment', Commission on Human Rights, UN Doc. E/CN.4/1998/44, 19 December 1997, Annex 1, para. 8.

[258] EOC, p. 118.

[259] *Ibid.*

[260] Boot *et al.*, 'Article 7', pp. 137–8, and see *Blaškić*, Trial Judgement, paras 691–2.

suggests that the term 'severe' would have to be decided by the court on a case-by-case basis, taking into account conditions of detention, whether the individual was cruelly treated and whether the detention was secret or the individual was denied contact with the outside world.[261]

The second element requires that the conduct must be so grave that it violates fundamental rules of international law. These are not defined as such, but it is submitted that the approach of *Krnojelac* could apply, which requires that a legal basis for the detention or continued detention exists either in national law, which does not violate international law, or in international law.[262] Therefore, in peacetime, detention justified by national law which does not violate the basic provisions of the Universal Declaration of Human Rights and International Covenant on Civil and Political Rights would not breach this provision.[263] During internal disturbances or emergencies, detention justified by proportionate and properly made derogations to human rights conventions would not violate international law. Lastly, in time of armed conflict, a detention justified under the Geneva Conventions would not constitute a violation of international law.[264]

The *mens rea* for this offence, taking into account the default mental element in Article 30, and the final element of this offence, would be an intention to imprison or severely deprive a person of physical liberty and an awareness of the factual circumstances which made the conduct so grave. Therefore, a legal evaluation is not required by the perpetrator, but there must be sufficient awareness of 'some sort of wrongfulness . . . to warrant individual criminal responsibility for participating in the imprisonment'.[265]

## Article 7(1)(f) Torture

The origins and development of torture have been discussed in depth with respect to torture as a grave breach and therefore it is necessary here to look at the EOC of torture only as a crime against humanity.[266] The first element of torture as a crime against humanity requires that the perpetrator 'inflicted severe physical or mental pain or suffering upon one or more persons'.[267] This is identical to the

[261] Boot *et al.*, 'Article 7', p. 138, and see *Blaškić*, Trial Judgement, para. 692, an example of detention which would amount to severe deprivation of physical liberty according to these criteria.

[262] *Krnojelac*, Trial Judgement, para. 114.

[263] The Working Group on Arbitrary Detention, n. 257 *supra*, cite Articles 7, 13–14 and 18–21, 1948, UDHR, and Articles 12, 18–19, 21–2 and 25–7 of the 1966 ICCPR.

[264] Articles 42–3, 1949, Geneva Convention IV and discussion *supra*, pp. 54–5.

[265] Lee (ed.), *ICC: Elements*, p. 89.

[266] See discussion *supra*, pp. 28–36. Note that ICTY cases have defined the elements of torture in the same way as both a war crime and a crime against humanity, see *Krnojelac*, Trial Judgement, para. 178; *Simić, Tadić and Zarić*, Trial Judgement, para. 79. and *Martic*, Trial Judgement, para. 74.

[267] EOC, p. 119.

first element of torture as a grave breach and should be interpreted in the same way.[268]

However, the remaining elements of this offence differ and require that '[s]uch person or persons were in the custody or under the control of the perpetrator' and that the 'pain or suffering did not arise only from, and was not inherent in or incidental to, lawful sanctions'.[269] Notably, a prohibited purpose is not part of torture as a crime against humanity and therefore 'random, purposeless or merely sadistic infliction of severe pain or suffering' could amount to torture for the purposes of Article 7(1)(e).[270]

The phrase 'in the custody or under the control' of the perpetrator is a fairly broad expression and would include unofficial *de facto* control or restraint of a person in addition to imprisonment following arrest.[271] The exclusion of pain and suffering arising from lawful sanctions from the offence of torture, in this context, prevents States which impose corporal punishment for certain offences from being accused of crimes against humanity. However, it is not clear whether 'lawful sanctions' in the EOC refers to sanctions which are lawful under national or international law. It is submitted that, whilst this primarily refers to national law, if such law was contrary to international law it could not shield the perpetrator from the offence of torture as a crime against humanity, or a State could avoid this provision simply by enacting draconian laws.[272]

The *mens rea* of torture, applying the default mental element in Article 30, requires an intention to inflict severe physical or mental pain or suffering on a person or persons in the perpetrator's custody or control. Further, there must be awareness that such pain or suffering was not being imposed as a result of a lawful sanction. This part of the *mens rea* could potentially lead to ignorance of the law as a defence, if the perpetrator genuinely believed that he was carrying out a lawful sanction.[273]

## Article 7(1)(g) Rape, sexual slavery, enforced prostitution, forced pregnancy, enforced sterilisation, or any other form of sexual violence of comparable gravity

The origins and development of offences described in Article 7(1)(g) have been discussed in detail in respect of sexual violence as a war crime.[274] Further, the basic EOC are identical in both contexts, with one minor exception. The

[268] Discussed *supra*, pp. 38–40.

[269] EOC, p. 119.

[270] Boot *et al.*, 'Article 7', p. 164, and see Lee (ed.), *ICC: Elements*, p. 91, and EOC, fn. 14 on p. 119.

[271] See Boot *et al.*, 'Article 7', p. 163, and K. Ambos and S. Wirth, 'The current law of crimes against humanity', n. 32 *supra*, p. 69.

[272] See Boot *et al.*, 'Article 7', p. 164, and Lee (ed.), *ICC: Elements*, p. 92.

[273] Article 32(2), Rome Statute.

[274] See discussion *supra*, pp. 143–51.

definition of this offence in the Rome Statute includes 'any other form of sexual violence of comparable gravity' as opposed to 'any other form of sexual violence also constituting a grave breach of the Geneva Conventions' or 'any other form of sexual violence also constituting a serious violation of article 3 common to the four Geneva Conventions' required for sexual violence as a war crime under Article 8(2)(b)(xxii) or 8(2)(e)(vi).[275] The Elements reflect this change of wording by stating that the 'conduct was of a gravity comparable to the other offences in article 7, paragraph 1 (g), of the Statute', but it is submitted that the seriousness of the conduct required for this offence in all three situations should be similar.[276]

## Article 7(1)(h) Persecution against any identifiable group or collectivity on political, racial, national, ethnic, cultural, religious, gender as defined in paragraph 3, or other grounds that are universally recognised as impermissible under international law, in connection with any act referred to in this paragraph or any crime within the jurisdiction of the Court

### Origins

The crime of persecution was included in the Nuremberg Charter as 'persecutions on political, racial or religious grounds'.[277] The same offence was included in CCL No. 10 and in the Tokyo Charter, except that the latter was restricted to 'persecutions on political or racial grounds' only, which reflected the factual pattern of persecution in the Far East.[278] The Nuremberg Judgement devoted a section to the persecution of the Jews. This set out the acts of persecution carried out by the Nazis, from discriminatory laws which restricted professions and family life to the creation of ghettoes, to the use of Jews as slave labour and, finally, to the mass execution of Jews by the *Einsatzgruppen* and in the gas chambers of the concentration camps.[279] Indeed, the ICTY tribunal in *Kupreškić* commented that it was clear from this part of the Judgement that 'the IMT accorded this crime a position of great prominence and understood it to include a wide spectrum of acts perpetrated against the Jewish people'.[280]

The ambit of persecution was explored by several US military tribunals operating under the auspices of CCL No. 10 at Nuremberg. In the case of *Weizsaecker* the court held that the civilian population of occupied territory had been persecuted on religious grounds, as many Catholic priests were removed from their posts and interned in terrible conditions in concentration camps

[275] See discussion *supra*, pp. 155–6.
[276] EOC, p. 121, and see comments in Lee (ed.), *ICC: Elements*, p. 93.
[277] Article 6(c), Nuremberg Charter.
[278] Article II(c), CCL No. 10, and Article 5(c), Tokyo Charter.
[279] *IMT Judgement*, pp. 463–6.
[280] *Kupreškić*, Trial Judgement, para. 597.

where a large number died.[281] The Judgement in *Altstötter* found the defendant guilty of racial persecution of the Jews, in particular because of the murders and atrocities committed against the Jews in concentration camps.[282]

The *Flick* Trial considered whether the compulsory taking of industrial property from Jews could amount to persecution.[283] The Court reviewed the Nuremberg Judgement and stated that 'it nowhere appears in the judgment that the International Military Tribunal (IMT) considered, much less decided, that a person becomes guilty of a crime against humanity merely by exerting antisemitic pressure to procure by purchase or through State expropriation industrial property owned by Jews'.[284] The Court held that, on a proper construction of CCL No. 10, 'other persecutions' must be interpreted *ejusdem generis* with the other crimes in the list, such as murder, extermination and torture, and therefore persecutions must 'affect the life and liberty of the oppressed peoples'.[285] However, the UN War Crimes Commission emphasised that the Court left open the question of whether offences against personal property, such as the burning of houses, would amount to an assault upon the health and life of a human being.[286]

## Development

The crime of persecution 'on political, racial, religious or ethnic grounds' is included in the 1996 ILC Draft Code.[287] However, the commentary does not provide an expansive definition of this offence, simply observing that '[t]he inhumane act of persecution may take many forms with its common characteristic being the denial of the human rights and fundamental freedoms to which every individual is entitled without distinction'.[288] The most thorough analysis of the content of this offence can be found in the Judgements of the ICTY, which has jurisdiction over 'persecutions on political, racial or religious grounds'.[289]

In the jurisprudence of the ICTY, persecution has consistently been defined as an 'act or omission which discriminates in fact and which infringes upon a fundamental right laid down in international customary or treaty law and was carried out deliberately with the intention to discriminate on one of the listed

[281] *In re Weizsaecker and Others* (*Ministries* Trial), 16 AD (1949), 344, p. 357.

[282] Trial of *Altstötter and Others* (*Justice* Trial), 6 LRTWC 1, pp. 62–4.

[283] *Flick* Trial, 9 LRTWC 1.

[284] *Ibid.*, p. 27.

[285] *Ibid.*, pp. 27–8. This was followed in the *IG Farben* Trial, 10 LRTWC 1, p. 64.

[286] *Flick* Trial, 'Notes on the case', 9 LRTWC 1, p. 50, and see M. Greenspan, *The Modern Law of Land Warfare* (Berkeley CA: University of California Press, 1959), p. 460.

[287] Article 18(e), 1996 ILC Draft Code.

[288] 1996 ILC Draft Code Commentary, para. 11, commenting on Article 18.

[289] Article 5(h), ICTY Statute. Note that there are fewer ICTR Judgements on persecution and they tend to follow the ICTY jurisprudence.

grounds'.[290] Therefore the *actus reus* of persecution initially requires a discriminatory act or omission but the principle of legality requires the prosecutor to charge the acts amounting to persecution, rather than persecution in general.[291]

The case law suggests that the act or omission must have discriminatory consequences in fact, rather than just be done with discriminatory intention, which alone is insufficient.[292] The *Kvočka* Trial Chamber persuasively suggested that an attack against a person because of their support or sympathy for the persecuted group should also amount to persecution, because that person would have been targeted as a result of his link with the specific group, but this issue has not been considered by an Appeal Chamber.[293] Further, the *Krnojelac* Appeal Chamber considered that 'a Serb mistaken for a Muslim may still be the victim of the crime of persecution', as the act committed against him 'institutes discrimination in fact, *vis-à-vis* the other Serbs who were not subject to such acts' and carried out with the intention of discriminating against a group on the grounds of ethnicity.[294] Another issue raised by the ICTY jurisprudence is whether a single act may be enough to satisfy the definition of persecution, and this has been answered in the affirmative by the *Vasiljević* Appeal Chamber.[295]

Not every denial of human rights constitutes a crime against humanity, and the *Tadić* Judgement explained that '[i]t is the violation of the right to equality in some serious fashion that infringes on the enjoyment of a basic or fundamental right that constitutes persecution'.[296] Furthermore, the *Kupreškić* Judgement explained that persecution requires a 'gross or blatant denial' of a fundamental right,[297] which reaches the same level of gravity as other acts prohibited as crimes against humanity in the ICTY Statute.[298] Nevertheless, the case law demonstrates that the crimes must be examined in terms of their cumulative effect, and thus, although individual acts may not be inhumane, if their overall consequences offend

[290] *Krnojelac*, Appeal Judgement, para. 185, followed by *Vasiljević*, Appeal Judgement, para. 113; *Blaškić*, Appeal Judgement, para. 131; *Kordić and Čerkez*, Appeal Judgement, para. 101; *Kvočka et al.*, Appeal Judgement, para. 320; *Deronjić*, Appeal Judgement, para. 109, and *Stakić*, Appeal Judgement, para. 327. See O. Swaak-Goldman, 'The crime of persecution in international criminal law', LJIL, 11 (1998), 145–54.

[291] *Vasiljević*, Trial Judgement, para. 246, *Stakić*, Trial Judgement, para. 735; *Simić, Tadić and Zarić*, Trial Judgement, para. 50, and *Brđanin*, Trial Judgement, para. 994.

[292] *Vasiljević*, Trial Judgement, para. 245.

[293] *Kvočka et al.*, Trial Judgement, para. 195.

[294] *Krnojelac*, Appeal Judgement, para. 185, followed by *Nahimana, Barayagwiza and Ngeze*, Trial Judgement, para. 1071, and *Martić*, Trial Judgement, para. 118.

[295] *Vasiljević*, Appeal Judgement, para. 113, followed by *Blaškić*, Appeal Judgement, para. 135, and *Kordić and Čerkez*, Appeal Judgement, para. 102.

[296] *Tadić*, Trial Judgement, para. 697.

[297] *Kupreškić*, Trial Judgement, paras 618–21, followed by *Kordić and Čerkez*, Trial Judgement, para. 195; *Krstić*, Trial Judgement, para. 534; *Krnojelac*, Trial Judgement, para. 434, and *Brđanin*, Trial Judgement, para. 995.

[298] *Ibid.*, and see *Blaškić*, Appeal Judgement, para. 135; *Kordić and Čerkez*, Appeal Judgement, para. 671; *Naletilić and Martinović*, Appeal Judgement, para. 574, and *Brđanin*, Appeal Judgement, para. 296.

humanity they could amount to the *actus reus* of persecution.[299] As a result of this, the *Kvočka et al.* and *Krnojelac* Trial Judgements held that it is not necessary that 'each discriminatory act alleged must individually be regarded as a violation of international law',[300] and other ICTY cases have held that there does not need to be a link between the persecutory acts and other acts defined as crimes against humanity.[301]

The ICTY case law on acts which may establish the *actus reus* of persecution demonstrate the level of seriousness required. Unlawful detention has been considered a sufficiently serious act, although the *Simić, Tadić and Zarić* Trial Chamber opined that unlawful arrest itself, without unlawful detention, may not constitute a gross or blatant denial of a fundamental right of the same level of gravity as other crimes against humanity.[302] Forced displacements have been also been accepted as of a sufficiently serious level to amount to the *actus reus* of persecutions.[303] The Appeal Chamber in *Kvočka* asserted that harassment, humiliation and psychological abuse, whilst not specific offences in themselves, reached such a degree of gravity in the camps, where detainees lived in overcrowded, lice-infected and cramped facilities and were forced to beg for water and relieve bodily functions in clothes, that their cumulative effect was serious enough to form the basis of a charge of persecution.[304]

Another controversial issue was whether the plunder or destruction of property was sufficiently serious to form the *actus reus* of persecution. The *Kupreškić* and *Kordić and Čerkez* Judgements held that the cumulative effect of the comprehensive destruction of homes and property was sufficiently severe, as it amounted to the destruction of the livelihood of a certain population and their removal from their homes, and this has been approved by the *Blaškić* Appeal Chamber.[305] The *Blaškić* Trial Chamber explained that 'persecution may take forms other than injury to the human person, in particular those acts rendered serious not by their apparent cruelty but by the discrimination they seek to instil within humankind'.[306] In this respect, the *Kordić and Čerkez* Judgement found that the

[299] *Kupreškić*, Trial Judgement, paras 615 and 622; *Tadić*, Trial Judgement, para. 715; *Kordić and Čerkez*, Trial Judgement, para. 199; *Kvočka et al.*, Appeal Judgement, para. 321, and *Naletilić and Martinović*, Appeal Judgement, para. 574.

[300] *Kvočka et al.*, Trial Judgement, para. 186, and *Krnojelac*, Trial Judgement, para. 434, approved by *Brđanin*, Appeal Judgement, para. 296.

[301] *Kupreškić*, Trial Judgement, para. 581, followed by *Kordić and Čerkez*, Trial Judgement, paras 193–4, and *Krstić*, Trial Judgement, para. 535.

[302] *Simić, Tadić and Zarić*, Trial Judgement, para. 62, and see *Blaškić*, Appeal Chamber, para. 155, on the issue of unlawful detention.

[303] *Krnojelac*, Appeal Judgement, para. 221, followed by *Blaškić*, Appeal Judgement, paras 152–3.

[304] *Kvočka et al.*, Appeal Chamber, paras 323–5.

[305] *Kupreškić*, Trial Judgement, para. 631, and *Kordić and Čerkez*, Trial Judgement, para. 205. See also *Naletilić and Martinović*, Trial Judgement, para. 699. Approach approved by *Blaškić*, Appeal Judgement, para. 146, and see *Kordić and Čerkez*, Appeal Judgement, para. 109.

[306] *Blaškić*, Trial Judgement, para. 227.

destruction of religious buildings was a clear case of persecution, as it amounted 'to an attack on the very religious identity of a people'.[307]

The mental element of persecution in the ICTY Statute requires that the act or omission was committed with the intention to discriminate on political, racial or religious grounds.[308] Consequently, the *mens rea* for persecution is higher than for other crimes against humanity.[309] According to the *Brđanin* Appeal Chamber it is not enough to show that the accused was merely aware that he was acting in a discriminatory manner, 'he must consciously intend to discriminate'.[310] Therefore, in addition to awareness of the context of the acts necessary for crimes against humanity and the intention to commit the underlying act (such as torture or rape) the accused must also have had the specific intention to discriminate on political, racial or religious grounds.[311] This means that the accused must have committed the *actus reus* with the 'specific intent to cause injury to a human being because he belongs to a particular community or group'.[312] However, the *Blaškić* Appeal Judgement emphasises that there is no requirement in law for a 'persecutory intent' over and above a discriminatory intent.[313]

The *Kupreškić* Judgement commented that the deprivation of rights in a case of persecution 'can be said to have as its aim the removal of those persons from the society in which they live alongside the perpetrators, or eventually even from humanity itself'.[314] It is unclear whether the Trial Chamber was merely observing a common factual situation in cases of persecution or was setting out part of the *mens rea*. The Trial Chamber in *Kordić and Čerkez* treated it as the latter,[315] but this has not been referred to by subsequent Judgements of the ICTY and would if followed set the *mens rea* of persecution practically as high as genocide. The *Kvočka* Appeal Judgement, however, makes it clear that motive and discriminatory intent are to be distinguished and on this basis refused to accept *Radić's* defence that his motive for acting in a discriminatory manner derived from reluctant obedience to his superior's explicit orders.[316]

The ICTY cases of *Tadić*, *Blaškić* and *Kvočka* also discussed the concept of a negative discriminatory intention, that is, the intention to target all those not belonging to a particular race, religion or political persuasion, and held that this

[307] *Kordić and Čerkez*, Trial Judgement, paras 206–7.

[308] Article 5(h), ICTY Statute.

[309] *Kupreškić*, Trial Judgement, para. 636.

[310] *Brđanin*, Appeal Judgement, para. 996.

[311] *Kupreškić*, Trial Judgement, paras 634–6; *Blaškić*, Trial Judgement, para. 235; *Kordić and Čerkez*, Trial Judgement, para. 212; *Kvočka et al.*, Trial Judgement, para. 200 and *Krnojelac*, Trial Judgement, para. 435.

[312] *Blaškić*, Trial Judgement, para. 235, approved by *Blaškić*, Appeal Judgement, para. 165.

[313] *Blaškić*, Appeal Judgement, para. 165, followed by *Kordić and Čerkez*, Appeal Chamber, para. 111, and see *Brđanin*, Appeal Judgement, para. 996.

[314] *Kupreškić*, Trial Judgement, para. 634.

[315] *Kordić and Čerkez*, Trial Judgement, paras 214 and 220.

[316] *Kvočka et al.*, Appeal Judgement, para. 367.

would be sufficient *mens rea* for the offence of persecution.[317] Additionally, the *Krnojelac* Judgement held that the intent to discriminate 'need not be the primary intent with respect to the act', provided that it was a significant one.[318] Finally, the ICTY case law demonstrates acceptance that in certain situations a discriminatory intention can be inferred from the surrounding circumstances, although this could be displaced by evidence that the accused had acted for other reasons.[319]

### The Rome Statute

Persecution is defined in Article 7(2)(g) of the Rome Statute as 'the intentional and severe deprivation of fundamental rights contrary to international law by reason of the identity of the group or collectivity'. This definition is reflected in the EOC, which commence by requiring that the perpetrator 'severely deprived, contrary to international law, one or more persons of fundamental rights' and 'targeted such person or persons by reason of the identity of a group or collectivity or targeted the group or collectivity as such'.[320]

Only fundamental rights are protected by this definition, such as non-derogable rights in human rights instruments.[321] However, the word 'severe' refers to the 'character of the deprivation of fundamental rights'[322] rather than the character of the act, and therefore, as suggested by the ICTY case law, the cumulative effect of several acts could be taken into account when judging the severity of the deprivation.[323] The second element is interesting, as it appears to protect groups *per se*, rather than simply individuals belonging to a group.[324] Kittichaisaree states that this formulation was adopted in order to ensure that those persons who were not part of the group, and yet were targeted because of their association with or support of the group, would also be protected.[325]

The third element requires that the targeting 'was based on political, racial, national, ethnic, cultural, religious, gender . . . or other grounds that are

317 *Tadić*, Trial Judgement, para. 714; *Blaškić*, Trial Judgement, para. 236; *Kvočka et al.*, Trial Judgement, para. 195, and see *Milosević*, Prosecutor's Second Pre-trial Brief, para. 1049. This approach can be seen in the *Kvočka et al.*, Appeal Judgement, para. 366.

318 *Krnojelac*, Trial Judgement, para. 435.

319 *Kvočka et al.*, Trial Judgement, para. 201; *Krnojelac*, Trial Judgement, para. 436; *Krnojelac*, Appeal Judgement, para. 184; *Blaškić*, Appeal Judgement, para. 164; *Kordić and Čerkez*, Appeal Judgement, para. 715; *Kvočka et al.*, Appeal Judgement, paras 366 and 460, and *Naletilić and Martinović*, Appeal Judgement, paras 129–31.

320 EOC, p. 122.

321 Boot *et al.*, 'Article 7', p. 167.

322 *Ibid.*, p. 166.

323 Discussed *supra*, pp. 227–8.

324 C. Byron and D. Turns, 'The Preparatory Commission for the International Criminal Court', ICLQ, 50 (2001), 420–35, p. 423.

325 K. Kittichaisaree, *International Criminal Law*, n. 247 *supra*, pp. 121–2, and see *Kvočka et al.*, Trial Judgement, para. 195, discussed *supra*, p. 227.

universally recognized as impermissible under international law'.[326] Therefore the grounds for the discrimination have been extended greatly, although the EOC do not provide any amplification of the individual bases for discrimination. It is submitted that the national, ethnic, racial and religious grounds should be interpreted similarly to those terms as used for the crime of genocide, which is set out in Article 6 of the Rome Statute.

Therefore, persecution on 'ethnic' grounds would include the targeting of those 'whose identity as such is distinctive in terms of common cultural traditions or heritage'.[327] 'Racial' grounds, applying the ICTR jurisprudence on genocide, would be persecution based on 'hereditary physical traits often identified with a geographical region'.[328] However, taking into account the comment of Schabas that '[a]s a way to classify humans into major subspecies . . . race has become virtually obsolete',[329] it may be preferable to take the two concepts of racial and ethnic groups together to cover relevant cases.[330]

Persecution on 'national' grounds should be understood as persecution of 'a collection of people who are perceived to share a legal bond based on common citizenship . . .'.[331] This would protect nationals of a particular State, targeted because of their citizenship, irrespective of their ethnic or religious backgrounds. According to the ICTR a 'religious' group is one 'whose members share the same religion, denomination or mode of worship'[332] and therefore the targeting of a group adhering to a particular system of faith and worship[333] would amount to persecution on religious grounds.

[326] EOC, p. 122.

[327] The Proxmire Act, para. 1093(5), and see the similar definition in *Akayesu*, Trial Judgement, para. 513, and *Kayishema and Ruzindana*, Trial Judgement, para. 98. Boot *et al.*, 'Article 7', p. 149, suggest that the term 'ethnic' in Article 7(1)(h) is narrower than the term 'ethnical' in Article 6; however, the terms 'ethnical' and 'ethnic' appear to be treated interchangeably by the ICTR, *Akayesu*, Trial Judgement, para. 583.

[328] *Akayesu*, Trial Judgement, para. 514, and *Kayishema and Ruzindana*, Trial Judgement, para. 98.

[329] W. Schabas, *Genocide in International Law* (Cambridge: Cambridge University Press, 2000), pp. 122–3.

[330] See M. Shaw, 'Genocide and international law', pp. 797–820, in Y. Dinstein (ed.), *International Law at a Time of Perplexity: Essays in Honour of Shabtai Rosenne* (Dordrecht: Nijhoff, 1989), p. 807.

[331] *Akayesu*, Trial Judgement, para. 512. This approach was taken by several participants in the Sixth Committee discussions of the Genocide Convention, UNOR Third Session of the General Assembly, 1948, Part I, Summary Records of the Sixth Committee Discussions on Article II of the Draft Convention on Genocide, Seventy-third Meeting, pp. 97–8, and Seventy-fourth Meeting, pp. 99 and 106, but some participants understood the word to refer to national minorities, Seventy-fourth Meeting, p. 99, and Seventy-fifth Meeting, p. 116. Compare opposing views of M. Lippman, 'The Convention on the Prevention and Punishment of the Crime of Genocide: fifty years later', Ariz J Int'l & Comp L, 15 (1998), 415–514, p. 456, with W. Schabas, *Genocide in International Law*, n. 329 *supra*, pp. 114–20.

[332] *Akayesu*, Trial Judgement, para. 515, and *Kayishema and Ruzindana*, Trial Judgement, para. 98.

[333] Taken from the definition of 'religion' in the *Concise Oxford Dictionary*, n. 38 *supra*.

Persecution on 'political' grounds would include targeting on the basis of 'party political beliefs and political ideology', according to the ICTR in *Kayishema and Ruzindana*.[334] However, Boot and Hall suggest an even broader approach, with 'political' grounds for persecution including a difference of opinion on 'public affairs issues such as environment and health'.[335] They also suggest a broad meaning of 'cultural' grounds of persecution, as relating to the 'customs, arts, social institutions, etc., of a particular group or people'.[336]

The ground for persecution which has provoked most comment is that of 'gender',[337] which Article 7(3) of the Statute states 'refers to the two sexes, male and female, within the context of society'. Whilst the inclusion of gender persecution was welcomed by many,[338] the definition in Article 7(3) has been criticised.[339] The definition of sex and gender accepted by most commentators is that 'sex refers to biologically determined differences between men and women' whereas 'gender refers to the social differences between men and women that are learned, changeable over time and have wide variations both within and between cultures'.[340] Therefore, Article 7(3) appears to reflect 'an unsuccessful attempt to combine the different concepts of "sex" and "gender"'.[341]

This compromise language was adopted because of the fear of some States that the expression 'gender' could render suspect laws criminalising

[334] *Kayishema and Ruzindana*, Trial Judgement, para. 130, and see *Akayesu*, Trial Judgement, para. 583.

[335] Boot *et al.*, 'Article 7', pp. 148–9.

[336] *Ibid.*, p. 149, referring to definition in the *Oxford Advanced Learner's Dictionary of Current English*.

[337] See 'What is gender?' on the website of the Women's Caucus for Gender Justice, available at: <http://www.iccwomen.org/resources/gender.htm>.

[338] The inclusion of gender as a basis for persecution was strongly supported by the NGO group Women's Caucus for Gender Justice, see <http://www.iccwomen.org/>. See also J. Campanaro, 'Women, war, and international law: the historical treatment of gender-based war crimes', Geo LJ, 89 (2001), 2557–92, p. 2590; G. McDougall, 'Contemporary forms of slavery, update to Final Report', n. 204 *supra*, para. 31, and B. Moshan, 'Women, war and words: the gender component in the permanent International Criminal Court's definition of crimes against humanity', Fordham Int'l LJ, 22 (1998), 154–84, p. 182.

[339] See H. Charlesworth, in K. Rittich *et al.*, 'The gender of international law', ASIL Proceedings, 93 (1999), 206–9, p. 207; K. Askin, 'Women's issues in international criminal law: recent developments and the potential contribution of the ICC', pp. 47–63 in D. Shelton (ed.), *International Crimes, Peace and Human Rights: The Role of the International Criminal Court* (New York: Transnational, 2000), pp. 60–1, and H. Charlesworth and C. Chinkin, *The Boundaries of International Law: A Feminist Analysis* (Manchester: Manchester University Press, 2000), p. 335.

[340] Report of the Secretary General, 'Integrating the human rights of women throughout the UN system', UN Doc. E/CN.4/1997/40, 20 December 1996, para. 10.

[341] K. Askin, 'Crimes within the jurisdiction of the International Criminal Court', n. 49 *supra*, p. 47, and see G. Robertson, *Crimes against Humanity*, n. 125 *supra*, p. 338. The tension between sex and gender in the context of the UN Fourth World Conference on Women in Beijing is discussed in S. Baden and A. Goetz, 'Who needs [sex] when you can have [gender]', Feminist Review, 56 (1997), 3–25.

homosexuality,[342] and Sadat suggests that the resulting vagueness in the language used allows both sides to assert that the definition reflects their understanding of the term.[343] However, McAuliffe deGuzman asserts that Article 7(3) 'represents an acceptance of the view that in applying and interpreting the law, the Court should be concerned not only with discrimination based on "sex" but with any discrimination related to socially constructed roles and power differentials'.[344] Therefore, it would seem that, for example, attacks against working women, as opposed to housewives, could amount to gender persecution under this definition, but it is still unclear whether attacks against homosexuals could amount to persecution under the Rome Statute.[345]

The final ground of persecution is the open-ended 'other grounds that are universally recognized as impermissible under international law'.[346] Boot and Hall comment that this final basis for persecution should be understood as other 'widely recognised' grounds and thus not all States would have to recognise a particular ground as impermissible in order for it to form the basis for persecution.[347] However, Robinson states that this is a very high threshold provision and that the Statute may simply be amended to reflect future developments in grounds of persecution.[348]

The EOC specific to the offence of persecution conclude with the requirement that '[t]he conduct was committed in connection with any act referred to in Article 7, paragraph 1, of the Statute or any crime within the jurisdiction of the Court'.[349] An attached footnote states that no additional *mens rea* is necessary as a result of this element and so the perpetrator does not have to be aware of any specific 'connected acts'.[350] Therefore, this element simply adds

[342] H. Charlesworth and C. Chinkin, n. 339 *supra*, p. 335, and L. Sadat, *The International Criminal Court and the Transformation of International Law*, n. 13 *supra*, p. 159.

[343] L. Sadat, *The International Criminal Court and the Transformation of International Law*, n. 13 *supra*, p. 160.

[344] M. McAuliffe deGuzman, 'Article 21, applicable law', pp. 435–46 in O. Triffterer (ed.), *Commentary on the Rome Statute*, n. 2 *supra*, p. 446, and V. Oosterveld, 'The definition of "gender" in the Rome Statute of the International Criminal Court: a step forward or back for international criminal justice?', Harv HRJ, 18 (2005), 55–84, p. 75. See also K. Askin, 'Crimes within the jurisdiction of the International Criminal Court', n. 49 *supra*, p. 49.

[345] G. Robertson suggests that transsexuals and homosexuals are not protected under this definition, in *Crimes against Humanity*, n. 125 *supra*, p. 338, and this interpretation is supported by R. Lehr-Lehnardt, 'One small step for women: female-friendly provisions in the Rome Statute of the International Criminal Court', BYU J Pub L, 16 (2002), 317–54, p. 340. However, see the opposing view of B. Bedont, 'Gender-specific provisions in the Statute of the ICC', pp. 183–210 in F. Lattanzi and W. Schabas (eds), *Essays on the Rome Statute of the ICC*, Vol. I (Naples: Editorale Scientifica, 1999), pp. 187–8.

[346] EOC, p. 122.

[347] Boot *et al.*, 'Article 7', p. 150.

[348] D. Robinson, 'Defining "crimes against humanity"', n. 99 *supra*, p. 54.

[349] EOC, p. 122.

[350] *Ibid.*, fn. 22, and see W. Rückert and G. Witschel, 'Genocide and crimes against humanity', n. 175 *supra*, p. 88.

a requirement for an objective contextual link between the persecution and at least one act described by the Statute in Articles 6, 7(1) or 8(2).[351]

Therefore the *actus reus* of this offence is to deprive, severely, at least one person of fundamental rights, in connection with at least one crime described in the Rome Statute. The *mens rea* requires the act to be carried out intentionally, against the person because of their connection with or identity as part of a group, or against the group as such, which was targeted on one of the listed grounds. Accordingly, the crime of persecution under the Rome Statute has a higher mental element than that of other crimes against humanity, because of the necessity to show discrimination on one of the listed bases, but it is clear that it need not be shown that the perpetrator intended to remove the targeted group from society.

## Article 7(1)(i) Enforced disappearance of persons

### Origins

The crime of enforced disappearance, although it was not so described at the time, appears to have been invented by Hitler in 1941 in his 'Night and Fog' decree.[352] The Nuremberg Judgement describes how those who committed crimes against the Reich or the German occupation forces, or were even suspected of opposing the policies of the German occupation forces, would be taken secretly to Germany for trial. No word was permitted to reach their relatives, even if they died, in order 'to create anxiety in the minds of the family of the arrested person'[353]

The term 'disappearance' was first coined in the 1960s in Guatemala, when many political opponents of the ruling regime were abducted and never heard from again.[354] During the 1970s enforced disappearances took place on a massive scale in Argentina and Chile – indeed, Lacabe estimates that between 20,000 and 30,000 people disappeared in Argentina alone.[355] This cruel practice then spread to other Latin American countries.[356] A typical enforced disappearance

[351] Lee (ed.), *ICC: Elements*, p. 97, but if the conduct was itself one of the acts referred to in Article 7(1) it would not be necessary to link the conduct to another act, K. Ambos and S. Wirth, 'The current law of crimes against humanity', n. 32 *supra*, p. 72. See also M. Badar, 'From the Nuremberg Charter to the Rome Statute: defining the elements of crimes against humanity', San Diego Int'l LJ, 5 (2004), 73–144, pp. 126–7.

[352] Boot *et al.*, 'Article 7', p. 151, and see M. Lippman, 'The prosecution of Josef Altstoetter *et al.*: law, lawyers and justice in the Third Reich', Dick J Int'l L, 16 (1998), 343–433, pp. 378–9.

[353] *IMT Judgement*, p. 453, and see Judgement of Keitel, p. 493.

[354] J. Mendez and J. Vivanco, 'Disappearances and the Inter-American Court: reflections on a litigation experience', Hamline LR, 13 (1990), 507–77, p. 510.

[355] M. Lacabe, 'The criminal procedures against Chilean and Argentinian repressors in Spain: a short summary', Revision One, 11 November 1998, available at: <http://www.derechos.net/marga/papers/spain.html>, and see A. Garro and H. Dahl, 'Legal accountability for human rights violations in Argentina: one step forward and two steps backward', HRLJ, 8 (1987), 283–344, pp. 287–301.

[356] C. Grossman, 'Disappearances in Honduras: the need for direct victim representation in human rights litigation', Hastings Int & Comp LR, 15 (1992), 363–89, pp. 366–8.

was described by the Argentine National Commission on the Disappeared. A kidnapping by security forces, who concealed their identities, would be followed by detention of the victim in inhuman conditions in a secret detention centre. There he or she would be humiliated and tortured, leading to death. The body would then be destroyed to prevent subsequent identification.[357]

## Development

Three important instruments have tried to tackle the practice of enforced disappearance. First, the General Assembly in 1992 passed a 'Declaration on the Protection of all Persons from Enforced Disappearances'.[358] Although enforced disappearance was not defined in the main body of the declaration, the preamble both described enforced disappearances as:

> persons are arrested, detained or abducted against their will or otherwise deprived of their liberty by officials of different branches or levels of Government, or by organized groups or private individuals acting on behalf of, or with the support, direct or indirect, consent or acquiescence of the Government, followed by a refusal to disclose the fate or whereabouts of the persons concerned or a refusal to acknowledge the deprivation of their liberty, which places such persons outside the protection of the law

and stated that the 'systematic practice of such acts is *of the nature* of a crime against humanity'.[359] The second instrument is the 1994 Organisation of American States Inter-American Convention on the Forced Disappearance of Persons.[360] The definition of enforced disappearance is in Article 2 of the main body of the Convention, which defines it as:

> the act of depriving a person or persons of his or their freedom, in whatever way, perpetrated by agents of the state or by persons or groups of persons acting with the authorization, support, or acquiescence of the state, followed by an absence of information or a refusal to acknowledge that deprivation of freedom or to give information on the whereabouts of that person, thereby impeding his or her recourse to the applicable legal remedies and procedural guarantees.

[357] 'Nunca más': The Report of the Argentine National Commission on the Disappeared (CONADEP), 1984, Recommendations and Conclusions, available at: <http://www.nuncamas.org/index2.htm>, and see 'Guatemala: memory of silence', Commission for Historical Clarification, Conclusions and Recommendations, para. 89, available at: <http://hrdata.aaas.org/ceh/report/english/toc.html>.

[358] General Assembly Resolution (GA Res.) 47/133, 18 December 1992, and see R. Brody and F. González, '*Nunca más:* an analysis of international instruments on "disappearances"', HRQ, 19 (1997), 365–405, pp. 371–4.

[359] GA Res. 47/133, 18 December 1992, emphasis added.

[360] Organization of American States 1994 Inter-American Convention on the Forced Disappearance of Persons, and see R. Brody and F. González, '*Nunca más*', n. 358 *supra*, pp. 374–5.

Furthermore the preamble states unambiguously that 'the systematic practice of the forced disappearance of persons *constitutes* a crime against humanity'.[361] The third instrument is the International Convention for the Protection of all Persons from Enforced Disappearance, adopted by the UN General Assembly in December 2006 and not yet in force.[362] Enforced disappearance is defined in Article 2 as:

> the arrest, detention, abduction or any other form of deprivation of liberty by agents of the State or by persons or groups of persons acting with the authorization, support or acquiescence or the State, followed by a refusal to acknowledge the deprivation of liberty or by concealment of the fate or whereabouts of the disappeared person, which place such a person outside the protection of the law.[363]

Article 5 of the Convention in stating that '[t]he widespread or systematic practice of enforced disappearance constitutes a crime against humanity as defined in applicable international law and shall attract the consequences provided for under such applicable international law' appears to make an oblique reference to the ICC.[364]

Although these definitions of enforced disappearance differ, a common core appears to be the deprivation of a victim's freedom by State agents or those acting with State approval,[365] followed by refusal to provide information on the whereabouts of the victim, resulting in the impeding or prevention of the legal protection of the victim.[366] Human rights cases before the Inter-American Court of Human Rights (IACHR) and the European Court of Human Rights (ECHR) have not tackled the definition of this phenomenon; rather they have listed a series of human rights protections breached by such enforced disappearances.[367]

[361] Emphasis added.

[362] Adopted 20 December 2006 by GA Res. 61/177. The Convention needs twenty ratifications to enter into force (none as of October 2007).

[363] For comments on this definition see S. McCrory, 'The International Convention for the Protection of all Persons from Enforced Disappearance', Hum Rts L Rev, 7 (2007), 545–66, pp. 551–2, and K. Anderson, 'How effective is the International Convention for the Protection of all Persons from Enforced Disappearance likely to be in holding individuals criminally responsible for acts of enforced disappearance?', Melb J Int'l L, 7 (2006), 245–77, pp. 271–5.

[364] K. Anderson, *ibid.*, pp. 269–70.

[365] The concept of enforced disappearances with the authorisation of a non-State body is an innovation of the Rome Statute, see *infra*, p. 238.

[366] See also Article 1, 1998 Draft International Convention on the Protection of all Persons from Forced Disappearance, which defines forced disappearance as 'the deprivation of a person's liberty, in whatever form or for whatever reason, brought about by agents of the State or by persons or groups of persons acting with the authorization, support or acquiescence of the State, followed by an absence of information, or refusal to acknowledge the deprivation of liberty or information, or concealment of the fate or whereabouts of the disappeared person'. Article 3 of the Draft Convention describes the systematic or massive practice of forced disappearance as a crime against humanity.

[367] *Velasquez Rodriguez* case, IACHR, 28 ILM (1989), 291, paras 155–7; *Çakici v. Turkey*, ECHR Judgement, paras 85–107, and *Timurtas v. Turkey*, ECHR Judgement, paras 83–98, and see J. Mendez and J. Vivanco, 'Disappearances and the Inter-American Court', n. 354 *supra,* and G. Sethi, 'The European Court of Human Rights' jurisprudence on issues of forced disappearances', HR Brief, 8 (2001), 29–31.

Despite these attempts to eliminate this most cruel of crimes, the Working Group on Enforced Disappearances, established by the Human Rights Commission in 1980,[368] has observed the practice of enforced disappearances spreading to such countries as Iraq, Sri Lanka and the former Yugoslavia.[369] The continuing relevance of enforced disappearance is also shown by its inclusion in the 1996 ILC Draft Code, the commentary of which states that 'the present Code proposes its inclusion as a crime against humanity because of its extreme cruelty and gravity'.[370] However, the Draft Code and commentary do not define enforced disappearances, but merely refer to the UN Declaration and Organization of American States Convention on the subject.[371]

## The Rome Statute

Enforced disappearance is defined in the Rome Statute as:

> the arrest, detention or abduction of persons by, or with the authorization, support or acquiescence of, a State or a political organization, followed by a refusal to acknowledge that deprivation of freedom or to give information on the fate or whereabouts of those persons, with the intention of removing them from the protection of the law for a prolonged period of time.[372]

This was based on the UN Declaration on Enforced Disappearance.[373] The EOC of this offence reflect the complex nature of the crime and the fact that its commission normally involves several participants over a prolonged period of time.[374] The Elements include alternative parts in order to deal both with those perpetrators who are involved in the initial detention as well as those who refuse

[368] For a discussion of the Working Group and its practices see M. Lippman, 'Disappearances: towards a declaration on the prevention and punishment of the crime of enforced or involuntary disappearances', Conn JIL, 4 (1988), 121–43, pp. 128–37.

[369] Report of the Working Group on Enforced Disappearances, Commission on Human Rights, 12 January 1998, UN Doc. E/CN.4/1998/43, para. 409. See I. Taqi, 'Adjudicating disappearance cases in Turkey: an argument for adopting the Inter-American Court of Human Rights' approach', Fordham Int'l LJ, 24 (2001), 940–87; D. Udagama, 'Taming of the beast: judicial responses to State violence in Sri Lanka', Harv HRJ, 11 (1998), 269–94; L. Black, 'Forced disappearances in Sri Lanka constitute a crime against humanity', 1 January 1999, available at: <http://www.disappearances.org/mainfile.php/articles_srilanka/9/>; J. Kaur, 'A judicial blackout: judicial impunity for disappearances in Punjab, India', Harv HRJ, 15 (2002), 269–97, and O. Ben-Naftali and S. Gleichgevitch, 'Missing in legal action: Lebanese hostages in Israel', Harv ILJ, 41 (2000), 185–252, pp. 199–205.

[370] Article 18(i), 1996 ILC Draft Code and Commentary, para. 15 to Article 18.

[371] *Ibid.*

[372] Article 7(2)(i), Rome Statute.

[373] C. Hall, 'The sixth session of the UN Preparatory Committee on the Establishment of an International Criminal Court', AJIL, 92 (1998), 548–56, p. 550, and T. McIntyre and C. de Gaston, 'Enforced disappearance of persons: its inclusion as a crime against humanity in the ICC', pp. 26–8, available from 'Law without Borders: Student Perspectives on International Law', at: <http://www.law2.byu.edu/lwb>.

[374] EOC, p. 122, fn. 23, and Lee (ed.), *ICC: Elements*, p. 99.

to give information, although they do not deal with those who dispose of the bodies of victims of enforced disappearance. In order to simplify the analysis of this crime, the following discussion will deal first with the EOC relating to detention and then with the EOC relating to refusal to give information.

The perpetrator must first have 'arrested, detained or abducted one or more persons'.[375] These terms cover a wide range of possibilities,[376] which are further widened by two footnotes which state that 'detained' includes a perpetrator who maintained an existing detention and that 'under certain circumstances an arrest or detention may have been lawful'.[377] Consequently, criminal liability may attach to an individual who takes charge of the detained victim and does not redress the situation and a perpetrator cannot avoid liability because the victim's initial arrest was lawful if the other elements of the offence are met.[378]

The arrest, detention or abduction must have been carried out 'by, or with the authorization, support or acquiescence of, a State or a political organization'.[379] The inclusion of a 'political organization' is a new development in this crime, but one which is supported by the approach of the Rome Statute that a crime against humanity must be committed pursuant to a 'State or organizational policy'.[380] However, the exact definition of 'political organization' is unclear. Would it, for example, include a well organised terrorist group which was carrying out disappearances as part of a violent secession campaign?

The deprivation of freedom must have been accompanied or followed by 'a refusal to acknowledge that deprivation of freedom or to give information on the fate or whereabouts of such person or persons' and the perpetrator must have been aware that the deprivation of freedom 'would be followed in the ordinary course of events by a refusal to acknowledge that deprivation of freedom or to give information on the fate or whereabouts of such person or persons'.[381] Therefore, because the perpetrator may not be involved after the initial arrest, it is not necessary to prove that he knew of an actual refusal to give information, but it is sufficient if he is aware that such a refusal would follow in the ordinary course of events.[382] A footnote to the mental element states that a perpetrator maintaining an existing detention would also be liable if he knew that a refusal to give information had already taken place.[383] Finally, it must be shown that the perpetrator 'intended to remove such person or persons from the protection of the law for a prolonged period of time'.[384] Askin comments that the

[375] EOC, p. 122, Element 1(a).
[376] Boot *et al.*, 'Article 7', p. 170.
[377] EOC, fns 25 and 26 on p. 122.
[378] See Lee (ed.), *ICC: Elements*, p. 101.
[379] EOC, p. 123, Element 4.
[380] EOC, Introduction, para. 3, p. 116, and see Boot *et al.*, 'Article 7', pp. 170–1.
[381] EOC, pp. 122–3, Elements 2(a) and 3(a).
[382] Lee (ed.), *ICC: Elements*, pp. 102–3.
[383] EOC, fn. 28 on p. 123.
[384] EOC, p. 123, Element 6.

expression 'prolonged period' should be 'interpreted generously on behalf of the disappeared'.[385]

In the alternative case of perpetrators refusing to give information, the perpetrator must have '[r]efused to acknowledge the arrest, detention or abduction, or to give information on the fate or whereabouts of such person or persons', and this must have been done 'by or with the authorisation or support of, such State or political organisation'.[386] For this type of perpetrator, State or political organisational acquiescence alone is insufficient.[387]

The perpetrator's refusal must have either accompanied the deprivation of freedom of the victim or followed that event, and the perpetrator must have been aware that the deprivation of freedom was occurring or had occurred.[388] Therefore an innocent denial that the victim had been deprived of his or her freedom would clearly not amount to an offence. The perpetrator must also, as is the case above, intend to 'remove such person or persons from the protection of the law for a prolonged period of time'.[389]

A final issue raised at the Preparatory Commission was whether the ICC would have jurisdiction over continuing enforced disappearances in the case of those persons who were deprived of their freedom in the past but whose whereabouts were still unknown and denied by the relevant authorities at the date the Rome Statute entered into force.[390] This issue was resolved in a footnote which explains that the crime of enforced disappearance falls under the jurisdiction of the Court only if the widespread and systematic attack against a civilian population of which it forms part occurs after the entry into force of the Statute.[391]

## Article 7(1)(j) The crime of apartheid

### Origins

The term 'apartheid' is an Afrikaans word meaning apartness or separation. The term was coined in 1944 by the South African Prime Minister, Daniel Malan, 'to denote South African policies of racial segregation between whites and various nonwhite racial groups' and it became official policy in South Africa after the National Party formed a government in 1948.[392] Nevertheless, the apartheid regime in South Africa was characterised not by a 'separate but equal' policy,

[385] K. Askin, 'Crimes within the jurisdiction of the International Criminal Court', n. 49 *supra*, p. 49.

[386] EOC, pp. 122–3, Elements 1(b) and 5.

[387] This was to harmonise the different language versions of the Rome Statute, Lee (ed.), *ICC: Elements*, p. 102.

[388] EOC, p. 123, Elements 2(b) and 3(b).

[389] EOC, p. 123, Element 6.

[390] C. Hall, 'The first five sessions of the UN Preparatory Commission', n. 121 *supra*, p. 781.

[391] EOC, fn. 24 on p. 122.

[392] L. Sunga, *Individual Responsibility in International Law*, n. 1 *supra*, p. 74.

even if such were possible, but by institutionalised racism, forced removals of populations, imprisonment without trial, torture and even murder.[393]

Apartheid was condemned by the General Assembly as a crime against humanity as early as 1966,[394] and in 1968 the Convention on the Non-applicability of Statutory Limitations to War Crimes and Crimes against Humanity expressly included apartheid as a crime against humanity.[395] In 1971 the International Court of Justice (ICJ) condemned apartheid as a denial of fundamental human rights and a 'flagrant violation of the purposes and principles' of the UN Charter.[396] Then in 1973 the General Assembly adopted the International Convention on the Suppression and Punishment of the Crime of Apartheid, which declared in Article 1 that 'apartheid is a crime against humanity'.[397]

The Apartheid Convention explained that the crime of apartheid would 'include similar policies and practices of racial segregation and discrimination as practised in southern Africa' and would apply to 'the following inhumane acts committed for the purpose of establishing and maintaining domination by one racial group of persons over any other racial group of persons and systematically oppressing them'.[398] The acts referred to included murder, the infliction of serious bodily or mental harm, torture, inhuman or degrading treatment, arbitrary arrest or illegal imprisonment of a racial group; imposition of living conditions calculated to cause a racial group's physical destruction wholly or in part; legislative and other measures to prevent a racial group from participation in the political, social, economic and cultural life of the country, including the right to work, the right to education and the right to freedom of movement and residence; measures to divide the population along racial lines by the creation of separate reserves and ghettoes; exploitation of the labour of members of a racial group and persecution of those opposing apartheid.[399] Practices of apartheid 'and other

[393] For background information on apartheid in South Africa see R. Abel, *Politics by Other Means: Law in the Struggle against Apartheid, 1980–1994* (New York: Routledge, 1995), and M. Coleman (ed.), *A Crime against Humanity: Analysing the Repression of the Apartheid State* (Johannesburg: Human Rights Committee of South Africa, 1998), and the Truth and Reconciliation Commission of South Africa (TRC) Final Report, 29 October 1998, available at: <www.polity.org.za/govdocs/commissions/1998/trc/index.htm>, particularly Vol. I, chapter 2, paras. 45–6 and 80.

[394] GA Res. 2202 (XXI), 16 December 1966.

[395] Article 1(b), 1968 Convention on the Non-applicability of Statutory Limitations to War Crimes and Crimes against Humanity, and see R. Slye, 'Apartheid as a crime against humanity: a submission to the South African Truth and Reconciliation Commission', Mich J Int'l L, 20 (1999), 267–300, pp. 290–2.

[396] *Legal Consequences for States of the Continued Presence of South Africa in Namibia (South West Africa) Notwithstanding Security Council Resolution 276 (1970)*, Advisory Opinion, ICJ Rep. (1971), 3, para. 131.

[397] Article 1, 1973 International Convention on the Suppression and Punishment of the Crime of Apartheid. See R. Slye, 'Apartheid as a crime against humanity', n. 395 *supra*, pp. 292–5.

[398] Article 2, 1973 Apartheid Convention.

[399] Article 2, *ibid*. As of October 2007 there were 107 States parties to the Apartheid Convention, details available at: <http://www.unhchr.ch/html>.

inhuman and degrading practices involving outrages upon personal dignity, based on racial discrimination' were also prohibited as a grave breach in AP I.[400]

## Development

The crime of apartheid was included expressly in the 1991 ILC Draft Code of Crimes, with a definition closely based on the Apartheid Convention.[401] A more generic version was included in the 1996 Draft Code, which prohibited 'institutionalized discrimination on racial, ethnic or religious grounds involving the violation of fundamental human rights and freedoms and resulting in seriously disadvantaging a part of the population'.[402] The ILC commentary states that this crime consists of three elements, 'a discriminatory act committed against individuals because of their membership in a racial, ethnic or religious group . . . the denial of their human rights and fundamental freedoms . . . and a consequential serious disadvantage to members of the group comprising a segment of the population'.[403]

The Truth and Reconciliation Commission (TRC) of South Africa published its report in 1998. However, whilst it stated that apartheid was a human rights violation and that 'as a system of enforced racial discrimination and separation' it was a crime against humanity,[404] the report did not define apartheid as such. The TRC instead concentrated upon its mandate to investigate gross violations of human rights, defined as 'killing, abduction, torture or severe ill-treatment' and so 'was restricted to examining only a fraction of the totality of human rights violations that emanated from the policy of apartheid'.[405]

## The Rome Statute

The crime of apartheid is defined in Article 7(2)(h) of the Rome Statute as 'inhumane acts of a character similar to those referred to in paragraph 1, committed in the context of an institutionalized regime of systematic oppression and domination by one racial group over any other racial group or groups and committed with the intention of maintaining that regime'. This definition was refined by the Elements, which require that the perpetrator 'committed an inhumane act against one or more persons' and that the act was 'referred to in article 7, paragraph 1, of the Statute, or was an act of a character similar to any of those acts'.[406]

Therefore the EOC clarify the Rome Statute definition by showing that other acts specified as crimes against humanity can, if the other elements of this offence

[400] Article 85(4)(c), AP I.

[401] Article 20, 1991, ILC Draft Code.

[402] Article 18(f), 1996, ILC Draft Code.

[403] 1996 ILC Draft Code Commentary, para. 12, commenting on Article 18.

[404] TRC Report, Vol. I, chapter 2, para. 22; Vol. I, chapter 4, appendix 'A crime against humanity', para. 1, and Vol. V, chapter 6, para. 101.

[405] TRC Report, Vol. I, chapter 2, para. 19.

[406] EOC, p. 123, and see Lee (ed.), *ICC: Elements*, pp. 104–5.

are satisfied, constitute apartheid. Although the expression 'inhumane act' is not defined, clearly any of the offences specified in Article 7(1) would amount to such. Furthermore, a footnote states that 'character' 'refers to the nature and gravity of the act', so an act which is similar in quality and seriousness to the other crimes against humanity could also constitute an inhumane act for the purposes of this offence.[407] Whilst the perpetrator need not have consciously evaluated his act as inhumane, he must have been 'aware of the factual circumstances that established the character of the act'.[408]

The conduct must have been 'committed in the context of an institutionalized regime of systematic oppression and domination by one racial group over any other racial group or groups'.[409] The TRC provides an insight into the concept of an 'institutionalized regime', by referring to the 'violence of the law or what is often referred to as *institutional or structural violence*'.[410] Applying this and dictionary definitions, an 'institutionalized regime' could be described as an established law or practice by a government or prevailing order.[411] The regime must impose 'systematic oppression and domination' over one or more racial groups, thus controlling and harshly treating them.[412] As Hall comments, this cumulative requirement will 'impose a significant burden on the prosecution'.[413] Racial groups are not defined, but 'racial' should be given the same definition as in the crime of persecution.[414] This offence is not restricted to regimes imposed by States and could feasibly be imposed also by an armed group with control over an area where it was not the recognised government.[415]

Finally, the Elements state that the perpetrator 'intended to maintain such regime' by his or her conduct.[416] Therefore, the *mens rea* of this offence requires that the perpetrator intended to commit the underlying act whilst being aware of the factual circumstances establishing its nature and gravity and did so with the intention of maintaining an institutionalised regime of systematic oppression and domination over a racial group. Hall criticises the specific intent to maintain the regime, as it 'could be interpreted to exclude both acts by those seeking to replace the regime with something worse and by those seeking to replace it with a regime which was less oppressive, but still imposing severe discrimination'.[417] Nevertheless, it seems likely that most acts criminalised under this provision would constitute another offence under Article 7(1) if the specific intent were not proved.

[407] EOC, fn. 29 on p. 123.
[408] *Ibid.*
[409] EOC, p. 123.
[410] TRC Report, Vol. I, chapter 2, para. 68, emphasis added, and see Vol. IV, chapter 1, para. 6.
[411] See *Concise Oxford Dictionary*, n. 38 *supra*.
[412] *Ibid.*
[413] Boot *et al.*, 'Article 7', p. 169.
[414] See discussion *supra*, p. 231.
[415] See Boot *et al.*, 'Article 7', p. 168.
[416] EOC, p. 123.
[417] Boot *et al.*, 'Article 7', pp. 169–70.

## Article 7(1)(k) Other inhumane acts of a similar character intentionally causing great suffering, or serious injury to body or to mental or physical health

### Origins

The expression 'other inhumane acts' was included in the Nuremberg and Tokyo Charters but was not defined.[418] Nevertheless, reference should be had to the similar expression 'inhuman treatment' described in the grave breach provisions of the Geneva Conventions, as both provide a 'catch-all' provision in the knowledge that not all war crimes or crimes against humanity can be explicitly defined in advance.[419] Attempts have been made to narrow the ambit of this offence in two Israeli decisions. First, the Tel Aviv District Court in the case of *Attorney General v. Enigster* stated that 'other inhumane acts' must be 'of a serious character and likely to embitter the life of a human being, to degrade him and cause him great physical or moral pain and suffering'.[420] Second, the Supreme Court in the case of *Eichmann* spoke of acts 'causing serious physical and mental harm'.[421]

### Development

The ILC 1996 Draft Code includes 'other inhumane acts' in its definition of crimes against humanity, but the offence is limited to those which 'severely damage physical or mental integrity, health or human dignity, such as mutilation and severe bodily harm'.[422] The commentary states that these requirements are intended to ensure that inhumane acts are 'similar in gravity to those listed in the preceding subparagraphs' and that the acts 'in fact cause injury to a human being in terms of physical or mental integrity, health or human dignity'.[423]

The ICTY Judgements treat inhumane acts as a residual category with the same basic elements as cruel treatment under Common Article 3 or inhuman treatment as a grave breach.[424] Essentially the international jurisprudence on this offence

[418] Article 6(c), Nuremberg Charter; Article 5(c), Tokyo Charter, and Article II(c), CCL No. 10.

[419] See discussion *supra*, pp. 29–30.

[420] *Attorney General v. Enigster*, 18 ILR, 540, p. 541.

[421] *Attorney General of the Government of Israel v. Eichmann*, Judgement, District Court of Jerusalem, 36 ILR, 18, p. 239.

[422] Article 18(k), 1996 ILC Draft Code.

[423] 1996, ILC Draft Code Commentary, para. 17, commenting on Article 18.

[424] Those cases commenting upon the status of inhumane acts as a residual category include: *Kupreškić*, Trial Judgement, para. 563; *Krnojelac*, Trial Judgement, para. 130; *Vasiljević*, Trial Judgement, para. 234; *Blagojević and Jokić*, Trial Judgement, para. 626; *Kordić and Čerkez*, Appeal Judgement, para. 117, and *Stakić*, Appeal Judgement, paras 315–16. Those cases confirming that the elements are the same as cruel or inhuman treatment include: *Jelisić*, Trial Judgement, para. 52; *Kupreškić*, Trial Judgement, para. 711; *Krnojelac*, Trial Judgement, para. 130, and *Vasiljević*, Trial Judgement, para. 234, and see discussion *supra*, pp. 36–7 and 177.

shows that the *actus reus* of inhumane acts requires that the act or omission must be of a similar seriousness to the other listed crimes against humanity and that the accused must have caused serious physical or mental suffering or injury or a serious attack on human dignity.[425]

The Trial Chamber in *Krnojelac* comments that the assessment of the seriousness of an act is by its nature relative and all factual circumstances must be taken into account, including 'the nature of the act or omission, the context in which it occurs, its duration and/or repetition, the physical, mental and moral effects of the act on the victim and the personal circumstances of the victim, including age, sex and health' and added that the suffering inflicted did not need to be lasting as long as it was 'real and serious'.[426] This interpretation of the assessment of the seriousness criteria has been followed by ICTY Trial and Appeal Chambers.[427]

The *mens rea* of inhumane acts has been generally accepted by the ICTY, the ICTR and the Special Court for Sierra Leone as either the intention to inflict the act or omission concerned or knowledge of the likely consequences of the act.[428] Finally, the ICTR in *Kayishema and Ruzindana* comments that whilst a witness may suffer serious mental harm as a result of witnessing an attack by the accused upon another person, the accused will have the *mens rea* for the offence only if he or she knew that the act was being witnessed and knew that his or her act was likely to cause serious mental suffering or was reckless as to whether such suffering would result.[429] In this respect the ICTR Trial Chamber in *Niyitegeka* found that the killing, followed by the decapitation and castration of a victim and the fact that his 'genitals were hung on a spike, and visible to the public' was an inhumane act, as it would cause 'mental suffering to civilians, in particular, Tutsi civilians, and constitute a serious attack on the human dignity of the Tutsi community as a whole'.[430]

[425] *Kupreškić*, Trial Judgement, para. 566; *Kordić and Čerkez*, Trial Judgement, paras 269–71; *Kvočka et al.*, Trial Judgement, para. 206; *Krnojelac*, Trial Judgement, para. 130; *Kayishema and Ruzindana*, Trial Judgement, para. 151; *Bagilishema*, Trial Judgement, para. 92; *Vasiljević*, Trial Judgement, para. 234; *Niyitegeka*, Trial Judgement, para. 460; *Galić*, Trial Judgement, para. 152; *Blagojević and Jokić*, Trial Judgement, para. 626; *Vasiljević*, Appeal Judgement, para. 165; *Kordić and Čerkez*, Appeal Judgement, para. 117; *Brima, Kamara and Kanu*, Trial Judgement, para. 698, and *Fofana and Kondewa*, Trial Judgement, para. 150.

[426] *Krnojelac*, Trial Judgement, para. 131.

[427] *Vasiljević*, Trial Judgement, para. 235; *Galić*, Trial Judgement, para. 153; *Blagojević and Jokić*, Trial Judgement, para. 627, and *Vasiljević*, Appeal Judgement, para. 165.

[428] *Kayishema and Ruzindana*, Trial Judgement, para. 153; *Krnojelac*, Trial Judgement, para. 132; *Galić*, Trial Judgement, para. 154; *Blagojević and Jokić*, Trial Judgement, para. 628, and *Fofana and Kondewa*, Trial Judgement, para. 152.

[429] *Kayishema and Ruzindana*, Trial Judgement, para. 153, and see *Muvunyi*, Trial Judgement, para. 529, and *Fofana and Kondewa*, Trial Judgement, para. 153.

[430] *Niyitegaka*, Trial Judgement, paras 462 and 465.

## The Rome Statute

The Elements of inhumane acts require that the perpetrator 'inflicted great suffering, or serious injury to body or to mental or physical health, by means of an inhumane act'.[431] The act must have been 'of a character similar to any other act referred to in article 7, paragraph 1, of the Statute' and the perpetrator 'was aware of the factual circumstances that established the character of the act'.[432] Therefore the Rome Statute takes the same two-stage approach as the ILC in order to circumscribe a potentially wide crime in two ways. First, the Elements restrict the *actus reus* of the offence to those acts similar in nature and gravity to other acts under Article 7(1).[433] Second, the Elements restrict the offence to those inhumane acts which result in a level of suffering or injury which should be interpreted as similar to that caused by the grave breach of wilfully causing great suffering or serious injury to body or health.[434]

The *mens rea* of this offence, applying the default mental element of Article 30, requires that the perpetrator intended to commit an inhumane act and intended or knew that in the usual course of events his or her actions would result in the infliction of great suffering or serious injury. Furthermore, the perpetrator must have been aware of the factual circumstances establishing the character of his or her act, but need not have made a conscious evaluation of the act as inhumane.

Ratner and Abrams suggest that inhumane acts would include 'medical experimentation, mutilations, severe beatings, food deprivation, sterilizations, violations of corpses, forced undressing, forced witnessing of atrocities against loved ones, and other egregious physical and mental assaults'.[435] However, Schabas questions whether acts condemned by the Rwanda tribunal such as forced nudity would still qualify as inhumane acts, given the restrictive language of the Rome Statute.[436] Equally, it is difficult to see how the violation of corpses could, of itself, amount to inhumane acts as defined by the Statute and Elements, although, as discussed above, if such acts were knowingly witnessed they could amount to inhumane acts with respect to the mental harm caused to the witnesses.[437]

[431] EOC, p. 124.

[432] *Ibid.*

[433] *Ibid.*, fn. 30, see discussion of the identical fn. 29 *supra*, p. 242.

[434] Lee (ed.), *ICC: Elements*, p. 108, and see discussion *supra*, pp. 41–4.

[435] S. Ratner and J. Abrams, *Accountability for Human Rights Atrocities*, n. 16 *supra*, p. 74.

[436] W. Schabas, *An Introduction to the International Criminal Court* (Cambridge: Cambridge University Press, 2001), p. 39.

[437] See discussion of *Kayishema and Ruzindana*, Trial Judgement, para. 153, and *Niyitegeka*, Trial Judgement, paras 462 and 465 *supra*, p. 24.

# 6

# Conclusion

This book has examined crimes against humanity and war crimes under the Rome Statute of the International Criminal Court (ICC). This concluding chapter commences by considering how this interpretation of crimes may be affected by national prosecutions of war crimes and crimes against humanity under the principle of complementarity. Next, consideration is given to the influence that reservations and interpretative declarations to the Conventions which form the basis of Article 8, or interpretative declarations to the Rome Statute, will have on the definition of crimes. Then, the question of whether some of the crimes are still insufficiently defined to enable a fair trial in accordance with the principle of legality is addressed.

This chapter also reviews the influence of human rights law upon the definition of crimes in the Rome Statute and questions whether human rights bodies may provide an effective alternative method of ending impunity for conduct described in Articles 7 and 8 rather than prosecutions before the ICC. The Rome Statute is praised for its approach to gender issues in the definition of crimes but criticised for failure to sufficiently address the issue of prohibited weapons. Finally, the particular problems of applying international humanitarian law in non-international armed conflicts and the extent to which Article 8(2)(e) of the Rome Statute addresses these concerns are discussed.

## Domestic prosecutions and the definition of crimes in the Rome Statute

The definitions of war crimes and crimes against humanity in the Rome Statute discussed in this book have already made an impact on national legislation worldwide, despite the fact that the ICC has only recently commenced prosecutions.[1]

[1] See generally, C. Kreß and F. Lattanzi (eds), *The Rome Statute and Domestic Legal Orders*, Vol. I: *General Aspects and Constitutional Issues* (Fagnono Alto: Editrice il Sirente, 2000), and D. Turns, 'Aspects of national implementation of the Rome Statute: the United Kingdom and selected

Since the Statute entered into force on 1 July 2002 States Parties have been obliged to investigate and prosecute not only grave breaches but also all the listed offences in the Rome Statute or they will risk action by the ICC.[2] Indeed, as Aldrich comments, 'the mere existence of the court should spur trials by national courts'.[3]

However, in certain circumstances, States alone will have jurisdiction over offences described in the Rome Statute. The *chapeau* to crimes against humanity in Article 7 ensures that only widespread or systematic incidences of this offence, with State or organisational involvement, will come within the jurisdiction of the ICC.[4] Furthermore, with respect to minor or isolated war crimes the ICC may be unable to act, as Article 8(1) establishes that the Court should deal with such offences '*in particular* when committed as part of a plan or policy or as part of a large-scale commission of such crimes'.[5] Whilst this restriction is not mandatory, it is submitted that when considered in conjunction with Article 17(1)(d), which allows the Court to find that a case is not of 'sufficient gravity' to justify further action, the ICC would be unlikely to find admissible a single or small number of war crimes unless they were of extreme gravity.[6]

Nevertheless, in such circumstances States Parties may still be obliged to take action under the grave breach system of the Geneva Conventions and Additional Protocol (AP) I.[7] Further responsibility is conferred on States under the principle of complementarity by which the Rome Statute concedes primacy to national jurisdictions even in the case of crimes serious enough to come within the jurisdiction of the ICC.[8] This, combined with the reluctance of States to relinquish their sovereignty in respect of criminal trials, makes it is very likely that more prosecutions will take place at a national level than at an international level even with respect to crimes serious enough to come within the jurisdiction of the ICC. Therefore, effective national implementation of the Rome Statute is of great importance in ensuring that consistent definitions of crimes are applied in the different national trials and before the ICC.

However, a review of national implementing legislation reveals that States are not simply enacting the definitions of crimes in the Rome Statute and Elements

other States', pp. 337–87 in D. McGoldrick, P. Rowe and E. Donnelly (eds), *The Permanent International Criminal Court: Legal and Policy Issues* (Oxford: Hart Publishing, 2004).

[2] Due to the principle of complementarity, Articles 1, 17 and 18, Rome Statute.

[3] G. Aldrich, 'The laws of war on land', AJIL, 94 (2000), 42–63, p. 55.

[4] See discussion *supra*, pp. 191–4 and 202–6.

[5] See discussion *supra*, pp. 16–17.

[6] Note that the reference to seriousness is repeated in the *chapeaux* to Article 8(2)(b), (c) and (e).

[7] See Articles 50/51/130/147 of the 1949 Geneva Conventions. See also para. 6 of the Preamble, Rome Statute, 'it is the duty of every State to exercise its criminal jurisdiction over those responsible for international crimes'.

[8] Articles 1, 17 and 18, Rome Statute, and see L. Yang, 'On the principle of complementarity in the Rome Statute of the International Criminal Court', Chinese J Int'l L, 4 (2005), 121–32.

of Crimes (EOC) without change.[9] For example, the definitions in the Canadian implementing legislation are extremely broad, essentially allowing prosecutions against any war crime or crime against humanity which 'at the time and in the place of its commission' constituted a crime 'according to customary international law', although to avoid confusion the Act confirms that the crimes set out in the Rome Statute are crimes according to customary international law.[10] The definitions of crimes in the German Code of Crimes against International Law are broadly similar to those in the Rome Statute, but extend national jurisdiction over several offences restricted to international armed conflict in the Rome Statute, to include those offences when committed in non-international armed conflicts.[11]

Differing definitions of international crimes in different States may cause conflicting case law in respect of the crimes in the Rome Statute. However, with regard to the issue of complementarity, the main difficulty for the ICC lies in the fact not that States may decide to prosecute a greater range of offences than those provided for in the Rome Statute[12] but that, owing to inadequate implementation, they may be unable to prosecute those crimes set out in the Rome Statute to the same extent as the ICC. This could occur, first, if the definition of an offence were drawn more narrowly than its equivalent in the Rome Statute. For example, the Australian ICC Act defines the crimes by way of detailed elements which differ somewhat from the EOC adopted by the Assembly of States Parties.[13] Under this Act the crime against humanity of persecution requires that the perpetrator severely deprived one or more person of specifically listed rights guaranteed by the International Covenant of Civil and Political Rights (ICCPR).[14] The EOC adopted by the Assembly of States Parties, in contrast, contain a far more open-ended definition in which deprivation of rights not mentioned in the ICCPR could still feasibly amount to the offence of persecution.[15]

[9] See International Criminal Court Act, 2001 (England, Wales and Northern Ireland), International Criminal Court (Consequential Amendments) Act, 2002, No. 42 (Australia), Crimes against Humanity and War Crimes Act, 2000, C.24 (Canada), and Act to Introduce the Code of Crimes against International Law, 2002 (Germany), available on the National Implementation database on the International Committee of the Red Cross website at: <http://www.icrc.org/ihl-nat> and on the Legal Tools database on the ICC website at: <http://www.icc-cpi.int/legaltools/>.

[10] Crimes against Humanity and War Crimes Act, 2000, C.24, Articles 4(3–4) and 6(3–4), and see D. Turns, 'Aspects of national implementation of the Rome Statute', n. 1 *supra*, pp. 358–61.

[11] For example, see Section 12 on prohibited means of warfare, 2002 Act to Introduce the Code of Crimes against International Law, and D. Turns, 'Aspects of national implementation of the Rome Statute', n. 1 *supra*, pp. 378–86.

[12] See Article 10, Rome Statute.

[13] International Criminal Court (Consequential Amendments) Act, 2002, No. 42, Schedule 1: Amendment of the Criminal Code Act 1995, subdivisions B–G, and see G. Boas, 'An overview of implementation by Australia of the Statute of the International Criminal Court', J Int'l Crim Just, 2 (2004), 179–90.

[14] International Criminal Court (Consequential Amendments) Act, 2002, No. 42, Schedule 1: Amendment of the Criminal Code Act 1995, subdivision C, para. 268.20.

[15] Elements of Crimes, Assembly of States Parties to the Rome Statute of the ICC, Official Records, First Session, ICC-ASP/1/3, 3–10 September 2002 (hereinafter: EOC), pp. 108–55, p. 122.

Second, failure to enact an equivalent of Article 25 on individual criminal responsibility, or Article 28 on command and superior responsibility, could result in inability on the part of a State to prosecute those who attempt to commit or assist in the commission of war crimes or crimes against humanity, or inability to prosecute commanders who fail to repress such crimes. For example, the Finnish ICC Crimes Act completely fails to mention command responsibility and, at present, provision is not made for command responsibility in the Norwegian penal code.[16] Third, if defences were more widely drawn in the national legislation than the Rome Statute, there would be the possibility of an accused escaping liability for an offence for which he or she would have been liable had they been tried before the ICC.[17] Finally, the different rules and procedures of evidence in different States could result in confessions being excluded or hearsay evidence disallowed when it might have been admissible before the ICC.

These problems of national implementation raise the question of whether, in circumstances such as those discussed above, the ICC could either find that a State Party was in such circumstances unwilling or genuinely unable to carry out the investigation or prosecution, or retry a person who had been acquitted by a national court under such circumstances.[18] It is practically unthinkable that the ICC would retry a person who had been acquitted by a national court solely because of evidence excluded owing to different rules of procedure and evidence or because of additional defences available under national law, provided that the prosecution was genuine and conducted with due diligence within a working judicial system. The ICC could retry a person for crimes arising from the same conduct in such circumstances only if the State concerned was attempting to shield the person from criminal responsibility or conducted a trial which was not independent or impartial and was inconsistent with an intent to bring the accused to justice.[19]

The situation if the State concerned had refused to prosecute because of provisions of national law, such as the absence of a law of command responsibility, is more complex. It would be difficult to find that the State was 'unwilling' to prosecute if an independent and impartial investigation had concluded that the

[16] See Human Rights Watch, 'Table 2, Implementation of the Rome Statute, Implementation Strategies adopted by: Norway, Finland, Estonia, the Netherlands and Germany', available at: <http://www.hrw.org/campaigns/icc/implementation.htm>, p. 6.

[17] The defence may also, of course, be drawn more narrowly in national law. For example, English law disallows the defence of duress on a charge of murder or attempted murder, see *R. v. Howe* [1987] 1 AC, 417, and *R. v. Gotts* [1992] 2 WLR, 284, although the defence may be available on such a charge before the ICC under Article 31(1)(d), Rome Statute. See R. Cryer, 'Implementation of the International Criminal Court Statute in England and Wales', ICLQ, 51 (2002), 733–43, p. 740.

[18] Article 17, Rome Statute, and see J. Terracino, 'National implementation of ICC crimes: impact on national jurisdictions and the ICC', J Int'l Crim Just, 5 (2007), 421–40.

[19] Article 20, Rome Statute. It is submitted that the ICC would not find that there was an intention to shield the accused simply because the application of that State's normal legal process resulted in an acquittal which would not have occurred if the trial had taken place before the ICC.

national laws simply did not allow such a prosecution.[20] The situation would be closer to one of 'inability', but this would be for the reason that such conduct was not criminalised under national law rather than because of the collapse of the State's judicial system. In determining whether a State is unable to carry out a prosecution, under Article 17(3) the ICC must consider whether 'due to a total or substantial collapse or unavailability of its national judicial system the State is unable to obtain the accused or the necessary evidence and testimony or otherwise unable to carry out its proceedings'.

The wording of this section could be interpreted as indicating that the ICC was intended to determine a case admissible only when the 'inability' of States Parties arose from the collapse of a national judicial system, rather than when the basis of the inability of a State Party with a working judicial system arose owing to inadequate implementation of the Rome Statute. Nevertheless, such an interpretation would allow States Parties to the Rome Statute to shield some or all of those accused of war crimes or crimes against humanity, simply by failing to legislate in order to criminalise such conduct. Such an interpretation would clearly be contrary to the object and purpose of the Rome Statute.[21]

Therefore, although the ICC must consider whether the judicial system of a country has collapsed or is unavailable, Article 17(3) does not state that this must be the Court's *only* consideration. It is submitted that the ICC may also take into account the inability of a State to prosecute as a result of insufficient provisions in national criminal law when making an admissibility decision.[22]

Nevertheless, it seems likely that most prosecutions of individuals for war crimes and crimes against humanity will take place in national jurisdictions. This will undoubtedly lead to some inconsistencies as different States interpret crimes in accordance with their national legislation and past jurisprudence. For example, the French cases of *Barbie* and *Touvier*, in their interpretation of crimes against humanity, included the unnecessary requirement that 'the acts charged were performed in a systematic manner in the name of a State practising by those means a policy of ideological supremacy' as a result of the background in which crimes against humanity took place in France during the Second World War.[23]

The approach of the UK International Criminal Court Act offers a constructive method of reducing the likelihood of inconsistencies between the definitions

[20] But see discussion of this in J. Gurulé, 'United States opposition to the 1998 Rome Statute establishing an International Criminal Court: is the Court's jurisdiction truly complementary to national criminal jurisdictions?', Cornell Int'l LJ, 35 (2001–02), 1–45, pp. 23–30.

[21] Paragraph 4 of the preamble to the Rome Statute affirms that 'the most serious crimes of concern to the international community as a whole must not go unpunished' and, in para. 5, determines 'to put an end to impunity for the perpetrators of these crimes'. See Article 31(1) and (2), 1969 Vienna Convention on the Law of Treaties.

[22] See also comments of C. Stahn, 'Complementarity, amnesties and alternative forms of justice: some interpretative guidelines for the International Criminal Court', J Int'l Crim Just, 3 (2005), 695–720.

[23] *Barbie*, 100 ILR, 330, p. 336, and *Touvier*, 100 ILR, 337, p. 352, discussed *supra*, p. 250.

of war crimes and crimes against humanity applied by UK courts and those applied by the ICC.[24] Section 50 of the Act allows the Court to 'take into account' the EOC adopted under Article 9 of the Rome Statute, 'any relevant judgement or decision of the ICC' and 'any other relevant international jurisprudence'.[25] Whilst the expression 'take into account' does not make ICC decisions binding upon national courts, in the absence of contradictory precedents it is highly likely that ICC jurisprudence would be applied by the UK courts. It is submitted that similar provisions should be enacted by all States Parties to the Rome Statute in order to encourage consistency of interpretations.

## The effect of reservations and interpretative declarations on the definition of crimes

Another issue which could influence national interpretation of crimes is reservations and interpretative declarations to the Geneva Conventions and Additional Protocols upon which many of the war crimes in the Rome Statute are based.[26] However, a more interesting question is the extent to which such reservations and declarations should have an effect upon the interpretation of crimes by the International Criminal Court.

According to Article 30 of the Vienna Convention on the Law of Treaties, if two treaties cover the same subject matter, with respect to States Parties to both treaties, 'the earlier treaty applies only to the extent that its provisions are compatible with those of the later treaty'.[27] Therefore, in the case of inconsistencies between the duty to prosecute under the grave breach system of the Geneva Conventions and Additional Protocols and a broader duty to prosecute under the Rome Statute, the Rome Statute would take precedence with respect to States Parties to both. This article also implies that States Parties to the Rome Statute could not rely upon a reservation to a similar provision in the Geneva Conventions or Protocols before the ICC, as the Rome Statute does not permit reservations.[28]

[24] International Criminal Court Act, 2001 (England, Wales and Northern Ireland). The International Criminal Court (Scotland) Act, 2001, in Article 9(2) and (4), contains a similar provision for Scottish courts. For a critical analysis of the UK approach see D. Turns, 'Aspects of national implementation of the Rome Statute', n. 1 *supra*, pp. 343–53.

[25] The latter would presumably allow the Court to take into account ICTY or ICTR jurisprudence.

[26] See, in particular, reservations and interpretative declarations to AP I, available at: <http://www.icrc.org>.

[27] Article 30, 1969 Vienna Convention on the Law of Treaties.

[28] Article 120, Rome Statute. The Geneva Conventions and Additional Protocols are silent on the issue of reservations and therefore under customary law, codified by Article 19 of the Vienna Convention on the Law of Treaties, States parties could make reservations compatible 'with the object and purpose of the treaty'.

Nevertheless, an interpretative declaration, or even in some cases a reservation,[29] can change the interpretation of a particular provision in customary international law if widely held. Indeed, under Article 31 of the Vienna Convention on the Law of Treaties, 'any subsequent practice in the application of the treaty which establishes the agreement of the parties regarding its interpretation' should be taken into account when interpreting treaty provisions.[30] Therefore, reference has been made to various reservations and interpretative declarations when discussing the interpretation of crimes in the previous chapters.[31] In this respect, the UK declaration upon ratification of the Rome Statute drew attention to its statements made upon ratification of AP I as evidence of customary international law to be taken into account by the ICC.[32]

A related question is the extent to which the ICC should take into account interpretative declarations to the Rome Statute. Interpretative declarations are not mentioned in Article 21 on law to be applied by the Court. Therefore, such declarations are relevant to the definitions of crimes only in so much as they provide evidence of the principles and rules of international law, or are applied by the Court as general principles of law derived from national legal systems, or as national laws of States that would normally exercise jurisdiction over the crime, 'provided that those principles are not inconsistent' with the Rome Statute or 'with international law and internationally recognized norms and standards'.[33]

One of the most contentious statements made upon ratification of the Rome Statute has been the French declaration, discussed in Chapter 3 with respect to Article 8(2)(b)(iv), that the provisions of Article 8 'relate solely to conventional weapons and can neither regulate not prohibit the possible use of nuclear weapons'.[34] It is submitted that if this were an interpretative declaration it would be considered under Article 21 as discussed above. In deciding whether this reflected customary international law the ICC could have regard, *inter alia*, to the New Zealand declaration that 'it would be inconsistent with principles of international humanitarian law to purport to limit the scope of article 8 . . . to events that involve conventional weapons only'.[35]

However, the French 'interpretative declaration' could be interpreted as purporting to 'exclude or to modify the legal effect of certain provisions of the treaty'

[29] As in the case of reservations with respect to second use of gas under the 1925 Gas Protocol, which arguably may create a defence under customary international law to a breach of Article 8(2)(b)(xviii) in such circumstances under Articles 31(3) and 21(1), Rome Statute.

[30] Article 31(3), 1969 Vienna Convention on the Law of Treaties.

[31] See *supra*, pp. 63 and 131.

[32] Declaration of the UK, made upon ratification of the Rome Statute on 4 October 2001, available at <http://www.icrc.org>. The ICC would not necessarily accept such a claim.

[33] Article 21(1)(b) and (c), Rome Statute.

[34] See *supra*, p. 88.

[35] New Zealand, declaration upon ratification of the Rome Statute on 7 September 2000, and see Swedish statement upon ratification of the Rome Statute on 28 June 2001, available at: <http://www.icrc.org>.

and so could be termed a reservation.[36] This approach of looking behind the label given by the State concerned was taken by the European Court of Human Rights in the case of *Belilos v. Switzerland*, which stated that '[i]n order to establish the legal character of such a declaration, one must look behind the title given to it and seek to determine the substantive content'.[37] Nevertheless, given that reservations are not permitted to the Rome Statute, would a classification of the French 'declaration' as being in effect a reservation invalidate France's ratification of the Rome Statute?

It is submitted that if this question were to arise before the ICC the Court should take the same approach as the European Court of Human Rights and the Human Rights Committee with respect to States Parties to the European Convention on Human Rights (ECHR) and ICCPR. The European Court in the case of *Belilos v. Switzerland*, having held that the Swiss declaration in effect amounted to an invalid reservation, proceeded to hold Switzerland bound by the ECHR without the benefit of the reservation, as 'it is beyond doubt that Switzerland is, and regards itself as, bound by the Convention irrespective of the validity of the declaration'.[38] The Human Rights Committee stated in General Comment 24 that '[t]he normal consequence of an unacceptable reservation is . . . [that] such a reservation will generally be severable, in the sense that the Covenant will be operative for the reserving party without benefit of the reservation'.[39] Therefore, unless it was absolutely clear that the invalid 'declaration', which in fact amounted to a reservation, constituted an essential condition of the State's consent to be bound, it should be nullified and the State should remain a party to the Rome Statute without the benefit of the 'declaration' in question.[40]

## Offences insufficiently defined?

A serious criticism which may be levelled at the Rome Statute is that the offences, or some of them, are not sufficiently well defined to enable a fair trial in accordance with the principle of legality. It is certainly true that most national

[36] Article 2(d), 1969 Vienna Convention on the Law of Treaties.

[37] *Belilos v. Switzerland*, ECHR Judgement (Merits and Just Satisfaction), 29 April 1988, Application No. 00010328/83, para. 49, and see R. Edwards, Jr, 'Reservations to treaties', Mich J Int'l L, 10 (1989), 362–405, pp. 368–72.

[38] *Belilos v. Switzerland*, ECHR Judgement (Merits and Just Satisfaction), 29 April 1988, Application No. 00010328/83, para. 60, and see *Loizidou v. Turkey*, ECHR Judgement (Preliminary Objections), 23 March 1995, Application No. 00015318/89, paras 96–8.

[39] Human Rights Committee (HRC) General Comment 24, UN Doc. CCPR/C/21/Rev.1/Add.6 (1994), para. 18.

[40] This is still controversial, see discussion in R. Goodman, 'Human rights treaties, invalid reservations, and State consent', AJIL, 96 (2002), 531–60, and M. Fitzmaurice, 'On the protection of human rights, the Rome Statute and reservations to multilateral treaties', SYBIL, 10 (2006), 133–73, especially pp. 146–70.

jurisdictions define offences with more clarity and precision than the vague expressions sometimes used in Articles 7 and 8.[41] Indeed, it was this concern that led to the US suggestion for the inclusion of Elements of Crimes, which have been drafted by the Preparatory Commission and adopted by the Assembly of States Parties, to assist the Court in the interpretation and application of the definitions of offences.[42]

However, the EOC fail to deal adequately with certain issues. A source of uncertainty is the standard of *mens rea* required for each crime. Whilst Article 30 provides a default mental element which applies, '[u]nless otherwise provided', it is not always clear whether the Statute, the Elements or customary international law displace this.[43] Furthermore, some of the expressions used in the Statute and EOC such as 'wilful' or 'wantonly', which appear to replace the default mental element, are not clear in their meaning. The question of *mens rea* for certain offences, such as wilful killing, murder contrary to Common Article 3 and murder as a crime against humanity, are particularly difficult to evaluate, given the conflicting decisions of the International Criminal Tribunal for the former Yugoslavia (ICTY) and International Criminal Tribunal for Rwanda (ICTR).[44]

With respect to some crimes the EOC can be criticised for doing little more than repeating the wording of the offence in the Statute, with inadequate or no amplification. A notable example of inadequate amplification is the crime of transfer, by the Occupying Power, of all or parts of its own civilian population into the territory it occupies.[45] Although, in this case, a vague definition was probably adopted purposely in order to avoid antagonising the State of Israel, which is sensitive to the accusation that it is breaching this provision in the West Bank and Gaza, such political considerations will not ease the future task of the ICC in interpreting the offence.

The EOC have avoided attempting to define the potentially broad and rather vague offence of 'violence to life and person', from Common Article 3 by providing Elements only to the crimes of murder, mutilation, cruel treatment and torture, which are listed as specific types of such violence.[46] Given the refusal of the ICTY Trial Chamber in *Vasiljević* to hold the accused guilty of this crime '[i]n the absence of any clear indication in the practice of states as to what the definition of the offence . . . may be under customary law',[47] it is unfortunate that

[41] See J. Murphy, 'The quivering Gulliver: US views on a permanent international criminal court', Int Law, 34 (2000), 45–64, p. 54, and see the Australian approach to implementing the Rome Statute, discussed *supra*, para. 6.1.

[42] See M. Politi, 'Elements of crimes', pp. 443–73 in A. Cassese, P. Gaeta and J. Jones (eds), *The Rome Statute of the International Criminal Court: A Commentary* (Oxford: Oxford University Press, 2002), pp. 445–6; W. Schabas, *An Introduction to the International Criminal Court* (Cambridge: Cambridge University Press, 2001), p. 29, and Article 9(1), Rome Statute.

[43] See discussion *supra*, p. 5.

[44] Discussed *supra*, pp. 26–7, 177 and 207.

[45] See Article 8(2)(b)(viii), Rome Statute, discussed *supra*, pp. 107–8.

[46] See Article 8(2)(c)(i), Rome Statute, discussed *supra*, p. 177.

[47] *Vasiljević*, Trial Judgement, para. 203.

the Preparatory Commission chose not to clarify the elements of 'violence to life and person'.

Two crimes against humanity which may be singled out as worryingly vague are persecution on the basis of 'other grounds that are universally recognized as impermissible under international law' and '[o]ther inhumane acts'.[48] However, with respect to the former, universal recognition is a very high threshold and so could be utilised only to reflect a basis of discrimination very widely accepted as customary international law.[49] Additionally, the existence of catch-all provisions such as '[o]ther inhumane acts' is arguably necessary, given that it is impossible to imagine and proscribe in detail every atrocity of which an evil mind could conceive. Therefore, provided that such crimes are limited by a level of intentional injury or suffering which would, in any case, offend against national laws, they are undeniably a necessary part of the ICC's weaponry.[50]

Despite the questions which remain with respect to the definitions of crimes, it must be remembered that the principle of legality is enshrined as a general principle of criminal law under Article 22 of the Rome Statute. This states that '[t]he definition of a crime shall be strictly construed and shall not be extended by analogy. In case of ambiguity, the definition shall be interpreted in favour of the person being investigated, prosecuted or convicted.'

## The Rome Statute and human rights law

The analysis of war crimes and crimes against humanity in the Rome Statute has revealed the interaction between international humanitarian law and human rights law. The convergence between these two fields can be seen in the subject matter of the ICC's jurisdiction, discussed in the preceding chapters.[51] For example, the war crime and crime against humanity of torture has been greatly influenced by the Torture Convention. Furthermore, the case law relied on by the ICTY with respect to this crime includes decisions of human rights bodies such as the Human Rights Committee, the ECHR and the Inter-American Commission of Human Rights.[52] Similarly, the definition of the grave breach of inhuman treatment or the crime against humanity of other inhumane acts has

[48] Article 7(1)(h) and (k), Rome Statute, and see the similarly vague war crimes in Article 8(2)(a)(ii) and (c)(i).

[49] See discussion *supra*, p. 233.

[50] See discussion *supra*, p. 245.

[51] On convergence between human rights and international humanitarian law see T. Meron, 'The humanization of humanitarian law', AJIL, 94 (2000), 239–78; A. Benison, 'War crimes: a human rights approach to a humanitarian law problem at the International Criminal Court', Geo LJ, 88 (1999), 141–75, pp. 155–8; H. Espiell, 'Humanitarian law and human rights', pp. 345–59 in J. Symonides (ed.), *Human Rights: Concepts and Standards* (Aldershot: Dartmouth and Paris: UNESCO, 2000), pp. 353–56, and C. Byron, 'A blurring of the boundaries: the application of international humanitarian law by human rights bodies', Va JIL, 47 (2007), 839–96.

[52] Articles 8(2)(a)(ii) and 7(1)(f), Rome Statute, see discussion *supra*, pp. 31–6 and 223–4.

been equally affected by human rights Conventions and jurisprudence.[53] The same influence can also be seen in the war crimes of sentencing or execution without due process and conscripting or enlisting children under the age of fifteen.[54]

Moreover, pursuant to Article 21 of the Rome Statute on applicable law, human rights law is directly relevant to the definitions of war crimes and crimes against humanity, as the interpretation and application of the Statute, the EOC and other sources of law applied by the ICC must be 'consistent with internationally recognized human rights'.[55] Article 21(3) also sets out the principle that no adverse distinction based on 'gender . . . age, race, colour, language, religion or belief, political or other opinion, national, ethnic or social origin, wealth, birth or other status' must affect the interpretation or application of the law.

This incorporation of human rights principles into the interpretation of crimes in the Rome Statute demonstrates recognition that human rights instruments and international humanitarian law 'share a common nucleus of non-derogable rights and a common purpose of protecting human life and dignity'.[56] It further leads to the realisation that the two systems are not mutually exclusive and can be applied simultaneously.[57] Therefore, victims of gross breaches of human rights, whether the breaches amount to war crimes or crimes against humanity, can potentially apply to human rights bodies for relief as an alternative to prosecutions before the ICC. Indeed, in cases of isolated war crimes or offences which fail to reach the threshold required for crimes against humanity, if national authorities refuse to investigate and prosecute, an application to a human rights body may be the only way for victims to achieve some form of redress.[58]

In this respect, human rights bodies have already shown themselves capable of tackling breaches of human rights in armed conflicts. The Inter-American Commission of Human Rights found itself competent to apply international humanitarian law in the *Abella* case, stating, *inter alia*, that in order to resolve violations of the right to life in an armed conflict, it is necessary to 'look to and apply definitional standards and relevant rules of humanitarian law' as authoritative guidance on whether a deprivation of life was arbitrary.[59] The Human Rights

[53] Articles 8(2)(a)(ii) and 7(1)(k), Rome Statute, see discussion *supra*, pp. 36–7 and 243–4.

[54] Articles 8(2)(c)(iv) and 8(2)(b)(xxvi), Rome Statute, see discussion *supra*, pp. 178–9 and 165–7.

[55] See R. Lehr-Lehnardt, 'One small step for women: female-friendly provisions in the Rome Statute of the International Criminal Court', BYUJ Pub L, 16 (2002), 317–54, p. 341.

[56] *Abella v. United States* (1997), Inter-American Commission of Human Rights [IA Com HR] Case 11.137, Report No. 55/97, para. 158.

[57] C. Sepulveda, 'Interrelationships in the implementation and enforcement of international humanitarian law and human rights law', Am ULR, 33 (1983), 117–24, p. 118.

[58] See C. Byron, 'A blurring of the boundaries', n. 51 *supra*, pp. 891–2.

[59] *Abella v. United States* (1997), IA Com HR, Case 11.137, Report No. 55/97, para. 161, but see criticism of this decision in L. Zegveld, 'The Inter-American Commission on Human Rights and international humanitarian law: a comment on the Tablada case', IRRC, 324 (1998), 505–11. See also *Legality of the Threat or Use of Nuclear Weapons*, Advisory Opinion, ICJ Rep. (1996), 226, para. 25.

Committee has also indicated that it will consider a State's duties under international humanitarian law in order to decide whether a derogation from the ICCPR is properly made and has confirmed that States Parties 'may in no circumstances invoke article 4 of the Covenant [on derogations] as justification for acting in violation of humanitarian law'.[60]

Furthermore, human rights bodies have shown that the duty of States Parties to ensure rights 'may imply an affirmative duty to prosecute violators'.[61] Therefore, when the subject matter of the application breaches the provisions of the relevant human rights Convention, applications to human rights bodies may result in domestic prosecutions for war crimes or crimes against humanity. This obligation to investigate and prosecute has been referred to by the Human Rights Committee in *Muteba v. Zaire*,[62] a case concerning torture, and by the Inter-American Court of Human Rights in the *Castillo Páez* case, which concerned forced disappearances.[63]

Whilst human rights law may often provide an alternative or complementary route of redress for victims of violations contained within the Rome Statute, there are problems with this approach. First, not only must the State concerned be a party to the human rights Convention in question, but either the Convention must automatically allow individual applications from victims complaining of abuse of their rights[64] or the State concerned must have specifically accepted the individual application procedure.[65] Second, human rights bodies may require that the victim complains within a certain time limit of the alleged abuse of human rights,[66] whereas the Rome Statute does not have any such limitations upon the prosecution of crimes committed after the entry into force of the Statute for the State concerned.[67]

Third, human rights bodies do not necessarily have jurisdiction over the actions of States Parties committed on the territory of other States during an international

[60] HRC General Comment 29, UN Doc. CCPR/C/21/Rev.1/Add.11 (2001), paras 10–11.

[61] G. Mugwanya, 'Expunging the ghost of impunity for severe and gross violations of human rights and the Commission of *Delicti jus gentium*: a case for the domestication of international criminal law and the establishment of a strong permanent international criminal court', Mich SU-Detroit Col L JIL, 8 (1999), 701–79, p. 748.

[62] *Mutaba v. Zaire* (124/1982), HRC Report, UNOR, GA Twenty-second Session, Supplement No. 40 (1984), para. 13, and see also *Muiyo v. Zaire* (194/1985), HRC Decision, UN Doc. CCPR/C/OP/2 (1990), 219, para. 11, and *Chongwe v. Zambia* (821/1998), HRC Decision, UN Doc. CCPR/C/70/D/821/1998, para. 7.

[63] *Castillo Páez* case, Inter-American Court of Human Rights [IACHR] Judgement, 3 November 1997, No. 34 (1997), para. 90, and see also *Velasquez Rodriguez* case, IACHR Judgement, 29 July 1988, No. 4 (1988), 28 ILM (1989) 291, para. 174.

[64] For example, see Article 34, ECHR.

[65] For example see Article 1, First Optional Protocol, ICCPR, and Article 22, Convention against Torture.

[66] For example, under Article 35(1), an applicant under the ECHR must apply within six months of exhausting domestic remedies for the alleged violation of human rights.

[67] See also the 1968 Convention on the Non-applicability of Statutory Limitations to War Crimes and Crimes against Humanity.

armed conflict. The ECHR case of *Banković v. Belgium* demonstrates the limits of jurisdiction in such cases.[68] The applicants (citizens of the Federal Republic of Yugoslavia, FRY) were relatives of those killed or were themselves injured in the NATO bombing of a television station during the Kosovo conflict. The Court found that 'recognition of the exercise of extraterritorial jurisdiction by a Contracting State is exceptional' and that in ECHR case law it had been restricted to situations 'when the respondent State, through the effective control of the relevant territory and its inhabitants abroad as a consequence of military occupation or through the consent, invitation or acquiescence of the Government of that territory, exercises all or some of the public powers normally to be exercised by that Government'.[69] It was not persuaded by the argument that in bombing the television station the NATO States exercised limited jurisdiction over FRY (a non-party to the ECHR) for the purposes of applying human rights,[70] and commented that the ECHR was not 'designed to be applied throughout the world, even in respect of the conduct of Contracting States'.[71]

Finally, even if the alleged incident takes place entirely within the territory of a State Party to a human rights convention, which has accepted the individual applications procedure, actions taken by rebels in a non-international armed conflict cannot in any case be examined, as human rights law 'does not extend to the conduct of private actors which is not imputable to the State'.[72] Peterson comments that '[t]his inherent unfairness might suggest a lack of legitimacy in the decisions of these human rights bodies' when they are 'left with the capacity to govern only one side of an armed conflict'.[73]

## Gender issues

The prohibition of adverse distinction on grounds of gender in Article 21(3)[74] represents the efforts of feminist groups which lobbied for the inclusion of

[68] *Banković v. Belgium*, ECHR Judgement (Admissibility), 12 December 2001, Application No. 52207/99, 41 ILM (2002), 517.

[69] *Ibid.*, para. 71. See the ECHR decisions in *Loizidou v. Turkey*, ECHR Judgement (Preliminary Objections), 23 March 1995, Application No. 00015318/89, para. 62, and *Cyprus v. Turkey*, ECHR Judgement (Merits), 10 May 2001, Application No. 00025781/94, paras 77–8.

[70] *Banković v. Belgium*, ECHR Judgement (Admissibility), 12 December 2001, Application No. 52207/99, 41 ILM (2002), 517, paras 74–5.

[71] *Ibid.*, para. 80. For further analysis of this case see C. Cerna *et al.*, 'Bombing for peace: collateral damage and human rights', ASIL Proceedings, 96 (2002), 95–108, and T. Schiers, 'European Court of Human Rights declares application against NATO member states inadmissible', Int'l Enforcement L Rep, 18 (2002), 154–6. See also *Issa v. Turkey*, ECHR Judgement (Merits), 16 November 2004, Application No. 31821/96, para. 589, and discussion of extraterritorial jurisdiction of the ECHR in C. Byron, 'A blurring of the boundaries', n. 51 *supra*, pp. 869–78.

[72] *Abella v. United States* (1997), IA Com HR, Case 11.137, Report No. 55/97, para. 175.

[73] A. Peterson, 'Order out of chaos: domestic enforcement of the law of internal armed conflict', Milit LR, 171 (2002), 1–90, p. 58, and C. Byron, 'A blurring of the boundaries', n. 51 *supra*, pp. 883–4.

[74] *Supra*, p. 256.

gender issues in the International Criminal Court (ICC), particularly with respect to the definition of crimes.[75] The incorporation of the offences of rape, sexual slavery, enforced prostitution, forced pregnancy, enforced sterilisation and sexual violence was a victory for groups, such as the Women's Caucus for Gender Justice, who were determined to ensure the responsiveness of the ICC to 'gender justice'.[76] The explicit inclusion of these offences as war crimes in both international and non-international armed conflicts, as well as within crimes against humanity, is a vast improvement over the ICTY Statute, which mentioned rape only as a crime against humanity,[77] and over the Nuremberg and Tokyo Charters, which ignored the subject altogether.[78]

The gender issue which caused the most controversy was forced pregnancy, which was included in the Rome Statute as a war crime and a crime against humanity.[79] Indeed, forced pregnancy proved difficult to define at the Rome Conference, owing to fears by delegates that it could be construed as guaranteeing women the right to an abortion.[80] Therefore the definition of this crime in Article 7(2)(f) explicitly states that the definition 'shall not in any way be interpreted as affecting national laws relating to pregnancy'. Additionally, the definition of forced pregnancy requires proof of intention to affect 'the ethnic composition of any population' or, alternatively, to carry out 'other grave violations of international law'. It is to be hoped that the alternative form of intention provides sufficient flexibility for this crime to remain relevant in conflicts which are not based on ethnic grounds.

Gender issues were also addressed specifically within crimes against humanity. First, enslavement was defined under Article 7(2)(c) as including the exercise of the powers of the rights of ownership 'in the course of trafficking in persons, in particular women and children'.[81] This fairly broad definition ensures that contemporary problems of trafficking, which affect predominantly women and children, are addressed within this offence. Second, gender was included as a basis of persecution, raising concerns among some delegates at the Rome Conference that such a ground would criminalise discrimination against homosexuals.[82] However, whilst the definition of gender in Article 7(3) of the Rome Statute is broad enough to cover discrimination related to socially constructed

[75] See comments on Article 21(3) by B. Bedont, 'Gender-specific provisions in the Statute of the ICC', pp. 183–210 in F. Lattanzi and W. Schabas (eds), *Essays on the Rome Statute of the ICC*, Vol. I (Naples: Editorale Scientifica, 1999), p. 185.

[76] See Women's Caucus of Gender Justice, now Women's Initiatives for Gender Justice, website available at: <http://www.iccwomen.org/>, and see discussion *supra*, pp. 143–56.

[77] Article 5(g), 1993 ICTY Statute, although Article 4(e), 1994 ICTR Statute, also included jurisdiction over rape, enforced prostitution and indecent assault as war crimes in non-international armed conflicts.

[78] See discussion *supra*, pp. 144–5.

[79] Discussed *supra*, pp. 153–4.

[80] *Ibid.*

[81] Article 7(1)(c) and (2)(c), Rome Statute, see discussion *supra*, pp. 217–18.

[82] Discussed *supra*, pp. 232–3.

roles,[83] it is unclear whether this would include discrimination on the basis of homosexuality as persecution.

Nevertheless, the impact of gender concerns upon the definitions of crimes against humanity and war crimes goes far beyond these specific crimes. Mainly owing to the jurisprudence of the ICTY, it must be acknowledged that grave breaches, such as torture or wilfully causing great suffering, may be committed through rape or sexual violence.[84] Additionally, the jurisprudence of the ICTY also shows that other war crimes, such as outrages upon personal dignity, may be committed through sexual violence.[85] Therefore the definitions of war crimes and crimes against humanity in the Rome Statute address gender concerns, both explicitly and implicitly, in a manner more comprehensive than previous treaties.

## Prohibited weapons

One of the most disappointing exclusions from the jurisdiction of the ICC was in respect of weapons of mass destruction.[86] Although agreement was reached on jurisdiction over the use of poisoned weapons, asphyxiating or poisonous gases or expanding bullets in international armed conflicts,[87] even this limited jurisdiction was not extended to the use of such weapons in non-international armed conflicts. Furthermore, on the contentious issue of weapons of mass destruction, agreement was rendered more difficult by the refusal of the nuclear weapon States to contemplate a proscription on their use.[88] The perceived inequity of a Statute silent with respect to nuclear weapons, whilst outlawing 'poor man's weapons of mass destruction' such as biological and chemical weapons, resulted in a Statute which prohibited neither.[89]

Nevertheless, it is arguable that, in international armed conflicts, the use of most chemical weapons would in any case be contrary to Article 8(2)(b)(xviii), which forbids the employment of 'asphyxiating, poisonous or other gases, and all analogous liquids, materials or devices'.[90] Alternatively, use of weapons of

[83] *Ibid.*

[84] Discussed *supra*, pp. 35–6 and 42–3.

[85] Discussed *supra*, pp. 140–2.

[86] See comments of E. Kalivretakis, 'Are nuclear weapons above the law? A look at the International Criminal Court and the prohibited weapons category', Emory Int'l L Rev, 15 (2001), 683–732, pp. 686–8, and discussion of 8(2)(b)(xx), Rome Statute, *supra*, pp. 138–9.

[87] Article 8(2)(b)(xvii), (xviii) and (xix), Rome Statute, discussed *supra*, pp. 130–5.

[88] E. Kalivretakis, 'Are nuclear weapons above the law?', n. 86 *supra*, p. 703. Note that even the International Court did not hold that the use of nuclear weapons would be illegal in all circumstances, *Legality of the Threat or Use of Nuclear Weapons*, Advisory Opinion, ICJ Rep. (1996) 226, decision, para. E.

[89] E. Kalivretakis, 'Are nuclear weapons above the law?', n. 86 *supra*, p. 703.

[90] See discussion *supra*, p. 133.

mass destruction during an international armed conflict could be judged under Article 8(2)(b)(iv) as causing excessive incidental loss of life or injury to civilians or widespread, long-term and severe damage to the natural environment.[91] Additionally, if such weapons were used at any time as part of a widespread or systematic attack upon civilians, irrespective of the type or existence of conflict, their employment could amount to crimes against humanity.[92]

Despite the possibility of adding new prohibited weapons in an annex to the Statute under Article 8(2)(b)(xx), Cassese is of the opinion that the necessary agreement to add new weapons will never be reached.[93] Given the political problems surrounding the prohibition of nuclear weapons and other weapons of mass destruction this is an understandable conclusion. However, a qualified jurisdiction over the use of weapons of mass destruction could provide a way to deal with the problem.[94] For example, ICC jurisdiction over the first use of nuclear, biological or chemical weapons (to the extent that they are not already prohibited under Article 8(2)(b)(xviii)) would be an improvement over the present situation and would counter the resistance of the nuclear weapon States, which defend the possession of such weapons on the basis of their deterrent value. Second use of such weapons should still be considered as a potential breach of Article 8(2)(b)(iv) or as a crime against humanity.

## Offences committed in non-international armed conflicts

An important achievement of the Rome Statute is the inclusion of jurisdiction over offences committed in non-international armed conflicts. It not only provides for jurisdiction over serious violations of Common Article 3, but a list of twelve other violations of laws and customs of war applicable in non-international armed conflict.[95] The inclusion of jurisdiction over these crimes is an indication of how far the international community has come in recognising that atrocities committed in internal conflicts are no less severe in their effects on the victims or post-conflict reconciliation than those committed in international conflicts. However, the distinction between the two, in terms of the reduced list of non-international war crimes and the failure to include prohibited weapons in Article

[91] See discussion *supra*, pp. 81–9.

[92] See T. Meron, 'Crimes under the jurisdiction of the International Criminal Court', pp. 47–55 in H. von Hebel, J. Lammers and J. Schukking (eds), *Reflections on the International Criminal Court* (The Hague: Asser, 1999), p. 54.

[93] A. Cassese, 'The Statute of the International Criminal Court: some preliminary reflections', EJIL, 10 (1999), 144–71, p. 152.

[94] See E. Kalivretakis, 'Are nuclear weapons above the law?', n. 86 *supra*, pp. 731–2.

[95] See J. Pejic, 'Accountability for international crimes: from conjecture to reality', IRRC, 845 (2002), 13–33, pp. 21–2.

8(2)(e), demonstrates that the desire to create an ICC did not totally overcome the reluctance of States to accept interference in internal conflicts.[96]

The inclusion of war crimes committed in non-international armed conflicts necessitates a distinction between mere riots or internal disturbances and armed conflict. The definition of the threshold for application of Article 8(2)(c) is vague, only making it clear that 'internal disturbances and tensions, such as riots, isolated and sporadic acts of violence' are excluded.[97] The threshold for the application of Article 8(2)(e) is somewhat clearer, requiring 'protracted armed conflict between governmental authorities and organised armed groups or between such groups'.[98] This is undoubtedly an improvement over the much higher threshold of AP II, which was restricted to internal conflict between the government of a state and organised rebel groups which controlled part of the territory.[99]

Nevertheless, the definitions used in Article 8(2)(c) and (e) cannot alter the practical problem that, when facing an armed rebellion, the State concerned may seek to exclude the application of international humanitarian law entirely by denying that the situation has escalated into a non-international armed conflict. A practical way that the Rome Statute could be used to make an impression, if such a situation was referred to the Prosecutor, would be an announcement that the investigation of alleged crimes were being conducted on the basis that the situation amounted to a non-international armed conflict. Alternatively, if the Prosecutor commenced a *proprio motu* investigation of the situation, the authorisation of this investigation by the Pre-trial Chamber should necessarily include a provisional analysis of the status of the situation as a non-international armed conflict.

A further complex issue is the distinction between international and non-international armed conflicts, which is particularly difficult to make in situations where *prima facie* internal conflicts may have been internationalised by the involvement of another State.[100] In this type of armed conflict it is possible that the State concerned may attempt to implicate another State, for political reasons,[101] even though the involvement is insufficient to internationalise an essentially internal conflict. Therefore, whilst it remains necessary to distinguish between the two types of conflict under the Rome Statute, an intricate legal and factual analysis of the situation will be necessary.

[96] Article 8(3), Rome Statute, is a reminder of the issue of State sovereignty but does not really restrict the jurisdiction of the ICC over non-international armed conflicts, see discussion *supra*, pp. 186–7.

[97] Article 8(2)(d), Rome Statute, discussed *supra*, pp. 171–2.

[98] Article 8(2)(f), Rome Statute, discussed *supra*, pp. 171–3.

[99] Article 1(1), AP II.

[100] See discussion *supra*, pp. 17–20, and C. Byron, 'Armed conflicts: international or non-international?', JCSL, 6 (2001), 63–90.

[101] For example, to justify governmental recourse to third State assistance, or in order to elicit world support.

Nevertheless, even when the situation in a particular State is accepted as amounting to a non-international armed conflict, there are problems peculiar to internal conflicts which jeopardise compliance with Common Article 3 and the other basic rules of international humanitarian law criminalised in Article 8(2)(e). Part of the problem is that the rebels are usually 'ex-civilians' with little or no training in international humanitarian law and in fact may never have heard of the Geneva Conventions or the ICC.[102]

The main problem in the application of humanitarian law in such conflicts, however, is the position of rebels *vis-à-vis* the government in terms of resources and infrastructure, which is a more difficult issue to overcome. In practical terms it will be harder for rebels to comply with rules of international humanitarian law which require resources than it will be for the State Party. Therefore, there is to some extent more pressure on the non-State Party to declare that no quarter will be given, as prohibited under Article 8(2)(e)(x), if it has insufficient soldiers to guard prisoners and perhaps insufficient infrastructure to house them or supplies to feed them. Additionally, if facing a better trained and equipped force with superior numbers, the rebels may be more likely to enlist anyone who can fight, including children under fifteen, as prohibited by Article 8(2)(e)(vii). The problems of rebels operating a 'regularly constituted court' as required under Article 8(2)(c)(iv) have already been discussed in Chapter 4 above.[103]

It is submitted that the ICC should take problems of infrastructure into account to some extent when, for example, deciding whether a rebel court was 'regularly constituted',[104] and with respect to available buildings and supplies when deciding whether the conditions in which government soldiers were held prisoner amounted to cruel treatment by rebels, particularly if they were no worse than the conditions faced by the rebel troops stationed in that area themselves. However, on the whole the individual problems of accused non-State actors with respect to non-compliance with international humanitarian law should be considered as potential mitigating circumstances only if they are found guilty of an offence under the Rome Statute. This approach is necessary in order to maintain an evenhanded approach between the rebels and the State Party. If a rebel group do not apply and are led to believe that they will not be required to apply basic international humanitarian law, it will be increasingly difficult to ensure that the State Party itself applies that law.[105]

In any case, the difficulties with enforcement of international humanitarian law in non-international armed conflicts are not restricted to the non-State Party.

[102] See Y. Dinstein, 'Humanitarian law and the conflict in Afghanistan', ASIL Proceedings, 96 (2002), 23–41, p. 29.

[103] See discussion *supra*, p. 180.

[104] *Ibid.*

[105] See comments of C. Nier III, 'The Yugoslavia civil war: an analysis of the applicability of the law of war governing non-international armed conflicts in the modern world', Dick J Int'l L, 10 (1992), 303–31, p. 320, and the discussion of reciprocity in I. Detter, *The Law of War* (Cambridge: Cambridge University Press, 2nd edn, 2000), pp. 400–13.

Particularly in the case of guerrilla warfare, commonly used in internal conflicts, the State Party may fail to distinguish between civilians and rebels. This is due to the nature of guerrilla warfare, which blurs the line between civilians and the military when a person may appear to be a civilian by day and a soldier by night and when civilians are actively involved in supporting and assisting a rebel movement.[106]

Under Article 8(2)(c)(i) of the Rome Statute the State Party may be prosecuted for directing attacks against 'the civilian population as such or against individual civilians not taking direct part in hostilities'. However, in internal conflicts involving guerrilla warfare, the definition applied to taking a 'direct part in hostilities' becomes crucial. Whilst this definition is still so uncertain the temptation in an internal conflict will be for the State Party to interpret it widely enough to include civilians who assist rebels by providing food and shelter.[107] Even if the State Party attacks only military objectives, the Rome Statute does not include jurisdiction over methods of warfare in an internal conflict which cause excessive collateral damage to civilians. This omission would leave the ICC powerless to deal with a situation such the Chechen conflict, where the Russian forces continued to use artillery and rocket fire in Grozny 'even after they became aware of the consequent high civilian casualty rate'.[108]

## Concluding comments

Whilst this book has concentrated upon the definitions that the ICC will apply to the war crimes and crimes against humanity set out in the Rome Statute, undoubtedly most prosecutions will take place before national courts, either with respect to crimes which do not meet the jurisdictional threshold of the ICC or as a result of the operation of the principle of complementarity.[109] Therefore, in order to promote consistency in the definitions of crimes in national prosecutions, it is essential that States Parties to the Rome Statute should be encouraged to pass legislation which allows their courts to take into account the EOC and the decisions and judgements of the ICC.[110]

The influence of human rights law can be seen throughout the book, both with respect to its influence upon specific definitions of crimes, such as torture, and as a result of the pervasive influence of Article 21 of the Rome Statute, which requires that the interpretation of the Statute and EOC are 'consistent with

[106] See K. Brown, 'Counter-guerilla operations: does the law of war proscribe success?', Nav LR, 44 (1997), 123–73, p. 152.

[107] *Ibid.*, pp. 152–5, and discussion *supra*, pp. 175–6.

[108] D. Hollis, 'Accountability in Chechnya: addressing internal matters with legal and political international norms', BCL Rev. (1995), 793–846, p. 829.

[109] Discussed *supra*, pp. 246–51.

[110] *Ibid.*

internationally recognized human rights'.[111] Whilst applications to human rights bodies cannot be discounted as an alternative solution for victims of atrocities, nevertheless, the worst atrocities often occur when human rights mechanisms have failed and, moreover, human rights bodies do not have jurisdiction over non-States parties in non-international armed conflicts.

The definitions of crimes in the Rome Statute are to be praised for their incorporation of gender concerns and their inclusion of jurisdiction over a substantial number of crimes in non-international armed conflict.[112] However, criticism must be made of the failure to include jurisdiction over weapons of mass destruction in international armed conflicts, or even over any prohibited weapons whatsoever in non-international armed conflicts.[113] Furthermore, uncertainty remains in respect of the exact *mens rea* required for each crime, or indeed whether crimes within the Statute may be committed by omission.[114]

To conclude, whilst this book raises many criticisms of the definitions of crimes in the Rome Statute, nevertheless the Statute and EOC contribute significantly to a contemporary interpretation of war crimes and crimes against humanity. Furthermore, the establishment of an International Criminal Court with jurisdiction over the most serious crimes of international concern, coupled with the principle of complementarity, should promote a resurgence of national and international prosecutions for war crimes and crimes against humanity. In the long term it is to be hoped that such denial of impunity for serious abuses of human rights will deter such offences from being committed and will break the cycle of violence, so ensuring that justice replaces revenge.[115] For the present, though, whilst we cannot prevent all atrocities from being committed, the ICC brings us one step closer to ensuring that those who commit such crimes are held accountable for their actions.[116]

[111] See discussion *supra*, pp. 255–8.

[112] Discussed *supra*, pp. 258–60 and 261–4.

[113] See discussion *supra*, pp. 260–1.

[114] See discussion *supra*, pp. 5–8 and 253–5.

[115] See C. Elliott, 'A permanent International Criminal Court: "a giant step towards universal human rights" or "dead on arrival"?', JCL, 64 (2000), 398–408, p. 398.

[116] See J. Roy, 'Strengthening human rights protection: why the Holocaust slave labor claims should be litigated', Scholar: St Mary's LR Min Issues, 1 (1999), 153–205, p. 205.

# Select bibliography

### Books


Askin, K., *War Crimes against Women: Prosecution in International War Crimes Tribunals* (The Hague: Nijhoff, 1997)

Bassiouni, M. Cherif, *Crimes against Humanity in International Criminal Law* (Dordrecht: Nijhoff, 1992)

Bernhardt, R. (ed.), *Encyclopaedia of Public International Law*, Vols III–IV (Amsterdam: North-Holland, 1982)

Bothe, M., K. Partsch and W. Solf, *New Rules for Victims of Armed Conflicts* (The Hague: Nijhoff, 1982)

Cassese, A., P. Gaeta and J. Jones (eds), *The Rome Statute of the International Criminal Court: A Commentary* (Oxford: Oxford University Press, 2002)

Clark, R., and M. Sann (eds), *The Prosecution of International Crimes: A Critical Study of the International Tribunal for the Former Yugoslavia* (New Brunswick NJ: Transaction, 1996)

Delissen, A., and G. Tanja (eds), *Humanitarian Law of Armed Conflict: Challenges Ahead* (Dordrecht: Nijhoff, 1991)

Detter, I., *The Law of War* (Cambridge: Cambridge University Press, 2nd edn, Cambridge, 2000)

Dinstein, Y., and M. Tabory (eds), *War Crimes in International Law* (The Hague: Nijhoff, 1996)

Doswald-Beck, L. (ed.), *San Remo Manual on International Law applicable to Armed Conflicts at Sea* (Cambridge: Cambridge University Press, 1995)

Draper, G., *The Red Cross Conventions* (London: Stevens, 1958)

Durham, H., and T. McCormack (eds), *The Changing Face of Conflict and the Efficacy of International Humanitarian Law* (The Hague: Kluwer, 1999)

Ferencz, B., *An International Criminal Court, A Step toward World Peace: A Documentary History and Analysis*, Vol. I (New York: Oceana Publications, 1980)

Fischer, H., C. Kreß and S. Lüder (eds), *International and National Prosecution of Crimes under International Law: Current Developments* (Berlin: Berlin Verlag, 2001)

Fleck, D. (ed.), *The Handbook of Humanitarian Law in Armed Conflicts* (Oxford: Oxford University Press, 1999)

Green, L., *The Contemporary Law of Armed Conflict*, Melland Schill Studies in International Law (Manchester: Manchester University Press, 2nd edn, 2000)

Greenspan, M., *The Modern Law of Land Warfare* (Berkeley CA: University of California Press, 1959)
Henckaerts, J., *Mass Expulsion in Modern International Law and Practice* (Dordrecht: Nijhoff, 1995)
Henckaerts, J., and L. Doswald-Beck, *Customary International Humanitarian Law* (Cambridge: ICRC and Cambridge University Press, 2005)
Jones, J., *The Practice of the International Criminal Tribunals for the Former Yugoslavia and Rwanda* (New York: Transnational, 1998)
Kuper, J., *International Law concerning Child Civilians in Armed Conflict* (Oxford: Clarendon, 1997)
Kwakwa, E., *The International Law of Armed Conflict: Personal and Material Fields of Application* (Dordrecht: Nijhoff, 1992)
Lee, R. (ed.), *The International Criminal Court, The Making of the Rome Statute, Issues, Negotiations, Results* (The Hague: Kluwer, 1999)
Lee, R. (ed.), *The International Criminal Court: Elements of Crimes and Rules of Procedure and Evidence* (New York: Transnational, 2001)
McCoubrey, H., *International Humanitarian Law: The Regulation of Armed Conflicts* (Aldershot: Dartmouth, 1990)
McCoubrey, H., and N. White, *International Law and Armed Conflict* (Aldershot: Dartmouth, 1992)
McDougal, M., and F. Feliciano, *The International Law of War: Transnational Coercion and World Public Order* (New Haven CT: New Haven Press, 1994)
Meron, T., *War Crimes Law Comes of Age* (Oxford: Clarendon Press, 1998)
Meyer, M. (ed.), *Armed Conflict and the New Law: Aspects of the 1977 Geneva Protocols and the 1980 Weapons Convention* (London: BIICL, 1989)
Ministry of Defence (MoD), *The Manual of the Law of Armed Conflict* (Oxford: Oxford University Press, 2004)
Morris, V., and M. Scharf, *An Insider's Guide to the International Criminal Tribunal for the Former Yugoslavia: A Documentary History and Analysis*, Vol. I (New York: Transnational, 1995)
Morris, V., and M. Scharf, *The International Criminal Tribunal for Rwanda* (New York: Transnational, 1997)
Pictet, J. (ed.), *The Geneva Conventions of 12 August 1949: Commentary I/II/III/IV Convention* (Geneva: ICRC, 1952–60)
Rogers, A., *Law on the Battlefield* (Manchester: Manchester University Press, 2nd edn, 2004)
Rowe, P. (ed.), *The Gulf War, 1990–1991, in International and English Law* (London: Routledge, 1993)
Sadat, L., *The International Criminal Court and the Transformation of International Law: Justice for the New Millenium* (New York: Transnational, 2002)
Sandoz, Y., C. Swinarski and B. Zimmermann (eds), *Commentary on the Additional Protocols of 8 June 1977 to the Geneva Conventions of 12 August 1949* (Geneva: ICRC and Nijhoff, 1987)
Schabas, W., *An Introduction to the International Criminal Court* (Cambridge: Cambridge University Press, 3rd edn, 2007)
Schmitt, M. (ed.), *The Law of Military Operations: Lieber Amicorum Professor Jack Grunawalt*, 72 US Naval War College International Law Studies (Newport RT: Naval War College, 1998)

Schmitt, M., and L. Green (eds), *Levie on the Law of War*, 70 US Naval War College International Law Studies (Newport RT: Naval War College, 1998)
Thomas, A., and A. Thomas, *Legal Limits on the Use of Chemical and Biological Weapons* (Dallas TX: Southern Methodist University Press, 1970)
Triffterer, O. (ed.), *Commentary on the Rome Statute of the International Criminal Court: Observers' Notes, Article by Article* (Baden-Baden: Nomos, 1999)
War Office, with the assistance of H. Lauterpacht, *Manual of Military Law*, Part III: *The Law of War on Land* (London: HMSO, 1958)

**Articles and essays**

Allen, C., 'Civilian starvation and relief during armed conflict: the modern humanitarian law', Georgia J Int Comp L, 19 (1985), 1–85
Ambos, K., 'General principles of criminal law in the Rome Statute', Crim LF, 10 (1999), 1–32
Bassiouni, M. Cherif, 'Establishing an international criminal court: historical survey', Milit LR, 149 (1995), 49–63
Bothe, M., 'The protection of the environment in time of armed conflict', Germ Yrbk Int'l L, 34 (1991), 54–62
Byron, C., 'Armed conflicts: international or non-international?', JCSL, 6 (2001), 63–90
Byron, C., and D. Turns, 'The Preparatory Commission for the International Criminal Court', ICLQ, 50 (2001), 420–35
Cottier, M., W. Fenrick, P. Viseur Sellers and A. Zimmermann, 'Article 8, war crimes', 173–262 in Triffterer, O. (ed.), *Commentary on the Rome Statute of the International Criminal Court: Observers' Notes, Article by Article* (Baden-Baden: Nomos, 1999)
Cryer, R., 'Implementation of the International Criminal Court Statute in England and Wales', ICLQ, 51 (2002), 733–43
DeSaussure, A., 'The role of the law of armed conflict during the Persian gulf war: an overview', AFLR, 37 (1994), 41–68
Dinstein, Y., 'Humanitarian law and the conflict in Afghanistan', ASIL Proceedings, 96 (2002), 23–41
Dörmann, K., 'The first and second sessions of the Preparatory Commission for the International Criminal Court', YIHL, 2 (1999), 283–306
Dörmann, K., 'Preparatory Commission for the International Criminal Court: the elements of war crimes', IRRC, 839 (2000), 771–95
Dörmann, K., 'Preparatory Commission for the International Criminal Court: the elements of war crimes', Part II 'Other serious violations of the laws and customs applicable in international and non-international armed conflicts', IRRC, 842 (2001), 461–87
Doswald-Beck, L., 'The legal validity of military intervention by invitation of the government', BYIL, 56 (1985), 189–252
Fenrick, W., 'International humanitarian law and criminal trials', Transnat'l L & Contemp Probs, 7 (1997), 23–43
Fenrick, W., 'Should crimes against humanity replace war crimes?', Colum J Transnat'l Law, 37 (1999), 767–85
Fenrick, W., 'The application of the Geneva Conventions by the International Criminal Tribunal for the Former Yugoslavia', IRRC, 834 (1999), 317–29

Fenrick, W., 'Article 28, responsibility of commanders and other superiors', pp. 515–22 in Triffterer, O. (ed.), *Commentary on the Rome Statute of the International Criminal Court: Observers' Notes, Article by Article* (Baden-Baden: Nomos, 1999)
Green, L., 'The environment and the law of conventional warfare', Can YBIL, 29 (1991), 222–37
Greenwood, C., 'International humanitarian law and the Tadic case', EJIL, 7 (1996), 265–83
Greenwood, C., 'International humanitarian law and United Nations military operations', YIHL, 1 (1998), 3–34
Henckaerts, J., 'Towards better protection for the environment in armed conflict: recent developments in international humanitarian law', RECIEL, 9 (2000), 13–19
Hwang, P., 'Defining crimes against humanity in the Rome Statute of the International Criminal Court', Fordham Int'l LJ, 22 (1998), 457–504
Hyland, K., 'The impact of the Protocol to Prevent, Suppress and Punish Trafficking in Persons, especially Women and Children', HR Brief, 8 (2001), 30–2
Kalshoven, F., 'Arms, armaments and international law', 191 Rec des Cours (1985) II, 183–341
Meron, T., 'The humanization of humanitarian law', AJIL, 94 (2000), 239–78
Mettraux, G., 'Crimes against humanity in the jurisprudence of the International Criminal Tribunals for the Former Yugoslavia and for Rwanda', Harv ILJ, 43 (2002), 237–316
Moir, L., 'The historical development of the application of humanitarian law in non-international armed conflicts to 1949', ICLQ, 47 (1998), 337–61
Momtaz, D., 'War crimes in non-international armed conflicts under the Statute of the International Criminal Court', YIHL, 2 (1999), 177–92
Müllerson, R., 'International humanitarian law in internal conflicts', JACL, 2 (1997), 109–33
Murphy, T., 'Sanctions and enforcement of the humanitarian law of the four Geneva Conventions of 1949 and Geneva Protocol I of 1977', Milit LR, 103 (1984), 3–77
Ni Aolain, F., 'The relationship between situations of emergency and low-intensity armed conflict', Israel Yrbk Hum Rts, 28 (1998), 97–106
Niarchos, C., 'Women, war, and rape: challenges facing the International Tribunal for the Former Yugoslavia', HRQ, 17 (1995), 649–90
Normand, R., and C. af Jochnick, 'The legitimation of violence: a critical analysis of the Gulf War', Harv ILJ, 35 (1994), 387–416
Nurick, L., 'The distinction between combatant and noncombatant in the law of war', AJIL, 39 (1945), 680–97
Oeter, S., 'Methods and means of combat', pp. 105–207 in D. Fleck (ed.), *The Handbook of Humanitarian Law in Armed Conflicts* (Oxford: Oxford University Press, 1999)
Paust, J., 'The Preparatory Committee's "definition of crimes": war crimes', Crim LF, 8 (1997), 431–44
Pejic, J., 'The International Criminal Court Statute: an appraisal of the Rome package', Int Law, 34 (2000), 65–84
Pejic, J., 'Accountability for international crimes: from conjecture to reality', IRRC, 84 (2002), 13–33
Peterson, A., 'Order out of chaos: domestic enforcement of the law of internal armed conflict', Milit LR, 171 (2002), 1–90
Piragoff, D., 'Article 30, mental element', 527–35, in O. Triffterer (ed.), *The Handbook of Humanitarian Law in Armed Conflicts* (Oxford: Oxford University Press, 1999)
Plattner, D., 'The penal repression of violations of international humanitarian law applicable in non-international armed conflicts', IRRC, 278 (1990), 409–20

Politakis, G., 'Stratagems and the prohibition of perfidy with a special reference to the law of war at sea', Austrian JPIL, 45 (1993), 253–308

Politi, M., 'Elements of crimes', 443–73, in A. Cassese, P. Gaeta and J. Jones (eds), *The Rome Statute of the International Criminal Court: A Commentary* (Oxford: Oxford University Press, 2002)

Rabus, W., 'Protection of the wounded, sick and shipwrecked', pp. 293–319 in D. Fleck (ed.), *The Handbook of Humanitarian Law in Armed Conflicts* (Oxford: Oxford University Press, 1999)

Rassam, Y., 'Contemporary forms of slavery and the evolution of the prohibition of slavery and the slave trade under customary international law', Va JIL, 39 (1999), 303–52

Rittich, K., *et al.*, 'The gender of international law', ASIL Proceedings, 93 (1999), 206–9

Robblee, P., 'The legitimacy of modern conventional weaponry', Milit LR, 71 (1976), 95–148

Robertson, H., Jr, 'The principle of the military objective in the law of armed conflict', pp. 197–223 in M. Schmitt (ed.), *The Law of Military Operations: Liber Amicorum Professor Jack Grunawalt*, 72 US Naval War College International Law Studies (Newport RI: Naval War College, 1998)

Robinson, D., 'Defining "crimes against humanity" at the Rome Conference', AJIL, 93 (1999), 43–57

Robinson, D., and H. von Hebel, 'War crimes in internal conflicts: Article 8 of the ICC Statute', YIHL, 2 (1999), 193–209

Rogers, A., 'Zero casualty warfare', IRRC, 837 (2000), 165–81

Ronzitti, N., 'Is the *non liquet* of the final report by the committee established to review the NATO bombing campaign against the Federal Republic of Yugoslavia acceptable?', IRRC, 840 (2000), 1017–28

Rosenblad, E., 'Area bombing and international law', Rev dr milit, 15 (1976), 53–104

Rottensteiner, C., 'The denial of humanitarian assistance as a crime under international law', IRRC, 835 (1999), 555–82

Rowe, P., 'The use of special forces and the laws of war: wearing the uniform of the enemy or civilian clothes and of spying and assassination', Rev dr milit, 33 (1994), 207–234

Rowe, P., 'Kosovo 1999: the air campaign: have the provisions of Additional Protocol I withstood the test?', IRRC, 837 (2000), 147–64

Rückert, W., and G. Witschel, 'Genocide and crimes against humanity in the Elements of Crimes', pp. 59–93 in H. Fischer, C. Kreß and S. Lüder (eds), *International and National Prosecution of Crimes under International Law: Current Developments* (Berlin: Berlin Verlag, 2001)

Ryan, S., 'From the furies of Nanking to the Eumenides of the International Criminal Court; the evolution of sexual assaults as international crimes', Pace ILR, 11 (1999), 447–86

Sadat-Wexler, L., 'The interpretation of the Nuremberg principles by the French Court of Cassation: from Touvier to Barbie and back again', Colum J Transnat'l Law, 32 (1994), 289–380

Sarooshi, D., 'The Statute of the International Criminal Court', ICLQ, 48 (1999), 387–404

Sassòli, M., and L. Olson, 'International decisions: Prosecutor v. Tadić (Judgement)', AJIL, 94 (2000), 571–8

Sassòli, M., and L. Olson, 'The Judgement of the ICTY Appeals Chamber on the merits in the Tadic case', IRRC, 839 (2000), 733–69
Schachter, O., 'United Nations law in the Gulf conflict', AJIL, 85 (1991), 452–73
Schindler, D., 'The different types of armed conflicts according to the Geneva Conventions and Protocols', 163 Rec des Cours (1979) II, 117–63
Schmitt, M., 'Future war and the principle of discrimination', Israel Yrbk Hum Rts, 28 (1998), 51–90
Schmitt, M., 'The principle of discrimination in twenty-first-century warfare', Yale HR & Dev LJ, 2 (1999), 143–82
Schwelb, E., 'Crimes against humanity', BYIL, 23 (1946), 178–226
Sethi, G., 'The European Court of Human Rights' jurisprudence on issues of forced disappearances', HR Brief, 8 (2001), 29–31
Shotwell, C., 'Food and the use of force', Rev dr milit, 30 (1991), 345–85
Slim, H., 'Protection of the Red Cross and Red Crescent emblems and the repression of misuse', IRRC, 272 (1989), 408–19
Slye, R., 'Apartheid as a crime against humanity: a submission to the South African Truth and Reconciliation Commission', Mich J Int'l L, 20 (1999), 267–300
Spaight, J., 'Legitimate objectives in air warfare', BYIL, 21 (1944), 158–64
Stephens, B., 'Humanitarian law and gender violence: an end to centuries of neglect', Hof LPS, 3 (1999), 87–109
Swaak-Goldman, O., 'The crime of persecution in international law', LJIL, 11 (1998), 145–54
Tigar, M., S. Casey, I. Giordani and S. Mardemootoo, 'Paul Touvier and the crime against humanity', Texas Int'l LJ, 30 (1995), 285–310
Toepfer, S., and B. Wells, 'The worldwide market for sex: a review of international and regional legal prohibitions regarding trafficking in women', Mich J Gender & L, 2 (1994), 83–128
Tomuschat, C., 'A system of international criminal prosecution is taking shape', Int Com JR, 50 (1993), 56–70
Totsuka, E., 'Commentary on a victory for "comfort women": Japan's judicial recognition of military sexual slavery', Pac Rim LPJ, 8 (1999), 47–61
Turns, D., 'War crimes without war? The applicability of international humanitarian law to atrocities in non-international armed conflicts', RADIC, 7 (1995), 804–30
Turns, D., 'Prosecuting violations of international humanitarian law: the legal position in the United Kingdom', JACL, 4 (1999), 1–39
Turns, D., 'Some reflections on the conflict in southern Lebanon: the "Qana incident" and international humanitarian law', JCSL, 5 (2000), 177–209

# Table of cases

**ICTY cases**

All cases *Prosecutor v.*

**ICTR cases**

All cases *Prosecutor v.*

**Second World War cases**

## Human rights cases

## ICJ cases

## Other international cases



## National cases

# Table of international instruments

1868 St Petersburg Declaration, Declaration renouncing the Use, in Time of War, of Explosive Projectiles under 400 grammes Weight, reprinted in 1 AJIL (Supp. 1907) 95

1899 Hague Declaration II concerning Asphyxiating Gases, reprinted in 1 AJIL (Supp. 1907) 157

1899 Hague Declaration III concerning Expanding Bullets, reprinted in 1 AJIL (Supp. 1907) 155

1907 Hague Convention IV respecting the Laws and Customs of War on Land, reprinted in 2 AJIL (Supp. 1908) 90

1907 Hague Convention IX concerning Bombardment by Naval Forces in Time of War, reprinted in 2 AJIL (Supp. 1908) 146

1919 Treaty of Peace between the Allied and Associated Powers and Germany (Treaty of Versailles), reprinted in 13 AJIL (Supp. 1919) 151

1920 Treaty of Peace between the Allied Powers and Turkey (Treaty of Sèvres), reprinted in 15 AJIL (Supp. 1921) 179

1923 Hague Rules of Aerial Warfare, reprinted in 17 AJIL (Supp. 1923) 245

1923 Treaty with Turkey and other Instruments signed at Lausanne (Treaty of Lausanne), reprinted in 18 AJIL (Supp. 1925) 1

1925 Geneva Protocol for the Prohibition of the Use in War of Asphyxiating, Poisonous or other Gases, and of Bacteriological Methods of Warfare, reprinted in 25 AJIL (Supp. 1931) 94

1926 Slavery Convention, reprinted in 21 AJIL (Supp. 1927) 171

1930 Convention concerning Forced or Compulsory Labour (ILO Convention No. 29), 39 UNTS 55

1937 Convention for the Creation of an International Criminal Court, reprinted in B. Ferencz, *An International Criminal Court, a Step toward World Peace: A Documentary History and Analysis*, Vol. I (1980, New York: Oceana), p. 355

1945 CCL No. 10, Punishment of Persons Guilty of War Crimes, Crimes against Peace and against Humanity, 20 December 1945, 3 Official Gazette Control Council for Germany (1946) 50

1945 Nuremberg Charter, reprinted in 39 AJIL (Supp. 1945) 257

1946 Tokyo Charter, reprinted in M. Bassiouni, *Crimes against Humanity in International Criminal Law* (1992, Dordrecht: Nijhoff), p. 606

1948 Convention on the Prevention and Punishment of the Crime of Genocide, 78 UNTS 277
1949 Convention for the Suppression of the Traffic in Persons and of the Exploitation of the Prostitution of Others, 96 UNTS 271
1949 Geneva Convention I for the Amelioration of the Condition of the Wounded and Sick in Armed Forces in the Field, 75 UNTS 31
1949 Geneva Convention II for the Amelioration of the Condition of Wounded, Sick and Shipwrecked Members of Armed Forces at Sea, 75 UNTS 85
1949 Geneva Convention III relative to the Treatment of Prisoners of War, 75 UNTS 135
1949 Geneva Convention IV relative to the Protection of Civilian Persons in Time of War, 75 UNTS 287
1950 European Convention for the Protection of Human Rights and Fundamental Freedoms (European Convention on Human Rights), 213 UNTS 221
1954 Hague Convention for the Protection of Cultural Property in the Event of Armed Conflict, 249 UNTS 240
1954 ILC Draft Code of Crimes against the Peace and Security of Mankind, UN Doc. A/2693 (1954)
1956 Supplementary Convention on the Abolition of Slavery, the Slave Trade, and Institutions and Practices similar to Slavery, 226 UNTS 3
1957 Convention concerning the Abolition of Forced Labour (ILO Convention No. 105), 320 UNTS 291
1966 International Covenant on Civil and Political Rights, 999 UNTS 171
1968 Convention on the Non-applicability of Statutory Limitations to War Crimes and Crimes against Humanity, 745 UNTS 73
1969 American Convention on Human Rights (Pact of San José), reprinted in 9 ILM (1970) 673
1969 Vienna Convention on the Law of Treaties, 1155 UNTS 331
1972 Convention on the Prohibition of the Development, Production and Stockpiling of Bacteriological (Biological) and Toxic Weapons and on their Destruction (Biological Weapons Convention), 1015 UNTS 163
1973 International Convention on the Suppression and Punishment of the Crime of Apartheid, 1015 UNTS 243
1976 UN Convention on the Prohibition of Military or any other Hostile use of Environmental Modification Techniques, 1108 UNTS 151
1977 Geneva Protocol I additional to the Geneva Conventions of 12 August 1949, and relating to the Protection of Victims of International Armed Conflicts (AP I), 1125 UNTS 3
1977 Geneva Protocol II additional to the Geneva Conventions of 12 August 1949, and relating to the Protection of Victims of Non-international Armed Conflicts (AP II), 1125 UNTS 609
1979 Convention on the Elimination of all Forms of Discrimination against Women, reprinted in 19 ILM (1980) 33
1979 International Convention against the Taking of Hostages, reprinted 18 ILM (1979) 1456
1980 UN Convention on Prohibitions or Restrictions on the Use of Certain Conventional Weapons which may be Deemed to be Excessively Injurious or to have Indiscriminate Effects, 1342 UNTS 137

1984 Convention against Torture and other Cruel, Inhuman or Degrading Treatment or Punishment (Torture Convention), reprinted in 23 ILM (1984) 1027

1989 Convention on the Rights of the Child, reprinted in 28 ILM (1989) 1457

1990 African Charter on the Rights and Welfare of the Child, OAU Doc. CAB/LEG/24.9/49 (1990)

1991 ILC Draft Code of Crimes against the Peace and Security of Mankind, UN Doc. A/46/10 (1991)

1993 Convention on the Prohibition of the Development, Production, Stockpiling and Use of Chemical Weapons and on their Destruction (Chemical Weapons Convention), reprinted in 32 ILM (1993) 800

1993 ICTY Statute, UN Doc. S/25704 (1993), reprinted in 32 ILM (1993) 1192

1994 ICTR Statute, UN. Doc. SC/5974 (1995), reprinted in 33 ILM (1994) 1598

1994 ILC Draft Statute for an International Criminal Court, ILC Report, Forty-sixth Session, UN Doc. A/49/10 (1994)

1994 Inter-American Convention on International Traffic in Minors, reprinted in 33 ILM (1994) 721

1994 Inter-American Convention on the Forced Disappearance of Persons, reprinted in 33 ILM (1994) 1529

1994 UN Convention on the Safety of United Nations and Associated Personnel, reprinted in 34 ILM (1995) 482

1996 Amended Protocol on Prohibitions or Restrictions on the Use of Mines, Booby-traps and other Devices (Amended Protocol II), reprinted in 35 ILM (1996) 1206

1996 ILC Draft Code of Crimes against the Peace and Security of Mankind, UN Doc. A/51/10 (1996)

1997 Convention on the Prohibition of the Use, Stockpiling, Production and Transfer of Anti-personnel Mines and on their Destruction (Ottawa Convention), 36 ILM (1997) 1507

1998 Draft International Convention on the Protection of all Persons from Forced Disappearance, 14 August, E/CN.4/Sub.2/1998/WG.1/CRP. 2

1998 ICRC Statute (revised), reprinted in 324 IRRC (1998) 537

1998 Rome Statute of the International Criminal Court, UN Doc. A/Conf.183.9

1999 Convention concerning the Prohibition and Immediate Action for the Elimination of the Worst Forms of Child Labour (ILO Convention No. 182), reprinted in 38 ILM (1999) 1215

2000 Optional Protocol to the Convention on the Rights of the Child on the Involvement of Children in Armed Conflicts, UN Doc. A/54/49 (2000)

2000 Statute for the Special Court for Sierra Leone, annexed to the Report of the Secretary General on the Establishment of a Special Court for Sierra Leone, 4 October 2000, UN Doc. S/2000/915

2000 UN Convention against Transnational Organised Crime, UN Doc. A/55/383 (2000)

2001 Protocol to Prevent, Suppress and Punish Trafficking in Persons, especially Women and Children, Supplementing the United Nations Convention against Transnational Organised Crime, UN Doc. A/45/49 (2001)

2005 Geneva Protocol III Additional to the Geneva Conventions of 12 August 1949 and relating to the Adoption of an Additional Distinctive Emblem, 8 December 2005 (AP III)

2006 International Convention for the Protection of all Persons from Enforced Disappearance, GA Res. 61/177 (2006)

# Table of national instruments

1863 Instructions for the Government of Armies of the United States in the Field, prepared by Francis Lieber, promulgated as General Orders No. 100, by President Lincoln, 24 April 1863 (Lieber Code), reprinted in D. Schindler and J. Toman, *The Laws of Armed Conflicts: A Collection of Conventions, Resolutions and other Documents* (Dordrecht: Nijhoff, 1998), p. 3

1988 Genocide Convention Implementation Act (Proxmire Act), 18 USC, Chapter 50A, §1091–3, reprinted in L. LeBlanc, *The United States and the Genocide Convention* (Durham NC: Duke University Press, 1991), p. 255

2000 Crimes against Humanity and War Crimes Act, 2000, C.24, available at: <http://laws.justice.gc.ca/en/e-45.9/38374.html>

2001 International Criminal Court Act, 2001, available at: <http://www.legislation.hmso.gov.uk/acts/acts2001/20010017.htm>

2001 International Criminal Court (Scotland) Act, 2001, available at: <http://www.scotland-legislation.hmso.gov.uk/legislation/scotland/s-acts.htm>

2002 Act to Introduce the Code of Crimes against International Law, 2002, translated by B. Duffett, available at: <http://www.iccnow.org/resourcestools/ratimptoolkit/nationalregionaltools/legislationdebates.html>

2002 International Criminal Court (Consequential Amendments) Act, 2002, No. 42, Schedule 1, Amendment of the Criminal Code Act, 1995, available at: <http://scaleplus.law.gov.au/html/comact/browse/TOCN.htm>

# Index